# MODERN ENGLISH

### a practical
### reference guide

PRENTICE-HALL INTERNATIONAL, INC., *London*
PRENTICE-HALL OF AUSTRALIA, PTY. LTD., *Sydney*
PRENTICE-HALL OF CANADA, LTD., *Toronto*
PRENTICE-HALL OF INDIA PRIVATE LIMITED, *New Delhi*
PRENTICE-HALL OF JAPAN, INC., *Tokyo*

# MODERN ENGLISH

## a practical
## reference guide

MARCELLA FRANK

*New York University*

PRENTICE-HALL, INC., Englewood Cliffs, New Jersey

ISBN: C 0-13-594010-9
ISBN: P 0-13-594002-8

Library of Congress Catalog Card Number: 70-163400

*Printed in the United States of America*

10 9

# Contents

## 19

## *Absolute Constructions*     355

# *Preface*

*Modern English: A Practical Reference Guide* presents detailed information about current English usage, some of which will not be found in other grammar texts. Although reference is made to spoken English, the emphasis of this book is on written English, both formal and informal. An accompanying workbook is available to help students develop habits of correct English usage.

This reference text is the product of fifteen years experience with foreign and American college students, at Queens College in New York City, at New York University, and at the University of Hawaii. It is also the product of a much longer period of research in modern and traditional English grammar, current English usage, and general linguistics.

*Modern English* represents a synthesis of the old and the new. The conceptual framework for the book has been determined by modern grammatical theories (both structural and transformational) because I believe they present a clearer and more accurate picture of the English grammatical system than the older views, which were often patterned on Latin grammar rather than on English grammar. The facts of usage themselves, however, have been checked against the works of earlier grammarians such as Curme, Jespersen, and Poutsma, as well as against modern books on usage.

In general, American usage is recorded in this book; however, differences between American and British usage have been pointed out. Also, different levels and varieties of usage have been accounted for.

In the preparation of this book, I had in mind especially the practical needs of advanced learners of English as a foreign language, both in English-speaking countries and elsewhere. For this reason there is a heavy concentration on grammatical usages that continue to trouble foreign students—articles, verb forms, prepositions and idioms, and such complex structures as dependent clauses and verbal constructions. Also, word order, which modern linguists have been emphasizing as an important feature of English grammatical structure, is dealt with at some length.

Native speakers of English should also find *Modern English* valuable because of its realistic description of the English language, which takes into account the many complexities of the language that often do not fit into the simple generalizations made by most grammar books, whether traditional or modern.

The grammatical information contained in this text has been presented in the simplest possible order—parts of speech, clauses, verbal constructions.

Chapters One to Eight, parts of speech, have been influenced by concepts from structural linguistics—that words in a sentence can be classified according to their form and/or the way they pattern in a sentence. I differ from those structural linguists who use form alone as the basic criterion, and from those who make a two-fold classification of parts of speech—one according to form and one according to syntactic function. Rather, I follow the practice of many recent college English handbooks of considering *function* as the basic criterion for classifying parts of speech. However, I include in my description of each part of speech *all* the structural characteristics that can be observed as a word patterns in a sentence—the function, position, form, and the "markers" that signal a part of speech.

For the sake of simplicity of presentation, I have included a description of structure words—determiners, auxiliaries, intensifiers, etc.—under the part of speech where they have been traditionally classified. However, I have pointed out their role in signaling a structure. Also, because my basic criterion was functional, I have followed the traditional practice of labeling the prepositions and the conjunctions as parts of speech because of their connective function, but have treated them differently from the other parts of speech.

Chapters Ten to Twelve, clauses and verbal constructions, are based on an important concept from transformational grammar—that most complex syntactic structures are derived from simple basic sentences. In the description of clauses and verbal constructions, therefore, the changes from the original subject-verb-complement base are pointed out. This kind of description helps the learner become aware of how such structures serve as grammatical shapes for predications. In addition, other features of usage in connection with each structure are given—position, punctuation, level and variety of usage, possible semantic content. Thus the description goes beyond grammar to the larger area of writing where stylistic choices are involved.

The appendix to *Modern English* gives rules for spelling and for punctuation. It also includes Latin and Greek roots and prefixes with their meanings and with examples.

The workbooks that accompany *Modern English* are correlated with the chapters in this reference text. The exercises on the parts of speech concentrate on word forms, position, and other problems connected with the use of a particular part of speech. The exercises on the syntactic structures are of a transformational type. Students combine sentences or clauses in order to become aware of the changes from the subject-verb-complement core and in order to practice using correct introductory words for each structure. They are also given practice in such matters as the position and punctuation of each structure, possible substitutions for the structure, possible abridgment of the structure. The purpose of these exercises is to enable students to write not only correct but effective sentences, and to prepare them for the next stages of writing, the development of the paragraph and the entire essay.

Many thanks are due to Milton G. Saltzer, Associate Director of the American Language Institute, New York University, for his careful reading of the manuscript of this book, for his valuable suggestions for making this book more useful, and most of all, for his kind encouragement. I am also indebted to Lawrence Terzian, of the English Language Institute, Queens College, New York, for his helpful comments on the manuscript.

Marcella Frank
*New York, New York*

# 1

## Introduction
## to
## Parts of Speech

English sentences consist of predications—something is said, or *predicated*, about a subject. The main grammatical divisions of a sentence are therefore the subject and the predicate.

---

Subject      **the boy** (who or what is being talked about)
Predicate    **threw the ball into the water.** (what is being said about the subject)

---

The sentence may be further divided according to the function each word has in the subject-predicate relationship. Each of these functions is classified as a different part of speech. The words that form the central core of the sentence—around which all the other words "cluster"—are the parts of speech known as nouns (or pronouns) and verbs; the words that modify the central core words are the parts of speech called adjectives and adverbs; the words that show a particular kind of connecting relationship between these four parts of speech are called prepositions and conjunctions.

PARTS OF SPEECH
FORMING THE CENTRAL CORE

The central core of a sentence, the part that is absolutely necessary for a complete sentence, consists of the *most important word in the subject* (often called the "simple subject") plus either:

1. A *predicating* word, which expresses action or some other kind of event. This word is frequently followed by another word that completes the predication (called an *object*).

Sentence: *The boy threw the ball into the water.*

| (central core) | BOY | THREW | BALL[1] |
|---|---|---|---|
| | (subject) | (predicating word) | (object) |

2. A *linking* word, which expresses state or condition. This linking word is *always* followed by another word which makes the actual predication (called a *subjective complement*).

Sentence: *Mary is a pretty girl.*

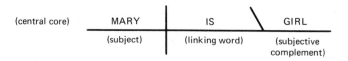

| (central core) | MARY | IS | GIRL |
|---|---|---|---|
| | (subject) | (linking word) | (subjective complement) |

The predicating word or the linking word is often termed the "simple predicate."

A word functioning as a subject, object, or subjective complement in a central core is called a *noun* in the part-of-speech classification. Thus, **boy, Mary, girl** in the above sentences are all nouns. (Other uses of the noun in a sentence will be given later.)

Certain words may be used to avoid repeating a noun already mentioned (or understood). For example, instead of saying **The *boy* threw the *ball*,** we can say **He threw it.** These substitutes for nouns (**He** and **it** in the example just given) are termed *pronouns* in the part-of-speech classification.

The predicating word or the linking word is given the part-of-speech name of *verb*. The form and arrangement of a verb with its subject and its complement (what completes it) determines not only the kind of central core—or "sentence pattern"—a sentence will have, but also what *type* of sentence it will be:

| | |
|---|---|
| Statement | He *is going* to the movies tonight. |
| Question | *Is* he *going* to the movies tonight? |
| Exclamation | **What a beautiful day it *is*!** |
| Command or Request | **Please *close* the door.**[2] |

---

[1] In traditional diagraming, the words in the central core are placed on the same horizontal line. All other words are shown as tied to this core by slanting lines drawn down from the core words.

[2] A command or request (imperative sentence) is the only kind of sentence with no subject expressed; the word **you** is understood as the subject.

PARTS OF SPEECH THAT MODIFY

If we go back to the central core of our sentence **The boy threw the ball into the water**

we find that we can attach further description to each of these words and thereby narrow them down, or *modify* them. Thus we can get

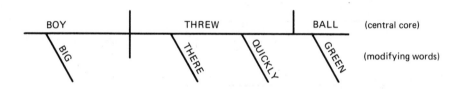

Those words that modify the nouns are called *adjectives* (**big, green**): those that modify the verb are called *adverbs* (**there, quickly**).

PARTS OF SPEECH
THAT EXPRESS A CONNECTING RELATIONSHIP

Certain words express a relationship of position, direction, time, etc., between two other words. In the sentence used above, we can join **water** with **threw** by **into** to show direction.

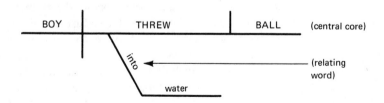

A word like **into** that indicates a physical relationship between two other words is called a *preposition*.

Another type of relating word, the *conjunction*, does one of two things:

1. It connects words or groups of words that are *equal grammatically* (*coordinate conjunction*).

Sentence:  *The boy and the girl threw the ball.*

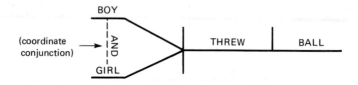

2. It connects groups of words that are *not equal grammatically* (*subordinate conjunction*).

Sentence:  *The girl caught the ball after the boy threw it.*

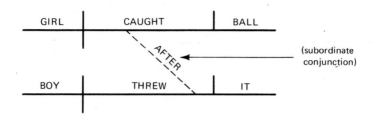

In presenting parts of speech, traditional grammarians often include another part of speech, the interjection. However, since the interjection is simply some expression of emotion or feeling (surprise, pleasure, pain, etc.) usually occurring at the beginning of the sentence (**oh, hurrah, ouch**) and does not perform any grammatical function, this part of speech will not be treated further in this text.

In the chapters that follow, each part of speech will first be classified into its various types. Such classifications will be based chiefly on differences in structural form or in grammatical behavior. After that, the part of speech will be described according to the observable signals that operate the grammar— function, position, form, markers. Under function will be a further consideration of how a part of speech serves either as part of the central core (noun or pronoun, verb), or a modifier (adjective, adverb), or a connector (preposition, conjunction). Under form will be included (1) inflectional endings, that is, endings for grammatical purposes (for example, **-s** for plural nouns, **-ed** for past verbs); and (2) derivational endings, or suffixes that indicate the part of speech (for example, **-tion** for a noun, **-ize** for a verb). Under markers will be included the kinds of words that act as signals for parts of speech that follow (for example, **the** before a noun; **very** before an adjective or adverb).[3]

---

[3] The "meaning" of each part of speech will not be given in this text, since we feel that such a definition is less useful in identifying a part of speech than a study of observable signals is.

From the discussion of these parts of speech we will see that only nouns, verbs, adjectives and adverbs have special inflectional and derivational endings, and use special markers for identification. The great bulk of our vocabulary falls into these four parts of speech, and new words enter into these categories only.

---

Because of the tendency in English for many words to shift freely from one part of speech to another (especially from noun to verb, or from verb to noun), the same word may actually belong to several parts of speech. Thus, in the sentence **The ship sails tomorrow,** *sails* is a verb; in **The sails of the boat are white,** *sails* is a noun. This is why a meaning-based definition, such as "a noun is the name of a person, place or thing" is often more confusing than helpful.

# 2

## Nouns

The noun is one of the most important parts of speech. Its arrangement with the verb helps to form the sentence core which is essential to every complete sentence. In addition, it may function as the chief or "head" word in many structures of modification.

### Classified by Meaning

Some nouns may belong to more than one of the types given below.

### Proper Nouns

A *proper* noun begins with a capital letter in writing. It includes (a) personal names (**Mr. John Smith**); (b) names of geographic units such as countries, cities, rivers, etc. (**Holland, Paris**); (c) names of nationalities and religions (a **Dutchman, Christianity**); (d) names of holidays (**Easter, Thanksgiving Day**); (e) names of time units (**Saturday, June**); (f) words used for personification—a thing or abstraction treated as a person (**Nature, Liberty**).

As opposed to proper nouns, all other nouns are classified as *common* nouns.

### Concrete or Abstract Nouns

A *concrete* noun is a word for a physical object that can be perceived by the senses—we can see, touch, smell the object (**flower, girl**). An *abstract* noun is a word for a concept—it is an idea that exists in our minds only (**beauty, justice, mankind**).

## Countable or Noncountable Nouns

A *countable* noun can usually be made plural by the addition of -*s* (one **girl**, two **girl***s*). A *noncountable* noun is not used in the plural. *Mass* nouns form one type of noncountable noun. They are words for concrete objects stated in an undivided quantity (**coffee, iron**). Abstract nouns (including names of school subjects and sports) are noncountable.

Some noncountable nouns may also be used in a countable sense and will therefore have a plural. In the sentence **We had chicken for dinner,** *chicken* is a mass noun; in **There were many chickens in the yard,** *chickens* is a countable noun. In addition, a noncountable noun may be used in the plural with the special meaning of *kinds of*—**Many *fruits* were displayed at the fair.**

## Collective Nouns

A *collective* noun is a word for a group of people, animals or objects considered as a single unit. Examples of collective nouns are **audience, committee, class, crew, crowd, enemy, faculty, family, flock, folk, government, group, herd, jury, majority, minority, nation, orchestra, press, public, team**.

In American English a collective noun used as subject usually takes a singular verb—**The committee has decided to make some recommendations**. However, if attention is being drawn to the individual members of the unit, then a plural verb is used—**The committee have disagreed among themselves**. With some of these collective nouns, British usage prefers a plural verb— **The government** (or **the public**) **were asked to cooperate**.

Collective nouns are countable nouns; they may be used in the plural— **All the committees have now made their recommendations.**

### Classified by Form

## Noun Compounds

The term compound, as it is used for a part of speech, refers to a group of words—usually two, but sometimes more—joined together into one vocabulary unit that functions as a single part of speech.

Noun compounds consist of the following composite forms.

1. *noun + noun*—**bathroom, department store, grammar book**
This kind of noun compound is most common. Noun + noun compounds are more likely to be hyphenated in British English than in American English.

2. *possessive noun + noun*—**lady's maid, artist's model, traveler's checks**
Sometimes the 's is omitted from the first noun—**a womens college, a citizens bank.**

3. *adjective + noun*—**blackbird, common sense, blue print**
An adjective + noun compound is usually not hyphenated.

4. *verb + noun*—**pickpocket, flashlight, dance team**
5. *noun + verb*—**handshake, garbage dump, lifeguard**
6. *gerund + noun*—**dining room, punching bag, wearing apparel**
7. *noun + gerund*—**fortune telling, housecleaning, water skiing**
8. *preposition + noun*—**overalls, by-way, downpour**
9. *verb + preposition-adverb*—**breakdown, makeup, grown-up**
10. *noun + prepositional phrase*—**son-in-law, editor-in-chief**

An *-er* may be added to noun compounds containing verbs to indicate "agent"—**bystander, baby-sitter, pressure cooker.**

Some less usual noun compounds with verbs are—**ne'er-do-well, a has-been, a might-have-been, newlyweds.**

Since compounds may be written as two separate words, as hyphenated words, or as single words, a good dictionary should be consulted if there is any doubt about how a compound is used. We must keep in mind however that because the usage of certain compounds may not yet be firmly established, dictionaries may differ in the way they record some compounds.

In speech many noun compounds are stressed more heavily on the first part of the compound (**ármchàir, bláckbìrd**); other noun compounds may receive even, or almost even, stress (**cómmon sénse, wóman dóctor**).

Words Having the Form
of Other Parts of Speech

**Adjective Forms Used as Nouns**

These nouns are often preceded by **the**. They take a plural verb when they refer to persons—**The *rich* grow richer and the *poor* grow poorer.** Adjectives of nationality are frequently used thus, especially adjectives ending in **-ch, -sh**, or **-ese**—**the French, the Irish, the Chinese.** Adjectives of nationality that end in **-an** are also used as nouns, but they have a regular plural with **-s**—**Americans, Italians.** The addition of **-man** or **-men** to adjectives of nationality changes them to regular nouns that may be singular or plural—**the Frenchmen, an Irishman.**

Adjective forms used as nouns may be in comparative form (**The *richest* are not always the *happiest***), and they may be modified by adverbs (**the *newly* rich, the *very* poor**), or even adjectives (**the *deprived* poor, the *arrogant, selfish* rich**).

A few **-ed** adjectives referring to persons may also be used in the singular—**his betrothed, the accused, the deceased.**

The adjective form used as a noun may also express an idea (**Greek philosophers were searching for the *good*, the *true* and the *beautiful*; The *best* is still not good enough for him**) or a thing (**Please buy some margarine for me; the *cheapest* is good enough**).

## Verb Forms Used as Nouns

*Swimming* **is a great sport**; **Seeing is believing**. Such nouns with **-ing** endings are called gerunds.

In addition, some words that usually function as adverbs may be used as nouns—**from** *there,* **by** *now.*

Nouns may function not only in the central core of the sentence, but also in structures of modification. These functions will be listed here along with their structural significance.

### Function in Central Core

## Subject of Verb

Who or what is being talked about. The verb agrees with the subject in person (first, second, third) and in number (singular, plural).

> The **girl** is resting.
> The **girls** are resting.

## Complement of Verb

This completes the predication after the verb.

OBJECT OF VERB.   This can be:

(a) A *direct object*—Who or what receives the action of the verb.

> We need some **money**.

A *cognate* object is a special kind of direct object that is either identical in form with the verb or has derivative form (**She laughed a bitter** *laugh*; **He lived a good** *life*).

(b) An *indirect object*. A second object *to* or *for* which the action of the verb is directed. The indirect object precedes the direct object.

> Please give that **man** some money.

The indirect object may also be expressed in a **to** or **for** phrase after the direct object.

> Please give some money to that **man**.

Some verbs that take indirect objects are—**bring, buy, give, make, owe, pay, sell, send, teach, write.**

## Subjective Complement (Predicate Noun)

Used after a linking verb to refer back to the subject. While an object of a verb has a different identity from the subject, a subjective complement has the same identity as the subject.

*Washington was the first **President** of the United States.*

The subjective complement is often referred to merely as a *complement*, in spite of the fact that, strictly speaking, a complement is any structure that completes a predication after a verb. Since both nouns and adjectives may function as subjective complements, we will generally confine ourselves to the narrower terms *predicate noun* or *predicate adjective* unless we are referring to the broader function of these words as complements.

### Objective Complement

An object following the direct object that has the same identity as the direct object.

*The country elected Washington **President**.*

The objective complement may be preceded by **as—The country elected Washington as President**. Among the small number of verbs taking objective complements are **appoint, consider, elect, name, nominate, select, think.**

Function in Modification Structures

### Object of Preposition

Completes the idea of time, direction, position, etc., begun by a preposition.

*The student sat at his **desk**.*

There is one kind of noun that is only technically an object of a preposition that precedes it. In the sentence **The children laughed at the clown,** *clown* is superficially the object of the preposition **at**, but at a deeper level it might also be interpreted as the object of the combined verb and preposition and therefore as a complement in the central core of the sentence. In general, this is the interpretation we are following in this text. Nouns used in this function will be called *prepositional objects*.

### Noun in Apposition (Appositive)

A second noun used after a first one to re-identify the first one.

*Mr. Johnson, my **lawyer**, is very intelligent.*

The first noun may be used in any of the functions already given.

### Noun in Direct Address (Vocative)

Usually a proper noun used to draw the attention of the person being spoken to.

***John,** please come here.*

The noun in direct address actually names the "subject" who is asked to perform in a request or a command.

**Noun Adjunct**

A noun used in adjective position before another noun, the two together forming a noun compound.

> *She's going to the **grocery** store.*
>
> *They have a **swimming** pool.*

Many other examples have already been given under noun compounds.

Most noun adjuncts are singular in form even when used with plural noun heads (**student activities, cigar boxes**), but some adjuncts may be plural (**a savings bank, women doctors, a clothes closet**).

Many noun compounds that contain noun adjuncts are merely set phrases that have been established by usage. New compounds are constantly coming into the language because of the increasing need for names for new products, new specializations (usually those that splinter off from larger fields of endeavor), and new agencies.

In addition to these names that are set by custom, new combinations may be coined for special situations. Such compounds often represent some form of collapsed predication that enables the user to achieve greater compression. These specially coined compounds are very common in technical and academic writing. Newspapers and news magazines also make great use of such compounds. Some random samples from the editorial section of the New York Times are—**a small military assistance operation in Laos, travel-hotel-tour industry, an American space research facility.**[1]

Other structures than nouns may perform noun function. We have already pointed out the noun function of adjectives (**the idle** *rich*) and of pronouns (***We* don't like** *him*). In addition, larger grammatical structures may function as nouns.

| | |
|---|---|
| Gerund phrases | *Seeing him once again* **made her very happy.** (seeing him once again is the subject of the verb **made**) |
| Infinitive phrases | **She wanted** *to see him again.* (to see him again is the object of the verb **wanted**) |
| Noun clauses | **She said** *that she had seen him again.* (that she had seen him again is the object of the verb **said**) |

Any structure that functions as a noun is called a *nominal* in modern grammar. (The older term *substantive* is also used for such structures.)

## POSITION OF NOUNS

The position of a noun is determined by its function in the sentence. The blanks in the following sentences indicate the position of nouns as they fulfill different functions.

[1] *New York Times,* January 12, 1969.

| | |
|---|---|
| Subject | The _____ is good. |
| Subjective complement (predicate noun) | Mary is a pretty _____. |
| Direct object | The child ate his _____. |
| Indirect object | The lawyer sent _____ a letter. |
| Objective complement | The members elected Mr. Jones _____. |
| Object of preposition | He deposited the money in the _____. |
| Noun adjunct | He bought some gas at the _____ station. |
| Appositive | Shakespeare, a great _____, wrote many fine plays. |
| Noun in direct address | _____, please come here. or Please come here, _____. |

While the usual position for a subject is before the verb, in some cases the subject comes *after* the verb:

1. in most questions—*Does* your *wife* like candy?
2. after certain adverbials:
   a. indicating place—**On the hill** *stood* a *tree.*
   b. expressing negation or near-negation—**Never (or Seldom)** *have* our *people* seen such a thing.
   c. so, such, only—I like candy, and so *does* my *wife.*
3. after there—**There** *is* a *lamp* on the table.

Occasionally an object is placed before the subject for greater emphasis— **That** *kind* **of man I admire above all others.**

FORM OF NOUNS

Inflectional Forms

Nouns in many European languages may be inflected, that is, changed in form, for certain grammatical properties. Usually these changes are made through special endings. Inflectional forms of nouns may indicate:

1. *gender.* Special endings mark nouns as masculine, feminine or neuter, not necessarily according to actual sex.
2. *case.* Special endings mark nouns according to their function in the sentence—subject, object of the verb, etc.
3. *number.* Special endings mark singular or plural nouns.

The English noun has very few inflectional forms. There are almost no special forms for gender, nor is there anything that might really be called case. Earlier grammarians, who were strongly influenced by Latin grammar, tried to model a description of English "cases" on the Latin case system. In Latin, special endings are used for nouns functioning as subjects (nominative case), as possessive modifiers (genitive case), as indirect objects (dative case), as objects of verbs (accusative case), and as objects of many prepositions (ablative case). However, since the English noun actually does not have special endings for most of these functions, traditional grammarians simply attached these case names to the noun functions themselves.

As a matter of fact, the only grammatical properties for which the English noun is inflected are: (1) *number*—the noun has a special ending for a plural, and (2) *"possession"*—the noun has a special ending that signals not only actual possession, but a number of other relationships for which **of** phrases may also be used. These inflected forms for number and "possession" will now be described along with all their variations and exceptions.

### Plural Inflectional Form

The general rule for writing the plural of English nouns is to add *s* to the singular form (**boy—boys, apple—apples**). However, this rule is complicated because of the many exceptions given below.[2]

1. After a sibilant sound spelled as *s, z, ch, sh, x, es* is added (**classes, churches, dishes**). However, if final *ch* is pronounced [k], only *s* is added (**monarchs, stomachs, epochs**).

2. After *y preceded by a consonant*, the *y* is changed to *i* and *es* is added (**lady—ladies, country—countries**). If final *y* is preceded by a vowel, no change is made (**attorney—attorneys, valley—valleys**).

3. In one-syllable words, final *f* or *fe* becomes *ves* in the plural (**wife—wives, leaf—leaves, thief—thieves**). However, some such words take the regular *s* ending (**chief—chiefs, roof—roofs**). A few words have either form for the plural (**wharves** or **wharfs, scarfs** or **scarves**).

4. After final *o, es* is sometimes added, especially in some common words (**heroes, Negroes, echoes, potatoes**). If a vowel precedes the final *o*, or if the word is a term used in music, only *s* is added (**studios, zoos, pianos, sopranos**). Sometimes the *es* alternates with a less common *s* ending (**cargoes** or **cargos, mottoes** or **mottos, volcanoes** or **volcanos**).

5. Irregular plurals based on older English may take the form of:
   (a) an internal change (**man—men, foot—feet, mouse—mice**).
   (b) an *en* ending (**child—children: ox—oxen**). **Brethren** (the older plural of **brother**) is found mainly in religious contexts.

6. The plural has the same form as the singular (**sheep—sheep, deer—deer**).

7. The singular has the same form as the plural (**series—series, means—means**).

8. Many foreign words retain their foreign plurals in English.
   (a) Singular *us* ending becomes plural *i* ending (**stimulus—stimuli, radius—radii**).

---

[2] The dictionary records the exceptional forms and spellings of nouns, verbs, adjectives and adverbs. It should be consulted if there is any doubt about the plural form of a noun, the past tense or participial form of a verb, or the comparative form of an adjective or adverb.

(b) Singular *a* ending becomes plural *ae* ending (**larva—larvae, vertebra—vertebrae**).

(c) Singular *um* ending becomes plural *a* ending (**memorandum—memoranda, stratum—strata**). Some such words are used chiefly in the plural (**data, bacteria**).

(d) Singular *is* ending becomes plural *es* ending (**crisis—crises, parenthesis—parentheses**).

(e) Singular *on* ending becomes plural *a* ending (**criterion—criteria; phenomenon—phenomena**).

(f) Singular *ex* or *ix* ending becomes plural *ices* ending (**vortex—vortices, matrix—matrices**).

(g) Singular *eau* ending becomes plural *eaux* ending (**bureau—bureaux, plateau—plateaux**).

There is an increasing tendency for regular *s* plurals to alternate with foreign plurals. The dictionary therefore also records such plurals as **memorandums, vertebras, vortexes, criterions, bureaus**.

9.  No plural is used for noncountable words such as **information, advice, clothing, furniture**.

10.  Some words ending in *s* are singular noncountable nouns, especially names of diseases and fields of study (**news, measles, economics**). However, when words that name fields of study are used for practical matters, such words are often considered plural—**His business ethics are very questionable; The acoustics in this room are not good**.

11.  Some words ending in *s* are used chiefly as plurals (**ashes, brains, goods, riches**). In this group are words for items that have two parts (**scissors, spectacles, pliers, trousers**).

### Possessive Inflectional Form

A singular noun is changed to possessive form by the addition of *'s* (**one *boy's* mother**). A plural noun becomes possessive by the addition of *'* alone to the final *s* (**two *boys'* mothers**). If an irregular plural noun does not already end in *s*, then *'s* is added for the possessive (**the *children's* mothers**). Proper nouns ending in *s* may take either *'* or *'s* (**Dickens' novels** or, less commonly, **Dickens's novels**). With a group of words functioning as a unit, *'s* is placed after the last word in the group (**the Queen of England's throne; his mother-in-law's interference; everyone else's opinions**).

The possessive form is generally preferred to the alternate **of** phrase when it refers to a *person* or a *living being*. However, the **of** phrase may be chosen if long or awkward modification is involved—**the very long and graceful tail of the old black cat**, vs. the more clumsy **the old black cat's very long and graceful tail**.

The **of** phrase occurs more often than the possessive form with nouns referring to *things*. However, there are many occasions when the possessive form may be used for nouns denoting things: (1) with expressions signifying time (**a day's journey, a month's time, today's newspaper**); (2) with words referring to natural phenomena (**the moon's rays, the earth's atmosphere, the tree's branches**: (3) with words referring to political entities (**Japan's industrialization, the city's parks, the country's tax system**); (4) with names that represent aggregates of people working together (**the newspaper's editorial policy, the railroad's employees, the company's new factory, the ship's crew**). Only with expressions of time is the possessive form the more usual one. In the other examples the possessive form alternates freely with the **of** phrase.

Some noun adjuncts that refer to things may be considered as more economical alternatives for **of** phrases (**the barn door** or **the door of the barn; the table leg** or **the leg of the table**).

When used in its customary position before another noun, a possessive noun is often considered as an adjective in function. However, the possessive form may also occur alone without a following noun, in which case it is sometimes regarded as a pronoun.

> *I want today's paper, not **yesterday's**.*
> *Whose book is this?—It's **John's**.*

The possessive form is often used alone to indicate a place of business—**at the doctor's, near the grocer's**). It may also appear in a "double possessive" with **of**—**a friend of John's** (=**one of John's friends**).

Derivational Form of Nouns

Only nouns, verbs, adjectives and adverbs have derivational forms. These forms may express some degree of lexical meaning, or they may be little more than part-of-speech indicators. Derivational forms consist chiefly of special endings that may:

(1) *change one part of speech to another*. This kind of ending is attached to a word that already exists (**engage** + **ment** = **engagement**), perhaps with some change in the original word (**destroy** + **tion** = **destruction**). Sometimes the original word has several derivational endings, the last one of which determines the part of speech (**nation** + **al** + **ize** + **ation** = **nationalization**, a noun).

(2) *distinguish one part of speech from another*, without being added to an already existing word (**distance**—noun, **distant**—adjective).

The derivational forms of nouns consist of the following suffixes.

1. Suffixes changing *verbs* to nouns:
    a. suffixes indicating **the state of** _____**-ing: -age -al, -ance** or **-ence**,[3] **-(e)ry, -ment, -t, -tion** or **-sion, -ure**

---

[3] Some nouns ending in **-ance** or **-ence** may have alternate forms in **-ancy** or **-ency**: **consistence** or **consistency** (more common); **permanence** (more common) or **permanency**; **hesitance** or **hesitancy**.

*marriage, arrival, allowance, persistence, bribery,*
*arrangement, weight, deviation, enclosure*

  b. suffixes indicating **a person who** _____**-s**, or **a person who is**
     **active in** _____, or **a person who comes from** _____
     (agent suffixes): **-ant** or **-ent, -er** or **-or** or **-eer, -(i)an** or **-arian, -ist**

*defendant, attendant, manager, governor, auctioneer,*
*New Yorker, antiquarian, Bostonian, librarian, typist*

  c. the suffix **-ing**, which expresses some of the verbal force of the
     word to which it is attached. Nouns with **-ing** derivational suffixes
     often refer to fields of endeavor, or recreational activities (**fishing,
     mining, dancing, engineering**), or are used as adjuncts in compounds
     (**swimming pool, ironing board**). Some of these **-ing** words have
     become so much like other nouns that they may take adjective
     modification (**a good cleaning, excellent hunting**) or they may be
     used in the plural (**blessings, weddings**).
2. Endings distinguishing nouns from verbs:

| *Verb* | *Noun* |
| --- | --- |
| belie*ve* | belie*f* |
| prove | proo*f* |
| li*ve* | li*fe* |
| defen*d* | defen*se* |
| recei*ve* | receip*t* |
| descen*d* | descen*t* |
| advi*se* | advi*ce* |

3. Suffixes changing *adjectives* to nouns to indicate **the state of being**
   _____: **-ity, -ness, -th**

*activity, sterility, happiness, usefulness, warmth, strength*

4. Suffixes distinguishing nouns from adjectives: **-ant** or **-ent** adjective—
**-ance** or **-ence** noun

*intelligent—intelligence, distant—distance,*
*brilliant—brilliance, radiant—radiance*

5. Suffixes changing concrete nouns to abstract nouns, to indicate **the
state of being a** _____: **-hood, -ism, -ship**

*brotherhood, childhood, heroism, despotism, fellowship, statesmanship*

6. Suffixes changing nouns to other nouns, to indicate (1) a doctrine,
theory, or school of belief—**-ism**; (2) a follower or advocate of such a doctrine,
theory, or school of belief—**-ist**.

*capitalism—capitalist, communism—communist,*
*impressionism—impressionist, terrorism—terrorist*

In a few cases these suffixes are added to adjectives rather than to nouns—
**realism—realist, idealism—idealist, socialism—socialist.** Sometimes what
precedes these suffixes is not a full word—**pessimism—pessimist, baptism—
baptist, chauvinism—chauvinist.**

7. The suffix **-ess,** to distinguish a female person from a male person—
**waiter—waitress, actor—actress, host—hostess, steward—stewardess.** Other
less frequently used suffixes denoting a female person are **-ine (hero—heroine),
-ix (aviator—aviatrix),** and **-ette (suffragist—suffragette).** Only by the use of
this type of derivational suffix does the English noun make a distinction for
gender. Other distinctions between the sexes have to be made entirely through
the vocabulary (**boy—girl, uncle—aunt; a woman doctor, a man servant**).

A very large group of nouns have *the same forms as verbs.* Some examples
are—**answer, control, cough, dance, defeat, dust, exchange, favor, fight,
honor, influence, load, mistake, outline, profit, quarrel, request.**

A smaller group of nouns have *the same forms as adjectives*—**average,
elastic, equal, ideal, native, principal, public, secret, square, standard.**

Spelling Rules for Adding
Noun-Forming Derivational Suffixes

1. Double the final consonant before a noun suffix beginning with a vowel:

> *If a **stressed** syllable before the added vowel ends in a single consonant
> preceded by a **single** vowel.*[4]

| | | | |
|---|---|---|---|
| Vowel suffix added to *one-syllable words* | rún | n | er |
| | bág | g | age |
| | wráp | p | er |
| Vowel suffix added to words of *two or more* syllables | occúr | r | ence |
| | begín | n | er |
| | rebél | l | ion |

The consonant is not doubled if the accent does not fall on the syllable
before the added vowel (**dífference, ópener**) or if the accent shifts to another
syllable than the one before the added noun suffix (**refér—réference, prefér—
préference**).

2. Change final *y* to *i* before a noun suffix *beginning with a vowel or consonant.*

---

[4] This part of the rule is sometimes stated as: "Double the final consonant if the preceding
vowel is 'short,' a 'short' vowel meaning the sound spelled by any of the vowel letters *a, e, i,
o, u* before a single final consonant."

| | | Exceptions: |
|---|---|---|
| *y* before a *vowel* | **carry + age = carriage**<br>**supply + er = supplier**<br>**ally + ance = alliance**<br>**bury + al = burial**<br>**vary + ety = variety** | **lobbyist** (before *i*)<br>**handyman** (in a compound) |
| *y* before a *consonant* | **happy + ness = happiness**<br>**lonely + ness = loneliness**<br>**classify + cation = classification** | |

3. Drop final silent *e* before a suffix beginning with a *vowel* (**-ion, -ation, -ition, -ance, -ence, -ure, -ing, -er, -or, -ist, -ant, -ent**)

    *admire + ation    =  admiration*
    *compete + ition   =  competition*
    *insure + ance     =  insurance*
    *confide + ence    =  confidence*
    *serve + ant       =  servant*
    *translate + or    =  translator*

4. Retain final silent *e* before a suffix beginning with a *consonant* (**-ment, -ness, -ty, -dom**)

    *arrange + ment  =  arrangement*
    *engage + ment   =  engagement*
    *strange + ness  =  strangeness*
    *safe + ty       =  safety*
    *bore + dom      =  boredom*

    Exceptions:  a. wisdom
                 b. judgment, acknowledgment, abridgment, argument
                    (American usage)

In some words, the form of the original words (the stem) changes when noun suffixes are added.

    NOUNS FROM VERBS
    *maintain + ance  =  maintenance*
    *describe + tion  =  description*
    *fly + t          =  flight*
    *pronounce + ation = pronunciation*
    *obey + ence      =  obedience*

    NOUNS FROM ADJECTIVES
    *curious + ity  =  curiosity*
    *strong + th    =  strength*

## MARKERS OF NOUNS

A marker, as we have already explained, is a structure word that signals the part of speech of a word following it. While markers also point to verbs, adjectives or adverbs that follow, their greatest usefulness is in signaling nouns.

A. Determiners
   1. articles
      (a) indefinite **a—an** (*a* **pencil,** *an* **eraser**)
      (b) definite **the** (*the* **pen**)
   2. possessives (*my* **aunt,** *John's* **book**)
   3. demonstratives (*this* **child,** *those* **boys**)
   4. numbers (*four* **girls, the** *fifth* **girl**)
   5. words of indefinite quantity (*some* **people,** *more* **books**)
B. Prepositions (*in* **the house,** *after* **the storm**)

In addition, descriptive adjectives help to "mark" the nouns that follow them (**the** *beautiful* **painting, a** *long* **speech**).

# 3

## Pronouns

Pronouns make up a small class of words of very high frequency. The traditional definition of a pronoun as "a word that takes the place of a noun"[1] is applicable to some types of pronouns but not to others. Those pronouns that are actual substitutes may refer not only to a preceding noun—its *antecedent*—but to a larger part of a discourse that precedes. Those pronouns that are not substitutes may simply have indefinite reference or express indefinite quantity.

Modern grammarians who regard *position* and *function* as the decisive factors in classifying a part of speech often consider pronouns as a subclass of nouns. However, they point out important formal differences: many pronouns are more highly inflected for grammatical properties (person, number, case and gender), and all pronouns lack the derivational endings (such as **-tion, -ment,** etc.) that nouns have.

Although there are a number of dissimilarities among the types of pronouns—some may be freely chosen and some may not, some are substitutes and some are not, some are inflected and some are not, some take adjective modification and some do not—there are two features that most pronouns have in common. One is their weak lexical content. Whatever meanings they have are derived from the context in which they are used. In addition, many pronouns have the ability to serve either of two functions—they may stand alone in noun function, or they may act as adjectives (determiners) that precede descriptive adjectives.

---

[1] The literal meaning of **pronoun** is "a word *standing for* a noun."

TYPES OF PRONOUNS

**Personal Pronouns**

Personal pronouns refer to:

1. the *speaker*, called the *first person*
   Singular—**I** (spelled with a capital letter)
   Plural—**we** (includes the speaker and one or more others)
2. the *person spoken to*, called the *second person*—**you** (singular and plural)
3. the *person or thing being spoken of*, called the *third person*
   Singular—**he** (for males), **she** (for females), **it** (for things; also for live beings whose sex is unknown or unimportant to the speaker)
   Plural—**they** (for all live beings and for all things)

The impersonal pronoun **one** is used to generalize for all persons—**One should always try to be kind to others**.

**Interrogative Pronouns**

Interrogative pronouns introduce direct or indirect questions.

| | |
|---|---|
| Direct question | ***Who* answered the phone?** |
| Indirect question | **He asked *who* had answered the phone.** |

There are three interrogative pronouns—**who** (for persons), **what** (for things), and **which** (for a choice involving either persons or things).

The three interrogative pronouns have generalizing forms: **whoever, whatever, whichever**—***Whoever* told you to do such a thing?**

The pronoun **what** also introduces exclamations—***What* beautiful flowers those are! What a** is used with a singular countable noun—**What a beautiful flower that is!**

**Relative Pronouns**

Relative pronouns refer to noun antecedents which immediately precede them. They introduce adjective clauses in which they serve as subjects or objects—**The man *who* answered the phone was rude. (Who** is the subject of the verb **answered** in the adjective clause **who answered the phone**). The most common relative pronouns are **who** (for persons), **that** (for persons or things), **which** (for things). **As** sometimes also serves as a relative pronoun—**She likes the same things as (=that) her husband does.**

**Demonstrative Pronouns**

Demonstrative pronouns point out someone or something. The most common demonstrative pronouns are **this** (plural **these**) and **that** (plural those). **This** generally refers to what is near at hand, **that** to what is farther away. This distinction in space is related to the distinction between the adverbs **here** and **there**—**This table** (over here) **is prettier than that one** (over there).

Demonstrative pronouns may also point to something that has just been said—**He told his wife he had just received an increase in salary.** *This* **pleased her very much.** Occasionally a demonstrative pronoun points to a part of a discourse that follows—**I must tell you** *this*. **I can no longer afford to go out to expensive restaurants for dinner.**

**That** or **those** may be more emphatic alternatives for **the.**

> *Those* (=the) *compounds that end in -one or -body take singular verbs.*
>
> *A sidewalk is* ***that*** *(=the) part of the street on which pedestrians walk.*
>
> **Such** or **so** may function as demonstrative pronouns.
>
> *His teacher was pleased with his composition and she told him so.* (*=this, that*)
>
> *They would like to buy a Cadillac or an Oldsmobile, but such* (*=those*) *cars are very expensive. Such a* is used before a singular countable noun.
>
> *If such* (*=this, that*) *was his intention, he did not make it clear.*

If an **as** phrase follows a noun used with **such, such** may appear before or after the noun.

> *Such men as these are dangerous.*
>
> or *Men such as these are dangerous.*

### Reflexive Pronouns

The reflexive pronoun is a combination of **-self** with one of the personal pronouns or with the impersonal pronoun **one.** The reflexive pronoun generally refers to an animate being, usually a person. The most common use of the reflexive pronoun is as an object that "reflects back" to the subject; in other words, it has the same identity as the subject. Thus, in the sentence **The child hurt himself, child** and **himself** are identical.

### Reciprocal Pronouns

Like the reflexive pronoun, the reciprocal pronoun has the same identity as the subject. The reciprocal pronoun indicates that the individual members of a plural subject mutually react one on the other. The reciprocal pronouns are **each other** and **one another.**

> *They amused* ***each other*** *by telling stories.* (Each one told stories *to the other one*[*s*].)
>
> vs. *They amused* ***themselves*** *by telling stories.* (The mutual interaction is not important here.)

The schoolbook rule that **each other** should be used for two persons and **one another** for three or more is not always observed by educated speakers.

**Indefinite Pronouns**

Such pronouns refer to indefinite (usually unknown) *persons or things*, or to indefinite *quantities*.

INDEFINITE PERSONS OR THINGS.    These pronouns are all singular in form and are used without noun antecedents. They consist of the following compounds:

|        | *-body*   | *-one*  | *-thing*[2] |
|--------|-----------|---------|-------------|
| some-  | somebody  | someone | something   |
| any-   | anybody   | anyone  | anything    |
| no-    | nobody    | no one  | nothing     |
| every- | everybody | everyone| everything  |

The forms with **no-** generally make a sentence negative rather than the forms with **any-** or **every-** plus a negative verb. Thus we say **Nobody is permitted to enter** rather than *\*Anybody is not permitted to enter*.[3] However, it is possible to say **Not anybody is permitted to enter**, with the special meaning that only certain qualified people may enter.

INDEFINITE QUANTITIES.    **All, another, any, both, each, either, few, least, less, little, a lot (of), lots (of), many, more, most, much, neither, none, one, other(s), plenty (of), several, some.**

All of these pronouns also function as adjectives except **none**, which has the corresponding adjective **no (I have no money). Every** is an indefinite pronoun that functions only as an adjective (**Every man should do his duty**). The pronouns with **of—a lot of, lots of, plenty of**—may be considered as single units functioning as adjectives in the same way that their synonyms **much** and **many** do.

Many grammarians also include the numerals (**one, first**, etc.) among the indefinite pronouns. Although the numerals refer to *definite* quantities, they resemble indefinite pronouns in many ways, especially in their ability to function as adjectives that precede descriptive adjectives.

Some distinctions in the use of indefinite pronouns need to be pointed out.

*No One—None*

**No one** refers only to *persons*. **None** specifies a *quantity* and is generally followed by an **of** phrase. **None** may refer to either persons or things.

> *No one* (=*nobody*) *passed the examination.*
> *None* (=*not one*) *of the students passed the examination.*

---

[2] The combinations with **-thing** are sometimes regarded as nouns rather than as pronouns.

[3] In accordance with common linguistic practice, all ungrammatical forms and sentences are being marked with an asterisk in this text.

In older usage, **none** could also be the equivalent of **nobody** (especially if it was followed by **but**), and is sometimes still used with this meaning.

> *None but the lonely heart can know my sorrow.*
>
> *None are so deaf as those that will not hear.*

### All—Every—Each—Any

All of these words refer to smaller components within a larger mass. **Each** may apply to as few as two items; **all**, **every**, **any** refer to three or more.

> *All the students contributed to the fund.*

**All** indicates the totality of items. The component units are part of an unbroken mass.

> *Every student contributed to the fund.*

**Every** gathers the separate items one by one into a whole. The component units are thought of as having something in common.

> *Each student contributed to the fund.*

**Each** draws attention to the individual items. The component units are thought of as having separate identities.

> *Any student may contribute to the fund.*

**Any** used within a mass signifies indifference to the component being referred to. It is the equivalent of *no matter who* or *no matter what*.

The phrase **each and every** places emphasis on both the individuality (separateness) and the commonality (togetherness) of components within a larger group—**Each and every student contributed to the fund.**

**All** is generally used with a *plural* noun or with a *noncountable* noun.

> *All (of) the **pies** were eaten.*
>
> *All (of) the **meat** was eaten.*

With *singular* countable nouns, including *collective* nouns, **the whole** is preferred to **all**.

> *The whole **pie** was eaten.*
>
> *The whole **class** was invited to the party.*
>
> *The whole **world** was astounded to learn that man could reach the moon.*

Note that in this last sentence **world** is regarded as a collective mass of people. In older usage **all** was also possible here—**All the world loves a lover.**

In some adverbial expressions, either **all** or **the whole** may be used.

> *He has searched **all** over the world* (or, less commonly, *over the **whole** world*) *to find a cure for his disease.*
>
> *She studied hard **all** the time* (or *the **whole** time*) *she was in college.*
>
> *She has had a headache **all** week long* (or *the **whole** week*).

*Both—Two*

The pronoun **both** is used only after the context has established the fact that *two* individual persons or things are being referred to.

**There were *two* dogs on the porch.** *Both* **were fast asleep. The both should be avoided in formal English—The two of them** (not **the both of them) were invited.** Formal English also requires **the two of you** rather than **you both— Notices will be sent to the two of you** (not **the both of you).**

*Some—Other—Another*

**Some** is generally used with a *plural* noun or with a *noncountable* noun. It represents an indefinite amount or portion.

| | |
|---|---|
| Indefinite amount | He bought some chairs. |
| | He bought some furniture. |
| Indefinite portion | He bought some of the chairs. |
| | He bought some of the furniture. |

**Some** used with a singular noun merely expresses indefiniteness in the same way as the article **a** does.

*Some borderline clash may set off a war between those two countries.*

*I read it in some book.*

**Or other** after a singular noun reinforces the indefiniteness of **some.**

*Some borderline clash **or other** may cause another war.*

*I read it in some book **or other**.*

**Another** occurs only with singular nouns—**This pen doesn't work. I must buy *another* one. Some** cannot precede **another,** since **some** with a singular noun already has the force of an indefinite article.

**Other** is generally used in the plural unless it is preceded by **the, this,** or an indefinite pronoun like **some, any, each.**

*I'll have to use our duplicate key. I lost **the other one**.*

***Any other person** than her husband would have lost patience with her.*

Both **another** and **other** may have the meaning of *different.*

| | |
|---|---|
| Singular | This route to Boston takes too long. There must be some (or *another*) *route* that is shorter. |
| Plural | This route to Boston takes too long. There must be (*some*) *other routes* that are shorter. (or there must be *some others* that are shorter.) |

**Another** may also signify one *additional* item—**I don't have enough plates. Please give me *another* one.** If an indefinite number of additional items are intended, **(some) more** is used—**I don't have enough plates. Please give me** (*some*) *more*.

See the chapter on adjectives for the distinctions between **some** and **any**, **much** and **many**, **little** and **few**.

### Pairs with *One, Other(s), Another, Some*

The pair **(the) one . . . the other** refers to individual persons or things in a set of *two*.

> *He held a book in* **one** *hand and his notes in* **the other**.
>
> *Here are two books.* **One** *is for Mary,* **the other** *is for Jack.*

**One . . . another** points to two individual items in an open set that may be extended.

> **One** *person may like to spend his vacation at the seashore, while* **another** *may prefer the mountains.*
>
> *Still another* introduces a third item—**One** *person may like to spend his vacation at the seashore,* **another** *may prefer the mountains, while* **still another** *may choose a large metropolis.*

**Some . . . (the) others** breaks up a set into two parts, each of which has an indefinite quantity. **Some** denotes the first part of the set, **(the) others** signifies the balance of the set. This pair might be considered a plural of **(the) one . . . the others**.

> *The search party was divided into two groups.* **Some** *went to the right,* (*the*) **others** *went to the left.*

**Some . . . some** may also express this kind of division—*Some* **went to the right,** *some* **went to the left.** The second **some** places less stress on the idea of remainder than does **(the) others**.

### Special Meanings of Certain Pronouns

Some pronouns from among the various types just described have special meanings when used in particular contexts.

EACH: *a piece*
> *How much are these oranges? Ten cents* **each**.

EITHER: *each of two*
> *At* **either** *side of the road were glaring neon signs.*
>
> *He came down the street with a package in* **either** *arm.*

SO, SUCH: *very* (informal)
> *I've had* **such** *a busy day.*
>
> *I've been* **so** *busy today.*

ONE: *a certain*
> **One** *night we were awakened by a loud noise.*

ONE:  *only*
>  The **one** person who can help you is Mr. Jackson.

SOME:  *about*
>  It happened **some** thirty years ago.

THIS:  *the present*
>  We are studying the use of pronouns **this** week.
>  I don't see him much **these** days.

THIS, THAT:  *so* (informal)
>  I've never seen him **this** angry before.
>  No one could be **that** stupid.

WHAT(EVER):  *all*
>  I gave him **what(ever)** (=all the) money I had in my pocket.
>  I gave him **what(ever)** (=all that) I had in my pocket.

NONE:  *not*
>  I am **none** the worse for that experience.
>  The food here is **none** too good.

## FUNCTION OF PRONOUNS

Pronouns have most of the same functions as nouns.

| | |
|---|---|
| *Subject of verb* | **They** were late for their appointment. |
| *Object of verb:* | |
| Direct object | We enjoyed **ourselves** at the party. |
| Indirect object | We will send **you** the goods immediately. |
| *Subjective complement* | That's the **one**. |
| *Object of preposition* | After **this**, be more careful. |
| *Appositive:* | |
| Nonrestrictive | Mary, **one** of the most intelligent girls I know, is planning to attend the university. |
| Restrictive | The men **all** got into the boat. |

The indefinite pronouns **all, both, each** are the most common pronouns used in close (restrictive) apposition. They may be in apposition to nouns (**The children *all* have colds**) or to pronouns (**You *each* may have two pieces of candy**).

**All, both,** or **each** used as an appositive to a subject may also appear in adverbial position after an auxiliary, or after the verb **be** used independently.

>  They were **both** invited to the party.
>  You may **each** have two pieces of candy.
>  The children are **all** sick.

Since **all, both, each** are in adverbial positions in such sentences, they have some adverbial force. In some sentences their meaning may be ambiguous. Thus, the sentence **The boards are** *all* **rotten** may be interpreted as *All* **the boards are rotten** or as **The boards are** *completely* **rotten.**

A pronoun in apposition may make a summarizing reference to some part of the sentence that has already been mentioned.

> *Men, women, children—**all** were killed.*
>
> *To be or not to be, **that** is the question.*

The pronouns **we** and **you** may also appear as the first part of a structure of apposition. Such usage is generally informal.

> ***We** girls often go to the movies together.*
>
> *He asked **us** boys to be quiet.*

We have already seen that many pronouns function not only as nouns, but also as adjectives.

---

| | |
|---|---|
| I need **some**. | **Some** is a pronoun functioning as the *object* of **need**. |
| I need **some** money. | **Some** is a pronoun functioning as an *adjectival modifier* of **money**. Pronouns functioning as adjectives are being called *determiners* in this text. |

---

### POSITION OF PRONOUNS

Pronouns have the same position as nouns do. Pronoun subjects appear before verbs, pronoun objects appear after verbs or after prepositions. With a certain type of verb-preposition combination, a pronoun object appears *between* the verb and the preposition—**Call** *him* **up.** (See the chapter on prepositions for a list of separable verbs.)

In American English, two personal pronouns do not usually occur together as an indirect-direct object combination. For this reason, the sentence **I gave it to him** would be preferred to **I gave him it** (but, **I gave him** *some*, **I gave him** *that*).

A third-person pronoun, a demonstrative pronoun, or a relative pronoun generally appears in some position *after* the noun it refers to.

> *The Browns said **they** might move to California. **This** news disturbed us very much. The Browns, **who** had been our next door neighbors for years, were our best friends.*

In a short introductory structure within a sentence, a personal pronoun may precede the noun it refers to—**Because** *he* **had a bad cold, Mr. Jackson decided to stay in bed the whole day.**

In a series of two (or more) subjects or objects, the pronoun **I** comes last for the sake of politeness—**My wife and** *I* **always go to bed early.**

## INFLECTIONAL FORMS OF PRONOUNS

### Forms of Personal and Reflexive Pronouns

The personal pronouns change their form for person (first, second, third), for case (subject, object, possessive), number (singular, plural), and gender (masculine, feminine, neuter). Except for case, the reflexive pronouns make the same kinds of changes.

| | Subject | Object | Possessive Adjective | Possessive Pronoun | Reflexive |
|---|---|---|---|---|---|
| | ___ *Did It* | *Show* ___ | ___ *Book* | *It Is* ___ | *Hurt* ___ |
| *Sing.* | I | me | my | mine | myself |
| | you | you | your | yours | yourself |
| | he | him | his | his | himself |
| | she | her | her | hers | herself |
| | it | it | its | | itself |
| *Plural* | we | us | our | ours | ourselves |
| | you | you | your | yours | yourselves |
| | they | them | their | theirs | themselves |

Note that the possessive forms of the personal pronouns are not written with '*s*. Note further that the reflexive ending **-self** changes to **-selves** in the plural. This change marks the only difference between singular **you** and plural **you**. Observe also that the reflexive pronouns begin with *possessive* forms (**my**self, **our**selves) except for the third person **him**self and **them**selves, which begin with *object* forms.

An older pronoun for the second person familiar singular is still found in religious contexts. Its forms are **thou, thee, thy, thine, thyself.** The second person plural has an archaic form **ye,** which was once used as a subject, and occasionally as an object.

Personal pronouns appearing after the verb **be** (usually for identification of a person), take subject form in formal English: **It is *I*, It is *they*.** In informal speech, where such pronouns are more likely to occur, the natural tendency of the language is for *object form* to be used with words in object position—**It's *me*, It's them.** Many native speakers are not comfortable with expressions like **It is *I*,** which they feel are learned expressions rather than natural ones.

If a **who** or a **that** clause follows a personal pronoun used after a form of **be,** the pronoun *must* be in subject form—**It's *I*** (or *he, they*) **who did it.**

After the infinitive **to be,** the following forms are used:

> *I didn't expect the winner to be **me**. (**Me** agrees with **winner**, the object of the verb **expect**.)*

*I would like to be **he**.* (**He** agrees with **I**, the subject of the verb *like*. Informal speech permits **I would like to be him.**)

Sometimes a pronoun occurring as the second element in a compound nominal is used incorrectly. Care must be taken that such a pronoun has the form required by its function.

*They invited my wife and **me** to dinner.* (**My wife, me** are both objects of the verb **invited**.)

*Between you and **me**, that is not a real diamond.* (**You, me** are both objects of the preposition **between**.)

The first person plural **we** is often preferred by an individual speaking for a corporate entity:

An employee in a business firm or in a government office

*We should like to duplicate the order we sent you last month.*

A newspaper writer or editor (editorial **we**)

*We do not necessarily support the views expressed in this column.*

The head of a monarchy (royal **we**)

*We have this day commissioned a memorial in the general's honor.*

The forms for feminine pronouns are sometimes used figuratively for things to suggest gentleness, beauty, fertility—**We thank the earth for *her* bounty; The moon shines *her* rays on all.** Feminine pronouns may also be used for nations, ships, machines, cars and other vehicles to reflect a feeling of affection or familiarity with the object.

Unlike nouns, personal pronouns do not generally have **of** phrase alternatives for the possessive forms.

*This is **my** hat.* (Compare with *This is **the young man's** hat* or *This is the hat **of the young man.***)

*He was tactful with the children and **their** parents.*

*The dog wagged **its** tail.*

The **of** phrase alternative is sometimes possible in referring to things—**the name of it** (or **its name**), **the end of it** (or **its end**), or to persons in uses other than possession—**for the life of me** (idiom), **the sight of him.**

Personal pronouns may appear in a double possessive construction—**He is a friend of *mine*; I found some old hats of *yours*.** A double possessive may be used before the word **own** functioning as a pronoun—**I would like to have a house of my *own*.** Such double possessive constructions place more emphasis on the idea of possession; they usually alternate with constructions with the possessive adjectives—**one of *my* friends; some of *your* old hats; *my* own house.**

Forms of Interrogative and Relative Pronoun WHO

---

| | |
|---|---|
| *Subject* form: **who** | *Who* is watering the plants? |
| | I know *who* is watering the plants. |
| | The man *who* is watering the plants is the gardener. |
| *Object* form: **whom** | |
| object of verb | *Whom* do you want? |
| | I know *whom* you want. |
| | The man *whom* you want is the gardener. |
| object of preposition | From *whom* did he receive the money? |
| | I know from *whom* he received the money. |
| | Then man from *whom* he received the money is the gardener. |

---

In informal usage, **who** often replaces **whom** as the object either of a verb, or of a preposition which has been moved to final position:

> *Who* do you want?
>
> The man *who* you want is the gardener.
>
> I know *who* he received the money from.

This usage is in line with the general tendency for speakers of the English language to use a *subject form* for a word in *subject position*.

The possessive form of **who** is **whose**. **Whose** may refer to either persons or things.

> *Whose* book is this?
>
> He pointed to an abandoned house whose roof had caved in.

It is sometimes claimed that **whose** should refer only to persons. The fact remains, however, that **whose** has long been used for things by reputable writers, and is often preferable to the awkward **of which** form (**the roof of which**) that some authorities recommend for formal English.

Other Pronoun Forms

**This** has the plural form **these**; **that** has the plural form **those**.

The impersonal **one** has a plural form **ones**, a possessive form **one's**, and a reflexive form **oneself** (or the older **one's self**).

The indefinite compounds with **-one**, **-body** have possessive forms—**somebody's, everyone's**. The *'s* follows the word **else** used after one of these compounds—**anybody else's, no one else's**. Other pronouns with possessive forms are **other's, another's**, and, in their reciprocal use, **each other's, one another's**.

## PRONOUNS FOR GENERIC PERSON

Personal pronouns and indefinite pronouns may serve to make statements about people in general.

Personal Pronouns

> ***We***—***We*** *all get into trouble sometimes.*
> (***We*** includes the speaker or the writer.)
> ***They*** (informal)—***They*** *grow coffee in Brazil.*
> (***They*** refers to a smaller group, or one that is removed from the speaker and his audience.)
> ***They*** *say that oil has been found in that area.*
> ***They*** *say that honesty is the best policy.*

In formal English, a passive construction is preferred to the use of **they** for generic person.

> *Coffee is grown in Brazil.*
> *It is rumored that oil has been found in that area.*
> *It is said that honesty is the best policy.*
>
> ***You*** (informal)—***You*** *have to study very hard at the university.*

Indefinite Pronouns

> ***One***—***One*** *should obey the law.*

**One** is the most formal of the pronouns of generic person.

> ***Everybody*** or ***Everyone***—*Everybody should obey the law.*

Equivalent to these pronouns of generic person are the combinations of **each** and **every** with **person**, or **all** with **persons, people**—**Every person** (or **all people**) **should obey the law.**

## REFLEXIVE PRONOUNS

A reflexive pronoun generally *points back to the subject*. It is used:

1. as the direct object of the verb:

   *You mustn't blame* ***yourself*** *for that mistake.* (The subject ***you*** and the object ***yourself*** have the same identity.)

2. as the indirect object of the verb:

   *I bought* ***myself*** *a beautiful watch.* (or *I bought a beautiful watch for* ***myself***.)
   *He has never denied* ***himself*** *anything.*

3. as a prepositional object:

   of a verb—*We should depend on* ***ourselves*** *rather than on others.*
   of an adjective—*She's angry with* ***herself*** *for making such a mistake.*

In some prepositional phrases with reflexive pronouns that do not refer back to the subject, the reflexive pronoun merely serves as a more emphatic alternative of a personal pronoun. This usage is often regarded as informal.

> *This is strictly between **ourselves** (or **us**).*
>
> *The fault lies in **ourselves** (or **us**), not in our stars.*
>
> *Did anyone see the money besides **yourself** (or **you**) ?*
>
> *To a schoolteacher like **myself** (or **me**), such a book is very useful.*

In popular speech, a reflexive pronoun is sometimes used as the last part of a compound subject or object.

> *My wife and myself were invited to the party.*
>
> *Her teacher asked her friend and herself to help with the decorations.*

A special use of reflexive pronouns is to intensify a noun or pronoun functioning as a subject, or less commonly, as an object. These reflexive pronouns are not essential to the structure of the sentence; they merely give added emphasis to the subject or object.

| | |
|---|---|
| Reflexive pronoun intensifying a *subject* | We ***ourselves*** will lead the discussion. (=**we** and no one else) or We will lead the discussion ***ourselves***. Shakespeare ***himself*** could not have said it better. (=Even **Shakespeare**) or Shakespeare could not have said it better ***himself***. |
| Note that a reflexive pronoun that intensifies a subject appears either right after the subject, or at the end of the sentence. | |
| Reflexive pronoun intensifying an *object* | I saw the chief ***himself***. They want us to lead the discussion ***ourselves***. We spoke to the victims ***themselves***. |

Reflexive pronouns sometimes have special meanings. Such pronouns generally occur in final position.

| | |
|---|---|
| = Alone | I don't like to go to a party (by) ***myself***. You should not walk by ***yourself*** at night. |
| = Unaided | It's impossible for anyone to move that piano (by) ***himself***. (This meaning is related to the meaning of *alone*.) |
| = Also | We'll give you a lift to the concert hall. We're going there ***ourselves***. |

## NUMBER AND AGREEMENT IN THE USE OF PRONOUNS

The compounds with **-body, -one, -thing** are singular in form. When used as subjects these compounds require singular verbs—**Everyone** (or **everybody**) *is* **bringing lunch**. Subjects with the modifiers **each** or **every** also take singular verbs—**Every man** *is* **an individual, each student** *is* **bringing lunch.**

Possessive pronouns that refer to compounds with **-body** or **-one**, and to nouns modified by **each** or **every** are usually masculine singular if the gender is not known, or if both males and females are being referred to—**Everyone is bringing** *his* **lunch. His or her** is sometimes used for a group consisting of males and females—**Everyone is bringing** *his or her* **lunch.** However, this construction is not only clumsy, but it gives the impression of being over-precise. In informal speech, **their** is frequently used in order to avoid having to make a choice for gender—**Everyone is bringing** *their* **lunch.**

When a general statement is made with the indefinite pronoun **one**, either **one** or **he** may make further reference to this pronoun:

> *One must do one's best.*
>
> or
>
> *One must do his best.* (preferred American usage)

In sentences or paragraphs about people in general, it is best to use the same pronoun for generic person throughout. For example, one should not shift from **we** to **one** to **you**, as in the following:

> *If* **we** *are making statements about people in general,* **one** *should not shift from one person to another, but* **you** *should be consistent in* **your** *use of pronouns of generic person.*

In this sentence, the boldface words should all be either **we**, **one** (or **he** after the first **one**), or **you**.

In sentences stating an addition, multiplication, subtraction or division of numbers, the verb **be** or **equal** may be singular or plural.

> *Three times five is* or *are fifteen.*
>
> *Ten and four equals* or *equal fourteen.*

If the subject of a sentence is an indefinite pronoun of quantity plus an **of** phrase, the number of the verb is determined by the *noun in the of phrase.*

> *All of the* **fruit was** *spoiled.*
> *All of the* **apples were** *spoiled.*
>
> *None of the* **pie was** *eaten.*
> *None of the* **pies were** *eaten.*

There is an old rule that **none** is always singular because of its singular form (which corresponds to that of **no one**), but many educated speakers today disregard this rule and use **none** as singular or plural in the manner noted above.

A noun that denotes indefinite quantity also takes a singular or a plural verb according to the number of the noun in the following **of** phrase.

> *One half* (or *one third*) *of the* **fruit was** *spoiled.*
> *One half* (or *one third*) *of the* **apples were** *spoiled.*

*The rest* (or *remainder*) *of the **pie was** eaten.*

*The rest* (or *remainder*) *of the **pies were** eaten.*

When the indefinite pronoun **one** is followed by an **of** phrase, the noun in the **of** phrase is *plural*—**He is *one* of the best scientist*s* in the world.**

**Any** may have singular or plural reference.

1. *In questions or negatives:*

*Do you need any **money**?—No, I don't need any.*

*Do you want any **flowers**?—No, I don't want any.*

2. *In affirmative statements:* (=No matter who, no matter which)

*Any pupil who is found smoking is liable to punishment.*

*Any pupils who are found smoking are liable to punishment.*

**Either, neither**, and **any**, when they *express a choice*, require singular verbs in formal English (the word **one** being understood after them)—**Either (or neither, any) of the children is willing to do that chore.** In informal English these words often take plural verbs.

The interrogative pronouns **who** and **what** are generally used with singular verbs—**Who is there? What is missing?** Occasionally a plural verb is heard if the speaker has a number of persons or things in mind—**Who *were* at the party last night?**

In a question with **who** or **what**, the verb **be** agrees with a noun or pronoun after it. This noun or pronoun has the same identity as the interrogative pronoun.

*Who **are** these **people**?*

*What **am I**?*

*Who **are you**?*

## MODIFICATION OF PRONOUNS

Only certain indefinite pronouns may take simple adjective modifiers.

1. The compounds with **-body, -one**, and **-thing**. The adjective modifier *follows* the pronoun—**somebody *else*, everything *new*, no one *interesting*.**

2. The indefinite pronoun **one**. The adjective modifier *precedes* the pronoun—*the green* **one**, *a bad* **one**.

Larger adjective constructions may follow many of the indefinite pronouns —**the one *on top of the table*, anybody *knowing the truth*, several *who were present*.**

Pronouns, like nouns, may be preceded by intensifiers—*even* **you**, *only* **this**, *just* **me**.

## EXPLETIVE *IT, THERE*

Although expletives are classified as pronouns in most dictionaries and conservative grammar books, they actually differ somewhat from other pronouns. Expletives have even less semantic content than other pronouns.

Their chief function is either to provide a sentence with a formal subject, or to anticipate a true subject that appears in the predicate. Because expletives are used merely for a grammatical purpose, modern grammarians often classify them among the *structure words* which do not belong to any part of speech.

### IT as Expletive

A singular form of a linking verb, usually **be**, is used with expletive **it**.

**Impersonal** *It*

Impersonal **it** often co-occurs with a predicate adjective (sometimes a predicate noun) plus an adverbial.

> *It's gloomy here.*
> *It's pleasant in the garden.*
> *It would be wise if you went there now.*
> *It's more fun when we all go together.*

Impersonal **it** may also introduce predicates that have the special meanings of:

| | |
|---|---|
| *identification* | Who is **it**? —**It's** Mary. |
| | What is this? —**It's** a lawn mower. |
| *weather* | **It's** cold outside. |
| | With verbs signifying weather—**It** was raining (or snowing, hailing, storming) yesterday. |
| *time* | **It's** Wednesday. |
| | **It's** January 25. |
| | **It's** ten o'clock. |
| *distance* | **It** is five miles from the library to my house. (in terms of space) |
| | **It** is a five-minute walk to my house. (in terms of time) |

In a special kind of construction, impersonal **it** co-occurs with a clause that modifies a subjective complement. This construction permits greater emphasis on the complement than does the alternate construction without **it**.

1. *Noun or pronoun complement:*

> *It is not **I** who am to blame.* (or *I am not to blame.*)
> *It was **some poet** who said we live in an age of anxiety.* (or ***Some poet** said . . .*)

2. *Adverb complement:*

> *It was **four years ago** that he died.* (or *He died four years ago.*)
> *It was **here** that I met him.* (or *I met him here.*)

Other linking verbs than **be** after impersonal **it** are:

| Appear | Can you tell me who is outside? —It *appears* to be a small child. |
| Seem | It *seems* to be hot outside. |
| Get or Become | It *gets* (or *becomes*) very cold here in the winter. |

## Anticipatory *It*

Anticipatory **it** merely fills subject position; the actual subject is a noun structure in the predicate.

> *It is important (**for you**) **to be there on time.***
>
> *It is important **that you be there on time.***
>
> *It is important, **your being there on time.***
>
> *It's unbelievable **what doctors can do these days.***
>
> *It's astonishing **the amount of work he can do in one day.***

The noun structures in the predicate after anticipatory **it** may also appear in their regular subject position.

> *(**For you**) To be there on time is important.*
>
> *What doctors can do these days is unbelievable.*
>
> *The amount of work he can do in one day is astonishing.*

Anticipatory **it** also occurs with passive verbs of believing or communicating. Such verbs are followed by **that** clauses which are the actual subjects.

> *It is suggested that you be there on time.*
>
> *It was believed that he had committed suicide.*
>
> *It is rumored that secret peace talks have already begun.*

The **that** clauses with such passive verbs only occasionally appear in subject position—**That there had been foul play was believed by many people.**

It is sometimes claimed that the noun structures in sentences with anticipatory **it** are in apposition with **it**. The apposition here is considered to be of the same nature as the apposition with **it** used as object of a verb.

| *Apposition with It as Subject* | *Apposition with It as Object* |
| --- | --- |
| It is hard *to do all this work.* | I find **it** hard *to do all this work.* |
| It is possible *that they may* arrive next week. | We think *it* possible *that they* may arrive next week. |

### THERE as Expletive

Expletive **there** occurs most often with a linking verb. This construction permits the subject and the important part of the predicate to be laid side by side without the linking verb between.

In a sentence with expletive **there**, the verb agrees with the actual subject that follows it:

> *There is a book on the desk.*
> *There are some books on the desk.*

If the subject consists of two or more parts, the verb is plural—**There are a pencil and a notebook on the table.** Often, however, the pull of a following *a* may result in the use of a singular verb in such a sentence—There *is a* pencil and a notebook on the desk. This usage is regarded as informal.

In most sentences the linking verb that accompanies expletive **there** is **be**. There are three common types of sentences with expletive **there**.

1. *there + be + (pro)noun + expression of place*

> *There's nobody here.*
> *There is a piano in the room.*
> *There is a big sale now at Macy's.*

Sometimes the expression of place is understood from the context.

> *How many students are there?* (in the class)
> *—There are fifteen students.*

Although some of these sentences with expressions of place are reversible (**Nobody is here; A piano is in the room**), these reversed sentences are not felt to be as natural as the sentences with expletive **there**.

2. *there + be + noun with adjective modifier(s)*

In many sentences with this type of expletive **there**, the verb **be** has the meaning of *exist*. Such sentences are especially common in setting up an enumeration.

> *There are three kinds of TV programs that she likes to watch.*
> *There are different ways to do it.*
> *There are two blankets for each bed.*
> *There are many doctors who can help you.*
> *There are (some) people who like him.*

These sentences are not reversible. However, some of those that contain adjective clause modifiers may be simplified structurally by omitting the words that have no semantic content.

> *(There are) many doctors (who) can help you.*
> *(There are) some people (who) like him.*

Occasionally there may be a choice between expletive **it** and expletive **there**. In such cases, **there** often emphasizes *existence*, **it** emphasizes *identification*.

> *There was a poet who said that we live in an age of anxiety.* (Such a poet exists)

*It was a poet who said that we live in an age of anxiety.* (A poet said this and not someone else)

3. *there* + *be* + *noun* + *-ing participle*

This alternate way of using a progressive verb permits greater emphasis to be placed on the progression of an event.

> *There is a storm **approaching** (=A storm is approaching.)*
>
> *There is a sale **going on** at Macy's. (=A sale is going on at Macy's.)*
>
> *There is a strong wind **coming up** from the west. (=A strong wind is coming up from the west.)*

Sometimes the past participle rather than the present participle is used—**There were many people** *killed* **in the last war.** This construction acts as a loose substitute for a passive verb—**Many people** *were killed* **in the last war.**

In sentences with expletive **there,** *a* or some expression of definite or indefinite quantity often accompanies the noun subject. If **the** appears with a subject, the introductory **there** is usually an *adverb* rather than an expletive.

> *There's **a** book I've been looking for since February.* (**There** is an expletive)
>
> *There's **the** book I've been looking for since February.* (**There** is an adverb)

A few other verbs besides **be** occur after expletive **there**—**appear, come, go, happen, live, remain, seem.**

> *Once upon a time there lived a wicked king.*
>
> *There seem to be two reasons for his success.*
>
> *There comes a time when we must all face our maker.*
>
> *There goes Jim.* But, with a pronoun subject: *There **he** goes.*

Expletive **there** with the verb **go** has a greater adverbial force of place than expletives used with other verbs. Its semantic opposite, **here** plus **come**, also requires the same arrangement of subject and verb—**Here comes Jim**, but **Here** *he* **comes.**

### SUBSTITUTION WITH *ONE(S)*, *THAT—THOSE*

A common type of substitution with **one** is related to its meaning of number, quantity. In this function, stressed **one** used for countable nouns contrasts with stressed **some** used for noncountable mass nouns.

> *Here are the apples* (countable noun). *Would you like óne?*
>
> *Here is the fruit* (mass noun). *Would you like sóme?*

In a second kind of substitution, **one** still retains some of its lexical meaning as a numeral. It also has some degree of stress.

> *I lose a neighbor and you gain one.*
>
> *Our company has representatives everywhere; Mr. Smith is one.*

These two are fairly simple substitutions that require no further explanation. Far more complicated is the use of **one(s)** as a substitute word, or "prop," to which adjective modification can be attached. In this kind of substitution, the adjective modifier may precede or follow **one(s)**. In addition, **that**, or especially **those**, may be an alternative for **one(s)**.

### Adjective Modification Precedes ONE(S)

This type of substitution occurs with countable nouns only. The adjective that precedes the word **one(s)** receives greater stress than **one(s)** does.

### Descriptive Adjectives as Modifiers

> *They sent us the large trays instead of the small **ones**.*
> *I don't like this book. Show me a more interesting **one**.*
> *There is a French translation of his book and a German **one**.*

Noun adjuncts, like descriptive adjectives, may also precede **one(s)**.

> *She bought a cotton dress and a silk **one**.*
> *She likes to cook in stainless steel pans, not in aluminum **ones**.*

With noncountable nouns, the descriptive adjective alone may substitute for the adjective plus the noun.

> *We prefer red wine to **white**.*
> *The old equipment works just as well as the **new**.*

In informal English, **one(s)** is sometimes omitted after descriptive adjectives that are *preceded by **the***.

> *I bought the green dress. The blue was too expensive.*
> *She's the older sister, not the younger.*

**One(s)** is often omitted with a superlative adjective.

> *Of all her friends, the prettiest (one) is Jane.*
> *The chairs you have chosen are the most expensive (ones) in the store.*

### Pronoun Determiners as Modifiers

The use of **one(s)** after pronoun determiners is often optional. With a few of the determiners, the **one** substitute has some of the force of the numeral **one**.

> INTERROGATIVE—**Which (one** or **ones)**.

> *Here are all the paintings. Which (one* or *ones) do you want?—I haven't decided yet which (one* or *ones) I want.*
> *I found his name listed in some directory, I can't remember which (one).*

**Whichever (one** or **ones)** may be used in a noun clause.

> *Here are some dresses. Choose whichever (one* or *ones) you like.*

DEMONSTRATIVE—**This (one), that (one)**. The plural **these** or **those** is not used with **one**.

> *Let's weigh the two bags. I believe this (one) is heavier than that (one).*
> *I like this hat. I don't like that (one).*
> *Please give me a clean cup. This (one )is dirty.*

INDEFINITE QUANTITY—**Another (one), any (one), each (one), either (one), every one, neither (one), the other (one or ones)**.

**Every** must be accompanied by **one**. Only **the other** can be used in the plural.

> *This cup isn't clean. Please give me another (one).*
> *We can seat you at a table in the back. The other ones* (or *the others*) *are all occupied.*
> *I'll check on évery óne of the tickets.*

**Every one** written as two separate words has roughly the same meaning as **each one**. (The form written as one word, **éveryòne**, is the equivalent of **everybody**.)

NUMERALS—**One(s)** is used only with *ordinals*, and with **next, last**.

> *Of the speakers, only the first (one) was interesting.*
> *The second and third (ones) were boring.*
> *I want the fifth volume, not the fourth (one).*

Cardinal numbers, like mass nouns, stand alone without any additional word substituting for an antecedent noun—**I ordered five lamps, not six.**

Sentences of the form *determiner* + ***one*** + ***of*** *phrase* may be restated in two other ways.

> *Which one of the clerks can wait on me?*
> *Which of the clerks can wait on me?*
> *Which clerk can wait on me?*
> *Any* (or *either, neither, each*) *one of the clerks can help you.*
> *Any of the clerks can help you.*
> *Any clerk can help you.*

### Adjective Modification Follows ONE(S), THAT—THOSE

This kind of substitution differs from the substitution with preceding adjective modification in several respects: (1) the substitute word may not be omitted; (2) more often than not, **one(s)** is preceded by **the**; (3) **those** alternates with **the ones** for the plural substitute; (4) in certain circumstances a nonpersonal **that** may be used as a substitute for a singular noun.

> *Do you see those men over there?* ***The one*** *with the gray hair is my father.*

*I must sort through my clothes. I'll keep **the ones** (or **those**) that fit me and give away **the ones** (or **those**) that are too small.*

Substitutes with modifiers that follow are very common in comparisons.

*Our new television set is more expensive than **the one** we had before.*

*The people in this town are less helpful than **those** (or **the ones**) in the first town we visited.*

*The tools which are manufactured here are as good as **those** (or **the ones**) made anywhere else in the world.*

In formal usage, comparisons may also be made with *a nonpersonal **that*** as a substitute. In such instances, **that** may stand for:

1. *a noncountable noun*

*The furniture which is manufactured here is as good as **that** made anywhere else in the world.*

This is the only kind of substitution that may be made for a noncountable word.

2. *a singular countable noun denoting a thing* (interchangeable with **the one**)

*The dialect spoken in this town is different from **that** (or **the one**) spoken in the next town.*

The thing denoted by **that** is likely to be more abstract than the thing denoted by **the one**.

If an **of** phrase follows a nonpersonal substitute word in a comparison, **that** or **those** is generally used rather than **the one(s)**.

*Robert's income is less than **that** of his wife.*

*I believe the prestige of our college is as great as **that** of any other college in this area.*

*Today's styles are not as attractive as **those** of a generation ago.*

If the **of** phrase is short, its alternate possessive form is often preferred in informal English—**Robert's income is less than his** *wife's*. In fact, **that of** would be inappropriate in some casual situations—**I want today's paper, not** *yesterday's* (not **that of yesterday**).

**One(s)** may occur without **the** if it has *indefinite or general reference*.

*A house built of bricks is more durable than **one** made of wood.*

*Your company has been recommended to us as **one** that is reliable and honest.*

Such substitution without **the** is common in appositives.

*That man has just finished a remarkable invention, **one** that will undoubtedly effect some profound changes in modern living.*

*He is a brilliant student, **one** who should be successful in whatever career he chooses.*

Note that in these sentences, **one** substitutes for a noun with the indefinite article **a** (**a house, a company**, etc.).

The **one** substitute, like any noun, may be both preceded and followed by adjective modification.

> *He was **the first** (one) **to climb that mountain.***
>
> *This book is fascinating. I'm going to read **another** (one) **by the same author.***
>
> *The child doesn't like this book. Show him **some more interesting** ones **with pictures in them.***

Note that even with preceding and following modification, the **one** substitute may be omitted after a pronoun determiner (**first, another**) but must be kept after a descriptive adjective (**interesting**).

### GENERALIZING FORMS WITH *-EVER*

The generalizing forms with **-ever, whoever, whatever, whichever** are used in questions or negatives, and in adverbial clauses or noun clauses.

#### *-Ever* Forms as Intensifiers in Questions

The **-ever** forms give additional emphasis to a question word. These forms may be the equivalent of such a phrase as **in the world.**

> *Who(ever) (or who in the world) told you to do such a thing?*
>
> *Whatever happened to those pleasant people who used to live next door to you?*
>
> *What (ever) did you say to upset her so much?*

#### *What(so)ever* as Intensifier in Negatives

**Whatever** adds more emphasis to a negative. **Whatsoever** is an even stronger intensifier.

> *I have no money whatever (or whatsoever).*
>
> *We know no one whatever (or whatsoever) in this town.*
>
> *He doesn't understand any English whatever (or whatsoever).*

#### *-Ever* Forms in Adverbial Clauses

The **-ever** forms in adverbial clauses connote the idea of *no matter* **who** (**what** *or* **which**).

> *Whatever happens, remember that your mother and father love you.*
>
> *Whoever knocks at the door, don't open it.*
>
> *What(ever) he does, he does well.*

#### *-Ever* Forms in Noun Clauses

The **-ever** forms appear in noun clauses that are derived from questions. They often also suggest the idea of *no matter who (what or which)*, some more vaguely so than others. Usually, the **-ever** forms are required for pronouns denoting persons, but may be optional for pronouns denoting things.

1. *Pronouns denoting persons:*

> *Whoever broke the window must pay for it.*
>
> *He tells the same story to whomever he meets.*
>
> *We'll employ whichever boy the agency sends us.*

2. *Pronouns denoting things:*

> *What(ever) is worth doing at all is worth doing well.*
>
> *I'll do what(ever) you say.*
>
> *You may have either of these books, whichever you prefer.*

**Whosoever** and **whatsoever** used in noun clauses are older forms that are now found chiefly in religious contexts.

> *Whosoever will may enter this church.*
>
> *We will preach whatsoever is written in the Holy Book to whosoever will listen.*

## PRONOUN REFERENCE

By providing the connections that make the parts of a discourse *cohere* (literally, *stick together*), pronouns help to achieve greater unity within the discourse. However, because pronouns come so easily to mind, there is the danger that they will be used carelessly. Vague or ambiguous pronoun reference, which sometimes passes unnoticed in informal speech, is not appropriate for formal writing. For this reason, attention is being drawn here to various types of careless or inexact pronoun reference which should be avoided in formal situations.

1. *A pronoun with two possible antecedents.*

> *Whenever John is able to help his brother financially, **he** is very happy.*
> Is John happy, or is his brother happy?

> Corrected to:   *John is happy when he is able to help his brother financially.*
>
> or   *John's brother is happy to receive financial help from John.*

A noun should not be inserted in parentheses to explain a pronoun with ambiguous reference—**Whenever John is able to help his brother financially, he (John) is very happy.**

2. *An unnecessary personal pronoun after a noun subject.*

> *My friends, **they** told me the whole story.*

> Corrected to:   *My friends told me the whole story.*

3. *A pronoun whose antecedent must be inferred from the preceding discourse.*

> *My father is an engineer. **This** is a profession I admire very much.* The antecedent of ***this*** (supposedly ***engineering***) is inferred from ***engineer***.
>
> Corrected to:     *My father is an engineer. **Engineering** is a profession I admire very much.*

4. *A pronoun whose antecedent remotely precedes it.* The antecedent is so far back in the discourse as to cause difficulty in associating the pronoun with its antecedent.

> *The author tells the story of a man who gambles away his entire fortune and has nothing left for his family to live on. The gambler, in despair, decides to commit suicide. **He** goes on to tell us how the man is helped by an old friend.*

The italicized **he** in the third sentence should be corrected to **the author** or **the writer** (or, the author's name can be given).

5. *Relative **which** with indefinite reference.* Relative *which* refers back to an entire part of a sentence rather than to a single noun antecedent.

> *He decided to spend his summer vacation playing golf, **which** didn't please his wife.*
>
> Corrected to:     *His decision to spend his summer vacation playing golf didn't please his wife.*

Not all authorities consider a **which** clause with indefinite reference as inappropriate in formal speech, and such clauses are used by many reputable writers. However, it is best for those who are not highly skilled in the use of the English language to avoid this construction in formal situations.

6. *Vague **this** or **that**.* It is not clear what part of the preceding discourse **this** or **that** refers to.

> *Stores sell many more toys than they did a few generations ago. **This** deprives children of the pleasure of making their own toys.*
>
> Corrected to:     *This abundance of ready-made toys deprives . . .*

7. *Vague **it**.* The personal pronoun it is used without a definite antecedent.

> *Because Jane had once had a bad accident while driving, she was afraid to try **it** again.*
>
> Corrected to:     *. . . She was afraid to try to drive again.*

In certain colloquial idioms, a definite antecedent is not required for the personal pronoun **it**.

> *I hope you will like **it** here.*
>
> *The strain of final examinations is too great. I can't take **it*** (or *stand **it**, bear **it***).
>
> *Don't bother to make the correction. Let **it** go.*

Vague **it** is sometimes used with an introductory **if** or **when** clause that should really be the subject.

> *If you sail a boat, **it's** fun.*
>
> Corrected to:    *Sailing a boat is fun.*
>
>       or    *It's fun to sail a boat.*

8. *Too many* ***it****'s near each other.* Personal **it** appears in close proximity with impersonal or anticipatory **it**.

> *We like **it** very much in this hotel. **It's** wonderful to relax in **its** comfortable atmosphere. **It** is possible we'll stay in **it** again on our next vacation.*

9. *Loose use of* ***it*** *or* ***they*** *as subject.* **It** or **they** is sometimes used as the subject of a verb, while the agent which should actually be the subject is put in a prepositional phrase.

> *In the newspaper, **it** says that the concert was canceled.*
>
> Corrected to:    *The newspaper says that the concert was canceled.*

> *At the university, **they** require an examination for all entering freshmen.*
>
> Corrected to:    *The university requires an examination for all entering freshmen.*

10. *Shift in pronoun number.* This kind of shift often occurs in generalizations that can be made with either a singular or a plural noun representing a class.

> *The **student** must be made to understand how each lesson can be of value to **them**.*

The sentence can be corrected either by changing **the student** to **students,** or by changing **them** to **him.**

11. *Omission of pronoun substitute in the second term of a comparison.*

> *The dialect in one town may be quite different from the next town.*
>
> Corrected to:    *The dialect in one town may be quite different from that of the next town.*

If one of a group is singled out for comparison, logic requires that the rest of the group be marked as **other.**

> *He is more efficient than any **other** person we have had working for us.*

# 4

## *Verbs*

The verb is the most complex part of speech. Its varying arrangements with nouns determine the different kinds of sentences—statements, questions, commands, exclamations. Like the noun, the verb has the grammatical properties of *person* and *number*, properties which require agreement with the subject. But the verb also has several other grammatical properties that are shared with no other part of speech. These properties are:

TENSE.   Special verb endings or accompanying auxiliary verbs signal the *time* an event takes place.

VOICE.   Special verb forms are arranged in certain positions with nouns to indicate whether the grammatical subject of a sentence is performing an action (**The policeman arrested the burglar**—active voice) or is itself being acted upon (**The burglar was arrested by the policeman**—passive voice).

MOOD.   Special verb forms mark (a) commands and requests; (b) statements expressing wishes, unreal conditions, or matters of urgency or importance.

ASPECT.   Certain verb forms, often with accompanying adverbial expressions, may indicate whether an event is to be regarded as a single point on a time continuum, a repetition of points, or a single duration with a beginning, a middle and an end. It is the aspect of duration that the English verb most readily expresses through the progressive forms of the tenses.

TYPES OF VERBS

### Classified by Complement of Verb

The types of verbs described here differ according to the kind of complement they may have. Because these types may cut across each other, a verb may belong to more than one type.

**47**

### Predicating or Linking Verbs[1]

A predicating verb is the chief word in the predicate that says something about the subject. The predicating word (or predicator) has traditionally been called a verb of "action" (**babies** *cry*; **She** *wrote* **a letter**), but has actually been interpreted to include most non-action verbs that are not linking verbs (for example, **I** *remember* **him**; **She** *needs* **more money**). The term *event* is probably a more exact way to refer to what is denoted by a predicating verb, and is the term that will be favored in this book.

A linking verb is a verb of incomplete predication; it merely announces that the real predicate follows. The important word in the complement is usually an *adjective* (**The girl is** *pretty*) or a *noun* (**She is a pretty** *girl*). The *-ly* adverbs of manner (**quickly, angrily**) are not used with linking verbs. The more common linking verbs are **appear, be, become, get** (in the sense of **become), look, remain, seem.**

Also functioning as linking verbs are the verbs of perception—**feel, taste, smell, sound.**

> *The milk tastes sour.*
>
> *The rose smells sweet.*[2]

Included among the linking verbs are certain verb-adjective combinations that express a state. Some of these combinations are actually little more than idioms. Many of these verbs have the force of **become—blow (open), blush (red), break (loose), grow (worse), fall (ill), prove (wrong), stand (quiet), turn (pale), wax (eloquent).**

The linking verbs are often subdivided by modern grammarians into **be** and all others. One of the most important differences is that, whereas the other linking verbs are followed mostly by predicate adjectives, **be** may be followed by many types of complements:

| | |
|---|---|
| Adjective | He is *handsome*. |
| Noun | He is a handsome *boy*. |
| Adverb | The man is *here*. (usually place) |
| Prepositional phrase | Mary is *in the house*. (Some of the prepositional phrases after *be* are idiomatic: We are *of the same opinion*; that is *out of the question*.) |
| Noun clause | We are *what we eat*. |
| Infinitive phrase | The problem is *to find the right house*. |
| Gerund phrase | The problem is *finding the right house*. |

In addition to differing from other linking verbs in the type of complements it takes, **be** also differs from *all* other verbs with respect to the position

---

[1] Linking verbs are also called copulative verbs.

[2] Verbs of perception may also be non-linking; they may indicate action and take an object— **She** *is tasting* **the soup now.**

of adverbs used with it, and with respect to its manner of forming questions and negatives. For this reason some grammarians separate **be** still further from other verbs and place it in a special category all by itself.

### Transitive or Intransitive Verbs

A transitive verb takes a direct object (**He *is reading* a book**); an intransitive verb does not require an object (**He *is walking* in the park**). Only transitive verbs may be used in the passive voice (**The book was returned by him quickly**). All linking verbs are intransitive.

Transitive verbs may take more than one object:

| | |
|---|---|
| Indirect object and direct object | He gave his **wife a present.** |
| Direct object and objective complement | They elected **Mr. Smith president.** |

Many verbs may be used either transitively (**He *was writing* a letter**) or intransitively (**He *was writing* at the library**). Other verbs are transitive only and *must* be followed by an object—**have, like, need, owe, remember.**

Some intransitive verbs have developed transitive uses, especially in a causative sense:

> He always walks his dog at night (=***causes his dog to walk***).
> The railroad runs additional trains during holidays (=***causes additional trains to be run***).

A few intransitive verbs are used transitively with cognate objects—**run a race, dream a strange dream, live a good life.**

Other intransitive verbs have different forms for transitive use.

| *Intransitive* | *Transitive* | |
|---|---|---|
| lie | lay | The book *is lying* on the table. |
| | | He *laid* the book on the table. |
| rise | raise | The sun *rises* in the east. |
| | | The student *raised* his hand. |
| sit | set | Please *sit* down. |
| | | She *set* the chair in the corner. |

Some transitive verbs may be used intransitively to express a passive idea. Their subjects usually denote things rather than persons.

> The books sold out (=***were sold out***) in a week.
> The bread baked (=***was baked***) too long.
> Such houses rent (= ***are rented***) easily.

Many verb-preposition combinations may be regarded as transitive, since they can be used in the passive.

| | |
|---|---|
| Active | He *looked up* all the new words. |
| Passive | All the new words *were looked up* (by him). |

A small class of verbs, called *middle* verbs, are transitive in that they take a formal object, but intransitive in that they cannot be used in the passive voice—among them are **cost, have, last, resemble, weigh**.

> *Bob resembles his father.*
> *This book costs $8.00.*

The expressions after verbs like **cost** and **weigh** may also be considered as adverbial expressions of quantity rather than as direct objects. (They are sometimes called adverbial objects.)

## Reflexive Verbs

A reflexive verb requires one of the compounds with **-self** (reflexive pronoun) as its object—**express oneself, wash oneself, pride oneself, avail oneself**. Some verbs may be used with or without the reflexive pronoun object—**He washed (himself) and dressed (himself) quickly**. Reflexive verbs often have a non-reflexive use also, and can take objects that do not refer back to the subject—**She washed the child and then dressed him quickly**.

### Classified by Form of Verb

## Auxiliary or Lexical Verbs

Two or more words may be joined together into a single verb phrase that functions as the full verb of the predicate. The first part of the verb phrase is the *auxiliary* (or auxiliaries), and the second part is the lexical verb (**will be, arriving**). The *lexical* verb[3] carries the chief burden of semantic content. The *auxiliary* verb acts as a "helping" verb to the lexical verb by adding either (1) a structural element that marks differences in tense, voice, mood and aspect, or that signals questions and negatives; or (2) a semantic coloring such as ability, possibility or necessity (*modal* auxiliary).

Some verbs used as auxiliaries may also occur independently—**be, have, do**. Other verbs function chiefly as auxiliaries and *must* be used with a lexical verb—**shall, will[4], can[4], must, may, should, would, could, might**.

Auxiliaries combine with lexical verbs that are in simple (unchanged) form (**will open**)[5], in -ing form (**is opening**), or in -ed form (**was opened**). The number of auxiliaries used with a lexical verb varies. A lexical verb may have

---

[3] The lexical verb is often called the *main* verb, but, in order to avoid confusion, we are reserving the term main verb for the verb in the main clause. Other names for lexical verb are *notional* verb, *principal* verb, *meaningful* verb.

[4] In special senses, **will** and **can** also function as independent verbs with regular forms.

[5] The unchanged form of the verb is also called the verb *stem*.

no auxiliaries (**he opens, he opened**), one auxiliary (**he *will* open**), two auxiliaries (**he *has been* opening**), or three auxiliaries (**he *may have been* opening**). Agreement with the subject occurs in the *first auxiliary only*. Only **be, have, do,** the verbs that may be used independently, can indicate person and number.

**Finite or Non-Finite Verbs**

The form for these verbs is determined by the *function* which the verb has in a sentence. A *finite* verb is a lexical verb with or without auxiliaries that acts as the full verb in the predicate. It is limited by all the grammatical properties a verb may have—person, number, tense, voice, etc.

*Non-finite* (or *infinite*) verbs are incomplete verb forms that *function as other parts of speech than verbs*. They consist of the *infinitive* forms (**to** + the simple form of the verb) and the *participial* **-ing** or **-ed** forms. Thus, in **The boy *talking* to the teacher is my brother, talking** is a participle used as an adjective to modify **boy**. In **He likes *talking* to the teacher, talking** is a noun (a gerund) used as the object of **likes**. The non-finite forms, which are also called *verbals*, are not limited by person or number, but they have voice and some tense.

Another kind of classification of verbs by form may be made in terms of *compound semantic* units. Such compounds may consist of two words joined together into one, or of two separate parts.

Two Words Joined into One

ADVERB + VERB. **Ill-treat, dry-clean, cold-shoulder.** Many of these verbs are hyphenated, whereas their noun equivalents are written as two separate words (**ill treatment, dry cleaning, the cold shoulder**).

NOUN + VERB. **Hamstring, waterproof.** Some of these compounds may represent "back formations" which have been coined by dropping an **-er** agent-denoting suffix—**sleep-walk** (from the original **sleep-walker**), **sun-bathe** (from the original **sun-bather**), **baby-sit** (from the original **baby-sitter**).

Two Separate Words
Functioning as One Vocabulary Unit

Such a verb is composed of a verb plus a prepositional form—**give up, look over, drop in, find out**. English makes great use of such two-part verbs for expanding the vocabulary.

FUNCTION OF VERBS

The verb functions as the grammatical center for the predication about the subject. As we have seen, it may be a grammatical center expressing mere linkage, or it may be the strongest predicating word in the central core of the sentence. The verb is so basic that other functions (subject, object, complement) are determined in relation to it.

The verb is used after a subject, or before an object or complement. The verb appears before the subject in most questions, and in sentences or clauses that begin with certain types of negative adverbs. (See the section on the position of nouns for more information about the position of verbs.)

The grammatical form of verbs is usually discussed in connection with *tense*. The description of verb forms differs according to the way the term *tense* is interpreted. The most common interpretation of tense is a semantic one; each tense roughly indicates a kind of time. On the basis of this interpretation by meaning, some grammarians present a three-tense system—present, past and future. Most grammarians, however, give a six-tense system, which includes these three plus three perfect tenses—the present perfect, past perfect and future perfect—each of which expresses time in relation to a particular point in the present, past or future respectively. The different tenses are signaled by verb endings or by auxiliary verbs.

A second interpretation of *tense* is based on the form of the verb alone. According to this interpretation, there are only two tenses—a present and a past—each of which is marked by different forms in the lexical verb itself or in the auxiliary used with it. The semantic component of time is only secondary to the structural form. Many modern grammarians favor this two-tense system based on form alone.

In this book we have chosen to work with the six-tense time system because it is the one most commonly found in English textbooks for non-native speakers and is therefore most familiar to them. We also believe it offers the most practical approach for learning the verb forms of English. However, we will also devote some attention to the two-tense formal system because of the additional insights it gives into the working of the English language.

The forms given below for these six tenses are the *finite* forms for the full verb in the predicate. Additional finite forms are constructed with the auxiliary **do**, and with modal auxiliaries such as **can, may, must.**

The tense forms that consist of one part only are usually labeled *simple*. Note that there are only two such forms—the *simple present* and the *simple past*.[9] All the other tense forms are verb phrases containing one or more auxiliaries.

---

[9] In some older grammars, the term *simple* merely distinguished the nonprogressive forms of the six tenses from the progressive forms.

Paradigm[6] of the Six-tense Time System

| Tenses | Active Voice | *Progressive*[7] | Passive Voice | *Progressive* |
|---|---|---|---|---|
| Present | offer, offers | am / is / are offering | am / is / are offered | am / is / are being offered |
| Past | offered | was / were offering | was / were offered | was / were being offered |
| Future | shall / will offer | shall / will be offering | shall / will be offered | —— [8] |
| Present Perfect | has / have offered | has / have been offering | has / have been offered | —— [8] |
| Past Perfect | had offered | had been offering | had been offered | —— [8] |
| Future Perfect | shall / will have offered | shall / will have been offering | shall / will have been offered | —— [8] |

[6] The term *paradigm* means a display of all the forms of a particular part of speech. A paradigm for a verb is often called a *conjugation;* for a noun, a *declension.*

[7] Another term for *progressive* is *continuous.*

[8] It is conceivable that forms corresponding to the ones left blank might be used, but these forms would be exceedingly rare.

The alternate progressive forms given for each of the six tenses are used for single temporary acts with limited duration. The passive forms given for each of the tenses are used when a "receiver" of an action is the grammatical subject.

Paradigm of the
Two-Tense Formal System

By enlarging the concept of auxiliaries to include not only independent structure words but also the inflectional endings of the simple present and the simple past tenses, modern grammarians are able to claim that differences between the present and past tenses are marked by the auxiliary alone.

| *Tense* | *Auxiliary + Lexical verb* |
|---|---|
| present | nothing |
| | or **-s** suffix ⎫ + **offer** |
| past | **-ed** suffix ⎭ |
| present | **am, is, are** ⎫ + **offering, being offered, offered** |
| past | **was, were** ⎭ |
| present | **have, has** ⎫ + **offered, been offering, been offered** |
| past | **had** ⎭ |
| present | **do, does** ⎫ + **offer** |
| past | **did** ⎭ |
| present | **shall** |
| past | **should** |
| present | **will** |
| past | **would** |
| present | **can** ⎬ + **offer, be offering, be offered, have been offering, have been offered** |
| past | **could** |
| present | **may** |
| past | **might** |
| present | **must** |
| past | |

This system of present and past tenses makes it possible to formulate the simple rule that most verbs have special forms for agreement with the subject only in the *third singular present* tense.

| *Singular subject* | *Plural subject* |
|---|---|
| The girl  arrive*s* today. | The *girls*  arrive today. |
| *is* arriving today. | *are* arriving today. |
| *has* arrived today. | *have* arrived today. |
| *does* not arrive today. | *do* not arrive today. |

Only **be** has different forms for all three persons in the present tense, and only **be** has two different forms for the past singular and past plural. **Shall, will, can, may, must** are not marked for person or number at all.

Spelling Rules
for Adding Inflectional Suffixes

By observing either the six-tense or the two-tense systems just given, we note that there are only four single forms of the lexical verb that enter into the construction of the finite verb—**open, opens, opened, opening**. In adding **-s**, **-ed**, or **-ing** to the simple form of the verb, we must be careful to make any spelling changes that may be required.

---

-s    1. After a sibilant sound spelled as *s, z, ch, sh, x, es* is added (**passes, buzzes, catches, pushes, mixes**).
      2. After *y preceded by a consonant,* the *y* is changed to *i* and *es* is added (**carries, tries,** but **plays**).

-ed   1. After *y* preceded by a consonant, the *y* is changed to *i* and *ed* is added (**carried, tried,** but **played**).
      2. After a single consonant preceded by a single stressed vowel, the final consonant is doubled before *ed* (**stopped, permitted,** but **offered, rained**).[10]
      3. After final *e*, only *d* is added (**changed, argued, agreed**).

-ing  1. Final silent *e* is omitted (**changing, arguing,** but **agreeing**).
      Note: The *e* is retained if it is needed to prevent a change in pronunciation (**singeing**), or if it is preceded by a vowel (**canoeing**).
      2. After a single consonant preceded by a single stressed vowel, the final consonant is doubled before *ing* (**stopping, permitting,** but **offering, raining**).[10]
      3. Final *ie* in one-syllable words is changed to *y* (**lying, dying, tying**).

---

VOICE

Voice in English grammar refers to the active or passive use of a verb. The active voice is used in making a straightforward statement about an action; that is, the "doer"[11] of the action is the grammatical subject, and the "receiver" of the action is the grammatical object. In the passive voice, the *same action* is referred to indirectly; that is, the original "receiver" of the action is the grammatical subject, and the original "doer" of the action is the grammatical object of the preposition **by**.

[10] In many words ending in *l* (and a few in *p* or *m*) preceded by a single vowel, the British often double the final consonant even when the accent is *not* on the last syllable (**trável̃led, cáncelling, wórshipped**).

[11] While it is convenient at this point to use the traditional terms of "doer" of an action for the grammatical subject and "receiver" of an action for the grammatical object, we must remember that such terms are not always accurate. Some active subjects cannot "do" anything (for example, the subject in the sentence *The thought of going into to the army* terrified him.), and some active objects do not "receive" any action (for example, the object in the sentence **We understand** *that he will do all the work himself*).

| | |
|---|---|
| Active voice | The janitor ("doer" of the action) always opens the door ("receiver" of the action). |
| Passive voice | The door ("receiver" of the action) is always opened by the janitor ("doer" of the action). |

Because the grammatical subject of a passive verb is the original object of an active verb, *only a transitive verb may be used in the passive voice.*

Since it is generally preferable to make a direct statement of an action, a good writer chooses the active voice wherever possible. However, the passive voice is desirable or even necessary when greater emphasis is to be placed on the "event" represented by a verb plus its complement than on the "actor" involved in this event. Thus the passive voice will be preferred in the following instances:

1. Attention is to be drawn especially to the "receiver" of the action— **My *dog* was hit by a car.**

In a piece of connected prose, the use of the passive voice permits the subject under discussion to remain a grammatical subject even when it is not the "doer" of an action.

> **William Faulkner** *wrote a number of books about a mythological county in the South.* **He** *was awarded the Nobel Prize for literature in 1949.*

2. The "doer" of an action is unimportant or is not known. The omission of the agent makes it possible for an impersonal tone to be maintained.

The use of the passive voice for impersonal statements occurs frequently in textbooks, in scientific, technical or business reports, and in newspaper stories.

> *The Yalta Agreement was signed during World War Two.*
> *The United Jewelry Store has been robbed several times.*
> *The report was confirmed yesterday.*

A direct or an indirect object may become the subject in the passive voice. Thus the active construction **The cashier gave *him the money*** becomes one of the passive constructions:

> **The money** *was given* (**to**) *him by the cashier.* (**to** is optional)
> or **He** *was given the money by the cashier.*

The objects of certain verb-preposition combinations can also become the subjects in passive constructions.

> *All the documents* **were handed over** *to the lawyer.*
> *The power* **is turned on** *in the morning and* **turned off** *in the evening.*
> *This lock* **has been tampered with** *and the house* **broken into.**

Sentences with infinitive phrase objects or with **that** clause objects may be changed to impersonal passive constructions.

*Many people believe him to be a dishonest man.*

becomes *He is believed (by many people) to be a dishonest man.*

*Many people believe that he is a dishonest man.*

becomes *It is believed (by many people) that he is a dishonest man.*

The passive voice may indicate an *action* or a *state* resulting from an action.

| | |
|---|---|
| Action | The door was locked by the janitor last night. |
| State | The door is locked (No **by** phrase is used with the passive indicating state.) |
| Action | The key was lost by the janitor last night. |
| State | The key is lost. |

**Get** or **become** may be used instead of **be** as a passive of transition.

*They're getting married tomorrow.*

*We're becoming better acquainted with our new neighbor.*

Many past participles customarily appearing after the verb **be** are now felt as adjectives and may be followed by other prepositions than **by**—**be interested *in*; be composed *of*; be delighted with** (or **by**); **be terrified *at*** (or *of, by*).

MOOD

It is customary to say that *mood* indicates the way we feel about our subject. However, it is perhaps more accurate to say that *mood* refers to the special forms used to express commands or requests (*imperative* mood), or to signal unreality, wishes, conjecture, or urgency (*subjunctive* mood). The *indicative* mood is used in all other situations that do not require imperative or subjunctive mood. All the forms given in the preceding verb paradigms are in the indicative mood.

**Imperative Mood**

For this mood the *simple form* of the verb is used for requests, commands, or instructions.

1. Second person, singular and plural

   ***Open** the door.*

   ***Don't open** the door.* (negative)

2. First and second person together

   ***Let's open** the door.*

   ***Let's not open** the door.* (negative)

Aside from **don't** and **let's**, the only types of words that may precede the imperative verb are:

1. An adverb of frequency:

> ***Always*** *open that door slowly.*
>
> *Don't **ever** open that door.*

2. A noun in direct address:

> ***Robert,*** *open the door.*

If the request is short, the noun may also follow the request—**Open the door, Robert**.

3. A pronoun, especially **you**:

> *To get there, **you** turn right at the bridge.*
>
> *Don't **you** listen to him.*
>
> ***Everyone,*** *listen to me.*

A sentence with **you** plus an auxiliary verb (usually a modal) is often the equivalent of a sentence with the verb in the imperative mood.

> *You **must** turn right at the bridge.*
>
> *You **shouldn't** listen to him.*
>
> *You **will** deliver this package at once.*

**Do**, for entreaty:

> ***Do*** *be careful.*
>
> ***Do*** *drive slowly.*

Certain formulas of politeness either precede or follow the imperative verb in a request.

1. Formulas of politeness before the verb:

> ***Please*** *open the door.*
>
> $\left.\begin{matrix} \textit{\textbf{Will}} \\ \textit{\textbf{Would}} \end{matrix}\right\}$ *you (**please**) open the door.*

2. Formulas of politeness at the end of the sentence:

> *Open the door, **please**.*
>
> *Open the door,* $\left.\begin{matrix} \textit{\textbf{will}} \\ \textit{\textbf{would}} \end{matrix}\right\}$ *you (**please**).*

3. Formulas of politeness split between the beginning and the end of the sentence:

> ***Please*** *open the door,* $\left.\begin{matrix} \textit{\textbf{will}} \\ \textit{\textbf{would}} \end{matrix}\right\}$ *you.*
>
> $\left.\begin{matrix} \textit{\textbf{Will}} \\ \textit{\textbf{Would}} \end{matrix}\right\}$ *you open the door, **please**.*

With other formulas of politeness for requests, the verbal forms of the verb are used:

> $\left.\begin{matrix} \textit{\textbf{Would}} \\ \textit{\textbf{Do}} \end{matrix}\right\}$ *you mind **opening** the door (**please**).*

$$\left. \begin{array}{c} \textit{Would you be so kind as} \\ \textit{good enough} \end{array} \right\} \textbf{\textit{to open}} \textit{ the door.}$$

## Subjunctive Mood

Most of the indicative verb forms are used for the subjunctive mood, but the time that they express is not usually the same. The forms used in the subjunctive are:

| Tenses | Active Voice | Passive Voice |
|---|---|---|
| Present (neutral time) | offer | be offered |
| Past (present time) | offered | were offered |
| Past Perfect (past time) | had offered | had been offered |

Each of these tenses has only one form that remains the same for the three persons (**I, you, he**). The verb **be** has the invariable form **be** for the present subjunctive (**We insisted that he** *be* **punished**) and the invariable form **were** for the past subjunctive (**If he** *were* **here, he would help us**).

The subjunctive mood may express:

1. *an unreal condition*, with the conjunctions **if, unless**, etc.

   *If I* **were** *you, I would go to bed early.* (present time)

   *If I* **had been** *you, I would have gone to bed early.* (past time)

2. *a wish*, only after the verb **wish**.

   *I wish that I* **were** *you.* (present time)

   *I wish that I* **had been** *you yesterday.* (past time)

3. *some degree of conjecture*, after verbs like **act, behave, talk, look** that may be followed by **as if** or **as though**.

   *He acts as if he* **were** *a king.* (present time)

   *He acts as if he* **had been** *a king once.* (past time)

4. *Some degree of urgency*, after verbs of requesting, commanding, urging, recommending; and after adjectives like **important, necessary, imperative**.

   *He insisted that his wife* **be** *on time.*

   *It is necessary that he* **be** *on time.*

Each of these uses of the subjunctive will be taken up in more detail under adverbial clauses and noun clauses.

DERIVATIONAL FORM OF VERBS

The number of derivational forms that mark verbs is quite small. Such derivational forms consist chiefly of the suffixes **-en, -ize, -fy, -ate**, and the prefixes **en-** and **be-**. These affixes are added to nouns or adjectives, often with causative force.

---

*Affixes added to nouns* = *causes a state of,* or *cause to be a*
Suffixes     beautify, colonize, frighten, salivate
Prefixes     endanger enslave, befriend, besiege

*Affixes added to adjectives* = *cause to become*
Suffixes     brighten, equalize, invalidate, simplify
Prefixes     endear, enlarge, befoul

---

Alternating with these verb affixes that denote causation is the verb **make** plus an adjective—**make the home beautiful** (or **beautify the home**); **make the chart simple** (or **simplify the chart**); **make the room bright** (or **brighten the room**).

The prefixes **en-** and **be-** sometimes function merely as verb intensifiers— **en**liven, **en**tangle, **be**deck, **be**smear.

We have already seen that many verbs have the same form as nouns— **the answer, to answer; a desire, to desire; an experiment, to experiment.** Often such verbs are interchangeable with phrases consisting of **make, give** or **have** plus the nouns of the same form—**to promise** or **to give a promise; to make an attempt** or **to attempt; to quarrel** or **to have a quarrel.**

A number of two-syllable verbs differ from the nouns of the same form only in the position of the accent, the nouns being stressed on the *first* syllable, the verbs on the *second.*

|        *Noun*        |     *Verb*      |
| --------------- | ------------ |
| the ínsult   | to insúlt  |
| the óbject   | to objéct  |
| the prógress | to progréss |

Sometimes the distinction between a noun and a verb is merely a difference in the voicing of the final consonant.

| *Noun—Final Voiceless* [s] | *Verb—Final Voiced* [z] |
| --- | --- |
| 1.  *change represented in the pronunciation and spelling* | |
|     the advice | to advise |
|     the device | to devise |
| 2.  *change represented in the pronunciation alone* | |
|     the house | to house |
|     the use | to use |
|     the excuse | to excuse |

Some verbs have the same form as adjectives, but are stressed differently.

| *Simple Form of the Verb* | *Past Tense* | *Past Participle* |
|---|---|---|
| | 7. Verbs that pattern like: SHAKE, SHOOK, SHAKEN | |
| forsake | forsook | forsaken |
| mistake | mistook | mistaken |
| partake | partook | partaken |
| shake | shook | shaken |
| take | took | taken |
| | 8. Verbs that pattern like: GIVE, GAVE, GIVEN | |
| forbid | forbad(e) | forbidden |
| forgive | forgave | forgiven |
| give | gave | given |
| | 9. Verbs that pattern like: MOW, MOWED, MOWN | |
| hew | hewed | hewn |
| mow | mowed | mown |
| sew | sewed | sewn |
| show | showed | shown (sometimes **showed**) |
| sow | sowed | sown |
| saw | sawed | sawn (more often **sawed**) |
| strew | strewed | strewn |
| | 10. Miscellaneous | |
| be | was | been |
| dive | dove (or **dived**) | dived |
| do | did | done |
| eat | ate | eaten |
| fall | fell | fallen |
| go | went | gone |
| lie | lay | lain |
| see | saw | seen |
| slay | slew | slain |
| (a)wake | (a)woke (sometimes (a)**waked**) | (a)waked (British (a)**woke** or (a) **woken**) |

**Second and Third Principal Parts Are Alike**

| *Simple Form of the Verb* | *Past Tense and Past Participle* |
|---|---|
| | 1. Verbs that pattern like: HANG, HUNG |
| cling | clung |
| dig | dug |
| hang | hung[15] |
| sling | slung |
| slink | slunk |
| spin | spun |

[15] When **hang** refers to death by suspension by the neck, the past tense as well as the past participle is **hanged**.

| Simple Form of the Verb | Past Tense and Past Participle |
|---|---|
| stick | stuck |
| sting | stung |
| strike | struck[16] |
| string | strung |
| swing | swung |
| wring | wrung |

### 2. Verbs that pattern like: FEED, FED

| | |
|---|---|
| bleed | bled |
| breed | bred |
| creep | crept |
| dream | dreamt |
| | (also **dreamed**) |
| feed | fed |
| feel | felt |
| flee | fled |
| keep | kept |
| kneel | knelt |
| | (also **kneeled**) |
| lead | led |
| leap | lept |
| | (also **leaped**) |
| leave | left |
| mean | meant |
| meet | met |
| sleep | slept |
| speed | sped |
| sweep | swept |
| weep | wept |

### 3. Verbs that pattern like: BRING, BROUGHT

| | |
|---|---|
| beseech | besought |
| | (also **beseeched**) |
| bring | brought |
| buy | bought |
| catch | caught |
| fight | fought |
| seek | sought |
| teach | taught |
| think | thought |

### 4. Verbs that pattern like: BEND, BENT

| | |
|---|---|
| bend | bent |
| lend | lent |
| rend | rent |
| send | sent |
| spend | spent |

### 5. Verbs that pattern like: BIND, BOUND

| | |
|---|---|
| bind | bound |
| find | found |

[16] **Stricken** is the past participle of **strike** when used figuratively as an adjective—**conscience-stricken, terror-stricken, stricken with a disease.**

| Simple Form of the Verb | Past Tense and Past Participle |
|---|---|
| grind | ground |
| wind | wound |

6. Verbs that pattern like: PAY, PAID

| | |
|---|---|
| lay | laid |
| mislay | mislaid |
| pay | paid |
| say | said |

7. Verbs that pattern like: SELL, SOLD

| | |
|---|---|
| sell | sold |
| tell | told |

8. Miscellaneous

| | |
|---|---|
| abide (literary) | abode |
| build | built |
| clothe | clad (literary) (also **clothed**) |
| forget | forgot (or past participle **forgotten**, American usage) |
| get | got (or past participle **gotten**, American usage) |
| have | had |
| hear | heard |
| hold | held |
|   behold (literary) |   beheld |
|   withhold |   withheld |
| light | lit[17] |
| lose | lost |
| make | made |
| shine | shone[18] |
| shoe | shod |
| shoot | shot |
| sit | sat |
| slide | slid |
| stand | stood |
|   understand |   understood |
|   withstand |   withstood |
| tread (literary) | trod (or past participle **trodden**) |
| win | won |

### All Three Principal Parts Are Alike

bet (sometime **betted** for the past tense and the past participle)
bid (meaning offer money at an auction)
broadcast (sometimes **broadcasted** for the past tense and the past participle)
burst
cast
cost
cost
cut
hit
hurt
knit (also **knitted** for the past tense and the past participle)

[17] Also, **lighted**, meaning *to provide light*, or as an adjective (**a well-lighted room**).
[18] **Shined** is used for the transitive verb—**The boy shined his shoes.**

let
put
read[19]
rid
set
shed
shut
slit
spit (sometimes **spat** for the past tense and the past participle)
split
spread
thrust

**First and Third Principal Parts Are Alike**

| | | |
|---|---|---|
| come | came | come |
| become | became | become |
| overcome | overcame | overcome |
| run | ran | run |

**First and Second Principal Parts Are Alike**

beat    beat    beaten (or **beat**)

---

### USES OF THE SIX TENSES

The time relationship of the six tenses may be roughly indicated by the diagram opposite.

Note that there are *three past tenses* and *two future tenses*. Note further that the past perfect is tied in time to the past tense, the present perfect to the present tense, and the future perfect to the future tense.

### PRESENT TENSE

**Forms of the Present Tense**

| *Simple* | | *Progressive* | |
|---|---|---|---|

*Active Voice*

| | | | |
|---|---|---|---|
| I | | I | am offering |
| you | | you | |
| we | offer | we | are offering |
| they | | they | |
| he-she-it | offers | he-she-it | is offering |

*Passive Voice*

| | | | |
|---|---|---|---|
| I | am offered | I | am being offered |
| you | | you | |
| we | are offered | we | are being offered |
| they | | they | |
| he-she-it | is offered | he-she-it | is being offered |

---

[19] **Read** as the past tense and the past participle is pronounced [r ɛ d].

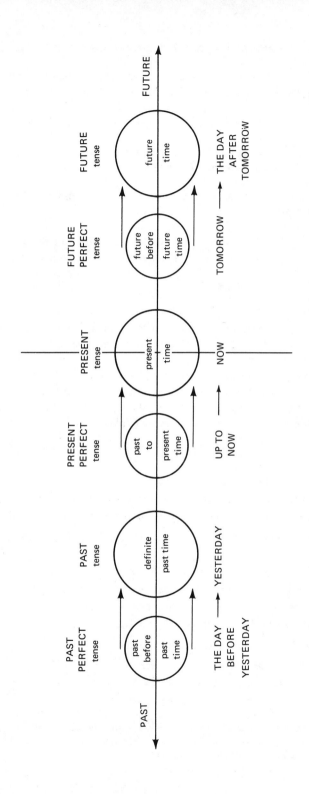

It should be noted that for the simple present tense, the form ending in *s* is actually used with every word denoting a singular subject except **I** and **you**.

A few verbs have irregular forms in the simple present tense:

1. **Go, do, have** in third person singular—**he goes; he does; he has.**
2. **Be**—**I am; you-we-they are; he-she-it is.**

Archaic forms of the present tense that are now found mainly in the Bible and in poetry are:

1. Second person—**thou** (singular) **help*est*,** ye (plural) **runn*est*.**
2. Third person singular (sometimes plural)—**he** (or **they**) **maketh.**

### Use of the Simple Present Tense

1. *To express general time.* In such a use, the simple present tense is usually "timeless." It has no terminal points in time—it can include the past, present and the future. Often it involves repetition—an event has been repeated before the present time and is open to future repetition.

The "timeless" time of the simple present is especially useful in general statements. Such general statements may range all the way from eternal truths to generalizations about the customs of single individuals. Examples of general statements with the simple present follow.

GENERAL TRUTHS.    Includes the laws or principles of the physical and the social sciences.

> The earth **revolves** around the sun.
>
> The sun **rises** in the east and **sets** in the west.
>
> Children **learn** faster when their needs and interests are provided for.

CUSTOM.    Includes the habitual actions of nations, communities, groups, individuals.

With an expression indicating frequency:

> The English **frequently drink** tea in the afternoon.
>
> The members of our club **play** tennis **once a week.**
>
> I **always**[20] **take** my umbrella with me when it rains.

Without an expression indicating frequency:

> Englishmen **drink** tea in the afternoon.
>
> The members of our club **play** tennis.
>
> I **take** my umbrella with me when it rains.

---

[20] With the frequency words **always, forever, continually, perpetually,** the progressive form may be used to express incessant action—**He is always getting into trouble.** The feeling here is that one action is continued with interruption.

2. *To express present time.* The simple present tense indicates present time with many non-action verbs, especially those expressing state or condition. Many of these verbs are durational without being limited by a beginning or an end.

LINKING VERBS. **Be, seem, appear, look.**

> She *seems* to be very tired today.
>
> He *is* an intelligent man.

VERBS OF PERCEPTION

1. **Feel, taste, smell,** used intransitively

> The medicine *tastes* bitter.
>
> Her skin *feels* smooth.

When these verbs are used transitively, the present progressive form is required for present action:

> The cook *is tasting* the soup.
>
> He's *feeling* the surface of the table.

2. **See, hear,** used transitively

> I *hear* music coming from the other room.
> but I *am listening* to the radio.
>
> From this window they *see* everything that goes on in the street.
> but We *are watching* (or *looking at*) all the people who are passing by.

Perhaps the reason for this difference in usage is that, while **see, hear** denote an unconscious taking in of impressions through the senses, **listen to, watch, look at** suggest a conscious act that requires some effort.

VERBS INDICATING A MENTAL STATE OR CONDITION. A partial list of such verbs would include **agree, believe, consider, guess, hesitate, imagine, know, prefer, realize, remember, suppose, trust, want, wish.** Many of these verbs are followed by **that** noun clauses or by verbal phrases (infinitive or gerund).

Included in this group are verbs signifying fulfillment in the future:

> I *hope* that you can come.
>
> We *expect* to go there next week.

VERBS EXPRESSING AN EMOTIONAL STATE. **Admire, appreciate, care, like, love, regret, trust.**

> We *love* each other very much.
>
> He *admires* his father more than he will admit.
>
> I *appreciate* a good meal.

OTHER NON-ACTION VERBS. Such verbs include **belong, contain, depend, equal, have, hold, indicate, mean, need, owe, require, resemble, tend.**

*We **need** more chairs.*

*I **owe** him ten dollars.*

*This jar **contains** honey.*

3. *With verbs of saying and telling*

*He **says** that he cannot come tonight.*

*We **suggest** that you take warm clothes with you.*

4. *To express future time*

A. with verbs like **come, go, arrive, depart**. A future time expression is usually required.

*The plane **leaves** tomorrow morning.*

*I **arrive** in Hong Kong on Saturday.*

B. with verbs in time clauses or conditional clauses

---

Time He will take a vacation in Europe after he **graduates** from college.
Condition If I **finish** my work early enough, I'll go to the movies tonight.

---

C. with verbs used for terse announcements of scheduled events or for making proclamations.

*Our club **gives** its annual dinner next week.*

*The boat races **take place** tomorrow.*

*The play **begins** a ten-week run next Saturday.*

5. *For the historic present or summaries of a story plot*

*The King **addresses** the soldiers and **asks** them to fight bravely for their country.*

*Goldilocks **enters** the room, **sees** three bowls of porridge on the table, and **goes** over to taste the food.*

6. *For stage directions*

*Mary **walks** to the window and **waves** good-bye to her departing guests.*

Use of the
Present Progressive Tense

In general, the progressive form of a tense is used for a *single temporary event that has a beginning and an end.* This form suggests that an event began and is continuing, but it *does not necessarily include the end* of the action. The progressive form occurs mostly with verbs that denote limited duration (**work, study, attend**). However, it can also occur with verbs that express some stage in a progression—either the beginning, end or continuation of an action:

*The play is beginning (or **ending**) now.*

*The book is getting (or **becoming**) more and more interesting.* (continuation)

Because of its ability to suggest action in progress, the progressive form often conveys greater vividness, emotion, or emphasis than the nonprogressive form does.

> *We reached the lake just as the sun was setting.*
>
> *I was coughing all night long.* (*All* and *long* reinforce the emphasis on duration that is established by the progressive verb.)

For most tenses, the progressive form often simply marks the aspect of duration. If emphasis on duration of an event is not desired, the nonprogressive form is used. It is only in the present tense that such a choice is generally not possible. A single action that is going on in the present must be expressed with a progressive verb. In terms of time, the progressive form is the real present. It may express relatively short duration, perhaps only momentary, or relatively long duration.

| | |
|---|---|
| Short duration | He *is opening* the book now. |
| | She *is studying* her English lesson at the moment. |
| Long duration | She *is studying* English this year. |
| | He *is writing* a book. |
| | How *are* you *getting along* these days? |

Like the simple present form, the present progressive form may signal future time if it is accompanied by a future time expression.

> *The tickets **are going** on sale next week.*
>
> *The gardener **is cutting** the grass tomorrow.*

The present progressive tense generally indicates that the future action is part of a plan made in the present, with the past possibly included. It is more frequently used with verbs that can show the intention of the subject or that can indicate the result of planning by some agent. Thus, we can say **I'm giving a party tomorrow**, but not *****It's raining tomorrow**.

A few verbs may occur in either the progressive or the simple form of the present tense, depending on the kind of emphasis desired.

PRESENT PROGRESSIVE. The emphasis is on the progression of one event.

> *He **is planning** (or **hoping, expecting**) to enter the university.*
>
> *Where **are** you **living** now?—I'm living in California.*
>
> *How are you feeling?—I'm feeling fine.*

SIMPLE PRESENT. The emphasis is on the general idea denoted by the verb.

> *He **plans** (or **hopes, expects**) to enter the university.*
>
> *Where **do** you **live** now?—I live in California.*
>
> *How **do** you **feel**?—I feel fine.*

Occasionally the present progressive form is found with non-action verbs that are ordinarily put in the simple form. In such cases the progressive verb may signal that an event is thought of as temporary.

> *I'm **remembering** how it used to be.*
>
> *He's **seeing** things clearer with his new glasses.*

Usually, however, when such verbs are used in the progressive form they have other meanings than those in the simple present.

> *He **is considering** entering the university.*
> but *He considers this university to be a good one.*
>
> *What **are** you **thinking** about ?*
> but *What do you think of him ?*
>
> *He **is trying** to get into the movies.*
> but *He tries very hard.*
>
> *They **are** all **having** a good time at the party. (**Have** as part of an idiom)*
> but *They have a lot of money.*
>
> *You **are being** silly* (=*You* are behaving in a silly manner).

Sometimes the progressive is used in a general statement to add a feeling of present action in progress:

> *They enjoy listening to good music while they **are eating** (vs. **eat**) their dinner.*
>
> *Millions of people **are watching** (vs. **watch**) television every night.*

## PAST TENSE[21]

**Forms of the Past Tense**

|  | *Simple* | *Progressive* |
|---|---|---|
| | | |

*Active Voice*

| *Simple* | *Progressive* |
|---|---|
| I, you, he—she—it, we, they   offered | I, he—she—it   was offering <br> you, we, they   were offering |

*Passive Voice*

| *Simple* | *Progressive* |
|---|---|
| I, he—she—it   was offered <br> you, we, they   were offered | I, he—she—it   was being offered <br> you, we, they   were being offered |

The regular ending for the simple past tense, for all persons, is **-ed**. Irregular forms of the past tense have been listed earlier in this chapter. Only the verb **be** has two separate forms for the past—**was** for the singular, **were** for the plural.

[21] The past tense is also called the *preterit(e)*.

In British usage, many verbs ending in **-n** or **-l** add **-t** rather than **-ed** for the past tense and for the past participle—**learnt, burnt, spelt, spilt, dwelt**.

An archaic form for the past that still appears in poetry is **-'d**—**open'd, fear'd**.

### Use of the Past Tense

The past tense indicates *definite time terminating in the past*, whether a time word is given or not. It is the required tense in statements about persons who are now dead (**Shakespeare lived in England**), unless the statement has some relevance to the present (**Shakespeare is the greatest playwright ever produced in England**).

The past tense may refer to:

1. *One* event completed in the past:

   *I **saw** him last night.*

   *They **left** two hours ago.*

The word **ago** requires the use of the past tense, even if the time indicated comes almost up to the present—**They left one minute ago**.

2. *Repeated* events completed in the past and no longer happening:

   *Last year it **rained** frequently in this area.*

   *(custom) When I was young, I **went** swimming every day.*

3. *Duration* of an event completed in the past:

   *He **lived** in New York for thirty years and then he decided to return to France.*

   *In Columbus' day, people **believed** that the earth was flat.*

The past form used as a subjunctive in **if** or **as if** clauses, and in **that** clauses after the verb **wish**, represents *present* time:

   *If he **studied** harder now, he would get better grades.*

   *She wishes she **were** rich instead of beautiful.*

### Past Progressive Tense

The past progressive form *emphasizes* the duration of one past event that has a possible beginning and ending. What is particularly stressed is the midst of the action.

   *What were you doing all day yesterday?*

   *When I arrived at the inn, the guests were already sitting down to dinner.*

The past progressive form may express duration of an event at *one point in the past*.

   *What were you doing at eleven o'clock last night?*

   *—At eleven o'clock last night I was sleeping soundly.*

The progressive form is required for a past action in progress which is suddenly or unexpectedly interrupted by another past action. The implication is that the action in progress is uncompleted (at least momentarily) because of the interruption.

|  | *Act in Progress* | *Interrupting Act* |
|---|---|---|
| | I was crossing the street | I saw an accident. |
| | She was doing her homework | The telephone rang. |
| | She was just (or already) clearing the table | A late dinner guest arrived. |
| | **WHEN** | |

*or*

| WHILE or AS | I was crossing the street | I saw an accident. |
|---|---|---|
| | She was doing her homework | The telephone rang. |

Note that the act in progress may be placed in the main clause or in the time clause. Sometimes **when** is used with the act in progress rather than **while** or **as**—*When* **I was crossing the street, I saw an accident.**

Note further that with an accompanying intensifier **just** or **already**, the act in progress may be placed only in the main clause.

In sentences referring to two past acts that are in progress simultaneously, the past progressive form may occur with both of the actions in progress, with only one, or with neither.

| He was watching television | | his wife was washing the dishes. |
|---|---|---|
| He was watching television | **WHILE** | his wife washed the dishes. |
| He watched television | | his wife was washing the dishes. |
| He watched television | | his wife washed the dishes. |

## FUTURE TENSE

### Forms of the Future Tense

| *Nonprogressive* | *Progressive* |
|---|---|

#### *Active Voice*

| I we } shall *or* will offer[22] | I we } shall *or* will be offering |
|---|---|
| you he—she—it they } will offer | you he—she—it } will be offering |

#### *Passive Voice*

| I we } shall *or* will be offered |
|---|
| you he—she—it they } will be offered |

---

[22] **Shall** originally meant *obligation, compulsion;* **will** meant *volition* (and is still so used as an independent verb). Today volition is more commonly expressed by other verbs—**want, wish, desire, intend.**

Use of the Future Tense

A rule is often given in schoolbooks that for future time, **shall** must be used with the first person **I** or **we** (and with **you** in questions expecting an answer in the first person); and **will** must be used with the second and third persons. This rule is probably observed more often in England than in the United States, where informal usage permits **will** for all persons for future time.

A second part of this textbook rule is that, for emphasis on meanings other than futurity, the reverse of the rule for simple futurity applies—that is, **will** is used for the first person and **shall** for the other two. This part of the rule is not always observed even in British usage. For example, in the following quotation, **shall** is used rather than **will** to express determination.

> *". . . We shall defend our island whatever the cost may be, we shall fight on the beaches, we shall fight on the landing grounds, we shall fight in the fields and the streets, we shall fight in the hills: We shall never surrender. . . ."* (Winston Churchill)

Actually, it is often difficult to separate futurity from its many other meanings. The following gives an indication of the different meanings, in addition to determination, that may blend with the future meaning of **will** or **shall**.

WILL (AMERICAN USAGE)

| | |
|---|---|
| 1. Promise | We *will see* you next week. |
| 2. Intention | The accountant *will do* all the work himself. |
| 3. Willingness | I *will be* glad to do that for you. |
| 4. Volition (=want to) | If you *will wash* the dishes, I will dry them. |
| negative volition | He *will not take* orders from anyone. |
| 5. Plans, arrangements, schedules | The stores *will stay* open late next month. |
| 6. Prediction | Flying *will* always *be* dangerous. |
| 7. Instructions | You *will deliver* this package to the bookstore and you *will bring* me *back* the signed receipt. |
| 8. Inclination, tendency (A general statement based on past observation is made about the future.) | Some *will praise* from politeness, and some *will criticize* from vanity. Accidents *will happen* in the best regulated families. (proverb) |
| 9. Obstinacy, insistence, willfulness (with emphasis on the word **will**) | Boys *will be* boys. |
| 10. Supposition | You *will see* from my post card that I am now in Paris. |
| **Will** may also be used in a special kind of concessive clause. | Say what you *will* (=no matter what you say), he deserves credit for at least trying. You can never find a better school, look where you *will* (=no matter where you look). |

SHALL

1. In *requests*—in the sense of **do you want me** (or **us**) **to**

    **Shall I close** the door?

    **Shall** we **go** inside now?

2. In *legal or commercial usage* (with third person—for regulations, specifications, requirements)

    A committee **shall be appointed** to study the matter further.

    The building **shall meet** all specifications set forth in the contract.

    Passengers **shall be permitted** to board only at regular bus stops.

3. In *moral injunctions* (with second person)—an archaic usage found especially in the Bible where **shall** was often used for futurity for all three persons

    Thou **shall** (older **shalt**) **honor** thy father and thy mother.

    Thou **shall** (older **shalt**) not kill.

4. In *literary usage* (with third person)

    There is much to be done before justice **shall prevail.** (more commonly, prevails, or will prevail)

    Who **shall decide,** when doctors disagree?

Use of the
Future Progressive Tense

This form of the future tense expresses duration of a single future event.

    She **will be working** on that book for a long time.

    He **will be having** trouble with his teeth all his life.

Like the past progressive form, it can also indicate duration *at some point.*

    What **will** you **be doing** tomorrow night at ten?

    —I'll **be sleeping** soundly tomorrow night at that hour.

The future progressive form often occurs when a word like **soon** relates the time of an event to the very near present.

    Soon the men **will be working** at this end of the building.

    We'll **be leaving** for the Orient soon.

    We'll **be writing** to you about that matter presently.

See and **hear** used in future progressive form have special meanings.

    I'll **be seeing** you. (meaning **I expect to meet you again.**)

    You **will be hearing** from us. (meaning **You will get a communication from us.**)

In both these sentences the immediate future is understood.

The future progressive form may denote supposition:

*If I don't get home soon, my wife **will be waiting up** for me and **getting** worried.*

In addition to the future tense, other means of expressing future time are the two forms of the present tense—simple and progressive—and **be going to**. We have already seen that the present tense often takes on future meaning from accompanying adverbial expressions of future time. **Be going to** is one of the most frequently used forms for indicating future time. It has stronger phonetic stress than **shall** or **will**, and is often the favored form in informal speech. Like the present progressive form, **be going to** suggests a connection of future plans with present time. When used with persons, this form expresses *intention*[23] more strongly than many of the other means of indicating future time.

*She's **going to** get married in June.*

*The manager **is going to** close the store early tonight.*

When used with either persons or things, **be going to** may also denote *certainty* or *expectation*.

| | |
|---|---|
| persons | Look out. You*'re going to* fall off that fence. |
| | I think I*'m going to* become sick. |
| things | There*'s going to* be an eclipse of the moon tonight. |
| | It's *going to* rain tomorrow. |

For the very immediate future, **be about to**, or **be on the point** (or **verge**) **of** is used:

*The boat **is about to** cast anchor.*

*I **am about to** sneeze.*

*The two countries **are on the verge of** war.*

### Perfect Tenses

Structurally the term *perfect* signifies that a form of **have** accompanies a verb as an auxiliary. Semantically, each of the three perfect tenses denotes time *completed in relation to a particular point*:

| | |
|---|---|
| *Present perfect* tense | time completed in relation to the *present* |
| *Past perfect* tense | time completed in relation to the *past* |
| *Future perfect* tense | time completed in relation to the *future* |

---

[23] **Be going to** may also indicate *past intention*—**He was going to write his report last night, but he received some unexpected visitors.** This kind of past intention is not carried out.

PRESENT PERFECT TENSE

**Form of the Present Perfect Tense**

|  *Nonprogressive* |  *Progressive* |
| --- | --- |

*Active Voice*

I
you
we
they
} have offered

I
you
we
they
} have been offering

he—she—it has offered

he—she—it has been offering

*Passive Voice*

I
you
we
they
} have been offered

he—she—it has been offered

For irregular past participles to be used with perfect tenses, see the list of irregular verbs given earlier in this chapter.

Use of the
Present Perfect Tense

In contrast with the past tense, which denotes definitely completed past time, the present perfect tense expresses *indefinite* time that begins in the past and extends to the present. It is a special kind of past time that *ends with the moment of speaking*. An event may continue beyond the present moment of speaking, but the statement is not concerned with this segment of time.

The kinds of past-to-present time that are possible are:

1.  *Actual* past-to-present time. An actual event starts in the past and continues up to the present.

*He has worked in the same company for ten years.*

2.  *Psychological* past-to-present time. The time exists only in the mind of the speaker. It is the time of *the statement itself*, not the time of an actual event, that extends up to the present.

*This author has often been praised by the critics.*

The actual time represented by the present perfect usually involves *duration of a single act* that ends with the moment of speaking or shortly before it. The psychological time connoted by the present perfect tense often involves possible *repetition* within the past-to-present period.

The expressions of time that mark a past-to-present event are indicated below.

1. *Duration of an event that ends with the moment of speaking* (actual time)

   A. *Prepositions indicating duration*

   (1) **During, in, over**

   *He has remained calm **during** the whole crisis.*

   *The population of this city has doubled **in** (or **during**) the last ten years.*

   *The car payments have been extended **over** a two-year period.*

   (2) **Since, for.** These are the most common prepositions that express duration with the present perfect tense. Both these prepositions refer to the same past-to-present time span: **since** gives the beginning point, **for** gives the entire extent of the past-to-present period. Thus, if a person who came to the United States in 1968 is speaking in 1972, he can say either:

   *I have lived in the United States **for four years**.*

(With **for**, the extended time is expressed as a *quantity*, often with a numeral.)

   or *I have lived in the United States **since 1968**.*

(With **since**, the beginning point of an extended period is often expressed as a *date*.)

   vs. *I came to the United States **four years ago**.*

(**Ago** marks a definite point completed in the past.)

The present perfect form of the verb suggests that the speaker is still living in the United States.

The word **for** may be omitted—**He has lived in the United States four years**. Also, the word **now** may be used at the end of the **for** phrase—**He has lived in the United States (for) four years now.**

**Since** used as an adverb, or as a conjunction introducing a clause may also indicate the beginning point of an extended past-to-present period.

| | |
|---|---|
| Adverb | She had the flu last month. She has not felt well *since*. |
| Conjunction | She has not felt well *since* she had the flu last month. |

   B. *Adverbial expressions meaning past-to-present time*—**so far, up to now, until now, up to the present.**

   *We have finished five chapters **so far**.*

   ***Up to now,** We have not found the kind of paint we need for the job.*

We can also add here such expressions as **all his life, in her whole life**—**He has lived in New York all his life.**

2. *Frequency within an extended past-to-present period* (psychological time)

The present perfect tense is used with frequency adverbs that involve repetition—**always, often, twice, sometimes,** etc.

> *He has **always** lived in the United States.*
>
> *We have **sometimes** gone to the beach, but we have **never** enjoyed the trip.*

Such frequency words usually appear in general statements about events that begin in the past.[24]

3. *Recency of an event* (actual time)

A. **Just (now), already** (or **yet** with negatives and questions), **finally, still** (negative only)

> *He has **just** (**now**) come in.*
>
> *I haven't seen that movie **yet**.*
>
> *The money has **finally** arrived.*

B. **Recently, lately, of late, in recent years,** etc.

> *He has **recently** come out of the hospital.*
>
> ***Lately**, the news about the war has not been good.*

C. Time expressions containing **this**—**this week, this month, this year, this Saturday, this morning.**[25]

> *He has been quite ill **this year**.*
>
> *They have gone shopping **this morning**.*

---

[24] If we compare the three tenses that may be used in such general statements, we see that each tense suggests a different end point.

*Present perfect tense*—the end point is the moment of speaking—**He has always gone to bed early.**

*Simple present tense*—the end point is some indefinite time in the future—**He always goes to bed early.**

*Past tense*—the end point is in the past—**He always went to bed early when he was a child.**

[25] Other tenses may also be used with a time expression containing *this,* depending on the *time the statement is made* and the *part of the time period being referred to.* For example, if a statement is made on *Friday of this week,* the following tense forms may be used.

| Part of the Week Being Referred To | Sentences Used on Friday |
|---|---|
| Monday | I **saw** the doctor this week. (past tense for a more remote part of the week) |
| Wednesday | I **have seen** the doctor this week. (present perfect tense for a recent part of the week) |
| Saturday | I **will** (or **am going to**) **see** the doctor this week. (future tense for a time that follows the day of speaking) |

## Present Perfect Tense in Dependent Clauses

The present perfect tense may occur in certain adverbial or adjective clauses.

A. Adverbial clauses of *time* or *condition*. The present perfect tense may be an alternative for the present tense used for future time.

---

| | |
|---|---|
| Time clause | He will not come to the party until he has *finished* (or *finishes*) his work. |
| Conditional clause | If he **has finished** (or *finishes*) his work he will come to the party. |

---

The present perfect tense in such clauses emphasizes the completion of the event mentioned in the time or conditional clause before the event in the main clause takes place.

B. Adjective clauses after *superlative* adjectives.

*This is the best book I have (ever) read.*

*She is the most beautiful woman that I have (ever) seen.*

## Choices with the Past Tense

If no time expression is contained within a statement about past time, the sentence may often be put in either the present perfect tense or the past tense. The choice depends on *how the time is felt* by the speaker.

Time felt as past to present—present perfect tense:

*I've finished the work.*

*Have you read this novel?*

Time felt as definite past—past tense:

*I finished the work.*

*Did you read this novel?*

In fact, except for **since** and **for**, most of the other past-to-present time expressions may be used informally with the past tense.

*We finished five chapters so far.*

*He always lived in the United States.*

*He just (now) came in.*

*He recently published his memoirs.*

When the time expressions that may represent past-to-present time refer to situations that no longer exist or are no longer possible, a past tense is required.

*World War Two lasted for five years.*

*The deceased man lived (or had lived) in the same town all his life.*

Present Perfect Progressive Tense

The progressive form of the present perfect tense stresses the duration of a single past-to-present action that has a beginning and an end. However, it suggests the middle of an event rather than the beginning or end of that event. The progressive form of the present perfect is even more closely related to the present than the nonprogressive form is; the action denoted by the verb is more likely to be continuing into the present.

> *He has been living* (vs. **has lived**) *in the United States since January.*
> *The professor has been lecturing* (vs. **has lectured**) *for over an hour.*

Occasionally the present perfect progressive form can be used for repeated events.

> *He has always been doing it this way.*
> *Recently we have been seeing each other every day.*

The present perfect progressive form does not occur with words like **just, already, ever, never, finally.**

### PAST PERFECT TENSE[26]

**Form of the Past Perfect Tense**

| *Nonprogressive* | *Progressive* |
|---|---|

*Active Voice*

| I you he—she—it we they } had offered | I you he—she—it we they } had been offering |
|---|---|

*Passive Voice*

| I you he—she—it we they } had been offered | |
|---|---|

Use of the
Past Perfect Tense

The past perfect tense expresses *one past time before another past time.* For this reason, this tense is always tied to past time, expressed or understood.

---

[26] The past perfect tense is also called the *pluperfect* tense.

A common use of the past perfect tense is to indicate time that precedes a particular point in a past narrative.

*The burglar alarm went off and a crowd began to gather. Soon the police arrived at the scene of the robbery. But they were too late. The thieves **had** already **gone**.*

The past perfect tense often occurs in sentences containing dependent clauses. The verb in the main clause is usually in the past tense, and the verb of the dependent clause is in the past perfect tense. In a few cases the reverse is true.

Past Perfect Tense
in Sentences with Adverbial Clauses

| | |
|---|---|
| A. *time clauses*—introduced by: | |
| **before** | |
|    past perfect in the *before* clause | The teacher took my paper before I *had finished* the test. |
|    past perfect in the main clause | I *had* never *seen* him before he visited our class yesterday. |
| **after** | After I *had spoken*, I realized my mistake. |
| **until** | The secretary did not leave until she *had finished* her work. |
| **when, as soon as** | When (as soon as) she *had finished* her work, she went to the movies. |
| **(had) just** ⎱ —**when**<br>    **already** ⎰ | He **had** just (already) **gone** to bed when the telephone rang.[27] |
| **(had) scarcely** ⎱ —**when**<br>    **hardly** ⎰ | I **had scarcely arrived** when I was put right to work. |
| B. *other adverbial clauses* | |
| cause | Because she **had** not **reported** the theft immediately, the police were unable to help her. |
| concession | Although she **had reported** the theft immediately, the police were unable to help her. |
| comparison | The weather was far worse than any of us **had anticipated**. |

The past perfect form used as a subjunctive in **if** clauses and in **that** clauses after the verb **wish** represents past time—**If he had studied harder last week, he would have passed the examination; I wish I had been there yesterday.**

Past Perfect Tense
in Sentences with Noun Clauses

*That he **had failed** once was no indication that he would fail again.*

[27] **Just** and **already** may also be used with the past progressive tense to indicate a continuous action that has just been *interrupted* rather than just completed—**He was just (or already) getting ready to go to bed when the telephone rang.**

> He said (or *believed, thought, remembered*) that he **had left** his wallet at home.
>
> He was worried about what he **had** just **heard**.
>
> His belief that he **had betrayed** his country could not be shaken.

The past perfect tense is used in the main clause with verbs like **hope, expect, intend, plan, think**. This tense indicates that the hope, expectation, etc., was not realized.

> *I* **had hoped** (or **intended, expected**) to take a vacation this summer, but I was forced to change my plans.

Past Perfect Tense
in Sentences with Adjectives Clauses

> The man who **had stolen** the money two weeks ago confessed last night.
>
> The house where he **had lived** as a child was right on a lake.
>
> He could still remember the good times he **had had** as a child.

In many of the sentences just given to illustrate the use of the past perfect tense, *informal usage also permits the past tense* if there is no desire or need to stress past time before another past time.

> The secretary did not leave until she finished her work.
>
> He said that he left his wallet at home.
>
> The man who stole the money two weeks ago confessed last night.

Only the sentences containing the time expressions **just** (or **already**)—**when, scarcely** (or **hardly**)—**when,** and **no sooner**—**than** permit no choice with the past tense.

Use of the
Past Perfect Progressive Tense

This form emphasizes the duration of one past event taking place before another past event.

> He **had been working** very hard; the doctor told him to take a vacation.
>
> We **had been waiting** in the doctor's office for an hour before we were told that he was still at the hospital.

The past perfect progressive form, like the past progressive form, may show a past event in progress before it is *interrupted* by another past event. The past perfect progressive, however, places greater emphasis on the fact that one event is completed before the other.

> She **had been planning** to go to the beach when it suddenly started to rain.
>
> He **had been working** on his painting for months when the order for it was suddenly canceled.
>
> Everybody **had** just **been talking** about him when he suddenly appeared.

## FUTURE PERFECT TENSE

**Form of the Future Perfect Tense**

|  | *Nonprogressive* | *Progressive* |
|---|---|---|

*Active Voice*

I
we } shall *or* will have offered

you
he—she—it } will have offered
they

I
we } shall *or* will have been offering

you
he—she—it } will have been offering
they

*Passive Voice*

I
we } shall *or* will have been offered

you
he—she—it } will have been offered
they

Use of the
Future Perfect Tense

In general, the future perfect tense may be characterized as *future-before-future* time. This tense emphasizes the fact that one future time is *completed* before another future time—or, to put it another way, that one future time is *"past"* in relation to a second future time. Often the event marked by the future perfect tense actually begins in the past and terminates in the future; we may then speak of *past-to-future* time.

The future perfect tense is usually accompanied by a time expression which signals *at*, *by*, or *before* which time a future event will be completed. Examples with such future end points follow. Many of these examples refer to *past-to-future* time.

THE FUTURE END POINT IS A TIME *AT WHICH* (TIME EXPRESSION **ON, AT, WHEN**)

*On June 10* (future) *she will have been a widow for two years.*

*At the end of this summer, I will* (or *shall*) *have been away from home for ten years.*

*When he retires from his work, he will have made more than a million dollars.*

THE FUTURE END POINT IS A TIME *BY WHICH* (TIME EXPRESSIONS WITH **BY**)

*My train arrives in New York at eight o'clock tonight. The plane I would like to take from there will have left by then.*

*By the time the wrestling matches end, many of the spectators will have left.*

*By the end of the school year, we will* (or *shall*) *have covered the entire grammar book.*

THE FUTURE END POINT IS A TIME *BEFORE WHICH*
(TIME EXPRESSIONS WITH **BEFORE**)

*The cook will have gone home **long before eight o'clock**.*

***Before his vacation is over,** he will have made many new friends.*

*They will have helped many people **before their money runs out**.*

In some instances the idea of completion of one future event before another is not absolutely necessary to the sense of a sentence. In such cases the future perfect alternates with the future tense, with the future perfect tense merely giving greater emphasis to the completion of the earlier event.

*By the end of the school year we will have covered* (or ***will cover***) *the entire grammar book.*

*Before we leave New York we will have seen* (or ***will see***) *every play on Broadway.*

In other instances the idea of completion makes a real difference in the meaning of a sentence. In such sentences the future perfect tense must be used.

*May I speak to your cook at eight o'clock tonight?*

*—I'm sorry. The cook will have gone home long before then.*

Sometimes the future perfect tense differs from the future tense in that it marks an event as *having already begun.*

*In the near future, many of the planets will have been explored.* (The action is stated as already begun)

*In the near future, many of the planets will be explored.* (The action is stated as not yet begun)

If the word **already** is used for future time, the future perfect tense is often required.

*When you wake up from your nap, I will have already done all the housework.*

*He will already have left by the time I get there.*

In some sentences with **already**, the future perfect tense may alternate with the present perfect tense.

*In some cases the process of decay will have begun* (or ***has begun***) *already.*

*Before anyone discovers his fraudulent operations, he will have already gone on* (or ***has already gone on***) *to another town.*

A special use of the future perfect tense is to express supposition in the past —**You *will have seen* from my post card that I was in Paris last week** (cf. with present supposition—**You will see from my post card that I am now in Paris**).

Use of the
Future Perfect Progressive Tense

This form of the future perfect tense does not occur very often. It stresses *duration* of a single event in the future that takes place before another future event.

On April 2, 1972, we **shall have been living** in this house (for) exactly thirty years.

They **will have been touring** for six months before they get to Japan.

The orchestra **will have been practicing** for three hours before the soloist gets there.

VERBS IN
NEGATIVES AND QUESTIONS

Except when single forms from the independent verb **be** are involved, all negatives and questions operate with auxiliaries. If the verb in a positive declarative sentence does not contain an auxiliary, a form from **do** is added for a negative statement or a question.

NEGATIVES

| | | | | | | |
|---|---|---|---|---|---|---|
| 1. | *Verbs with no auxiliaries* (simple present and simple past tenses only) | | | | | |
| | **be** | Mary *is* late. | Mary | **is** | not | late. |
| | all other verbs | Mary **arrived** late. | Mary | **did** (auxiliary added) | not | **arrive** late. |
| 2. | *Verbs with 1–3 auxiliaries* | | | | | |
| | 1 auxiliary | Mary **has arrived** late. | Mary | **has** | not | **arrived** late. |
| | 2–3 auxiliaries | Mary **has been arriving** late. | Mary | **has** | not | **been arriving** late. |

Note that with a single form of **be, not** is simply inserted after this form— **Mary is *not* late**. With the other verbs, **not** is placed after the auxiliary (the first one if there are two or three auxiliaries).

In informal usage, **not** is contracted with the auxiliary or the single form of **be**.[28] (See the chapter on auxiliaries for further details about contractions.)

The *simple present* tense of **have** meaning *possess* is made negative in either way given under 1. in the preceding chart.

*I **haven't** any money.* (negative form like that of **be**)

or *I **don't** have any money.* (negative form like that of other verbs than **be**)

An older usage still occasionally met with is the occurrence of **not** after an auxiliary-less verb other than **be**.

*If I mistake **not**, you should be the son of my old friend.*

---

[28] Because the single form of **be** functions so much like auxiliaries in negatives and questions, it will simplify further generalizations about negatives and questions in this section if we use the term *auxiliary* to include the single form of **be**.

*I know **not** what course others may take, but as for me, give me liberty, or give me death!* (Patrick Henry)

There are three kinds of questions in English:

YES-NO QUESTIONS.    These are simple questions eliciting the answer yes or no only.

ATTACHED (OR TAG) QUESTIONS.    These are also yes-no questions, but the special form into which they are put shows which of these two answers is actually expected.

INTERROGATIVE-WORD QUESTIONS.    These are questions that elicit specific information—a person, place, time, etc.

As in negation, the verb in each of these questions is handled differently depending on whether the verb is or is not accompanied by an auxiliary in the declarative sentence.

### YES-NO QUESTIONS

| | |
|---|---|
| 1. *Verbs with no auxiliaries*<br>(simple present and simple past tense only)<br>**be**          Mary *is* late.<br>all other     Mary ***arrived*** late.<br>verbs | **Is**          Mary                          late?<br>**Did**         Mary        **arrive**     late?<br>(auxiliary<br>added) |
| 2. *Verbs with 1–3 auxiliaries*<br>   1 auxiliary      Mary ***has arrived*** late.<br>   2–3 auxiliaries  Mary ***has been arriving***<br>                    late. | **Has**         Mary        **arrived**   late?<br><br>**Has**         Mary        **been<br>                          arriving** late? |

Note that all these questions begin with an auxiliary or a single form of **be** that has been reversed with the subject.

As in the case of the negative, the *simple present* tense of **have** meaning *possess* may have either form given in the previous chart.

> ***Have you*** *any money?* (question form like that of **be**)

or   ***Do you have*** *any money?* (question form like that of other verbs than **be**)

A short answer to a yes-no question contains only a personal pronoun as subject, and the same verb as the one that initiated the question. Negative answers of course also contain the word **not**.

> *Is Mary late?*          *—Yes, she is.*
> *—No, she isn't.*

*Did Mary arrive late?*    —*Yes, she did.*
                           —*No, she didn't.*
*Has Mary arrived late?*   —*Yes, she has.*
                           —*No, she hasn't.*

In addition to the personal pronouns, the expletives **there** and **it** may also appear in a short answer to a yes-no question.

*Are **there** enough chairs?*    —*No, **there** aren't.*
*Is **it** raining?*              —*Yes, **it** is.*

Sometimes the first two auxiliaries of a verb in a question are given in the short answer.

*Should he have done that?*    —*Yes, he **should** (**have**).*
*Has the machine been working properly?*    —*Yes, it **has** (**been**).*

In negative yes-no questions, **not** is contracted with the auxiliary that starts the question.

*Isn't Mary late?*
*Didn't Mary arrive late?*
*Hasn't Mary arrived late?*
*Hasn't Mary been arriving late?*

In formal usage, **not** is placed in adverbial position right after the reversed auxiliary and subject.

*Is Mary not late?*
*Did Mary not arrive late?*
*Has Mary not arrived late?*
*Has Mary not been arriving late?*

This form may be preferred if the user wishes to place more emphasis on the negation—**Has he *not* done what I requested**? Generally, the uncontracted form is avoided in questions because of its formal tone.

Negative questions often expect the answer yes (**Isn't she beautiful?**). They may connote such feelings as surprise (**Haven't the books arrived yet?**) or irritation (**Can't you move any faster?**).

In highly informal conversation, the auxiliary and the subject of a yes-no question are frequently omitted.

*Need any money?* (for *Do you need any money?*)
*Leaving so soon?* (for *Are you leaving so soon?*)

### ATTACHED QUESTIONS

These alternatives for yes-no questions consist of two parts. The first part makes a *statement;* the second part asks the question that expects

| | Statement Part of Sentence | Question Part of Sentence | Expected Answer |
|---|---|---|---|
| 1. *Verbs with no auxiliaries* (simple present and past) | | | |
| **be** | Mary is late, | isn't she? | Yes, she is. |
| | Mary isn't late, | is she? | No, she isn't. |
| all other verbs | Mary arrived late, | didn't she? | Yes, she did. |
| | Mary didn't arrive late, | did she? | No, she didn't. |
| 2. *Verbs with 1–3 auxiliaries* | | | |
| 1 auxiliary | Mary has arrived late, | hasn't she? | Yes, she has. |
| | Mary hasn't arrived late, | has she? | No, she hasn't. |
| 2–3 auxiliaries | Mary has been arriving late, | hasn't she? | Yes, she has. |
| | Mary hasn't been arriving late, | has she? | No, she hasn't. |

agreement with the statement. The second part contains the regular question auxiliary plus the personal pronoun that stands for the subject.

Note that if the statement part of the question is positive, the question part is negative; if the statement part is negative, the question part is positive.

As in the regular yes-no questions, **there** and **it** are the only words other than the personal pronouns that may be used in the second part of such questions.

> *It's not raining, is* ***it*** *?—No,* ***it*** *isn't.*
>
> *There is still some bread left, isn't* ***there*** *?—Yes,* ***there*** *is.*

Negative or near negative adverbs may appear in the first part of the question.

> *They never (or seldom, rarely) go anywhere, do they?*

## INTERROGATIVE-WORD QUESTIONS

Such questions begin with either interrogative adverbs or pronouns.

Questions Beginning
with Interrogative Adverbs-
WHY, WHEN, WHERE, HOW

| Interrogative Adverb | Auxiliary | Subject | Balance of predicate | |
|---|---|---|---|---|
| Why | **is** | Mary | | late? |
| Why | **did** (auxiliary added) | Mary | **arrive** | late? |
| Why | **has** | Mary | **arrived** | late? |
| Why | **has** | Mary | **been arriving** | late? |

Note that the interrogative adverb is merely placed before the auxiliary that ordinarily begins a yes-no question.

The interrogative adverb **how** may combine with an adjective or an adverb.

> ***How tall*** *are you?*
>
> ***How quickly*** *can you get here?*
>
> ***How long*** *will it take you?*

The interrogative adverb **where** is generally not used with other prepositions than **from (Where do you come from?)**. Although **Where are you going to?** and **Where is he at?** are often heard, such usage is regarded as non-standard.

Questions Beginning
with Interrogative Pronouns

| Pronouns | who (whom for object, whose for possessive)—for persons<br>what—for things<br>which—for persons or things, when a choice is involved |
|---|---|

| Interrogative<br>pronoun as: | | | | |
|---|---|---|---|---|
| Object of verb | Whom | **do** | you | **want**? Informal—Who do you<br>want? |
| | What | **can** | I | **do** for you? |
| Object of preposition | To whom | **is** | he | **speaking**? Informal—Who(m)<br>is he speaking to? |
| | On what | **will** | he | **lecture**? Informal—What will<br>he lecture on? |
| Subject of verb | | | Who | **invented** the telephone? |
| | | | What | **has caused** the accident? |

From this chart you will note that:

1.  When the interrogative pronoun *functions as subject*, there is no reversal of word order.
2.  When **whom** used as object introduces a question, it may be replaced informally by **who**.
3.  In informal English, the preposition may be placed at the end of the question rather than at the beginning.

Interrogative pronouns may function as adjectives.

*What time is it?*

*Whose book did you borrow?*

The choice of the adjective **which** or **what** depends on the speaker's emphasis.

*Which bus should we take?*

This question is asked in terms of a *choice* of buses.

*What bus should we take?*

This question is asked to obtain some general information about the buses.
Interrogative adjectives may also be contained within prepositional phrases that function as adverbs.

*At what time should I pick you up?*

*In whose name was the reservation made?*

*From which clerk did you buy your ticket?*

The interrogative adverb **how** plus **much** or **many** may function as a subject or an object in a question.

*How much (money) do you need?* (**How much** [**money**] is the object of the verb.)

An informal equivalent of **why** is **what—for.**

*What did you do that for?*

Even less formal than **what—for** is **how come.**

*How come you didn't tell me about this before?*

Interrogative pronouns and adverbs may be intensified by:

1.  the suffix **-ever**

*However did you get here so early?*
*Whoever heard of such a thing?*
*Whatever will he do with that?*

Only **why** does not take this suffix.

2.  expressions such as **in the world, on earth, in heaven's name,** or stronger expressions that shade into the profane—**the devil, the hell.**

*How in the world did you get here so early?*
*What in heaven's name will he do with that?*

**Else** may be used after interrogative words in the sense of *other* or *otherwise.*

*Who else would do such a thing?*
*What else should I have done?*
*How else can I get there?*

In questions beginning with **why,** informal usage permits the omission of the auxiliary (or a single form of **be**) and the subject.

*Why so early?* (for **Why are you so early?**)
*Why not go at once?* (for **Why shouldn't we go at once?**)

In older times, an interrogative-word question could be formed without adding **do** to a single form of a verb.

*What care I, though death be nigh, I'll live for love or die.* (from the opera *Carmen*)
*What say (or think) you?*

Yes-no questions could also be formed this way—**Think you the king will survive this terrible illness**?

# 5

## Auxiliaries

Auxiliary verbs,[1] as we have seen, are "helping" verbs that add structural meaning or a semantic coloring to verbs carrying the full burden of lexical meaning. All auxiliaries share the ability to be directly followed by **not** in negatives, often in contracted form (**They** *have not* **gone, We** *shouldn't* **wait**), and to be reversed with the subject in questions (*Have they* **gone**? *Should we* **wait?**).

There are three types of auxiliaries, each serving a different purpose.

### Tense Auxiliaries—*Be, Have, Will—Shall*

The tense auxiliaries perform a structural function only. **Be** occurs with the **-ing** present participle in the progressive forms of the tenses, and with the **-ed** past participle in the passive forms of the tenses. **Have** is used for the perfect tenses. (**Be** and **have** are also independent verbs.) **Shall** and **will** are used for the future tenses.[2]

### *Do* Auxiliary

The **do** auxiliary is accompanied by the simple form of the verb (the infinitive without **to**). It is used only in the *simple present* tense (**do** or **does offer**)

---

[1] Auxiliary verbs are also called *anomalous* verbs.

[2] Grammarians who work with the two-tense formal system classify **shall** and **will** among the modal auxiliaries because of similarities in grammatical form and behavior.

and in the *simple past* tense (**did offer**). It provides an auxiliary to auxiliary-less verbs to enable them to function in the following grammatical patterns.

1. *Questions*

   **Do** *you like my new hat?*

2. *Negative statements*

   *I* **don't** *like your new hat.*

3. *Abridgment—omission or substitution*

   *Do you like my new hat? Yes, I* **do**.
   *I don't like coffee and neither* **does** *my wife.* (or *my* **wife doesn't either.**)
   *Mary works harder than her sister* **does**.
   *He should study hard. Whenever he* **does**, *he gets good grades.*

4. *Emphasis*
   a. a positive contrasting with a negative (often introduced by **but**)

   *My teacher thinks I didn't study for my test, but I* **did** *study.*

   b. with a negative expression

   *The letter we were expecting never* **did** *arrive.*

   c. with a concessive type of contrast

   *Although I have little time for entertainment, I* **do** *go to the theater once in a while.*
   *He* **does** *have money, but it's all tied up in property.*

   d. as a positive resolution after some doubt

   *We're very pleased that she* **does** *intend to come.*

   e. with emphatic adverbs—**definitely, positively, certainly.**

   *Do you remember how beautiful she was? I certainly* **do** *remember.*

5. *Entreaty*

   **Do** *come to the party tonight.*

In older usage, **do** often appeared in positive statements, in variation with the simple present form.

   *Thus conscience does make cowards of us all.* (Shakespeare)

## Modal Auxiliaries

These auxiliaries add to the verb a special semantic component such as ability, obligation, possibility. Some of the modal auxiliaries express the same kinds of semantic coloring as verbs in the subjunctive mood (note the relationship between *modal* and *mood*).

Modal auxiliaries generally have no **-s** suffix for third person, and no infinitive or participial form. They have only two formal tenses, the present and the past, which are used with the simple form of the lexical verb (**may** *offer*, **might** *offer*), the progressive form (**may** or **might** *be offering*), the perfect form (**may** or **might** *have offered*) or the passive form (**may** or **might** *be offered*).

MODAL AUXILIARIES

The following chart of modal auxiliaries outlines the special meanings these auxiliaries have, and the present, past and future time they express.

| *Meaning Added to the Verb by the Modal Auxiliary* | *Present Time* | *Past Time* | *Future Time* |
|---|---|---|---|
| *ability* | | | |
| can | *can* offer | *could* offer | *can* offer |
| be able to | *am* *is* *are* } *able to* offer[3] | *was* *were* } *able to* offer | *shall* *will* } *be able to* offer |
| *permission* | | | |
| may | *may* *might* } offer | *might* offer (only for sequence of tenses) | *may* *might* } offer |
| can | *can* *could* } offer | *could* offer (only for sequence of tenses) | *can* *could* } offer |
| *obligation, advisability* | | | |
| should | *should* offer | *should have* offered | *should* offer |
| ought to | *ought to* offer | *ought to have* offered | *ought to* offer |
| *necessity* | | | |
| must | *must* offer | *had to* offer | *must* offer |
| have to | *have* *has* } *to* offer[3] | *had to* offer | *will* *shall* } *have to* offer |
| *possibility* | | | |
| may | *may* *might* } offer | *may* *might* } *have* offered | *may* *might* } offer |

Note that three of these verbs may be followed by the **to** infinitive—**be able to, ought to, have to.**[4] The verbs of **be able to** and **have to** are also independent; they may therefore be used in any of the six tenses, and in infinitive and participial form.

Note further that in most cases the present tense is used for future time. Actually, unless accompanied by an expression of present or future time, the present form of one of these auxiliaries may indicate "timeless" time (**He**

[3] These present forms may also express future time.

[4] It is customary to include these verbs followed by **to** among the modals not only because they are semantic equivalents of the modals listed here but also because they form negatives and questions in the same way as modal auxiliaries do.

**can swim**) or present-to-future time (**It may rain**, meaning *at any time beginning with this moment*).

Where the chart indicates alternate past forms along with the present forms (**may** or **might, can** or **could**), the past form has the effect of softening the idea, or lessening its force. Thus, **Could I borrow your pencil** makes a less strong request than **Can I borrow your pencil**. Also, in **It might rain**, the possibility of rain is considered less than in **It may rain**.

A number of observations need to be made about each type of modal auxiliary given in the chart.

### Ability

Three kinds of ability may be indicated by **can** and **be able to**. One is *physical ability* (**I can lift this stone**); a second is a *learned ability*, in the sense of knowing how to do something (**She can type**). The third type of ability is more general—it is equivalent to *have the power to* do something. (**I can see you tonight**). While the first two kinds of ability are used mostly for live beings, especially human beings, the third type can be used for things as well as persons (**This factory can produce dozens of machines a day**). It is only in this sense of ability, which is related to possibility, that **can** and **be able to** may be used for future time.

### Permission

Strict schoolbook rules say we must use only **may** for permission. However, in informal speech, cultivated speakers frequently also use **can** for permission. Of the two past forms denoting permission, **might** is more deferential in tone than **could** is.

A request for permission often takes the form of a question. The request may be in first person or in third person.

| | Question (*asking for permission*) | Answer—*Granting or Denying Permission* |
|---|---|---|
| First person | May (or can) I borrow your car? | Yes, you may. <br> No, you may not (or **cannot**). |
| Third person | May (or can) John come to the movies with us? | Yes, he may. <br> No, he may not (or **cannot**). |

The past forms of **may** and **can** are also used in requests—**Might** (or **Could**) **I borrow your car?** The answers, however, are generally given in present form, with **may** being preferred for granting permission. In these requests for permission, **can** retains some of its meaning of ability, and **may** some of its meaning of possibility.

Both **may** and **can** also occur in a simple request that does not involve permission—**May** (or **can**) **I have a drink of water?** For a simple request with **you**, only **can** is used—**Can** (or **could**) **you cash this check, please**?

**May** or **can** are used not only in a request for permission but in the sense of *be permitted*. In this sense, the past forms **might** and **could** express only past time.

| | |
|---|---|
| Present or "timeless" time | Anyone may (or **can**) enroll for this course. |
| | No visitor may (or **can**) remain in the hospital after eight P.M. |
| Past time | In those days, anyone might (or **could**) enroll for this course. |
| | Until recently, no visitor might (or **could**) remain in the hospital after eight P.M. |

In the sequence of tenses **might** and **could** also indicate only past time.

| | |
|---|---|
| Present time | John's mother *says* that he *may* (or *can*) go with us. |
| Past time | John's mother *said* that he *might* (or *could*) go with us. |

**May** used in indirect speech is sometimes ambiguous. In the two preceding sentences **may** and its past, **might**, can be interpreted as meaning either permission or possibility.

### Obligation or Advisability

**Should** and **ought to** occur in statements about one's duty or one's advantage which one is free to accept or reject.

| | | |
|---|---|---|
| Obligation | (What one is expected to do) | You should (or **ought to**) do your homework every day. |
| Advisability | (What is wise for one to do) | She should (or **ought to**) eat less if she wants to lose weight. |

The forms listed in the chart under past time, **should have offered** and **ought to have offered**, imply that *the action was not performed.* Thus the statement **John** *should have gone* **to the dentist yesterday** tells us that although it was advisable for John to have gone to the dentist, he did *not* go. This special meaning of non-fulfillment also applies in the sequence of tenses, and so when positive obligation or advisability is meant, the present form **should** or **ought to** remains unchanged after a past main verb—**He** *said* **that he** *should* (or **ought to**) **go to the dentist.**

In a question with the perfect form, the action has in fact been performed —**Should he have gone to the dentist yesterday?** Here the speaker is merely questioning the advisability of an event that has occurred.

Another auxiliary that denotes advisability is **had better**—**You had better study hard if you want to pass that examination.** This auxiliary has no past form.

**Necessity**

The difference between obligation and necessity is often one of degree only. While statements with **should** and **ought to** suggest a desirable course of action, which may possibly not be acted upon, **must** and **have to** suggest a more urgent course of action which does not allow for the possibility of rejection—**You must** (or **have to**) **do your homework every day; I must** (or **have to**) **keep my word.**

This difference in degree also operates when these auxiliaries are used to make a recommendation.

> *This is an excellent book. You should* (or ***ought to***) ***read it.*** (moderate recommendation)
>
> *This is an excellent book. You must* (or ***have to***) *read it.* (strong recommendation)

**Must** is generally felt as stronger than **have to.** Its use ranges from a compulsion forced on us by life itself to a constraint we impose on ourselves through a strong sense of duty or moral conscience.

> *We must eat in order to live.* (A compulsion imposed on us by life.)

**Must** in this use suggests inexorable fate, and is sometimes interchangeable with **will**—**What must** (or **will**) **be, must** (or **will**) **be.**

> *You must obey the law.* (A constraint imposed on us by others in authority —the government, our teachers, parents, employers, etc.)
>
> *I must save some money every week.* (A constraint placed on us by ourselves.)

In the sense of necessity, the past form for **must** is **had to**—**I** *had to* **meet my cousin yesterday.** This past tense is used in the sequence of tenses.

> *He **tells** me I **must do** it.*
>
> becomes *He **told** me I **had to do** it.*

However, in informal English the present form **must** is often heard in such sentences—**He told me I must do it.**

The negative of **must** often has a different meaning from the negative of **have to.**

1. *Must not*—denotes that it is strongly recommended *not* to take a certain course of action:

> *He mustn't go there alone. It's too dangerous.*
>
> *You mustn't spend so much money. You'll soon have none left.*
> (the negative refers to the *lexical verb*)

2. *Do not have to*—denotes that it is *not* necessary to take a certain course of action:

*He doesn't have to go there alone. Someone will go there with him.*
*You don't have to spend so much money. You can get a cheaper car.*
(the negative refers to the *auxiliary*)

**Must not** often has the effect of a prohibition, especially when used with you—**You mustn't smoke near the gasoline tank.**

Other verbs that express necessity are **need to** and **have got to**. **Have got to** is confined to use in informal speech. Like **had better, have got to** has only a present form and so cannot be used for past time.

### Possibility

The chart indicates that **may** is the regular auxiliary expressing possibility.

*It may (or **might**) rain tonight.*

*He may (or **might**) have gone to the party last night.*

In addition, depending on the context, other modal auxiliaries—particularly **can, should, must**—may signify varying degrees of possibility, ranging from mere chance to strong probability. We will point out here how **may** and **can** differ from each other in denoting possibility, and how **may, should** and **must** differ from each other in denoting probability.

### *May* vs. *Can* for Possibility

According to dictionary definitions, anything that is possible *may* or *can* be, or *may* or *can* happen. **May** simply indicates a possible chance, often with the negative implied as the other possibility (**It may or may not rain**). **Can** suggests what is within the limits of possibility; it often connotes greater certainty. The forms used for past possibility are **may** (or **might**) **have** and **could have**.

| | |
|---|---|
| present or future time | Something can (or **may**) go wrong. |
| | or Something could (or **might**) go wrong. |
| past time | Something could (or **may, might**) have gone wrong. |

Note that **could have** is used only for *past possibility*, not for ability in the past. The present form **may** does not occur in questions that involve possibility.

*Why hasn't Mabel arrived yet?*

*Could (or **might**) she have missed her train?*

*Can (or **could, might**) she still be at the station?*

### *May* vs. *Should* vs. *Must* for Probability

Each of these auxiliaries indicates a surmise from some kind of evidence. **May** expresses the greatest uncertainty. **Should** suggests a reasonable degree of probability; however, it can only be used where the idea of *expectation* is possible. **Must** denotes the greatest degree of probability; it is used when the speaker or writer is fairly certain that his inference from the available evidence is correct.

---

inference about:
present time    *He left home an hour ago.*
          He *may* (or *might*) possibly *be* at the office by now. (uncertainty)
          or He *should be* at the office by now. (expectation)
          or He *must* certainly *be* at the office by now. (certainty)
past time      *He left home an hour ago.*
          He *may* (or *might*) possibly *have arrived* at the office by now.
          or He *should have arrived* at the office by now.
          or He *must* certainly *have arrived* at the office by now.
Sometimes when **should have** is used for past probability, the expectation is not realized—**He should have arrived last night, but his train was delayed.** Here **should have** is the equivalent of **was supposed to. Must have** is used only for *past probability*, never for past necessity.
future time     *He is leaving home now.*
          He *may* (or *might*) get to the office in half an hour.
          or He *should get* to the office in half an hour.
          *Must in the sense of probability is not used for future time.*

---

The sentences with **may** or **might** can also be stated with **could**, and the sentences with **should** can be stated with **ought to**.

Sentences with the modal auxiliaries **may, should** and **must** in the second and third persons may be the equivalent of imperative sentences that range from mild suggestions to stern commands.

      *You may (or can) put your things there.*
      *You might check this information further.*
      *All new students should report to the dean today.*
      *You must put your toys away immediately.*

**Should** and **must** are often used in instructions—**You should** (or stronger **must**) **wash the floor before you wax it.**

*MAY—MIGHT*

In addition to denoting possibility and permission, the auxiliary **may** or **might** may express:

---

1.  a wish      *May* all your dreams come true.
2.  purpose     She is saving her money so that she *may* go to Europe next summer.
3.  concession  Try as he *might,* he could not find her.
               He *may* be poor (=**although he is poor**) but he is honest.
4.  reproach    You *might* try to be more helpful.
               You *might have* tried to shield me from criticism.

---

## Conditional SHOULD, WOULD

The form **should** or **would** plus a lexical verb is sometimes classified as the conditional tense in traditional grammar; and the past **should have** or **would have** plus a lexical verb is considered the conditional perfect tense.

This conditional form is required for the verb in the main clause of a sentence with an **if** unreal condition. Examples of the use of the conditional forms are:

*Present* unreal condition:

> If I were you, I **would** (or **should**) go to bed early.

*Past* unreal condition:

> If I had been you, I **would** (or **should**) **have** gone to bed early. (unrealized)

(See conditional clauses for a more detailed discussion of the forms used with unreal conditions.)

## Other Uses of SHOULD, WOULD

Since **should** and **would** have many other uses than with the main verb in sentences with conditions, it might be advisable to give a summary of these uses here. In some of the uses outlined below, **should** and **would** merely represent weakened alternatives for the present **shall** or **will**.

### *Should*

#### USES OF *SHOULD* ALREADY GIVEN

1. To express *obligation*:
   a. present   **You should do what your parents tell you.**
   b. past   **You should have done what your parents told you.** (You didn't)
2. To express *advisability*:
   a. present   **He should go to bed earlier.**
   b. past   **He should have gone to bed earlier.** (He didn't)
3. To express *expectation*:
   a. present   **They should be arriving now.**
   b. past   **They should have arrived by now.** (They might or might not have arrived)

#### ADDITIONAL USES OF *SHOULD*

1. As the past form of **shall** in sequence of tenses after a past verb.

   > We told them that we **should** (or **would**) be ready to leave in a few days.

2. As the past form of **shall** in requests meaning *do you want me to*.

***Should*** (vs. ***shall***) *I open the window?*

**Should** has the effect of softening the request.

3.   As a less formal alternative to the subjunctive form after verbs or adjectives expressing some degree of urgency.

> *The committee urged* (or ***requested, recommended***) *that the work* ***should*** *be finished as soon as possible.*
>
> *It is urgent* (or ***important, advisable***) *that the work* ***should*** *be finished as soon as possible.*

4.   In **that** clause subjects after the verb **be** plus certain adjectives (often alternates with an infinitive construction).

> *It's natural that people* ***should*** *like their comfort.* (or ***for people to like their comfort***).
>
> *It's not good that man* ***should*** *live alone.* (or ***for man to live alone***)

5.   In noun clause objects (often alternates with an infinitive construction).

> *We must ask our host how we* ***should*** *dress for dinner* (or ***how to dress for dinner***).

6.   In adjective clauses (often alternates with an infinitive construction).

> *The person whom you* ***should*** *see* (or ***the person to see***) *is away on vacation now.*

7.   In time clauses (often to express future time in relation to past time).

> *She asked for financial assistance until her check* ***should*** *arrive* (or *arrived*).

8.   After **for fear (that), lest** (alternates with the subjunctive form of the verb).

> *For fear* (*that*) (or *lest*) *news of the treaty* ***should*** *be made public prematurely, negotiations were held in secret.*

9.   In **if** clauses, in the sense of *if it happens that, by chance.*

> *If I should see him, I'll let you know.*

10.   To express a dilemma (this use is related to advisability).

> ***Should*** *we take train today or tomorrow?*

11.   To express conjecture.

> *Why* ***should*** *they have destroyed those paintings?*

12.   To make a correction.

> *This name is wrong; it* ***should*** *be spelled Smythe, not Smith.*

## *Would*

In addition to its function with the main verb in sentences with conditions, **would** may be used in the following situations.

1.  As the past form of **will** in sequence of tenses after a past verb.

*He said that he **would** leave soon.*

2.  As the past form of **will** with requests (to make the request less strong).

***Would** (vs. **will**) you bring me some paper, please?*

3.  To express past custom.

*When the Pilgrims needed food, they would go hunting and fishing.*

In a sequence of events representing past custom, often only the verbs for the first few events occur with **would**; the verbs that follow are used in the past tense.

4.  With certain verbs of liking, appreciating, wanting, etc.

*I **would** (or **should**) appreciate receiving your check.*

5.  Combined with **rather** or **sooner** to mean *prefer*.

---

| | |
|---|---|
| Present or "timeless" time | I **would rather** be right than President. |
| Past time | I **would rather have** stayed home than gone to the movies. |

---

The past form implies that the action was not performed.

6.  In wishes that are possible to realize in the present or future.

*I wish it **would** stop raining.*

In older usage, the word **would** could be used alone to mean *I wish—**Would that I could leave this wicked world***. This form has a literary, often a poetic effect.

7.  In **if** clauses, often in the sense of *be willing to*.

*You would get over your cold if you **would** stay in bed.*

*Take these books over there for me, if you **would** be so kind.*

8.  In sentences with conditional clause equivalents.

*It **would** be foolish of (or **for**) you to do that (=**It would be foolish if you did that**)*

*I **would** (or **should**) feel too encumbered with all that equipment (=**I would feel too encumbered if I had all that equipment**)*

*I am glad he came; otherwise (=**if not**) the party **would** be very dull.*

*John **would** go to the beach every day, but his mother doesn't allow him to (=**John would go to the beach every day if his mother allowed him to.**)*

9.  With concessive clauses or their equivalents.

*Although he was hungry, he **wouldn't** eat anything.*

*Try as he **would**, he could not make the grade.*

*He was hungry, but he **wouldn't** eat anything.*

10. For a cautious or modestly expressed present.

> *It **would** seem that he never understood the instructions.*
> *I **would** suggest that you get more sleep.*

11. To mean desire, volition.

> *The one objection that I **would** (or **should**) raise is that the plan will take too long.*
> *He **would** not have anyone think badly of him.*

An older use of **would** in the sense of **want to** is exemplified in:

> *If you **would** understand a nation, you must know its language.*
> *He raised his hand as if he **would** speak.*

Volition in the negative:

> *He was embarrassed and **would not** do as he was asked.*
> *She **wouldn't** admit that she was wrong.*

12. To mean probability.

> *That's what most people **would** do.* (an *if* clause such as *if they had the chance* is understood here)

**Dare** meaning *have the courage to* and **need** meaning *have to*[5] are sometimes classified among the modal auxiliaries. They might better be called "quasi-auxiliaries," because, while they function in all respects like regular verbs, they may also form negatives and questions in the same way as auxiliaries do.

|  | *Need to* | *Dare (to)* |
|---|---|---|
| *Positive* | He **needs to go** there. | He **dares (to) go** there. |
| *Negative* | | |
| (like auxiliaries) | He **need not go** there. | He **dare not go** there. |
| or | or | or |
| (like regular verbs) | He **doesn't need to go** there. | He **doesn't dare (to) go** there. |
| *Question* | | |
| (like auxiliaries) | **Need** he **go** there? | **Dare** he **(to) go** there? |
| or | or | or |
| (like regular verbs) | **Does** he **need to go** there? | **Does** he **dare (to) go** there? |

These choices for negative and question forms are similar to the choices for the independent verb **have** in the sense of possession:

---

[5] **Dare** in the sense of *challenge*, and **need** meaning *require* are regular verbs with the usual forms for all six tenses.

> *I haven't a pencil.*     **or**     *I don't have a pencil.*
>
> *Have you a pencil?*     **or**     *Do you have a pencil?*

With all three verbs—**need, dare, have**—the American preference is for the forms with **do**.

In the past tense, only **dare** has the same kind of choices for negatives or questions.

> *He dared not go there.*     **or**     *He didn't dare (to) go there.*
>
> *Dared he go there?*     **or**     *Did he dare (to) go there?*

Past time with **need** may be expressed either by **did need** or by **need have**.

> *He **didn't need** to make such harsh remarks.*
>
> **or**
>
> *He **needn't have** made such harsh remarks.*
>
> ***Did** he **need** to make such harsh remarks?*
>
> **or**
>
> ***Need** he **have** made such harsh remarks?*

### OTHER AUXILIARIES

A few other auxiliaries that cannot be classified under the types we have given in this chapter also deserve some attention here.

#### *Used to*, **for Past Custom**

The implication of past custom is that the situation no longer exists.

---

| | |
|---|---|
| Positive | When I was young, I **used to** play tennis very often. (but now I don't) |
| Negative | I **didn't use** to get tired when I played tennis. (but I do now) |
| Question | **Did** you **use to** play tennis when you were young? |

---

**Used to** places greater emphasis on the idea of past custom than do the two other means of indicating this kind of time—**When I was young I** *would play* (or **I** *played*) **tennis very often.**

**Used to** as an auxiliary for past custom must be distinguished from **be used to;** in this phrase **used** is an adjective synonymous with **accustomed** and **to** is a preposition—**I'm now used to** (or **accustomed to**) **eating the food in this country.**

#### *Be To*

1. Meaning *be required to, be expected to*

> *You **were to** do your homework in ink.*
>
> *Everyone **is to** hand in his paper immediately.*

2. Meaning *hope to*

> *If I **am to** succeed, I must work hard.*
> *If we **are to** get there on time, we should leave now.*

3. Meaning be *destined to* (a future outcome)

> *They **were to** fail miserably in their plot against the government.*
> *She **was to** become the wife of a prominent attorney.*

4. Meaning *planned or scheduled*

> *The baseball game **was to** have been played today, but it was canceled.*
> *The judge who **was to** take the case suddenly became ill.*

## *Be Supposed To*

1. Meaning *it is believed that*

> *Milk **is supposed to** be good for our health.*

2. Meaning *be required to, be expected to*

> *You **were supposed to** do your homework in ink.*

3. Meaning *planned or scheduled*

> *The train **is supposed to** leave late tonight.*

Where there is a choice with **be to** (for a requirement, or a scheduled event), **be supposed to** expresses less definiteness.

### CONTRACTIONS WITH AUXILIARIES

A special characteristic of informal speech is the use of contractions. An auxiliary may contract with the negative **not** that follows it, or with the subject that precedes it.

#### Contractions with NOT

**Not** can form contractions with most of the auxiliaries, as well as with the independent verbs **be** and **have**. These contractions are made by joining **not** to the auxiliary, then eliminating the *o* from **not** and substituting an apostrophe. Thus **do** + **not** becomes **donø't**. Exceptions are **can't** and **won't**.

A few auxiliaries that do not contract with **not** are:

1. **Am.** An illiterate contraction for **am not** is **ain't** (which many uneducated people use for all the persons in the present tense of **be**—he **ain't, you ain't,** etc.). In informal British usage, **aren't** often replaces the contraction for **am not** in questions—**Aren't I good enough?**

2. **Shall.** In British usage the form **shan't** occurs as a contraction for **shall not.**

3. **May.** The contraction of the past form, **mightn't,** is occasionally found.

Contractions with Subjects

Tense auxiliaries form contractions not only with a following **not**, but with a subject that precedes. Such contractions with a subject are:

| Be | | Have | | Shall-Will | |
|---|---|---|---|---|---|
| am | 'm | has | 's | shall-will | 'll |
| is | 's | have | 've | should-would | 'd |
| are | 're | had | 'd | | |

Note that the contraction **'s** stands for both **is** and **has**; **'d** stands for **had, should** and **would**; **'ll** stands for **shall** and **will**.

These contractions may be made with a *pronoun* as subject (**They're here, Who'll do it, It's ready**), or with a *noun* as subject (**John'll come; The boy's arrived; Mary'd rather eat lunch now than later**). **Let us** is contracted to **let's**.

A positive auxiliary does not contract with the subject when the auxiliary is stressed, as in short answers.

*Are they planning to go ?—They* ***are.***

but with a negative answer—***They aren't*** or ***They're not.***

Contractions with a subject are made with the independent verb **be** (**He's here**) but not with the independent verb **have** (**I have the money**—but **I've got the money**).

Contractions with **it** that are found in poetic usage are **'tis** and **'twas**.

# 6

## *Adjectives*

The adjective is a modifier that has the grammatical property of comparison. It is often identified by special derivational endings or by special adverbial modifiers that precede it. Its most usual position is before the noun it modifies, but it fills other positions as well.

TYPES OF ADJECTIVES

**Determiners**

Determiners consist of a small group of structure words without characteristic form.

1. *Articles*—**the, a–an**
2. *Demonstrative adjectives*—**this**, plural **these**
   **that**, plural **those**
3. *Possessive adjectives*
   a. from pronouns—**my, your, one's,** etc.
   b. from nouns—**John's, the girl's,** etc.
4. *Numeral adjectives*
   a. cardinal—**four, twenty-five, one hundred,** etc.
   b. ordinal—**fourth, twenty-fifth, one hundredth,** etc.
5. *Adjectives of indefinite quantity*—**some, few, all, more,** etc.
6. *Relative and interrogative adjectives*—**whose, what, which**

All of these determiners except the articles and the possessive adjectives of the personal pronouns may function as pronouns when not followed by nouns. Personal pronouns have separate forms for the possessive used without a noun—**my** (adjective) **book** vs. **the book is mine** (pronoun).

### Descriptive Adjectives

Descriptive adjectives usually indicate an inherent quality (**beautiful, intelligent**), or a physical state such as age, size, color. Inflectional and derivational endings can be added only to this type of adjective.

Some descriptive adjectives take the form of:

1. *proper adjectives*— **a Catholic church, a French dish, a Shakespearian play**

2. *participial adjectives*

   a. present participle—**an interesting book, a disappointing experience, a charming view, a trifling gift**

   b. past participle—**a bored student, a worn tablecloth, a tired housewife, a spoiled child**

3. *adjective compounds*

   a. with *participles*

      (1) present participle—**a good-looking girl, a heart-breaking story, a Spanish-speaking student, a long-suffering widow**
      past participle—**a turned-up nose, a broken-down house, newborn kittens, ready-made clothes**

   b. with *-ed added to nouns* functioning as the second element of a compound. The first element is usually a short adjective—**absentminded, ill-tempered, tear-stained, far-sighted**

Such compounds are especially common with nouns that denote parts of the body—**left-handed, kind-hearted, blue-eyed, barefooted** (or **barefoot**).

These compounds are usually written with hyphens, but sometimes they are not. Reflecting the general tendency to use fewer hyphens, some dictionaries give as single words a number of the compounds we have just listed—**heartbreaking, absentminded, newborn.**

Other adjective compounds include various syntactic combinations.

1. *a prepositional phrase*—**a wall-to-wall carpet, a fly-by-night scheme, an up-to-the-minute office**

2. *an infinitive*—**a hard-to-please employer, a never-to-be-forgotten plot, a well-to-do banker**

3. *coordinate elements* (joined by **and**)—**a life-and-death struggle, a black and blue mark, a hit-and-run driver**

Some *set phrases* or specially *coined phrases* may also function as adjective compounds—**a get-rich-quick scheme, a catch-as-catch-can policy, a publicity-shy actor.**

An adjective compound may express measurement. The compound may either precede the noun it refers to (**a ten-foot-high pole, a six-year-old child**) or follow the noun (**a pole ten feet high, a child six years old**). Note that the unit of measurement is *singular* in the compound that *precedes* the noun. Note also that the compound following the noun is not hyphenated.

Noun compounds may function as adjective compounds. Such compounds usually require hyphens—**a high-school girl** (vs. **she goes to high school**), **twentieth-century literature** (vs. **literature of the twentieth century**). Compound numerals from **twenty-one** to **ninety-nine** must also be hyphenated, whether used as adjectives or as nouns.

### FUNCTION OF ADJECTIVES

The adjective modifies a noun or a pronoun.

1. Adjective modifying a *noun*

    *a. the **small** boy*         *b. The boy is **small**.*

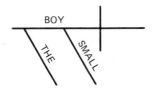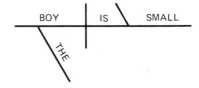

2. Adjective modifying a *pronoun*

    *a. everybody **else***         *b. He is **small**.*

A number of grammatical structures may function as adjective modifiers of nouns. Most of these *follow* the nouns they refer to.

| | |
|---|---|
| Adjective clause | the girl *who is sitting at the desk over there* |
| Participial phrase | the girl *sitting at the desk over there* |
| Prepositional phrase | the girl *at the desk over there* |
| Adverb | the girl *over there* |
| Infinitive phrase | the only girl *to finish on time* |

Sentence structures functioning as adjectives are called *adjectivals.*

Words that generally function as adjectives sometimes serve as *other parts of speech:*

1. As *nouns*

> None but the **brave** deserves the **fair.**

   a. objects of prepositions, in idioms

> by **far,** in **general,** for **long,** at **random**

2. As *adverbs.* These modify:

   a. verbs

> hold **tight,** break **loose,** make **uneasy**

   b. adverbs

> **better** off, **far** ahead, **close** by, **straight** ahead

   c. other adjectives

> **boiling** hot, **dead** drunk, **stark** naked, **dark** red

   d. prepositional phrases

> **deep** in her heart, **early** in the year, **long** before noon

## POSITION OF ADJECTIVES

Adjectives occur most frequently before the nouns they refer to or after linking verbs. However, they also appear in several other positions, not only in relation to nouns and verbs, but also in relation to pronouns. All the possible positions of adjectives will therefore be described here.

### Position of Adjectives
### in Relation to Nouns (Attributive Position)

A noun head may have adjective modifiers that appear before and after it in what is called a *noun phrase.* We have already pointed out the adjectival structures that follow a noun head. In this section we will be concerned chiefly with the position of *single-word* modifiers that precede or follow a noun head.

### Adjectives Preceding
### a Noun Head (Pre-Position)

Determiners and descriptive adjectives appear in this position before a noun. The determiners precede the descriptive adjectives.

> **The tall** man sat down quickly.

Adverbs are sometimes used in this position as adjectivals—**a *nearby* church, the *then* Miss Smith, a-*bygone* day.**

## Adjectives Following
## a Noun Head (Post-Position)

1. In set phrases coming from old French—**court-*martial*, the body *politic*, postmaster *general*.** Also in phrases possibly inflenced by such French expressions—**accounts *payable*, the best car *possible*** (or ***available***), **president-*elect*.**

2. with units of space or time—**a well fifteen feet *deep*, a ruler twelve inches *long*, two months *ago*.**

3. place or time words that usually function as adverbs—**the sky *above*, a village *nearby*, the world *hereafter*, the day *after*.**

4. Cardinal numbers used for identifying or naming—**chapter *five*, paragraph *three*, line *two*; World War *Two*.** Ordinal numbers preceding the nouns are also used in such instances—**the fifth chapter, the third paragaph, the second line, the Second World War.**

5. The adjective **enough**—**I have time *enough*. Enough** may also precede the noun head—**I have *enough* time.**

A. After the linking verbs **be, seem, appear, look** (as subjective complements in predicate position).

> *The boy is **tall**.*

Certain adjectives are used only in predicate position (**glad, content, exempt**), especially those beginning with the prefix **a-** (**alone, alike, asleep, aware**).

In the literary language, predicate adjectives may take initial position in inverted sentences. Such inversions usually occur with the linking verb **be.**

> ***Fair*** *was she as the roses in May.*
> ***Great*** *was his consternation to learn the news.*

B. After certain verbs and their objects, as objective complements.

> *The storm has made me **uneasy**.*
> *All his friends considered him **intelligent**.*

When such a construction is changed to the passive voice, the adjective remains in the position after the verb.

> *I was made **uneasy** by the storm.*
> *He was considered **intelligent** by all his friends.*

C. In the special verb-adjective combinations that express a state—**hold *tight*, stand *still*, lie *quiet*, break *loose*, open *wide*, slam *shut*.**

> *She held the child **tight**.*
> *The ship broke **loose** from its moorings.*

Position of Adjectives
in Relation to Pronouns

A. *After* the pronoun

*He is looking for something **new** and **exciting** to do.*

B. *Before* the pronoun (only with **one**)

*Did you buy the green dress or **the blue** one?*

Sequence of Adjectives
in a Noun Phrase

When more than one adjective precedes a noun in a noun phrase, the adjectives follow a set order. This order is determined by the degree of generality of each type of adjective. Adjectives that can be used with the greatest number of nouns, the determiners, always come first. Then come descriptive adjectives, those with more general application preceding those that are more specific. This sequence of adjectives is indicated on the chart on the following page.

The order of determiners that come at the beginning of a noun phrase is more or less fixed; numbers follow the other kinds of determiners, and cardinal numbers follow ordinal numbers. Also, the order of modifiers at the other end, just before the noun head, is usually fixed—the noun adjuncts come closest to the noun head, then come proper adjectives, then adjectives denoting color. The position of adjectives of general description and of physical state, however, may sometimes be reversed—**a young, beautiful girl; a new, streamlined mimeograph machine; a small, remote village.**

The order of two or more adjectives of general description may be a matter of personal preference; thus we may say **beautiful, long-lasting flowers** or **long-lasting, beautiful flowers.** Sometimes the length of the descriptive adjective determines the order; usually a shorter adjective precedes a longer one—**a quick, efficient method.**

Determiners may be preceded only by the indefinite adjectives **all, both, half,** used in a partitive sense—**all** the money, *both* my friends, *half* that amount. Such "predeterminers" may be interpreted as preceding a prepositional phrase from which **of** has been omitted—**all (of) the money, both (of) my friends, half (of) that amount.** Occasionally fractions also appear informally without the **of** in pre-determiner position—**one-third the amount.**

Adverbial "multipliers" may also appear in pre-determiner position—*twice* the amount, *ten times* the size. However, such expressions differ from the pre-determiners just mentioned in that they do not permit alternatives with **of** phrases.

The indefinite adjective **other** may follow any of the different types of determiners—*the other* men, *that other* student, *my other* suit, *several other* students. **Other** may also *precede or follow a numeral.*

SEQUENCE OF ADJECTIVES IN A NOUN PHRASE[1]

| Determiners | | Descriptive Adjectives | | | Noun Adjuncts | Nouns |
|---|---|---|---|---|---|---|
| | Numerals | General Description | Physical State | Proper Adjectives | | |
| 1. partitive **all, both, half** (pre-determiners) | 1. ordinals | (often inherent quality) | 1. size | nationality, religion, etc. | | |
| 2. articles (or) demonstratives (or) possessives | 2. cardinals | Includes most adjectives with derivational endings (**-y, -ous, -ful, -ing,** etc.) | 2. shape | | | |
| 3. indefinite adjectives | | | 3. age | Also in this position are some adjectives ending in **-ic(al), -al,** etc., that function almost like noun adjuncts | | |
| | | | 4. temperature | | | |
| | | | 5. color | | | |

**Examples**

| Determiners | Numerals | General Description | Physical State | Proper Adjectives | Noun Adjuncts | Nouns |
|---|---|---|---|---|---|---|
| both the | five | air-conditioned | white | Lincoln Continental | | cars |
| her | | gifted | young | Negro | college | students |
| a | | beautiful, exclusive | large | Chinese | cloissoné | bowls |
| those | three | self-conscious | little | residential | | district |
| Jane's | two | spacious | old | | | ladies |
| | | daringly-cut | | American colonial | | houses |
| the | | excellent | | Parisian | evening | gown |
| several | first ten | multi-purpose | | automatic | bottling | equipment |
| an | four | well-known | | commercial | jet | planes |
| that | | expensive | | | aluminum kitchen | utensils |
| every | | temperamental | brand-new | French Catholic | | priests |
| | | streamlined | | Italian | four-lane | highway |
| | | | | electric | opera | singer |
| | | | | | mimeograph | machine |

[1] For the purpose of demonstrating more clearly the sequence of adjectives before a noun, some of these examples contain more adjectives than would normally occur in pre-position.

(The numbers in each column indicate the usual sequence for the type of adjective in that column)

       *The employer wanted to interview **the other two** men.*

or  *The employer wanted to interview **the two other** men.*

The indefinite adjective **more** may follow an adjective of definite or indefinite quantity—*Several* (or *ten*) *more* **students brought their lunch. Few** usually follows the sequence adjectives **last, first, next**—He expects to call on **us in the next few days.**

Some adjectives with the derivational endings -ic(al), -(i)al, -en, -ary, often form a close relationship with the noun head, in some cases almost like a noun adjunct. Such adjectives, like noun adjuncts, are not usually separated from the noun head—**a fascinating new** *historical* **novel; the very best** *photographic* **equipment; costly and far-flung** *military* **installations.** Like the adjectives of general description, these "noun adjunct-like" adjectives may also be coordinate—**many hard-working** *political* **and** *social* **organizations.**

Gerunds used as noun adjuncts in compound nouns are inseparable from the noun heads—*looking* **glass,** *ironing* **board,** *dancing* **school.** These are to be distinguished from participles used as adjectives, which may be separated from the nouns; thus, **a dancing bear** may be changed to **a dancing, prancing bear.** Even here, however, when the participle and the noun combination is a familiar one, such a separation is not likely—**hot and cold** *running* **water.**

### Modification of Adjectives

We have seen that each succeeding type of adjective narrows down the class of the noun. For this reason we may consider that each adjective modifies everything else that follows it. Thus, in the noun phrase **the beautitul young French girl:**

    *The* modifies *beautiful young French girl;*

    *Beautiful* modifies *young French girl;*

    *Young* modifies *French girl:*

    *French* modifies *girl.*

A possessive noun may also be modified by a descriptive adjective. In **the pretty girl's mother,** *pretty* modifies **girl.** Descriptive adjectives occurring before possessive nouns sometimes cause ambiguity. In **the** *stout* **colonel's wife,** for example, **stout** may refer to the colonel or to his wife.

A modifier that precedes a compound noun may also be ambiguous. In **an old clothes dealer**, it is not clear whether the clothes dealer is old or the clothes are old. A hyphen between **old** and **clothes** makes one of the these meanings clear—**an old-clothes dealer.**

A possessive adjective may be intensified by the use of **own,** or **very own,** after it—**the boy's** (*very*) *own* **spending money; their** (*very*) *own* **beautiful summer home.**

An adverbial modifier of an adjective used in a sequence before a noun is placed directly before the adjective it modifies—**strong,** *very* **hot coffee;** *about* **fifty** *badly* **hurt soldiers.**

Numerals may be modified by adverbial expressions of indefinite quantity —**about, approximately, at least** (*about* fifty dollars, *at least* the first two years). Adjectives of general description and physical state are most often modified by adverbs of degree (*very* ambitious, *quite* diffcult, *extremely* cold). Some of these adverbs of degree have the form of *adjectives* (*bright* red, *wide* open), or of *nouns* (*stone* deaf, *jet* black). Adjectives with participial form, however, may also be modified by -ly adverbs of manner—a *stiffly* starched dress, a *beautifully* designed home. When adverbs of manner appear with the other descriptive adjectives, these adverbs often suggest degree to some extent— *easily* obtainable, *curiously* silent, *painfully* correct.

The entire noun phrase may be modified by an intensifying adverb that precedes the phrase—*even* that brave young French soldier; *only* the best students.

### Commas with Adjectives

No commas separate the different types of adjectives—determiners, descriptive adjectives, noun adjuncts—nor does any comma precede the noun itself.

Adjectives of general description may be joined coordinately by **and** (less frequently by **but**), or separated by commas. One test for a required comma is to see whether **and** can be substituted for the comma. In the phrase **many charming, intelligent French actresses,** we can replace the comma before **intelligent** with **and** but we cannot do so before **charming** or **French.** Another check for the comma is to see whether the order of the adjectives can be reversed—**many** *intelligent, charming* **French** actresses.

The comma before the word **and** in a series of three or more adjectives of general description is optional—**many charming, intelligent (,) and well-dressed French actresses.**

For other types of descriptive adjectives, no commas appear before proper adjectives (**beautiful Arabian women**) or before the adjectives functioning like noun adjuncts (**an excellent literary magazine**). However, there is some flexibility in the use of commas between adjectives of general description and those of physical state—**a large, old wooden house or a large old wooden house.** Commas are more likely to be used if a modifier precedes an adjective of physical state (**a large,** *very* **old wooden house**), or an adjective functioning like a noun adjunct (**expensive,** *fully* **automatic equipment**).

### FORM OF ADJECTIVES

### Inflectional Form

Determiners do not change their form except for the possessive of nouns and pronouns used adjectivally ('s for the singular and ' for the plural are added) and the demonstratives, which have separate forms for the plural (**these, those**). Descriptive adjectives have special forms only for *comparison*. These forms are given below.

| | | | | | | | |
|---|---|---|---|---|---|---|---|
| *Positive degree*<br>*Two units* are<br>    compared to an<br>    *equal* degree | **as**<br>**as** | tall<br>beautiful | **as**<br>**as** | **not so** (or **as**)<br>**not so** (or **as**) | tall<br>beautiful | **as** | |
| *Comparative degree*<br>*Two units* are<br>    compared to an<br>    *unequal* degree | **more** | taller<br>beautiful | **than**<br>**than** | **less**<br>**less** | tall<br>beautiful | **than**<br>**than** | |
| *Superlative degree*<br>*Three or more*<br>    *units* are compared<br>    to an *unequal*<br>    degree | **the**<br>**the most** | tallest<br>beautiful | | **the least**<br>**the least** | tall<br>beautiful | | |

**Less, least** are more likely to be found with longer adjectives, usually those that are compared with **more, most**.

The rules for constructing the comparative and superlative degree of adjectives are:

| | *Comparative Degree* | *Superlative Degree* |
|---|---|---|
| Adjectives of<br>*one syllable* | Add **-er** to the adjective<br>Add **than** after the adjective<br>    (tall)**-er    than** | Add **-est** to the adjective<br>Add **the** before the adjective<br>        **the**    (tall)**-est** |
| Adjectives of<br>*three or more*<br>*syllables* | Add **more** before the adjective<br>Add **than** after the adjective<br>    **more**    (beautiful) **than** | Add **the most** before the adjective<br>        **the most**    (beautiful) |

The rules for adjectives of *two syllables* are more complicated. Some adjectives form the comparative and superlative with **-er, -est**, some with **more, most**, others in either of these ways.

| *Two-Syllable Adjectives*<br>*with* **-er, -est** | *Two-Syllable Adjectives*<br>*with* **more, most** | *Two-Syllable Adjectives*<br>*with* **-er, -est** *or* **more,**<br>**most** (*The* **-er, -est** *Forms*<br>*Are Less Formal*) |
|---|---|---|
| 1.  adjectives ending in<br>    **-y** preceded by a<br>    consonant<br><br>    prettier<br>    dirtier | 1.  most adjectives ending<br>    in derivational<br>    suffixes: **-ous, -ish,**<br>    **-ful, -ing, -ed,** etc.<br><br>    more famous | 1.  adjectives ending in:<br><br>    **-er**    cleverer<br>            tenderer<br>            bitterer |

| Two-Syllable Adjectives with -er, -est | Two-Syllable Adjectives with more, most | Two-Syllable Adjectives with -er, -est or more, most (The -er, -est Forms Are Less Formal) |
|---|---|---|
| noisier<br>happier (also unhappier) | more useful<br>more childish<br>more interesting<br>more tired | **-ow** narrower<br>shallower<br>mellower |
| 2.  adjectives ending in -ple, -ble, occasionally -tle, -dle | 2.  many adjectives ending in -ct, -nt, -st | **-some** handsomer<br>wholesomer<br>lonesomer |
| simpler<br>nobler<br>humbler<br>subtler<br>idler | more exact<br>more recent<br>more honest<br>more urgent | 2.  others<br><br>stressed on first syllable:<br>  pleasanter, crueler, quieter, stupider, commoner<br>stressed on second syllable:<br>  politer, profounder, remoter, obscurer, sincerer, severer, securer |

With the exception of the adjectives ending in a consonant plus **-y** or **-le**, grammarians are not in complete agreement about which two-syllable adjectives will accept **-er, -est** endings for comparison. A good rule to keep in mind, however, is that **more, most** may actually be used with all two-syllable adjectives except the **-y** or **-le** adjectives just mentioned. In fact, when emphasis on the idea of comparison is desired, the **more, most** forms are used for any adjective, even monosyllables—**The *more* rich we are, the more *wise* we seem.** However, it is important to remember that the two forms of comparison never occur together; thus a form like *****more happier** would be ungrammatical.

In adding **-er** or **-est** for comparison, a writer must keep in mind that:

1.  final *y* preceded by a consonant is changed to *i*—**livelier, tastier, luckier.**

2.  a final single consonant preceded by a single vowel is doubled in one-syllable adjectives—**bigger, thinner, hottest.**

3.  final *e* is dropped—**simpler, largest, wider.**

Some adjectives do not logically lend themselves to comparison—**dead, left, open, perfect, round, unique, wrong,** and the adjectives used only in the predicate (**alive, asleep, alone**). However, in special circumstances, especially in figurative language, even these words may be compared—*deader* **than a doornail,** *more dead* **than alive, you could not be** *more wrong*, **the** *rounder* **the better.**

A few adjectives are compared irregularly.

| Positive Degree | Comparative Degree | Superlative Degree |
|---|---|---|
| good | better | best |
| bad | worse | worst |
| far | farther | farthest |
|  | further | furthest |
| little | less | least |
| much ⎫ much | | |
| many ⎭ | more | most |
| old | older | oldest |
|  | elder | eldest |

Conservative handbooks insist that when distance is referred to, only **farther** and **farthest** are "correct." Actually, however, except for the most formal situations, educated speakers use **further, furthest** for distance (**the** *furthest* **corners of the earth**) as well as for addition (**further details**).

**Elder, eldest** occur today mainly in the restricted sense of family relationships of children to parents—**She is the eldest of the three children; He is the elder of my two sons.**

In comparison, prepositions following adjectives in the superlative degree can cause some difficulty. A general tendency seems to be the use of **of** with members of the group being compared (**the tallest** *of* **all the students**) and the use of **in** for the place involved in the comparison (*in* **the class**).

**More, most** may occur with coordinate adjectives regardless of the number of syllables each of the adjectives has.

> He was **more** vain, **more** self-centered, and **more** hatefully rude than I had remembered him.

More often a single **more** or **most** serves for all such parallel adjectives.

> She was the **most** innocent, gentle, and delightful person I had ever known.

**Very** or **too** serving as an intensifier of a comparative or superlative adjective must be followed by **much.**

> Before he was very (or **too**) much older, he learned the folly of his ways.

Comparative and superlative adjectives may function as nouns before **of** phrases.

> She is **the taller** of the two.

> He is **the most intelligent** of all the foreign students.

In informal usage, the requirement that the comparative form be used for two units is often ignored—**She is the tallest of the two.**

**Inner, outer, upper, lower, the former, the latter** represent comparative forms that have no corresponding superlative forms. **Inner, outer, upper** may be strengthened by **-most**—**innermost, outermost, uppermost.**

Derivational Form of Adjectives

Most adjective derivational suffixes have little semantic content; they merely serve as part-of-speech indicators. Adjective suffixes are usually added to nouns or verbs.

1. Suffixes changing *nouns* to adjectives: **-(i)al, -ar, -ary** or **-ery, -ed, -en, -esque, -ful, -ic(al), -ish, -istic, -less, -like, -ly, -ous, -ward, -wide, -y.**

> *monumental, familiar, elementary, talented, picturesque, hopeful, historic(al), stylish, characteristic, useless, lifelike, friendly, famous, backward, world-wide, windy*

2. Suffixes changing *verbs* to adjectives: **-able** or **-ible, -ent** or **-ant, -ed, -ile, -ing, -ive, -(at)ory.**

> *sensible, dependent, frustrated, hostile, boring, attractive, congratulatory*

In many words of Latin origin, the first part of the adjective merely represents a Latin root rather than a complete word in English. Examples of such words are **generous, native, peculiar, annual.**

We have already seen that adjectives may have the same form as verbs—**average, complete, empty, equal, faint, open, welcome.**

A number of adjectives end in either **-ic** or **-ical**—**geographic(al), philosophic(al), alphabetic(al).** It is sometimes claimed that the **-ic** ending is preferred for scientific matters, the **-ical** ending for practical matters. However, American dictionaries do not make this distinction; they merely indicate which form is more common by recording the definition under this form (without necessarily agreeing with each other).

The adjective suffix **-en** is usually added to nouns denoting materials—**a woolen suit, wooden shutters, an earthen bowl.** Other **-en** adjectives are found in literary usage (**a golden chain, silken hair**) or in older usage (**the old oaken bucket, a waxen image**).

The choice between the adjective suffixes **-ible** and **-able** may cause difficulty. A general rule is to add **-able** to an already existing word (**enjoyable, drinkable, comfortable**) and to add **-ible** to an incomplete word (**edible, incredible, possible**).[2] Most of the words ending in **-ible** are actually derivatives from Latin past participles.

Whether used as a participial or a derivational ending, the **-ing** form often represents the original *subject* of a simple sentence; the **-ed** form, the original *object*.

Sentence—**The game excited the audience.**

---

[2] A good mnemonic device for remembering this rule is the advertising slogan (for a margarine)—It's so **spreadable**, it's **incredible.**

Participle used with:

---

| the subject **game** | The *exciting* game (=**the game was exciting**) |
| the object **audience** | The *excited* audience (=**the audience was excited**) |

---

The spelling rules that apply in adding adjective suffixes have already been given under noun derivational suffixes.

    1.   Double the final consonant before a vowel (or *y*)—**regrettable, rotten, foggy**

    2.   Change *y* to *i*:
        a.  before a consonant—**beautiful, pitiless, daily**
        b.  before a vowel—**envious, industrial, victorious**

    3.   Final silent *e*:
        a.  Drop silent *e* before a vowel—**nervous, observant, valuable**;
          but **noticeable, courageous** (*e* retained to prevent a change in pronunciation)
        b.  Keep silent *e* before a consonant—**careful, lonely, tasteless**

## MARKERS OF ADJECTIVES

Adjectives are signaled by adverbs of degree like **very, quite, rather, extremely** (*very* **quiet**, *rather* **useless**, *quite* **pretty**). These adverbs also mark other adverbs.

Adverbs of degree are used with **-ing** adjectives but not with participles or with gerunds. Since these two verbal forms occur in the same position as participial adjectives, the adverbs of degree help to distinguish the participial adjectives from these other forms.

---

| Adjective | a very charming girl |
| Participle | *a very burning house (**very** is ungrammatical here) |
| Gerund | *a very dancing school (**very** is ungrammatical here) |

---

## SPECIAL USAGES OF ADJECTIVES

### *Some-Any*

**Some** is used in positive statements, **any** in negative statements.

    *I have **some** money.*
    *I don't have **any** money.*

In such sentences, **some** and **any** fill a grammatical position that can be left empty (but usually is not). **Some** indicates the *presence* of a small quantity,

**any** the complete *absence* of a quantity. Such absence may actually be reinforced by the phrase **at all** after the noun—**I don't have *any* money *at all*.** In questions **any** or **some** may be used.

> *Do you have **any** money?*
>
> *Do you have **some** money?*

Here **some** refers to the *presence* of a small quantity, **any** has little meaning beyond serving structurally to fill a grammatical slot.

**Any** may be used in a positive statement. Here it means *it doesn't matter which,* or *any at all.*

> *Take **any** book you like.*
>
> ***Any** seat will be satisfactory.*
>
> ***Any** student caught cheating will fail the course.*

## Much-Many, Little-Few, Less-Fewer

The use of these adjectives of indefinite quantity is determined by whether they appear with noncountable nouns or with plural countable nouns.

| | Noncountable Nouns (singular form, no s ending) | | Plural Countable Nouns (plural s ending) |
|---|---|---|---|
| *Much* | furniture is needed. | *Many* | chairs are needed. |
| *(A) little* | furniture is needed. | *(A) few* | chairs are needed. |
| *Less* | furniture is needed. | *Fewer*[3] | chairs are needed. |

It is helpful to associate **many, few, fewer** with the *s* ending of a plural noun, only keeping in mind that some irregular plural nouns do not end in *s* (**many people, few children, many deer**), and a few singular nouns do end in *s* (**much news, too much politics**).

There is a difference in emphasis between **little** and **a little, few** and **a few**. **A little, a few** have positive force—they stress the *presence* of something, although in a small quantity (**I have *a little* money; I have *a few* friends**). **Little** and **few**, on the other hand, have negative force—they stress the *absence* of almost all quantity (**I have *little* money; I have *few* friends**).

Like descriptive adjectives, these words of indefinite quantity may be modified by adverbs of degree.

| too very | much | furniture |
|---|---|---|
| so not | many | chairs |

---

[3] In informal speech **less** is also used with plural nouns—**less chairs.**

**Much** and **many** may also modify the adjective **more**:

| | | |
|------|------|-----------|
| much | more | furniture |
| many | more | chairs |

Informal substitutes for **much—many** are **lots of, a lot of, plenty of**. These expressions are used with countable or noncountable nouns.

> *Please buy lots of* (or *a lot of, plenty of*) *soap.*
>
> *Please buy lots of* (or *a lot of, plenty of*) *towels.*

A more formal substitute for **much** is **a great** (or **good**) **deal of**—a great deal of money, a good deal of trouble. **Many** may be intensified by **a great** or a **good—a great** (or **a good**) **many books were lost.**

**Quite a few** is another equivalent of **many—Quite a few people came to hear his lecture.** In literary English, **many a,** while plural in meaning, requires a singular verb—**Many a man has tried and failed.**

## *No* Used as an Adjective

A sentence may be made negative not only by using **not** with a verb but by using **no** with a noun.

> *I have no money.*
>
> *No news is good news.*

**No** places more emphasis on the idea of negation than does **not**.

## Adjectives Used in the Comparison of Nouns— *Like, Simillar, Same*

| | | | |
|------------|----|-------------|--------------|
| | | like | |
| Mary's hat | is | similar to | Jane's (hat). |
| | | the same as | |

**or**

| | | | | |
|------------|-----|-------------|-----|----------|
| | | | | alike. |
| Mary's hat | and | Jane's (hat) | are | similar. |
| | | | | the same. |

**The same** may also immediately precede the noun—**Mary is wearing** *the same* **hat as Jane** (is).

# 7

## *Articles*

The two articles are **the** and **a**. **The** may be used with a singular or a plural noun; **a** is generally used with a singular countable noun. Each of the articles undergoes a change before a word beginning with a vowel sound—**the** changes in pronunciation, **a** changes in both pronunciation and spelling.

The chief structural function of articles is as determiners that precede nouns. However, they differ from other determiners in one important respect —they do not have the additional power of serving alone as pronouns.

The chief semantic function of articles is to mark nouns as *definite* or *indefinite*. **The** signals a *particular* person or thing that has been singled out from others—*the* **student sitting next to you**. **A** signals an *unspecified one* of others—**a student sitting in the front row**.

Actually a number of factors, both semantic and structural, determine the use or non-use of articles. These factors are related to: (1) whether the noun head is singular, plural or countable; (2) whether the referent[1] is familiar or unfamiliar to the speaker; (3) whether the statement which contains the noun head has general or specific application; (4) whether or not the noun head has a classifying function; (5) whether or not the noun head has a post-modifier.

The choices involved in the use of articles will be presented here under four headings: (1) **a** vs. **the** vs. no article; (2) uses of **the**; (3) uses of **a**; (4) no article.

### A vs. THE vs. NO ARTICLE

The choices that will be examined in this section represent some of the most basic uses of the article.

---

[1] The person or thing in the outside world that the noun head refers to.

Articles with Singular Countable Nouns

If we compare the sentences

I need _____ **furniture.**
I need _____ **chairs.**
I need _____ **chair.**

we see that only the singular countable noun **chair** in the third sentence requires an article, either **a** or **the** depending on the meaning intended. Although no article is necessary with the noncountable **furniture** or with the plural **chairs** in the other two sentences, it is possible to use **the** to particularize the nouns, or **some** to quantify the nouns in these sentences.

The article is required with a singular countable noun even when a descriptive adjective accompanies the noun—**I need a** *new* **chair.** The only time the article is not obligatory is when another determiner is used:

I need that ⎫
        my ⎬ chair.
       one ⎭

No Article
with Noncountable Nouns

Because of its meaning of singularity, **a** does not generally accompany nouns used in a noncountable sense.

Noncountable nouns that are *unrestricted by following modifiers* frequently also occur without **the.**

1. *Noncountable concrete nouns*—**Babies need to drink** *milk*. **The** is omitted especially in general statements. (But in statements about known objects in an actual situation, **the** is often used with such noncountable nouns—**Please put** *the* **milk** [or *the* **butter,** *the* **bread**] **in the refrigerator.**)

2. *Noncountable abstract nouns:*

| | |
|---|---|
| Concepts | The French Revolution was fought for *liberty*, *equality* and *fraternity*. |
| Areas of Study | She's studying *history* this year. |
| Recreational Activities | *Baseball* is my favorite sport. |

**The** is omitted even if these noncountable nouns are preceded by descriptive adjectives.

I like to drink **fresh milk.**

She's studying **American history** this year.

(The use of **a** or **the** with noncountable nouns that have post-modifiers, or the use of **the** with noncountable nouns that represent known objects will be taken up later in the individual sections on **a** and on **the.**)

Generic Use of Articles

In a general statement, it is possible to use **the, a,** or no article with a concrete countable noun that represents a class.

| | | |
|---|---|---|
| **the** | *The* lion is a wild animal. | The emphasizes the *class itself*, without regard for concrete representatives of the class. |
| a | *A* lion is a wild animal. | A emphasizes an individual representative of a class. It has the sense of *any*. |
| no article | *Lions* are wild animals. | The plural form without an article emphasizes *all* the representatives of this species. |

Strictly speaking, only *the* **lion** is generic. **The** represents the *concept* of class and is not used with the plural. The article-less plural **lions** is the plural of **a lion** only.

All three of the choices just given are common with nouns that represent names of actual species, especially names of plants and animals.

> *The rose smells sweet.*
> *A rose smells sweet.*
> *Roses smell sweet.*
> *The dog is man's[2] best friend.*
> *A dog is man's best friend.*
> *Dogs are man's best friends.*

With other types of concrete countable nouns, these three choices may not all be possible. For example, an article cannot be used generically if it may be interpreted in its usual sense of marking a particular or an unspecified member of a class. The following examples of articles in general statements will illustrate this point.

1. *The automobile has changed our way of life.* (*The* is used for the class itself)

   *Automobiles have changed our way of life.* (*Automobiles* includes all representatives in the class)

   but not *\*An automobile has changed our way of life.* (*An* is interpreted here as indefinite *a*)

   but *An automobile is a necessity today.* (*An automobile* is used for *any one* representative of the class)

2. *A student should work hard.* (*A student* is used for *any one* representative of the class)

[2] **Man** here has the sense of the noncountable **mankind** and therefore does not require an article.

    *Students should work hard.* (*Students* includes all representatives of the class)

    but not *\*The student should work hard.* (*The* is no longer interpreted as generic here, but as particularizing)

USES OF THE

    **The** is traditionally called the *definite* article. It is pronounced [ði] before words that begin with vowel sounds. **The** developed historically from a word meaning **this** and still retains some of the basic meanings of the pointing demonstrative. **Ye** is an archaic form of **the**.

    **The** serves to *particularize* a noun. It helps to distinguish the known from the unknown. It may narrow down a class, or it may even limit the class to *one:*

    *This is **the** way to do it.* (this is the *only* way)

    vs. *This is **a** good way to do it.* (this is one of several ways)

    The particularization in which **the** operates is often established by a special context. This context may be provided from outside the language or from inside the language. The context outside the language is the *actual physical environment*; the context inside the language is the *verbal discourse that surrounds the noun head.*

Particularization from the
External Physical Environment

    **The** occurs with names for familiar objects in the manmade environment of the home and the community, and in the natural environment of the geographic terrain and the universe. In this use, **the** limits a noun to the one specimen *we are familiar with or that we have in mind*, although other specimens in the class may exist.[3]

    *He walked into **the** house and hung his coat in **the** closet.*

    *As she was strolling along **the** street she looked at **the** clothes in **the** store windows.*

    *They were sailing along **the** river watching **the** clouds in **the** sky.*

    The familiar environment includes people in certain occupations, as well as their places of business. The names for these people and places of business also require **the**.

    *The doctor, the plumber, the president*

    *The doctor's, the hairdresser's, the barber's*

---

[3] Actually, with names for objects in the broader environment, **the** has very little semantic content, but serves rather as a structural "filler" in a position that seems to require a determiner.

Particularization
from the Verbal Context

The particularization is established by what precedes or follows the noun head.

A. Particularization occurs in the *preceding discourse* (anaphoric **the**). Anaphoric **the** refers back to a person or thing introduced previously as an unknown entity, often with the article **a**. At the second mention, the referent is considered as known, even if only on a verbal level.

> *A strange dog came on the porch.* **The** *dog seemed very friendly.*

B. Particularization occurs *within a noun phrase.*
(1) A restrictive modifier *follows the noun head*

| The man | who is standing near the window<br>standing near the window<br>near the window<br>over there | will be our guest speaker<br>tonight. |

**The** anticipates the post-modifier and works together with it to limit the reference of the noun head.

With certain post-modifiers, **the** may be omitted, or **a** may also be used. The following chart is intended to make clear the linguistic features that determine these choices with **the**, **a**, or no article.

*Post-Modifier*
*Limits Noun to:*

**Singular Countable Noun**

| one unit of a class | **The** chair *over there* | has just arrived. | (one event) |
| | **The** chair *over there* | is very attractive. | (generalization) |
| smaller class | **The** (or **A**) chair *from Denmark* | has just arrived. | (one event) |
| | **A** chair *from Denmark* | is very attractive. | (generalization) |

**Plural Countable Noun**

| one unit of a class | **The** chairs *over there* | have just arrived. | (one event) |
| | **The** chairs *over there* | are very attractive. | (generalization) |
| smaller class | **The** chairs *from Denmark* | have just arrived. | (one event) |
| | (**The**) chairs *from Denmark* | are very attractive. | (generalization) |

**Noncountable Noun**

| one unit of a class | **The** furniture *over there* | has just arrived. | (one event) |
| | **The** furniture *over there* | is very attractive. | (generalization) |
| smaller class | **The** furniture *from Denmark* | has just arrived. | (one event) |
| | (**The**) furniture *from Denmark* | is very attractive. | (generalization) |

Note that **the** must be retained if the post-modifier is in a generalization that refers to only *one unit of a class* (**The furniture** *over there* **is very attractive**);

or if the post-modifier of a plural or noncountable noun is in a statement about *one event* (**The furniture over there *has just arrived***).

Note also that **the** may be omitted in a generalization in which the post-modifier of a plural or noncountable noun merely *narrows down the class* rather than limits it to one unit of a class—(**The**) **furniture** *from Denmark* **is very attractive.** Indeed, in some such generalizations, **the** is not used at all.

> *Eggs* which are carefully packed will not break.
>
> *Milk* which is pasteurized is safe to drink.
>
> He is a manufacturer of *parts* used in the automobile industry.

This omission of **the** seems to be determined by (1) the degree of generality of the modifier and/or the degree of generality of the rest of the sentence; (2) the extent to which the post-modifier is felt as similar to a pre-modifier (**carefully packed eggs, pasteurized milk, automotive parts**).

(2) A restrictive adjective modifier *precedes the noun.* **The** works together with a "ranking" adjective to narrow down the reference of the noun, often to *only one* person or thing.

a. **The** plus the superlatives of adjectives—**She is *the best* cook I know; They bought *the most expensive* furniture in the store. *The richest* are not always *the happiest*.** (superlatives of adjectives used as nouns) (**The** with the superlative of adverbs [**He works *the hardest*; Mary dances *the most* gracefully of all the girls**] is actually functioning as an adverb rather than as a determiner.)

b. **The** plus ordinals—**the fifth row; the ninth day**

The ordinals may be used alone without the nouns—**Which one do you want? The eighth?**

For chapters of books, it is possible to use the form with **the** (**the second chapter**) or without **the** (**chapter two**).

Ordinals in dates are spoken with **the**; thus the written form **July 4** is spoken as **July the fourth**, or **the fourth of July**. Ordinals used after names are also spoken with **the**; thus the written form **Henry VIII** is spoken as **Henry the Eighth**.

c. **The** plus adjectives in a time or space sequence—**the next, the following, the last.**

> A student in *the last* row was asleep.
>
> He arrived in town on Wednesday. On *the next* (or *the following*) day he gave his lecture.

**Next, last** are not used with **the** when they refer to a *point* in time rather than to a *sequence* in time.

> He will give his lecture *next* week.
>
> He gave his lecture *last* week.

d. **The** plus other adjectives that rank nouns—**chief, principal, main, only.**

> *The chief reason for his resignation was bad health.*
> *He is the only person who can do this job.* but *He is an only child.*

THE in Special
Grammatical Constructions

Certain grammatical constructions require the use of **the.**

1. **The** with adjectives used as nouns

> *The British fought the French in the French and Indian War.*
> *A philanthropist tries to help the poor and the unfortunate.*

**The** also occurs with a few indefinite pronouns.

> *I want to try on a hat like the one in the window. The others don't appeal to me.*
> *The greedy few often exploit the helpless many.*

2. **The** with gerunds or abstract nouns followed by **of** phrases

---

| | |
|---|---|
| *gerund* | *The* instructing *of young children* is difficult. *but* Instructing young children is difficult. |
| *abstract noun* | *The* instruction *of young children* is difficult. |

---

3. **The** in **of** phrases after words expressing quantity

*Most*
*All*
*Many*
*One-third* } *of the students (in this class) passed the examination.*
*Five*
*The majority*

4. **The** used adverbially in older aphoristic constructions—**the more, the merrier.** This older type of construction is still in common use today. **The** may appear adverbially with single words (adverbs, adjectives or nouns), or with whole clauses.

> *The sooner, the better.*
> *The harder he works, the less he succeeds.*
> *The prettier the girl (is), the more foolishly he behaves.*

THE with Place Names

Some place names occur with **the** and some do not. For purposes of comparison, this section on place names with **the** also includes references to place names that do not take **the.**

*Geographic names.*

a. names composed entirely or partially of common nouns (the last noun usually refers to a political union or association):

> *the Soviet Union, the United Kingdom, the United Arab Republic, the British Commonwealth*

b. names composed of common nouns plus proper names contained within **of** phrases:

> *the Dominion of Canada, the City of New York, the Province of Quebec, the Republic of Venezuela, the Union of Soviet Socialist Republics (the USSR), the Isthmus of Panama, the Kingdom of Thailand*

This rule actually applies not only to geographic names but to all place names that take the form of a common noun plus a proper noun within an **of** phrase.

c. plural names

(1) *Continents* (and other geographic groups of nations)—**the Americas, the Balkans**

(2) *Countries*—**the Netherlands (Holland), the United States**

(3) *Mountain ranges*—**the Rocky Mountains, the Himalaya Mountains** The word **mountains** may be omitted and **the** used alone with the pluralized proper noun—**the Rockies, the Alps. The** is not used with a single mountain —**Mount Everest, Mount Blanc, Bear Mountain.**

(4) *Groups of islands*—**the Philippines** (for **the Philippine Islands**), **the West Indies, the Hawaiian Islands. The** is not used for one island—**Coney Island, Long Island, Wake Island.**

(5) *Groups of lakes*—**the Great Lakes, the Finger Lakes. The** is not used for one lake—**Lake Geneva, Lake Erie, Salt Lake** (but **the Lake of Lucerne, the Lake of Constance**).

d. all bodies of water except lakes and bays

> *the Mississippi River, the Pacific Ocean, the Mediterranean Sea, the English Channel, the Panama Canal (but the Sea of Japan, the Sea of Marmora).*

The names of most bays, gulfs and straits are given in **of** phrases—**the Gulf of Mexico, the Gulf of Bengal, the Gulf of Finland** (but **the Persian Gulf**). The word **ocean, sea** or **river** may be omitted from the name—**the Atlantic, the Mediterranean, the Mississippi.**

e. deserts, forests, peninsulas, and archipelagos—**the Sahara Desert** (also **the Sahara**), **the Black Forest, the Iberian Peninsula, the Malay Archipelago.**

f. points of the compass used as names for geographic areas—**the South, the Middle West, the Near East, the Orient.**

g. points on the globe—**the North Pole, the South Pole, the Equator, the 42nd Parallel.**

*The is not used with* continents, countries, and cities:

(1) *Continents*—**Europe, Africa, Asia.** The use of a modifier like **north** or **southern** does not affect this usage—**South America, Eastern Europe, West Africa.**

(2) *Countries*—**France, Peru, Algeria.** Exceptions requiring **the** have already been mentioned (names composed of common nouns, plural nouns). Other exceptions are **the Congo, the Sudan.**

(3) *Cities*—**Boston, London, Rio de Janeiro.** An exception is **the Hague,** which retains the article used in the Dutch language. For some cities, the foreign article has become part of the name—**Le Havre, El Paso, Las Vegas, La Plata.**

2. *Other names.*

a. Universities, and colleges.

**The** is used with **university** or **college** when the proper noun follows in an **of** phrase—**the University of Notre Dame.** Most of the state universities in the United States take this form—**the University of Michigan, the University of Hawaii.** Other names of universities or colleges are not used with **the**—**Columbia University, Oxford University, Harvard University, Boston College.**

b. Buildings—**the Empire State Building, the Woolworth Building, the Civic Auditorium, the Coliseum** (but **Carnegie Hall, Jefferson Hall**).

c. Hotels—**the Statler Hotel, the Carlyle Hotel** (but **Hotel Ambassador**). Sometimes the forms with or without **the** are interchangeable—**Hotel Ambassador** or **the Ambassador Hotel.**

The word **hotel** is often omitted—**the Statler, the Commodore.**

d. Libraries, museums—**the Forty-second Street Library, the Louvre, the Metropolitan Museum, the London Museum, the Library of Congress.**

e. Bridges, tunnels, towers—**the Brooklyn Bridge, the Golden Gate Bridge, the Hudson Tunnel, the Eifel Tower.**

f. No **the** with names of streets, parks, boulevards—**Fifth Avenue, Downing Street, Central Park, Hyde Park.**

Other Uses of THE

In addition to the general uses of **the** for particularization and the more special use of **the** with place names, there are a number of other limited uses of **the** that need to be mentioned.

1. **The** with points of time:
   a. points in a progression—**the beginning, the middle, the end**
   b. points in a time continuum—**the past, the present, the future**
   c. parts of the day—**in the morning, in the afternoon, in the evening** (but **at noon, at midnight**)
   d. seasons—**in the winter** (or **summer, autumn, spring**). **The** is sometimes omitted here, especially in a general statement—**In (the) winter we go skiing in the Alps.**
   e. Time expressions meaning **this**—**at the** (=**this**) **moment, for the time being, during the year, all the while.**

2. **The** with physical positions—**the top, the bottom, the middle; the back, the front, the side; the center, the inside** (or **interior**), **the outside** (or **exterior**)

3.   **The** with names of historical periods or events—**The Ming Dynasty, The Middle Ages, The Renaissance, The French Revolution, The Civil War, The First World War** (but **World War II**)

4.   **The** with names of bills, acts, and other legislative deliberations—**the Magna Carta, the Taft-Hartley Bill, the Missouri Compromise**

5.   **The** with official titles—**the Secretary of State, the Foreign** (or **Prime**) **Minister, the King, the Premier, the Mayor**

6.   **The** with names of law enforcement bodies, civil and military—**the Army, the Navy, the Air Corps, the State Militia, the police, the highway patrol**

7.   **The** with names of branches of the government—**the executive** (or **the legislative, the judicial**) **branch**

8.   **The** with names of institutions, foundations, organizations—**the United Nations, the Ford Foundation, the Girl Scouts**

9.   **The** with names of political parties—**the Labor party, the Conservative party, the Democratic party, the Communist party**
The name of the party is often used in the plural without the word **party**—**the Democrats, the Republicans, the Conservatives.**

10.   **The** with names of parts of the body

*A cape is worn over the shoulders.*

*He was wounded in the leg.*

But *I have a pain in my shoulders* (or *in my leg*).

11.   **The** with names of musical instruments, especially after **play**—**play the piano** (or **the violin, the flute, the saxophone**)

12.   **The** with names of planets—**the planet Mercury, the planet Venus** but **Mercury, Venus** when used without the word **planet**

13.   **The** with the plural of family names to refer to two or more members of a family—**the Johnsons, the Smiths, the Jones(es)**

14.   **The** with names of newspapers—**the New York Times, the Manchester Guardian, the Christian Science Monitor, the Washington Post**

15.   Stressed **the** to indicate uniqueness

*He is **thé** pianist of the day.*

*He is **thé** Shakespeare of our times.*

*He is **thé** specialist* (or ***lawyer, accountant***) *to see.*

USES OF *A*

**A** is traditionally called the *indefinite* article. Its alternate form **an** is used before words beginning with vowel *sounds*—**An apple, an obstruction, an ink bottle; an hour, an honor, an heir, an honest man** (words beginning with silent *h*)[4]

---

[4] Some words spelled with initial *h* may be pronounced with or without the *h*; we may therefore hear **a historical novel** or **an historical novel, a hotel** or **an hotel, a herb** or **an herb.** (The pronunciation with initial *h* is probably more common in the United States.)

A occurs before words beginning with *u* pronounced as [ju]—**a union, a united front, a usual occurrence** but **an unusual man, an utter fool, an ugly man, an undercurrent.**

A developed historically from a word meaning the number **one.** This basic meaning of singularity today manifests itself in three distinct senses of **a**: (1) the actual numeral **one**; (2) *one* undifferentiated specimen in a class (**We saw** *a* **lion at the zoo**); (3) *one* specimen representing a class (**That animal is** *a* **lion**). These three uses require further explanation.

### *A* Meaning the Numeral *One*

> *I waited **an** hour.*
>
> *He paid **a** hundred dollars for his suit.*

Closely related to the numerical use of **a** is the distributive use of **a** in the sense of *each*—**His rent is $200** *a* **month; these apples cost $.25** *a* **pound.**[5]

### *A* Signaling
### One Undifferentiated Specimen
### in a Class

In this use, no attempt is made to distinguish one individual member of a class from any other specimen in the same class. **A** occurs most often in a statement about one event.

> *He ate **an** apple.*
>
> ***A** prize will be given to the best student.*
>
> ***A** man is here to see you.*

This is the *true indefinite use* of **a.** Such indefinite use is far more common than any other use of **a.**

### *A* Signaling One Specimen
### that Represents a Class

A is used in a general statement to *classify* a noun. In this use, **a** points to *any* representative of a class—**a lion (=***any* **lion) is very strong.** This is the generic **a** that we have already looked at.

A often appears with a class word in the predicate after a form of the verb **be.** The class word after this verb may serve to:

1. *identify an individual*

> *John is **a** student.*
>
> *John is **a** good student who is not discouraged by failures.* (class word with modifiers)

2. *define a smaller class*

> *The lion is **an** animal.*
>
> *The lion is **a** large, powerful mammal of the cat family, found in Africa and*

---

[5] **The** sometimes replaces distributive **a**—**These apples cost $.25 the pound.** In commercial language, **per** may also be employed in the sense of *each*.

> *Southwest Asia, with a tawny coat, a tufted tail, and, in the adult male, a shaggy mane.*[6] (class word with modifiers)

With these class words after a form of **be, any** cannot substitute for **a**.

Classifying **a** may also introduce an appositive.

> *John, a student at our university, will compete in the Olympic Games.*

**A student at our university** may be considered as a derivation from the sentence **John is a student at our university.** This use of **a** is therefore related to its use for identifying an individual.

Under the classifying use of **a** we might also put the use of **a** in figures of speech.

| | |
|---|---|
| In a simile | He is as brave as *a* lion. |
| | He carries himself like *a* king. |
| In a metaphor | Hawaii is *a* paradise for bird lovers. |

Indefinite **a** and classifying **a** display some differences in forming their plurals.

| *Singular* | *Plural* |
|---|---|
| *Indefinite A*—The plural is **some** or no article | |
| He ate *an* apple. | He ate *some* apples. |
| *A* prize will be given to the best student. | (*Some*) prizes will be given to the best students. |
| *A* man is here to see you. | *Some* men are here to see you. |
| *Classifying A*—The plural is used without any determiner | |
| *A* lion is very strong. | Lions are very strong. |
| He is *a* good student. | They are good students. |

### A with Nouns
### Usually Considered Noncountable

Many nouns, more than are generally realized, have a countable as well as a noncountable sense. **A** may be used with the singular countable form.

| *Noncountable Sense* | *Countable Sense* |
|---|---|
| Life is hard in many countries. | Money can buy *a* life of ease. (singular) |
| | Many lives were lost in World War Two. (plural) |
| Everyone should eat fruit. | An apple is *a* fruit. (singular) |
| | Fruits of several kinds are grown in the orchard. (plural) |

[6] Definition in the *American College Dictionary*.

Nouns that have both countable and noncountable forms are often derived from verbs, and end in such suffixes as **-ment, -ion, -ure, -ance, -ary**. The noncountable word refers to the act itself—**operation, mixture, shipment, government**—and the countable word to the concrete product or result of the act—**an imitation, a shipment, a government**.[7]

> *The child learns through imitation.*
> but *Art is **an** imitation of life.*
> *This picture is **a** good imitation.*

Certain noncountable nouns that do not have a plural form may nevertheless be used with **a**, especially if they have adjective modifiers.

> *He exhibited **a** courage that surprised me.*
> *We encountered **an** unexpected friendliness wherever we went.*

**A** may also occur with a noncountable noun that is in apposition with another noun used earlier. Often the appositive noun repeats the noun it refers to.

> *He felt remorse over what he had done, **a** remorse that grew with the passing of time.*

When the referent of a noun that is usually noncountable is thought of as a contained item, the noun becomes countable and may be used with **a**—**Please bring us *a* milk and two coffees**. This usage is regarded as informal.

**A** used with noncountable nouns may have the sense of *a kind of, the kind of,* or *some.*

| | |
|---|---|
| a kind of | That restaurant serves *a* special French wine. |
| the kind of | *An* education which prepares the student for his role in life is the best kind of education. |
| some | *A* knowledge of history is important for all of us. |

Special Uses of *A*

### 1. A after **such, what**

**A** is required after **such** or **what** used with a singular countable noun.

> $\left. \begin{array}{l} such \\ what \end{array} \right\}$ *a pretty face*  vs.  $\left. \begin{array}{l} such \\ what \end{array} \right\}$ *pretty eyes*  or  $\left. \begin{array}{l} such \\ what \end{array} \right\}$ *pretty hair*

### 2. A after certain adverbs or adjectives—**not a, many a, quite a, rather a**

> *There was quite **a** large crowd in the street.*

---

[7] Other nouns of this type are never used in a countable sense—**information, equipment, furniture**. Since cognates of such words in other languages are often countable, only extensive experience with the English language can help the learner of English to recognize which of these nouns are countable and which are noncountable.

*Not **a** man volunteered.* (=***not one man volunteered.***) (The idea of *not one* can be strengthened by adding the word ***single*** [*not **a single** man volunteered*].)

*Many **a** man has volunteered to fight for his country.* (literary usage)

*Rather **a** large crowd gathered to hear the speaker.* (It is also possible to say *a rather large crowd.*)

3. **A** before noun quantifiers—**a few, a lot of, a little**

$\left.\begin{array}{l} a\ few \\ a\ lot\ of \end{array}\right\}$ *chairs    a little furniture*

4. **A** with proper names, meaning *a certain*

    ***A** Mr. Smith called you.*

5. **A** with **most** in the sense of *very* (often considered informal usage)

    *She is **a most** beautiful woman.*

    but *She is **the most** beautiful woman I know.* (***Most*** marks the superlative degree.)

6. **A** after **so** or **too** + an adjective + a singular noun

    *She is too sensible **a** girl to do a thing like that.*

    *She is so sensible **a** girl that she could not do a thing like that.*

7. **Half an hour** or **a half hour**

Either form may be used—**She waited for half an hour** (or **a half hour**).

NO ARTICLE

We have already seen that the article is not used:

    1.   in general statements, with noncountable and plural nouns that do not have post-modifiers.

    ***Milk** is good for children.*

    *Children should eat **eggs**.*

    2.   with many place names—continents, countries, cities, lakes, streets, parks—**Europe, Japan, Paris, Lake Geneva, Fifth Avenue, Central Park.**

Further usages that do not require the article are given below.

    1.   No article with names of holidays—**Thanksgiving, Christmas, Easter**—but **the Fourth of July.**

    2.   No article with names of magazines—**Life, Vogue, Punch, Holiday**—but **the Reader's Digest, the Saturday Review of Literature.**

    3.   No article with nouns denoting certain places in the environment

| *He is going to* | *church.* |
| | *school.* (or **elementary school, high school**), |
| | but **the university** |
| | *prison.* (or **jail**) |
| | *town.* |
| *He is going* | *home.* |
| | *downtown.* |

4. No article with names for most physical ailments or disorders

| *He has* | *pneumonia.* |
| | *heart trouble.* |
| | *polio.* |
| | *acne.* |

| but *He has* | *a headache* (or **a fever, a cold**). |
| | *the flu* (or **the measles**). |

5. No article with certain nouns used coordinately in set phrases

*Heart and soul, body and mind, mother and child, man and wife, field and farm*

6. No article in headlines, notices and telegrams, lists and outlines

*Man found dead in car.*

*Please wire answer immediately.*

## SPECIAL IDIOMS WITH *A, THE* OR NO ARTICLE

Many idioms involving the use of articles take the form of verbs plus objects, or of prepositional phrases.

### VERBS PLUS OBJECTS

| Objects with *a* | |
|---|---|
| after **make** | make a fool of, make a difference, make a living, make a remark, make a point of |
| after **take** | take a trip, take a break, take a picture, take a vacation, take a look at |
| after other verbs | do a favor (or **a job, a service**), become a reality, tell a lie, play a joke (or **a trick**) on, call a halt |
| Objects with *the* | make the beds, clear the table, wash the dishes, tell the truth, play the fool |
| Objects with **no article** | make friends, beg pardon, make haste, make conversation, take care of, take heart, take revenge, talk shop, talk sense, play football (or any other ball game), shake hands, take pity on, take pride in, take part in, take revenge on, take notice of, make love to, give way to, have faith in |

PREPOSITIONAL PHRASES

| | |
|---|---|
| Objects with *a* | in a hurry, as a rule, as a result, for a long time, as a matter of fact |
| Objects with *the* | by the way, in the long run, in the least, at the mercy of, on (the) one hand, on the other hand, on the contrary, on the whole |
| Objects with *no article* | by hand, by heart, by mistake, by train, by accident |
| | in addition, in fact, in front of, in case (of), in trouble, in general |
| | on purpose, on occasion, on foot, at last, at times |

Many phrasal prepositions having the form preposition + noun + preposition also occur without an article—**on account of, with regard to, in comparison with, on behalf of, in addition to, by means of.**

# 8

## *Adverbs*

It has been customary to include the most disparate elements among the adverbs, frequently those that cannot be put into any other part-of-speech classification. Adverbs range in *meaning* from words having a strong lexical content (those that describe the action of the verb, or those that indicate such meanings as time and place) to those that are used merely for emphasis. They range in *function* from close to loose modifiers of the verb; from close modifiers of single words, prepositional phrases or clauses, to loose modifiers of the entire sentence. They range in *form* from words clearly marked as adverbs to those that have the form of other parts of speech. For these reasons the dividing lines between the classification *adverb* and that of other parts of speech are not clearcut. Some adverbs merge with nouns or prepositions because of their form; some merge with interjections because of their ability to express emotion and to serve as sentence modifiers; some merge with conjunctions because of their ability to perform a connecting function.

Types of Adverbs
Classified by Meaning

### Manner—*Quickly, Neatly, Awkwardly*

The manner adverb has the most characteristic adverbial form (an **-ly** ending added to a descriptive adjective).

**Place and Direction—**
*Here, Away, Outside, Left, Straight, West*

Among the adverbs of place and direction may be included some prepositional forms appearing after the verb—**He came in; They walked down**.

Some archaic forms for adverbs of place and direction are still found
in the literary language—**hither** (=*here*), **thither** (=*there*), **yonder** (=*over
there*), **hence** (=from *here*), **thence** (=from *there*), **whither** (=*where*).

**Time**

DEFINITE TIME.    These adverbs have a fixed boundary in time—**yesterday,
today, tomorrow**. Most of these words have noun form[1] and some may be
used in plural form[2]—**Saturdays, nights (He works *nights* and sleeps *days*)**.
In addition, a group of words may function as a single time expression—**last
week, a month ago, the day before yesterday**.

INDEFINITE TIME.    This kind of time has no fixed boundary.

1.    Words like **recently, nowadays, soon, already, still, just, immediately**.

2.    Words denoting a sequence in time—**now, then, before, after(wards),
next, first, later**.

3.    Words denoting frequency. Frequency words range in meaning from
*at all times* to *at no time*—**always, often, sometimes, never**

**Intensifying Adverbs**

Such adverbs serve as quantifiers or emphasizers.

Adverbs of Degree (Quantifiers)

1.    Adverbs of degree denoting **how much** with respect to *adjectives* or
*adverbs*—**very, too, quite, somewhat, rather, extremely, exceedingly, fairly,
more (She became *quite* angry with the insolent boy; He always walks *rather*
quickly)**.

**Not** is sometimes included among such adverbs of degree on the basis that
it excludes all degree.

Certain adverbs of degree are characteristic of informal speech only—**so,
pretty, awfully, terribly, dreadfully, horribly, mighty**.

> *I feel so **terribly** tired tonight.*
>
> *The movie was **pretty** bad.*
>
> *She's been working **awfully** hard lately.*

Adverbs of manner sometimes also express degree—**She is breath-
takingly beautiful; He works devilishly hard**. These add the stronger lexical

---

[1] Adverbs of definite time are sometimes called adverbial nouns.
   Definite time word used as an adverb—**I saw him yesterday**.
   Definite time word used as a noun—**Yesterday was a busy day**.
[2] These -*s* forms are actually from an older genitive form.

meaning of the adjectives from which they are derived to the weaker semantic component of degree.

Those verbs that are capable of being expressed with a quantifying degree may be intensified by **much**, or more commonly **very much**.

| | |
|---|---|
| active verb | Everyone loves her very much. |
| | His work bores him very much. |
| passive verb | She is very much loved by everyone. |
| | He is very much bored by (or **with**) his work. |

Often an **-ed** participle after a form of the verb **be** is felt as an adjective rather than as part of a passive verb. This is particularly true with words denoting mental states. In such cases **very** is frequently used without **much**, especially in informal usage—**He was very bored** (or **pleased, annoyed**). **Very** may also occur with these participial adjectives when they appear before nouns—**a very bored** (or **pleased, annoyed**) **expression**.

2. Adverbs of degree denoting **how complete**—**almost, entirely, nearly, partially, practically, utterly, wholly**. Most of these adverbs have the same **-ly** form as adverbs of manner do and are often classed with manner adverbs.

a. degree of completion with respect to *verbs*

They have ***almost*** finished the work.

He has now ***partially*** recovered from his stroke.

He ***completely*** misunderstood his wife's remarks.

b. degree of completion with respect to *adjectives*

They're ***practically*** ready to begin the show.

The men were ***utterly*** exhausted.

***Entirely*** oblivious of all protests, the mayor went ahead with his plans.

**Almost, nearly** may also denote degree of completion with the indefinite adjectives **any, no, every** (*Nearly* **every woman loves a bargain**), even when these adjectives function as the first part of a pronoun (*Nearly* **everybody loves a bargain**).

Among the adverbs of completion may be included the word **enough** (**The patient will soon be well** *enough* **to leave the hospital**), as well as **all, half,** or words denoting fractions (**The mural was** *one-third* **completed before the painter received part of his fee**).

The **-ly** adverbs of degree do not usually occur together with adverbs of manner because of the awkward juxtaposition of two **-ly** forms (for example, in the sentence **He works completely independently**).

## Distinguishing Adverbs (Emphasizers)

These adverbs emphasize particular words or grammatical constructions— **especially, even, exactly, just, merely, not** (used for contrast), **only, purely,**

**simply, solely.** Such adverbs usually appear immediately before the words or constructions they modify.

Distinguishing adverbs often intensify *adjectives* (**She was not *especially* pretty; This isn't *exactly* right**), and, to a lesser extent, *verbs* (**He *even* began to dress more neatly**).

Unlike the other types of adverbs, some of the distinguishing adverbs also modify:

| | | |
|---|---|---|
| 1. | nouns | *Even* John agreed to come. |
| | | We ordered two dozen roses, *not* one dozen. |
| 2. | pronouns | *Only* she could not come. |
| | | *Even* they came late. |
| 3. | prepositional phrases[3] | He went to the party *only* because of his wife. |
| | | *Even* during the performance he didn't stop talking. |
| 4. | subordinate clauses[3] | I don't know *exactly* when I can come. |
| | | You shouldn't work so hard, *especially* after you've been ill. |

Certain adverbs of time may serve as distinguishing adverbs before prepositions or conjunctions of time—**immediately, just, right, soon** (***Soon* after dinner he fell asleep; *Just* when we left the house it started to rain**).

Types of Adverbs
Classified by Function

**Sentence Adverbs**

These adverbs often have a loose grammatical connection with the rest of the sentence, and are looked upon as modifying the whole sentence rather than the verb—**fortunately, presumably, actually, obviously, evidently.** Such adverbs may be considered as equivalents of a sentence or a clause; thus **presumably** may be interpreted as representing **as may be presumed.** Many of these words have the **-ly** form of manner adverbs, but actually they often reflect the *independent opinion of the speaker* rather than the manner of an action—*Fortunately*, **no one was hurt; He *evidently* thinks that he can do no wrong.** Many words ending in -ed + ly are sentence adverbs—**unexpectedly, allegedly, decidedly, advisedly.**

Sentence adverbs can serve as single word answers to questions, especially if they express *affirmation* (**yes, certainly, surely, absolutely, precisely, undeniably**), *negation* (**no**), *possibility or probability* (**perhaps, maybe, possibly, probably**).

---

[3] Some grammarians consider that the distinguishing adverbs in these instances modify only the preposition or subordinate conjunction rather than the whole construction.

Interjections expressing a mild degree of feeling are sometimes classified among the sentence adverbs—**well, indeed, now**.

Word groups may also function as sentence adverbs—**by all** (or **no**) **means, in my opinion, strangely enough**.

### Conjunctive Adverbs

These adverbs establish a relationship between one sentence or clause and the preceding sentence or clause. As in the case of sentence adverbs, they probably should be considered as modifying the whole sentence or clause rather than the verb alone.

Conjunctive adverbs indicate such relationships as result (**therefore, accordingly**), addition (**moreover, besides**), contrast (**however, nevertheless**), condition (**otherwise**), time (**then**). Groups of words may be used to establish the same kinds of relationships as conjunctive adverbs do—**in addition, for this reason, after this, if not**.

(The chapter on Sentences and Clauses contains more information about conjunctive adverbs.)

### Explanatory Adverbs

These adverbs illustrate or enumerate—**namely, for example, as, i.e.** (=*that is*), **e.g.** (=*for example*), **viz.** (=*namely*).

### Relative, Interrogative Adverbs—
*When, Where, Why, How*

1. relative adverbs—These adverbs introduce adjective clauses.

   *We visited the house **where** a famous poet once lived.*

2. interrogative adverbs
   a. in questions—***When* will he arrive?**
   b. in noun clauses derived from questions—**I asked *when* he would arrive**.

### Exclamatory Adverb—*How*

This adverb is used with adjectives and adverbs.

   ***How** beautifully she dresses !*
   ***How** beautiful she is !*

## FUNCTION OF ADVERBS

An adverb modifies a verb, adjective, adverb or an entire sentence.
1. *Adverb as modifier of a verb*

   Sentence: *The boy threw the ball **quickly**.*
   or *The boy **quickly** threw the ball.*

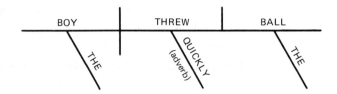

Adverbs of manner modify the verb most directly. Adverbs of place and time may also be considered as modifying the verb, although some grammarians consider these as modifying the entire sentence.

Sentence:   *The boy **quickly** threw the ball **there twice yesterday**.*

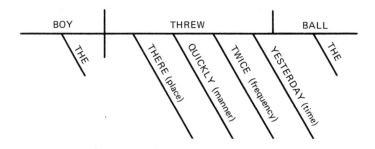

2. *Adverb as modifier (intensifier) of an adjective or an adverb*
  Intensifying adverbs of degree modify adjectives or adverbs in the same way as **very** in the diagram below.

Sentence:   *The **very** small boy threw the ball **very** quickly.*

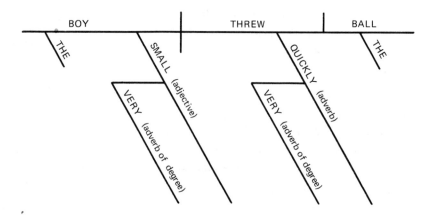

3. *Adverb as modifier of an entire sentence*

    Sentence: **Fortunately,** *the boy threw the ball quickly.*

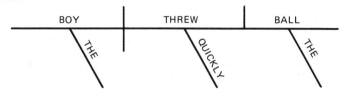

    Adverbs of degree can participate in several layers of modification— **He drank** *far too much* **coffee; He can finish this job** *ever so much more* **quickly than I can.**

    Functioning as a sentence adverbial may be an entire noun phrase with pre- and post-modification of a noun head. The noun head of such a phrase usually denotes definite time.

        **Two days before the show was to open,** *one of the stars became ill.*
        (**Days** is the noun head of the adverbial construction.)
        **The very first moment that he met her,** *he fell in love with her.*
        (**Moment** is the noun head of the adverbial construction.)

    Other complex structures that function as adverbials are:

| | |
|---|---|
| Prepositional phrases | He put the book *on the table*. (**On the table** modifies the verb **put**.) |
| Adverbial clauses | I'll do it *when I have time*. (**When I have time** modifies the verb **do**.) |
| Infinitive phrases | Turn right *to get to the bridge*. (**To get to the bridge** modifies the verb **turn**, or it may be interpreted as modifying the entire sentence.) |

### POSITION OF ADVERBS

    The adverb has a greater degree of maneuverability than any of the other parts of speech. It can fill one of three positions.

|  | *Sentences* |
|---|---|
| 1. *Initial position* before the subject (position of greatest emphasis) | *Sometimes* she comes late. |
| 2. *Mid-position* with the verb (position of close modification of the verb) | She *sometimes* comes late. |

*Sentences*

| | |
|---|---|
| 3. *Final position*<br>after the verb plus object or<br>other complement<br>(position less emphatic than<br>initial position, but more<br>emphatic than mid-position) | She comes late *sometimes*. |

Some types of adverbs and adverbial word groups may occupy all three of the possible adverbial positions, others only one or two of these positions. The following chart summarizes the most usual positions for the different classes of adverbs as well as their less common positions.

| Type of Adverb | Most Usual Position | Other Possible Positions |
|---|---|---|
| Adverbs of *manner* | final position:<br>The army advanced toward the enemy *slowly* and *silently*. | mid-position (mostly for one-word adverbs)<br>The army *slowly* and *silently* advanced toward the enemy. |
| | **Hard, fast, well, slow, nicely, badly, poorly** are used only in end position | initial position (for emphasis, often has a more literary tone):<br>*Slowly* and *silently* the army advanced toward the enemy. |
| Adverbs of *place* and *direction* | final position:<br>**Go home** (or **there, here, away, inside, east**) | initial position is occasionally used. In such cases the word order is often reversed:<br>*There* sat a mean-looking man. |
| Adverbs of *time*<br>　A. definite time | final position:<br>We submitted the report to the committee *yesterday*. | initial position:<br>*Yesterday* we submitted the report to the committee.<br>mid-position is rare for definite time—We have *today* sent the books you requested. |
| 　B. indefinite time<br>　　1. adverbs like **soon, recently** | mid-position:<br>We *soon* found our mistake. | initial position:<br>*Soon* we found our mistake.<br>final position:<br>We found our mistake *soon*. |
| 　　2. adverbs of sequence | initial position:<br>*Next*, we take up the use of adverbs. | mid-position:<br>We *next* take up the use of adverbs.<br>final position:<br>We take up the use of adverbs *next*. |

| Type of Adverb | Most Usual Position | Other Possible positions |
|---|---|---|
| 3.  adverbs of frequency | mid-position:<br>They *often* (or *sometimes*) have trouble with their television set.<br>**Always** and **never** appear mostly in mid-position:<br>He *always* (or *never*) does his work well.<br>**Never** is not used in final position; **always** sometimes appears there.<br>**Always** does not usually occur in initial position.<br>**Never** is occasionally found there; in such a case a reversal of word order is required:<br>*Never* has he done such a thing before. | initial position:<br>*Often* (or *sometimes*) they have trouble with their television set.<br>final position:<br>They have trouble with their television set *often* (or *sometimes*).<br>(only if the sentence or clause is short)<br><br>mid-position is rare for word groups such as **many times, once or twice** |
| *Intensifying* adverbs<br>A.  adverbs of degree | position preceding the word being intensified:<br>The weather is *very* hot this summer.<br>They have *completely* won our hearts. | adverbs of degree used with verbs may occur in final position:<br>They have won our hearts *completely*. |
| B.  distinguishing adverbs | position preceding the word or structure being emphasized:<br>*Only* Mary passed in Greek.<br>Mary passed *only* in Greek.<br>You can *only* guess my anguish. | distinguishing adverbs may follow nouns or pronouns:<br>Mary *only* passed in Greek.<br>Mary passed in Greek *only*.<br>**Alone** is used after a noun or pronoun:<br>He *alone* is responsible for that job. |
| *Sentence* adverbs | initial position:<br>*Obviously* they will not finish on time. | mid-position:<br>They *obviously* will not finish on time.<br>final position (only if the sentence or clause is short):<br>They will not finish on time, *obviously*. |
| *Conjunctive* adverbs | initial position:<br>I have a great deal of work to do. *Therefore* I must go to the office on Sunday.<br><br>mid-position:<br>I have a great deal of work to do. I must *therefore* go to the office on Sunday. | final position (only if the sentence or clause is short):<br>He quit his job. He needs to look for work *therefore*. |

In sentences that contain two verbs, adverbs in certain positions may cause ambiguity, especially in the written language. These troublesome adverbs usually express time or manner. Such sentences should be recast to make the meaning clear.

Ambiguous adverb in *mid-position*

> A man who lies **frequently** will cheat also.

Corrected to:   A man who **frequently** lies will cheat also.

> or   A man who lies will **frequently** cheat also.

Ambiguous adverb in *final position*

> She mentioned finding the money **yesterday**.

The tendency is to interpret such an adverb in final position as belonging with the second verb. If the adverb is intended as modifying the first verb, the sentence should be corrected to—**Yesterday she mentioned finding the money.**

Adverbials in Final Position

When two or more types of adverbials appear in final position, they follow the order of *place, manner, time* after the complement.

> The witness walked to the stand hesitantly when he was called.

In the position between adverbials of place and adverbials of time may also appear adverbials denoting instrument, agent, accompaniment, degree, purpose.

> He was walking along the street (place) *quietly* (manner) *with his dog* (accompaniment) *last night* (time).

> This toy can be made at home (place) *by young people* (agent) *very easily* (manner) *with a few simple tools* (instrument).

> They put the box in a dry place (place) *for safe keeping* (purpose) *during the storm* (time). (Purpose may also come last.)

Adverbials may precede prepositional objects, especially if these objects are long. Such adverbials usually denote manner, and, less commonly, time.

> He believes **wholeheartedly** in the cause he is fighting for.

> They were talking **for a long time** about the places they had visited.

Sometimes adverbs of place precede adverbs of manner. Actually, only one-word adverbs of place and direction require the position right after the verb—**He walked *home* quickly**. The position of adverbial word groups of place and direction, and of adverbs of manner is not so rigidly set—**He walked *into the house* quickly** or **He walked *quickly* into the house**.

There is less flexibility of position with adverbs of time, especially definite time. These adverbs are usually placed last in a series of adverbs in final position.

Sometimes the order of adverbs in final position is determined by the length of the adverbial expressions; usually the shorter one comes before the longer one—**We ran into him** *twice at the fair*. In addition, in informal speech, the order of adverbs in final position may depend on what comes to the speaker's mind first.

When several adverbial expressions are used in a sentence, the tendency is to distribute them among the various positions that are natural for them rather than to string them all along in the final position—*Every day* he *eagerly* **checked the stock market reports** *to see if his stocks had gone up*.

### Adverbs in Mid-position

The position of an adverb with the verb varies according to the number of auxiliaries that accompany the verb.

|  | *Usual Position of Adverb* | *Sentences* |
|---|---|---|
| 1. *Verbs with no auxiliaries* (Simple present and simple past tenses) | | |
| a.  the verb **be** | after the verb | She is *sometimes* late. |
| b.  all other verbs | before the verb | She *sometimes* comes late. |
| 2. *Verbs with one to three auxiliaries* | after the first auxiliary | She has *sometimes* come late. She has *sometimes* been coming late. |

It should be noted that the negative adverb **not** appears in the same position with the verb as the examples just given.

Usually only single-word adverbs appear in mid-position. Adverbs used in mid-position may be moved forward to precede the entire verb. This less usual position serves to emphasize the verb form immediately following it (**He never** *has* **been and never** *will* **be successful**), or sometimes the adverb itself.

| *Forwarded Position of Adverb with Verb* | *vs. the More Usual Position* |
|---|---|
| She *sometimes* is                    late. | is *sometimes* late. |
| She *sometimes* has been              late. | has *sometimes* been late. |
| She *sometimes* has been coming       late. | has *sometimes* been coming late. |

However, no choice is possible with auxiliary-less verbs other than **be**; thus, only **She** *sometimes* **comes late** may be used.

Adverbial expressions do not usually occupy the position between a verb and its object (or any other kind of complement)—*She eats *sometimes* steak. An exception to this usage occurs with an object that has long modification—**Please read** *carefully* **all the sections in the book that deal with adverbs.**

**Two types** of adverbs may occur in sequence with an auxiliary-less verb or a one-auxiliary verb. The second adverb usually denotes manner or degree of completion.

1. *Auxiliary-less verbs*

> She is **now thoroughly** competent to do supervisory work.
>
> The doctor **no doubt carefully** watched his patient's progress.

2. *Verbs with one auxiliary*

> The report was **next**[4] **carefully** checked for errors.
>
> I was **evidently**[4] **completely** misunderstood.

With verbs having more than one auxiliary, adverbs of manner and degree of completion generally appear before the lexical verb rather than after the first auxiliary.

1. *Passive verbs*

> He will be **severely** punished.
>
> vs. He will **surely** be punished.
>
> She has been **fully** restored to health.
>
> vs. She has **obviously** been restored to health.
>
> The soldiers must be **thoroughly** trained.
>
> vs. The soldiers must **first** be trained.

2. *Progressive verbs* (less common)

> The doctor has been **carefully** watching his patient's progress.
>
> vs. The doctor has **undoubtedly** been watching his patient's progress.
>
> The customs officials will be **painstakingly** inspecting all baggage.
>
> vs. The customs officials will **now** be inspecting all baggage.

It is also possible to use two adverbs with verbs having more than one auxiliary. These adverbs are distributed in two different positions with the verb.

> He will **surely** be **severely** punished.
>
> I have **evidently** been **completely** misunderstood.
>
> She has **always** been **well** provided for.
>
> They have **obviously** been **deliberately** instigating the recent riots.

When **not** occurs with another adverb in mid-position, it may (1) precede the other adverb, (2) follow the other adverb, or (3) do either.

1. *Not precedes the other adverb* (most common order)

> He will **not** be severely punished.
>
> He **doesn't** fully understand her letter.

---

[4] In these examples and in those that follow, all adverbs after the first auxiliary, except manner and degree of completion, may also precede the first auxiliary—**The report** *next* **was carefully checked for errors;** I *evidently* **was completely misunderstood.**

She **didn't** deliberately tell a lie.

2. *Not follows the other adverb*

He will surely **not** be punished.

She deliberately **didn't** tell the truth.

He still **hasn't** paid his bills.

3. *Not precedes or follows the other adverb*

He's **not** usually (or **generally**) interested in such things.

or He's usually (or **generally**) **not** interested in such things.

He **didn't** actually understand the question.

or He actually **didn't** understand the question.

## Reversal of Word Order
## after Certain Adverbial Elements

The order of subject and verb is reversed after the following adverbial elements.

1. Adverbial expressions of negation with **no, not, never, neither**

**In no** (or **in neither**) **case** can an exception be made.

**Never** have I seen such a stupid person.

**Not** until he loses all his money will he stop gambling.

The same reversal of word order takes place after negative conjunctions— **neither, nor, not only—but also, no sooner—than**.

I cannot attend the meeting tonight, and **neither** can my wife.

**Not only** is she very beautiful, but she is also very intelligent.

**No sooner** had he begun his vacation than he became ill.

2. Adverbial expressions of near negation—**scarcely, seldom, rarely, barely, hardly**

**Scarcely** had he entered the room when he was approached by a bearded stranger.

**Seldom** (or **rarely**) has anyone succeeded in this kind of business.

3. Adverbial expressions with **only**

**Only** after an operation will he be able to walk again.

**Only** once has he done such a thing.

In **only** one instance has he ever failed me.

4. Adverbial expressions with **so**

**So** greatly did he admire the beautiful actress that he asked her to marry him.

Everyone wildly applauded the violinist, **so** thrilling was his performance.

The word order is also reversed after the conjunction **so—I caught a cold, and so did my wife**.

5. Adverbial expressions of place

> *There* stood the tallest man he had ever seen.
>
> *Before them* lay a vast expanse of desert.
>
> *Inside the room* were a few dilapidated pieces of furniture.
>
> *Among those present* were the governor and his wife.

After certain other adverbials in initial position, a reversal of subject and verb is optional. Inverted sentences of this type have a literary effect.

> *Loud and clear* rang the bells.
>
> *In God alone* should we place our trust.
>
> *Often* (or *many a time*) did we sit together without saying a word.

## Position of Adverbs with Nouns

Adverbs used with nouns may take one of two positions:

1. *before* a noun and its determiners. (Such adverbs are usually intensifiers.)

> *Almost* (or *nearly, about, approximately*) a year, *exactly* the right thing,[5] *even* Robert.

2. *after* a noun—adverbial expressions of place, some time

> The view *outside*, the discussion *afterward*, the day *after*, the year *before*

An expression of time appearing in final position after a noun may sometimes be interpreted as either an adjectival or an adverbial.

> Where are you planning to go for your vacation *next year*?

## Position of Adverbs in Questions and Requests

In questions, only mid-position and final position are used for adverbs.

In questions with one auxiliary, adverbs in mid-position are placed before the lexical verb.

> Does he *usually* work so late?
>
> Has he *fully* recovered?
>
> Can you *honestly* say you have done your best?

In questions with two auxiliaries, adverbs occupy the same position with verbs as they do in statements.

> Will he be *severely* punished?
>
> Haven't they *ever* been invited to her house?

[5] **Exactly** may also be used after the noun—**the right thing exactly.**

In requests, most adverbs are placed in final position.

> *Do it* **quickly.**
>
> *Go there* **tomorrow.** (Sometimes, **Tomorrow, go there**)

The frequency adverbs **never** and **always** usually take initial position in requests—*Never* (or *always*) **buy expensive clothes.** Sometimes sequence adverbs occur in initial position—*First* **deliver the package,** *then* **go to the post office.**

### PUNCTUATION OF ADVERBIALS

Commas used to set off adverbials are often optional; in many cases they are determined by whether the writer would pause in speech. A pause is likely to occur if the adverbial is felt as loosely connected with the subject-verb-complement core, or if emphasis is being placed on the adverbial. In sentences that appear too "chopped up" with commas, the optional commas used with adverbials are preferably omitted. In general, the omission of optional commas reflects the modern trend toward less punctuation.

Because of the relative freedom in the punctuation of adverbials, the following uses of commas with adverbials must be interpreted as general tendencies rather than as definite rules.

### Adverbials in Initial Position

Commas often occur after adverbials in initial position. The longer the adverbial or the adverbial expression, the more likely that commas will be used. Sentence adverbs and conjunctive adverbs especially are likely to be cut off by commas.

> **Obviously,** *Mr. Jones doesn't care to work very hard.*
>
> *It's raining very hard;* **therefore,** *the club will cancel the picnic.*
>
> **Strangely enough,** *she won't accept any pay for the work she is doing.*

### Adverbials in Final Position

Commas generally do not cut off adverbials of time and place appearing in final position.

> *I saw him* **there Sunday night.**
>
> *We'll meet you* **at the airport the day after tomorrow.**

The occasional sentence adverbs or conjunctive adverbs that appear in final position are usually cut off by commas.

> *Mr. Jones doesn't care to work very hard,* **obviously.**
>
> *It's raining very hard; the club will cancel the picnic,* **therefore.**

Sometimes a comma before an adverb in final position is necessary to clarify the meaning. This is especially true when a final **-ly** adverb may be interpreted as either a manner adverb or a sentence adverb.

*He didn't understand the question, **clearly**.* (i.e., it is evident that he didn't understand the question)

vs. *He didn't understand the question **clearly**.* (i.e., the question was not clear to him)

## Adverbials in Mid-position

In this position, sentence adverbs and conjunctive adverbs are likely to be set off by commas. Such commas must appear *before and after* the adverbial element.

*Mr. Jones, **obviously**, doesn't care to work hard.*

*It's raining very hard; the club, **therefore**,[6] will have to cancel the picnic.*

*The shipment, **unfortunately**, has been delayed because of a dock strike.*

Short adverbs of frequency or manner appearing in mid-position are rarely cut off by commas.

*They **always** went to the movies Saturday night.*

*She **quickly** ran to the door.*

FORM OF ADVERBS

Inflectional Form

The adverb has an inflectional form only for comparison. Short adverbs (mostly one-syllable adverbs) that have the same form as adjectives are compared by the addition of **-er, -est**. These adverbs are of several types.

1. adverbs of *manner*—**hard,**[7] **fast**
One group of manner adverbs has two forms, one with, and one without, an **-ly** ending—**slow—slowly, quick—quickly, cheap—cheaply, dear—dearly, loud—loudly, clear—clearly**. The forms without **-ly** are less formal; they generally appear only directly after the verb.

*Drive **slow**(**ly**). but He **slowly** drove out of sight.*

*Please drive **slower** (or **more slowly**).*

2. adverbs of *time*—**early, late,**[8] **long, often,**[9] **soon**
3. adverbs of *distance and direction*—**close, far, near, straight, low, high**

The **-ly** adverbs of manner are compared by the use of **more—than, the most**.

*She dresses **more elegantly than** her sister.*

*He works **more efficiently** in the morning **than** in the afternoon.*

*She is **the most beautifully** dressed woman I have ever met.*

---

[6] The comma may be omitted in this sentence.
[7] The **-ly** form of **hard, hardly,** is synonomous with *scarcely, barely*.
[8] The **-ly** form of **late, lately,** is synonomous with *recently*.
[9] **Often** is also compared with **more** and **most**.

**Less—than, the least** are also used in the comparison of manner adverbs.

*He spoke **less eloquently than** usual.*
*He always contributes **the least generously** of all the members.*
*She works **less hard** now **than** she ever did.*

A few short adverbs have an irregular comparison:

| | | |
|---|---|---|
| well | better | best |
| badly | worse | worst |
| far | farther[10] | farthest |
| | *or* | *or* |
| | further | furthest |
| much | more | most |
| little | less | least |

Derivational Form

Most adverbs of manner, many sentence adverbs, and some adverbs of frequency and degree are formed by adding the derivational suffix **-ly** to a *descriptive adjective*:

| | |
|---|---|
| Manner adverbs | intelligently, laughingly, cold-bloodedly |
| Other adverbs | allegedly, frequently, extremely, fully |

Adjectives that already end in **-ly** are often used in unchanged form as adverbs:

| | |
|---|---|
| Adverbs of manner | friendly, leisurely, lively, orderly[11] |
| Adverbs of time | early, weekly, daily, monthly |

In formal usage, the manner adverbs of this type are avoided; instead, a phrase with the word **manner** or **way** is used—**He behaved *in a friendly way*; He spoke *in a lively manner*.**

Because of their special meanings, some descriptive adjectives are not used adverbially with **-ly** adverbial forms—**inferior, colonial, sick, indicative.**

A few spelling rules need to be observed when adding **-ly** to adjectives.

1. Final *y* preceded by a consonant is changed to *i*—**happily, busily, merrily.** Some adverbs from one-syllable adjectives ending in *y* may be written with a *y* or an *i*—**gayly** or **gaily, dryly** or **drily** (but **coyly**).

---

[10] See the inflectional form of adjectives for the distinction between **farther** and **further**.

[11] The dictionary also gives such adverbial forms as **friendlily, livelily**; however, these forms are rarely used.

2. With adjectives ending in *ble, ple, tle, dle,* the *le* is dropped before **-ly—possibly, simply, gently, idly.**

3. With adjectives ending in **-ic, -al** is added before **-ly—basically, hygienically.**[12] In the case of adjectives that end in either **-ic** or **-ical**—**geographic(al), historic(al)**—The **-ly** is added to the **-ical** form—**geographically, historically.**

Some caution must be observed in adding **-ly** to adjectives with other endings:

1. With adjectives ending in silent *e,*  the *e* must be retained before **-ly—extremely, entirely, sincerely.**[13]

2. With adjectives ending in *l*, the *l* must be kept before **-ly—beautifully, accidentally, totally.**[14]

Derivational suffixes other than **-ly** that distinguish adverbs are——*ward(s)*—**frontward(s), backward(s), downward, onward;** *-wise*—**lengthwise, otherwise, counterclockwise.**[15]

The last element in certain compound words may also be classed among derivational endings that signal adverbs—*-where*—**anywhere, nowhere, else-where;** *-ever*—**forever, however, whenever;** *-place*—**someplace, anyplace.**[16]

There is one derivational prefix that signals adverbs—**a**——**apart, apiece, aside, along, ahead, aloud.** This **a-** prefix is attached mostly to nouns.[17]

### MARKERS OF ADVERBS

Adverbs of degree mark the adverb, just as they do the adjective—*very* **quickly,** *too* **slowly,** *quite* **well,** *much more* **pleasantly.**

### SPECIAL USAGES OF ADVERBS

**Adverbs Used
in the Comparison
of Adverbs and Adjectives**

The comparative and superlative forms of adjectives and adverbs may be intensified by:

---

[12] **Publicly** is an exception to this kind of spelling change.

[13] Exceptions are **truly, duly, wholly.**

[14] In the case of a few one-syllable adjectives that end in a double *l*, one *l* is dropped before -ly—**dully, fully, shrilly.**

[15] There is a tendency to coin new adverbs with **-wise** added to a noun—**budgetwise, timewise, saleswise.** Such adverbs should be avoided in formal English.

[16] The forms with **-place** are not fully acceptable in formal English.

[17] The **a-** prefix may also signal adjectives—**aware, alive, asleep.**

| | |
|---|---|
| much | He works *much* more rapidly than the other employees. |
| | He eats *much* less heartily than he used to. |
| | She has become *much* prettier since she went on a diet. |
| | **Much** may be further intensified by **very**, or less formally, **ever so** or **so very**—He works *very* (or *ever so, so very*) *much* more rapidly than the other employees. |
| far or by far | His wife is a *far* better cook than most women he knows. |
| | He works *by far* the hardest of anyone in his office. |
| | **By far** may also follow the word it intensifies. |
| | His wife is a better cook *by far* than most women he knows. |
| | He works the hardest *by far* of anyone in his office. |

The superlative form of the adverb may be used in implied comparisons. In such cases the word **the** may be omitted.

> *We like this (**the**) **most**.*
>
> *He has worked here (**the**) **longest**.*

### *So* Substitution

The **so** substitute is used to avoid repeating a part of a predicate that appears with a preceding verb. **So** substitution occurs after the verbs **be afraid, believe, expect, hope, imagine, say, suppose, tell, think**.

> *Do you think it will rain?—Yes, I think **so**.*
> *(**so** = **it will rain**)*
> *I know he's going to be married because he told me **so**.*
> *(**so** = **he's going to be married**.)*

Except for **say** and **tell**, the negative substitute for **so** is **not** in such sentences.

> *Do you think it will rain?—No, I think **not**.*

The linking verbs **appear, be, remain, seem** may also be followed by a **so** substitute.

> *You are my best friend and I hope you will always remain **so**.*
> *Do you think he will be found guilty?—It appears **so** from all the evidence.*

Of these linking verbs, only **appear** and **seem** have the negative substitute **not**.

> *Have the police found the stolen jewelry?*
> *—It appears **not**, from what I have read in the newspapers.*

When the pro-verb **do** takes the place of a verb of action previously mentioned, **so** substitutes for the part of the predicate after the verb. **It** (informal) or **this** may be alternatives for **so** in this kind of substitution.

> *His lawyer suggested that he sue the man whose car hit him, but he is unwilling to do **so**. (or **it, this**.)*
> *Mr. Elsworth has asked our company to recommend him, and we have already done **so**. (or **it, this**.)*

In some sentences **so** may be the equivalent of the adverb **thus**.

> *She is very cynical. Her hard life has made her* ***so.***
> *She made life interesting because she found it* ***so.***
> *He is a friend and I treat him* ***so.*** (or ***as such.***)

## Negation with *Not, No*

**Not** precedes all the layers of degree that can be used with adjectives.

| Not | so | very | many | more | people | showed up. |
|---|---|---|---|---|---|---|
|  |  |  | much |  | work | was done. |

**Not** may be used with pronouns or other adverbs in short answers.

> *Were there any students at the rally?—**Not** many.*
> *Do you ever go to the movies?—**Not** often.*
> *Was the theater crowded?—**Not** very.*
> *Is any disturbance expected at the meeting tonight?—Certainly (or **probably**) not.*

Note that in these short answers **not** comes first except when it occurs with a sentence adverb (**certainly not**).

**No** may be used adverbially with comparative forms of adjectives or adverbs.

> *He is **no** better than I.*
> ***No** more work was done that day.*
> *I can bear this situation **no** longer (or I can **no** longer bear this situation).*

In some cases, either **no** or **not** may be used with a comparative.

> ***No** (or **not**) more than twenty people came to the lecture.*
> *This room will hold **no** (or **not**) more than twenty people.*

Intensifiers that strengthen the negation of **no** or **not** are:

| | |
|---|---|
| **whatever** or **whatsoever** follows **no** plus a noun | I have **no** money ***what(so)ever.*** <br><br> *No* exceptions ***what(so)ever*** will be made. |
| **at all:** follows **no** plus a noun <br> follows **not** or **never** plus a verb | I have **no** money ***at all.*** (**At all** here is synonomous with **whatever.**) <br> He **can't** be persuaded ***at all.*** <br> She **isn't** pretty ***at all.*** <br> This radio has ***never*** worked ***at all.*** <br> **At all** may follow **not**—I'm ***not at all*** sure he's right. |

**Not** is used before adjectives of quantity.

> *Not a (single) man showed up. (**A** here has the sense of one.)*
> *Not many people showed up.*
> *Not much work was done.*

**Not** may set up an opposition between two similar grammatical structures.

> *We need help, **not** sympathy.*
> *Please put the flowers in the green vase, **not** in the blue one.*
> *We went to the movies **not** because the picture interested us, but because we were bored.*

**Not** used with another negative, usually a word with a negative prefix, has a positive meaning—**not infrequently** means **frequently**. Further examples of such double negatives are **not unlikely, not unaware, not distasteful, not for nothing**. Other types of double negatives are considered substandard:

> *I didn't do **nothing**.*
> *We **never** (or **hardly ever**) give **nobody** any trouble.*

### *Already* vs. *Yet*

**Already** occurs in a positive statement, **yet** in a negative statement.

> *He has **already** left the office.*
> (less commonly, *He has left the office **already**.*)
> *He hasn't left the office **yet**.*
> (less commonly, *He hasn't **yet** left the office.*)

**Yet** is also used for questions.

> *Has he left the office **yet**?*
> *Hasn't he left the office **yet**?*

Sometimes **already** occurs in a positive question—**Has he left the office already**? There is little difference in meaning here between **yet** and **already**; we might say that **already** has a stronger semantic component of time than **yet**, and perhaps a greater expectancy of a yes answer. If the sentence stress is on **already**, the feeling of surprise may be indicated.

> *What! Have you run out of money alréady?*

### *Too* vs. *Very*

Both **too** and **very** mean "a high degree," but **too** has the added meaning of "more than enough," "an excessive amount," "going beyond a limit"—**This dress is *too* tight; This dress is *too* expensive for me to buy**. Some uses of **too** also include a value judgment on the part of the user, often disapproval.

> *He smokes **very** much. (**Very** here simply means "a great quantity")*
> *He smokes **too** much. (**Too** here implies that the user disapproves of the great quantity)*

*Ever*

---

Ever is used:

| | |
|---|---|
| In questions | Do you *ever* see him? (**Ever** here means "at any time.") |
| In negative statements | I don't *ever* see him any more. (Both **ever** and **any more** emphasize the idea of negation.) |
| In positive statements | If I (*ever*) see him, I'll tell him. (**Ever** here means "at any time.") |
| | This is the best book I have (*ever*) read. (**Ever** after the superlative means "in all my life.") |

---

## *Most* **Meaning** *Very*

The adverb **most** used without **the** is an informal equivalent of **very**.

*He worked **most** diligently.*

*She is a **most** beautiful girl.*

# 9

## Prepositions
## and
## Prepositional Phrases

The preposition is classified as a part of speech in traditional grammar. However, prepositions as well as conjunctions differ from other parts of speech in that (1) each is composed of a small class of words that have no formal characteristic endings; (2) each signals syntactic structures that *function as one of the other parts of speech*. For these reasons modern linguists prefer to classify prepositions as structure words rather than as parts of speech.

Prepositions range in meaning from such definite semantic notions as time, place, etc., to such purely structural meanings as those shaped by the subject-verb-complement relationship (**The murder *of* all the prisoners *by* their captors**).

A preposition signals that a noun or a noun structure follows it; the preposition + noun combination constitutes a *prepositional phrase* (**He walked *into the house***). A prepositional phrase may function as an adverb, adjective or noun. Since the preposition is an integral part of the prepositional phrase, both prepositions and prepositional phrases will be taken up together in this chapter.

### TYPES OF PREPOSITIONS

A highly detailed classification of all prepositions would be fruitless in a text on grammar, since such a classification would have to include many items that more properly belong in the lexicon of the language than in the grammar of the language. The following list will therefore give only the more common meanings that prepositions can have. Many of these meanings correspond to the adverbial meanings already given in the chapter on adverbs. Some meanings however are common only to prepositions.

Physical Relationships

TIME

---

**One point of time.**

| | |
|---|---|
| on | I saw him *on* Saturday. (**On** used with a day of the week) |
| | I saw him *on* September 16 (**On** used with a day of the month) |
| | **On** as a preposition of time may be omitted—I saw him Saturday. |
| at | I saw him *at* noon (or night, midnight). (**At** used with a part of the day considered as a point) |
| | But: He heard strange noises *in* (or *during*) the night. (**In** or **during** here imply duration rather than a point) |
| | I saw him *at* five o'clock. (**At** used with an hour of the day) |
| | Occasionally, in informal usage, **at** may be omitted—I saw him five o'clock. |
| in | I saw him *in* September. (**In** used with a month) |
| | I saw him *in* 1968. (**In** used with a year) |
| | I saw him *in* the morning (or **afternoon, evening**). (**In** used with a part of the day) |
| | I saw him *in* the spring (or **summer, autumn, winter**). (**In** used with a season) |

**Extended Time.   Starting at one point and ending at another (duration).**

| | |
|---|---|
| since | I have not seen him *since* Monday. (**Since** gives the beginning point. If it is used with the present perfect tense, the end point is *now*). |
| by | I can see you *by* Monday. (**By** implies *no later than, at any time up to this point*.) |
| from—to (or until, till) | I can see you *from* ten o'clock *to* two o'clock. A beginning point with **from** generally requires an end point with **to**. But: From now on (or **from ten o'clock on**), I will study very hard; From then on I studied very hard. |
| | If only the end point is given, **until** is used—**I cannot see you *until* five o'clock**. In speech, **till** is frequently heard. |
| for | I can see you *for* one hour. (**For** gives a quantity of time. It is usually accompanied by a number (**I waited for *two* hours**) or by an adjective of indefinite quantity (**I haven't seen him for *some* time; He has been working very hard for *many* weeks**). In informal use, **for** may be omitted before a number (**I waited two hours**). |
| during | I can see you *during* the week. (**During** gives a block of time, usually thought of as undivided.) |
| in *or* within | I can see you *in* an hour from now. (**In** gives a quantity of time before which something will happen.) |
| | The population has doubled *in* the last ten years. (**In** corresponds to **during**, but is used with a quantity rather than with a single block of time. With a word like **decade** that denotes an expanse of time, **in** or **during** may be used, depending on whether the time is felt as a quantity or as a single block of time—**The population has doubled *in* (or *during*) the last decade.** |

**Sequence of time.   Events that follow one another.**

| | |
|---|---|
| before | I will see you *before* Wednesday. (The event *precedes* the time given in the **before** phrase.) |
| | **Prior to** is a literary equivalent of **before**. |

after            I will see you *after* Wednesday. (The event *follows* the time given in the
                       **after** phrase.)
                       **Subsequent to** is a literary equivalent of **after.**

Prepositions of time may introduce not only adverbial prepositional phrases, as in those just given, but they may also introduce adjective phrases that modify nouns or pronouns.

> *on September 16*
> *The meeting*    *at five o'clock*   ⎫    *has been canceled.*
> *in September*        ⎬
>                     ⎭

### PLACE—POSITION AND DIRECTION

**Position**
(a) The point itself

in *or* inside    Hang your coat *in* the closet. (**In** gives the area of something enclosed—
                   a container, a drawer, a room, a building, the world).
                   There was no one *inside* the house. (**Inside** emphasizes the containment.)

on             Put the dishes *on* the table. (**On** indicates the surface of something—a
                   floor, a wall, a ceiling, a desk, a street).
                   **On top of**—He's standing *on top of* the desk. (**On top of** emphasizes
                   the uppermost horizontal surface. It is used with an object that has
                   some height.)

at             He's *at* school (*at* church, *at* the store). (**At** refers to a general vicinity.
                   Mere presence at a place is indicated.)
                   **At** is also used for addresses with street numbers—He lives *at* 200 Park
                   Avenue (but He lives *on* Park Avenue).

After the verb **arrive, at** refers to a place *smaller than a city or town*— **He has arrived at the airport** (or **the station, the library**); **in** refers to a place *larger than a city or town*—**He arrived in California** (or **Brazil, Europe**). For a city, **in** is more usual, but **at** may also be used, especially in reference to traveling—**the plane arrived in** (or **at**) **Singapore an hour late.**

(b) Higher or lower than a point
*Higher*

over          The plane flew *over* the mountains. (**Over** is felt to be *generally* higher
                   than a point)

above        He lives on the floor *above* us. (**Above** is felt to be *directly* higher than
                   a point.)
                   This distinction between **over** and **above** is not always carefully
                   observed.

*Lower*

under        A subway runs *under* this street. (**Under** is felt to be *generally* lower than
                   a point.)

| | |
|---|---|
| underneath | He swept the dirt **under(neath)** the rug. (**Underneath** expresses the idea of *close under*, especially so as to be hidden.) |
| beneath | ***Beneath*** a tree lay a dog fast asleep. (**Beneath** expresses the idea of directly under, with some space between) |
| below | He lives on the floor ***below*** us. (**Below** is felt to be *directly* lower than a point.) |
| | The distinction between **under** and **below** is not always carefully maintained. |

(c) Neighboring the point

| | |
|---|---|
| near | He lives *near* the university. (**Near** has the most general meaning of neighboring a point.) **By** is a synonym for **near**. **Close to** means very near. |
| next to | The theater is right ***next to*** the post office. (with nothing else between them) |
| alongside | The tug pulled up ***alongside*** the tanker. (adjoining persons or things considered as lined up, or side by side) |
| beside | He sat ***beside*** his wife during the party. (on one side of a person or thing that has two sides) |
| between | He sat ***between*** his two sons. (on each side of a person or thing that has two sides) If more than two persons or things are positioned around a point, **among** is used—**He sat *among* all his grandchildren.** [1] |
| opposite | The museum is just ***opposite*** the post office. (directly facing someone or something else) |

---

**Direction (Movement in regard to a point)**

The kind of movement designated by each preposition given below is illustrated by the diagram below.

to—from
He always walks *to* school *from* his home.

---

[1] This distinction between **between** and **among** is often made even for uses other than physical position. For example, formal usage requires **among** for more than two persons or things after such words as **distribute, divide, choose**—**He divided his money equally *among* his four children.** In informal usage, **between** also occurs here—**He divided his money equally between his four children.** However, the distinction between **between** and **among** cannot be maintained after other words, where the use of **between** is practically idiomatic—**to judge** (or **discriminate**) **between the three candidates; a similarity** (or **difference, distinction**) **between the three men; a relationship** (or **agreement, treaty**) **between the three nations.**

toward(s)

The pilgrims headed *toward(s)* Mecca.

away from

They moved *away from* their old neighborhood.

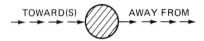

in(to)—out of

He ran *into* the house quickly. After a few minutes he ran *out of* the house with an umbrella under his arm.

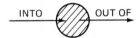

up—down

He climbed *up* (or *down*) the stairs.

around

The ship sailed *around* the island.

through

You can drive *through* that town in an hour.

past (or by)
He walked *past* (or *by*) his old schoolhouse without stopping.

PAST

as far as (up to)
We'll walk only **as far as (up to)** the old schoolhouse. Then we'll turn back.

AS FAR AS

---

Many of these prepositions of place can also begin adjective phrases
that modify a noun or pronoun.

> *The cabinet above the sink is very dirty.*
>
> *Everyone in the room was shocked by his remarks.*
>
> *The parade from Wall Street uptown*
> *     up the hill*
> *  around the town* } *is a long one.*
> *  through* (or *past*) *the town*

### Other Semantic Relationships

Many of the prepositions listed below introduce phrases that are adverbial
clause equivalents.

Those prepositions that introduce only adverbial phrases are marked **adv.**;
those that introduce only adjective phrases are marked **adj.**; and those that
introduce either type of phrase are marked **adv., adj.**

CAUSE OR REASON (ADV): *because of, for*[2], *for the sake of, on account of*

> ***Because of** his selfishness he has very few friends.*
>
> *He went to the spa **for** (**the sake of**) his health.*

**For lack of** or **for want of** might be considered as negative prepositions of cause—

---

[2] A **for** prepositional phrase is adjectival when used after the word **reason**—**His reasons for refusing such a good offer do not seem convincing.**

**During the war many children died for lack** (or **want**) **of food. (For lack of food** is
the equivalent of **because they didn't have food.**)
**As a result** (or **consequence**) **of** gives the reason for a resulting action—**As a result
of the engineer's carelessness, many people were injured.**
**What with** is an informal equivalent of **because of**—**What with all these reports to
do, I have to work overtime every night.**

CONCESSION (ADV): *in spite of, despite* (formal), *notwithstanding* (formal),
*regardless of*

> Helen Keller succeeded in life **in spite of** her physical handicaps.

> He went ahead **regardless of** all warnings about the danger of his mission.

**Irregardless,** which is sometimes used for **regardless,** is not considered an acceptable
form.
**With** may also express concession—**With all his faults, she still loves him.**

CONDITION (ADV): *in case of, in (the) event of*

> **In case of** (or **in the event of**) rain, the picnic will be canceled.

(See prepositions of *possession and origin* for the use of **with** in the combined sense
of condition and possession.)

PURPOSE (ADV): *for, for the purpose of*

> She went to the grocery store **for** milk.

> He came to the United States **for the purpose of** setting up a business
> office there.

**For the purpose of** usually requires the gerund form of the verb. It is a more emphatic
expression of purpose than the infinitive form **to** or **in order to.**

ACCOMPANIMENT (ADV, ADJ): *with, along with, together with*

> He went (**together, along**) **with** his wife to do the shopping.

ADDITION (ADJ): *as well as*

> John, **as well as** his wife Mary, has often expressed a desire to live in
> Europe.

In this use, **as well as** is a prepositional equivalent of the conjunction **and**—**John
and his wife Mary have often expressed a desire to live in Europe.** The prepositional
forms for addition are usually set off with commas and do not affect the form
of the verb, which agrees with the first noun only. These prepositional forms are
used when emphasis on the idea of addition is desired.

COMPARISON (ADV, ADJ): *like, as*

> He is living **like** a millionaire.

> He conducts himself **like** a king.

> Bold **as** a lion, he leaped into the fray.[3]

---

[3] Many comparisons of this type have become clichés because of overuse and should be
avoided. Other such trite comparisons are—**cool as a cucumber, sly as a fox, wise as an
owl, cold as ice, busy as a bee, white as a sheet.** In formal English **as** also appears before
the word being compared—**as cool as a cucumber, as sly as a fox.**

DEGREE (ADV): *according to*

> From each **according to** his abilities, to each **according to** his needs.
> (Karl Marx)

INSTRUMENT (ADV): *with*

> He cut the meat **with** a sharp knife.

MEANS (ADV): *with, by (means of)*

> You can get there **by** subway (or bus, train, plane).

> He has worked his way up to the top **by** (**means of**) hard work.

MANNER (ADV): *with*

> He always does his work **with** great care (=carefully or in a careful manner).

**Like** used for comparison after verbs of action like **act, behave, live** also conveys a strong degree of manner—**She acts like a martyr.** In informal or popular speech, **like** may replace a conjunction of manner—**It looks like** (=**as if**) **it may snow soon; The battle turned out like** (=**as**) **he had predicted.**

IN THE CAPACITY OF (ADV): *as*

> **As** a man of science he was admirable; **as** a husband he was less so.

> A gerund phrase functions **as** a noun.

MATERIAL (ADV, ADJ): *of, out of, from*

> This table is made **of** (or **out of**) mahogany.

> She made herself a dress **from** (or **out of**) an old lace curtain.

SOURCE (ADV, ADJ): *from*

> We get honey **from** bees.

> The honey **from** these bees is very expensive.

SEPARATION (ADV, ADJ): *from, with*

> Two inmates escaped **from** prison last night.

> He is always reluctant to part **with** his money.

POSSESSION OR ORIGIN (ADJ): *of*

> The father **of** the bride was very nervous at the wedding.

> The song **of** the nightingale has been much celebrated in English poetry.

**With** and its negative **without** may imply the kind of possession denoted by the verb **have.**

> ADJ: The girl **with** the red hair (=the girl having or who has red hair) is very pretty.

> She doesn't want to marry a man **without** money. (=a man not having or who doesn't have money)

Occasionally **with** may be the equivalent of **have** in a sense other than possession— **the girl with the blue dress on** (=**the girl having** or **who has the blue dress on**).

> ADV: With enough life insurance (=if he has enough life insurance), a man will worry less about leaving his family destitute.

> Without money (=if one does not have money) one cannot live.

Used in an adverbial phrase, **with** or **without** often combines a conditional meaning with the sense of **have**.

PARTITION (ADJ): *of*
> *Some **of** the guests stayed for dinner; the rest **of** the guests went home.*

APPOSITION (ADJ): *of*
> *The city **of** New York is governed by a mayor and a city council.*

CHARACTERIZED BY (ADJ): *of*
> *He is a man **of** the highest reputation.*
> *This is a matter **of** great importance.*

ARITHMETICAL FUNCTIONS (ADJ): *plus, minus*
> *Two **plus** three equal(s) five.*

EXCEPTION (ADV, ADJ): *except (for), but (for), save (for), apart from*
> *Everyone came **but** you.*
> ***Except for** a slight limp, he has fully recovered from his terrible automobile accident.*

REFERENCE (ADV, ADJ): *with (or in) regard to, with (or in) respect to, with (or in) reference to, regarding, as to, as for*
> ***With reference to** your recent letter, we regret to learn that the goods arrived in damaged condition.*
> *Your letter **regarding** the damaged goods has just been received.*

EXAMPLE (ADJ): *like, (such) as*
> *An adjective is used after a verb **like** (or **such as**) seem, appear, become.*

## FUNCTION OF PREPOSITIONS

The preposition has the function of connecting a noun or a pronoun to another word, usually a noun, verb or adjective.

> Sentence: *The girl **with the red hair** is beautiful.*

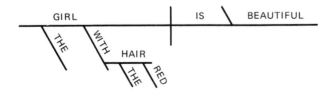

**With** connects **hair** with the *noun* **girl**.

Sentence: *They arrived **in the morning.***

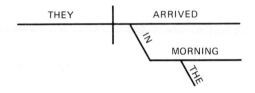

**In** connects **morning** with the *verb* **arrived**.

Sentence: *She is fond **of roses.***

**Of** connects **roses** with the *adjective* **fond**.

Other nominals than nouns or pronouns that may be joined to a sentence by prepositions are:

| | |
|---|---|
| Gerund phrases | The jeweler did not object to ***showing the diamond ring to her.*** |
| Noun clauses | The jeweler showed the diamond ring to ***whoever might be a potential buyer.*** |

After a verb of motion, a preposition of position or direction may be used without a noun object. Such a prepositional form is usually classified as an adverb.

| | |
|---|---|
| *Preposition* | He fell ***down*** the stairs. |
| | Please come ***in*** the house. |
| *Adverb* | He fell ***down.*** |
| | Please come ***in.*** |

In the spoken language these two prepositional forms are stressed differently.

*He féll down the stáirs.* (***Down*** as a preposition is unstressed)

*He féll dówn.* (***Down*** as an adverb is stressed)

### VERB-PREPOSITION COMBINATIONS

A preposition may combine with a verb to form a new vocabulary item. This verb-preposition combination goes by several names—two-part verbs, composite verbs, phrasal verbs. The prepositional form used with the verb may be referred to as an adverb, a prepositional adverb (or preposition-adverb) or by the more general term "particle."[4]

The verbs in such combinations are mostly one-syllable words; the most common prepositions are those denoting place—**in, out, on, off, over, up, down, through.**

Some of these verb-preposition combinations may be separated by their objects (**Please** *hand in* **your paper** or **please** *hand* **your paper** *in*); others are nonseparable (*call on* **one's neighbors;** *run across* **an old friend**).

Listed below are some of the more common verb-preposition combinations. Those that are intransitive are marked *Intrans.;* those that are nonseparable are marked **NS.** It is of course impossible in a book of this size to include all verb-preposition combinations or even to give all the uses of those that have been included. Fuller listings and explanations of these verbs are given in such dictionaries of idioms as:

Harold C. Whitford and Robert J. Dixson, HANDBOOK OF AMERICAN IDIOMS AND IDIOMATIC USAGE (New York: Regents Publishing Co., 1953)

Thomas Crowell, INDEX TO MODERN ENGLISH (section on prepositions), or A GLOSSARY OF PREPOSITIONS WITH PHRASES (New York: McGraw-Hill Book Co., 1964)

W. McMordie, ENGLISH IDIOMS AND HOW TO USE THEM (London: Oxford University Press, 1954)

BRING :  bring about—*cause*
*I wonder what **brought about** his strange behavior?*

bring on—*result in*
*His long exposure in the rain **brought on** a bad cold.*

bring up—*raise a subject*
*He **brings up** that subject at every opportunity.*

—*rear*
*They **brought up** their children to behave well.*

CALL :  call up—*telephone*
*He **calls up** his wife from the office every day.*

call (up)on (NS)—*visit* [5]
*We'll **call on** you tonight.*

call down—*reprimand*
*He was **called down** by his boss for laziness.*

call off—*cancel*
*The ball game was **called off** because of rain.*

---

[4] The *Standard College Dictionary* defines particle as "a short, uninflected part of speech, as an article, preposition, interjection, or conjunction."

[5] Where a choice between **on** or **upon** is possible, **upon** has a more formal effect.

COME:     come up (NS, Intrans.)—*arise*
          *A serious problem has just come up.*

          come out (NS, Intrans.)—*be published*
          *The new grammar book will come out in August.*

          come to (NS, Intrans.)—*total*
          *How much do these purchases come to?*

                              —*regain consciousness*
          *He fainted from the heat, but he soon came to.*

DO:       do over—*redo, redecorate*
          *We plan to do over our entire apartment.*

          do without (NS)—*sacrifice, not need*
          *No one can do without sleep.*

GET:      get up (NS, Intrans.)—*wake up*
          *What time do you get up in the morning?*

          get over (NS)—*recover from*
          *It took him a long time to get over his cold.*

GIVE:     give up—*surrender*
          (Intrans.)  *The enemy gave up after a long battle.*
          (Trans.)  *The enemy gave up the fort after a long battle.*

          give out—*distribute*
          *Please give out these papers to all the students.*

GO:       go over (NS)—*review, rehearse*
          *The actors went over their parts.*

          go with (NS)—*harmonize*
          *That hat goes with the color of her eyes.*

                              —*date*
          *Mary has been going with John for a year.*

HAND:     hand in—*submit*
          *Assignments should be handed in on time.*

          hand down—*transmit*
          *This ring has been handed down for generations.*

HOLD:     hold up—*rob*
          *Our gasoline station was held up last night.*

                    —*delay*
          *What could be holding up the delivery of the mail?*

          hold down—*suppress*
          *When people are held down too long, they often rebel.*

KEEP:     keep on (NS)—*continue*
          *If he keeps on coming late to work he'll be fired.*

keep off (NS)—*refrain from going on*
**Keep off** the grass.

**Keep off** may also be causative—**Keep your dog off the lawn.** Other combinations with **keep** that may have causative force are:

keep out

keep back

keep away

*Keep out of this room* (meaning, do not enter this room).

vs.  *Keep your dog out of this room* (meaning, restrain your dog from entering this room).[6]

LOOK:  look after (NS)—*take care of*
*While we're gone, Grandmother will look after the children.*

look over—*review*
*Before the test, he looked over his notes carefully.*

look up—*search for information*, usually in a dictionary, encyclopedia, telephone directory, or some other source of written information
*I must look up that word in the dictionary.*

MAKE:  make out—*understand*
*I can't make out what he really wants.*

*make up—become reconciled* (Intrans.)
*They had a quarrel, but they soon made up.*

*—put on cosmetics*
*Give me a few minutes to make up.*

*—invent*
*That story is a lie. It was made up on the spur of the moment.*

PASS:  pass out—*faint, lose consciousness* (NS, Intrans.)
*He passed out from the heat.*

*—distribute*
*Please pass out these papers.*

pass up—*neglect to take advantage of*
*He passed up a good job because of poor health.*

PICK:  pick on (NS)—*annoy, tease*
*Stop picking on your little brother.*

pick out—*select*
*Please pick out a nice tie for me.*

PUT:  put off—*postpone*
*Don't put off for tomorrow what you can do today.*

---

[6] Note that in such causatives with **keep**, the object must come between the two parts of the verb.

put on—*don* (clothes)
*She'll **put on** her best dress for the dance tonight.*

put out—*extinguish*
***Put out** your cigarette before you go into the elevator.*

RUN:  run across (NS)—*meet or find by chance*
*On the subway I **ran across** an old acquaintance.*

run down (NS)—*say unkind things about*
*If she keeps on **running down** her friends, she won't have any left.*

run over—*(get) hit by a car*
*The child was **run over** by a truck.*

TAKE:  take after (NS)—*resemble*
*She **takes after** her mother in everything she does.*

take over—*assume control*
*In time of war the government may **take over** all means of transportation.*

take up—*consider, discuss*
*We are **taking up** prepositions this week.*

TURN:  turn down—*reject*
*Their bid was **turned down** because it was too high.*

turn off—*stop some kind of power*
*Please **turn off** the light (gas, stove, radio, tv, record player)*

turn on—*start some kind of power*
*Please **turn on** the light (gas, stove, radio, tv, record player).*

turn out (NS, Intrans.)—*happen*
*The fortune teller's prediction **turned out** right.*

turn up (NS, Intrans.)—*appear*
*He always **turns up** when we least expect him.*

Nouns that follow the type of verb-preposition combinations given above may become subjects of passive constructions.

| Active | Passive |
|---|---|
| The students handed in *the test papers*. | *The test papers* were handed in by the students. |
| They called off *the game*. | *The game* was called off. |
| The company turned down *the bid*. | *The bid* was turned down by the company. |

For this reason, these verb-preposition combinations may be regarded as transitive verbs.

Some of the verb-preposition combinations function transitively in one of their meanings and intransitively in another of their meanings.

| *Transitive* | *Intransitive* |
|---|---|
| Take off your shoes. (**Take off** means *remove.*) | The plane will take off in ten minutes. (**Take off** means *leave the ground.*) |
| We must break down these figures accurately. (**Break down** means *make an analysis of.*) | My car broke down last night. (**Break down** means *go out of order.*) |
| Please pass out these papers. (**Pass out** means *distribute.*) | He passed out from the heat. (**Pass out** means *faint, lose consciousness.*) |

Other verb-preposition combinations are transitive only when they are used as causatives:

| *Intransitive* | *Transitive* |
|---|---|
| I usually wake up at nine o'clock. | The loud noise woke me up. (=caused me to wake up) |
| Keep out please. | Keep your dog out. (=cause your dog to keep out) |

With separable verbs, a personal pronoun object *must* be placed between the verb and the prepositional form.

> *Take off **your shoes**.*
> or   *Take **your shoes** off.*
> but   *Take **them** off.*

> *We must break down **these figures** accurately.*
> or   *We must break **these figures** down accurately.*
> but   *We must break **them** down accurately.*

Other types of pronouns are also usually placed between the two parts of a separable verb—**put** *this* **on, pick** *one* (or *some, a few*) **out**—but, sometimes **pick out** *one*.

If an object has long modification, it is used only after the two parts of the separable verb.

> *Take off **those tight shoes that are hurting you so much**.*
> *We must break down **all the figures that might be questioned by the auditor**.*

Certain verbs combine with prepositions that merely intensify the action of the verb, or that emphasize the completion of the action—**eat up, finish up, clean up, drink down, add up, type up, fasten down, gather in, freeze over.**

> *Let's **finish** (**up**) our work quickly and then go to a movie.*
> *He **drank** (**down**) the whiskey at one gulp.*
> *It will take hours to **clean** (**up**) this room.*

FUNCTION OF PREPOSITIONAL PHRASES

Many prepositional phrases, like the complex syntactic structures that will be considered later, function on two levels. One level is the purely physical arrangement of prepositional phrases in relation to a head word. On this level we find that some prepositional phrases function as adjectival modifiers and others as adverbial modifiers. The other level is based on a deeper kind of relationship—the relationship of elements in a simple sentence, especially the subject and complement. Some of the adjectival prepositional phrases are also involved in this function; the nominals given below are involved only in this function. In the pages that follow we will take into consideration both the more superficial level of the modifying function and the deeper level of the predication function.

Nominal Function

**Prepositional Object**

Many prepositions used after verbs are not actually part of the verb but are required before a noun can follow the verb—**dispose** *of* **the goods; wait** *for* **John; recover** *from* **pneumonia; listen** *to* **the radio.** Following the practice of some traditional grammars, we are referring to such prepositional phrases that follow verbs as "prepositional objects."

Sometimes it is difficult to distinguish these verbs that take prepositional objects from nonseparable two-part verbs. Both types of verb, for example, require that the preposition remain with the verb in passive and verbal constructions.

|  | *Verb-Preposition Combinations* | *Verbs Plus Prepositional Objects* |
|---|---|---|
| Passive | All the lessons were gone *over* carefully. | He was laughed *at* by everybody. |
|  | Here are the papers that must be given *out*. | He was highly thought *of*. |
| Verbals | The lessons to be gone *over* are very difficult. | That is nothing to laugh *at*. |
|  | Here are the papers to be given *out*. | Everybody would like to be highly thought *of*. |

In the spoken language, however, there is a difference between these two types of verbs:

| Verb-preposition combinations | Please túrn ón the light. (The prepositional form as well as the verb is stressed.) |
|---|---|
| Verbs plus prepositional objects | You can cóunt on mé. (The prepositional form is unstressed. Compare with **She líves on the bóulevard,** which contains an adverbial prepositional phrase.) |

The following list of verbs that take prepositional objects has been arranged according to the preposition that is required. Some of these prepositions retain a degree of their physical meaning. For example, with certain verbs, **at** implies direction *toward* (**glance at, spring at, look at**); **from** implies *separation from* (**flee from, escape from**) or *source* (**collect from, abstain from**); **with** implies *association with* (**cooperate with, join with**) or *separation* (**part with, fight with**). For this reason we cannot always draw a distinct line between prepositional objects and adverbial prepositional phrases.

(Verbs that may also be used with direct objects without prepositions [sometimes with other meanings] are marked *also* **DO**.)

### AT

| | |
|---|---|
| connive | rebel (*usually with the gerund*) |
| frown (*or* on, upon) | rejoice (*or* over) |
| gaze (*or* on, upon) | shudder |
| glance | smile (*or* on, upon) |
| grasp | snap |
| hint | sneer |
| jeer | spring |
| laugh | stare |
| look | wink |
| marvel | wonder (*or* about) |
| point | |

*All the children were laughing at the antics of the clown.*

*The mother looked at her child tenderly.*

*I shudder at the thought of another world war.*

### OF

admit (*also* **DO**)
beware
consist (*in the sense of* be composed of; **in** *usually with the gerund*)
despair (*only with the gerund*)
(dis)approve
dispose
dream (*or* about)
repent
smell (*also* **DO**)
talk (*or* about)
think (*or* about)

*The boy's mother disapproves of his late hours.*

*Water consists of hydrogen and oxygen.*

*They finally disposed of all the old rubbish in the attic.*

FOR

| | |
|---|---|
| atone | mourn |
| call (*also* **DO**) | pray |
| care (for someone, about something) | qualify (*also* **DO**) |
| clamor | shop |
| crave | strive |
| cry | suffice |
| grieve (for someone, over *or* about something) | thirst |
| hope | wait |
| long | watch (*also* **DO**) |
| look | wish |

*I'll wait for you until ten o'clock.*

*We all hope for a better world.*

*Please look for the letter you lost.*

TO

| | |
|---|---|
| accede | listen |
| accrue | object |
| adhere | point |
| allude | reply |
| appeal | resort |
| aspire | respond |
| assent | revert |
| conform | subscribe |
| consent | yield |
| defer (*meaning show respect to*) | |

*Which radio programs do you listen to?*

*Pearls have always appealed to me.*

*I subscribe to several news magazines.*

ON, UPON

| | |
|---|---|
| act | impose (*also* **DO**) |
| agree (agree on something, *but* agree with someone about something) | insist |
| | knock |
| border | lecture (*or* about) |
| count | live |
| decide | plan |
| depend | operate (*also* **DO**) |
| devolve | reflect |
| embark | rely |
| encroach | shine |
| exist | resolve |
| feed (*also* **DO**) | |

*It is not wise to impose on one's friends.*

*The doctor will operate on the patient immediately.*

*He insisted on paying the check for everybody.*

## WITH

| | |
|---|---|
| associate (*also* **DO**) | interfere (with a person, in a matter) |
| coincide | join (*also* do) |
| cooperate | meddle |
| consult (*also* **DO**) | part |
| cope | rank (*also* **DO**) |
| deal | side |
| dispense | unite (*also* **DO**) |
| expostulate | vie |

*I will cooperate with you completely.*

*No one can dispense with money altogether.*

*There are some problems that children cannot cope* (or *deal*) *with.*

## FROM

abstain

cease (*usually with a gerund or infinitive; also* **DO**—*Cease your chatter.*)

desist

deter

deviate

differ

dissent

emerge

escape

flee

recede

recoil

recover (*meaning get well; otherwise* **DO**)

refrain (*usually with a gerund*)

result (from *means cause,* in *means effect*)

retire

shrink

suffer

withdraw

*He withdrew from the club after a quarrel with the president* (*but he withdrew all his money from the bank.*)

*She was suffering from a bad cold.*

*Every once in a while we saw the dolphin emerge from the water.*

## IN

| | |
|---|---|
| abound | engage |
| acquiesce | excel |
| believe | indulge |
| concur | participate |
| confide | persevere |
| consist | persist |
| deal | result |
| delight | succeed (*also* **DO**, *in the sense of follow*) |
| end | |

*All the children participated in the game.*

*I hope you will succeed in your work.*

*That boy excels in all sports.*

### FOR or AGAINST

contend

declare

demonstrate

fight

strike

vote

*I shall vote for* (or *against*) *the proposal.*

*We are fighting for a good cause.*

### BETWEEN

arbitrate

discriminate

distinguish

intervene

judge

*Sometimes it is difficult to distinguish between good and evil.*

*We must learn to discriminate between our friends and our acquaintances.*

### AGAINST

immunize (*also* **DO**)

plot

rebel

strive

struggle

*A vaccine has been found to immunize people against polio.*

### INTO

transform

turn

*Clothes can transform a Cinderella into a princess.*

### OVER

reign

rule (over *may be omitted*)

*He ruled (over) his people with an iron hand.*

Some of the prepositions used after the verbs given above are modern equivalents of inflectional endings once used with the objects of these verbs. Thus **of** represents an older genitive ending; **to, for, from, on** represent former dative endings.

Prepositional objects may also be used with two-part verbs. Such verbs are usually nonseparable.

BEAR DOWN ON: *put pressure on*
  *Unless his boss bears down **on** him, he is very lax about his work.*

BEAR UP UNDER (or AGAINST): *withstand*
  *He has borne up well **under** the most trying circumstances.*

DROP IN ON: *visit unannounced or informally*
  *Please drop in **on** me whenever you are in town.*

DROP OUT OF: *discontinue (membership, attendance)*
  *It's unfortunate that he dropped out **of** school in his last semester.*

FALL OUT WITH SOMEONE ABOUT (or OVER) SOMETHING: *quarrel with someone about (over) something*
  *He fell out **with** his partner about the amount of work each was to do.*

GET ALONG WITH: *agree*
  *He's so easy-going that he gets along **with** everybody.*

GET OUT OF: 1. *go away from*
  *Let's get out **of** town before the summer heat begins.*
          2. *avoid keeping a promise or obligation*
  *He won't get out **of** that contract very easily.*

GET TOGETHER WITH: *meet informally*
  *When I get together **with** some of the other club members, I'll bring up your proposal.*

GIVE IN TO: *surrender, accede to someone's wishes*
  *Parents who give in **to** children too often will have spoiled children.*

GO ALONG WITH: *accept*
  *That proposal seems reasonable. I'll go along **with** it.*

GO BACK ON: *fail to fulfill a commitment*
  *He promised to pay his share, but he has gone back **on** his word.*

GO ON WITH: *continue*
  *She plans to go on **with** her studies at the university.*

GO THROUGH WITH: *carry out an intention*
  *He has tackled a very hard job, and we hope he will have the strength to go through **with** it.*

KEEP UP WITH: *maintain the same pace*
  *Even though John has been ill, he has kept up **with** the others in his class.*

LOOK DOWN ON: *consider as inferior*
  *We should not look down **on** a person just because he is poor.*

LOOK UP TO: *consider as superior*
  *Everyone looks up **to** a great scientist like Einstein.*

MAKE OFF WITH: *run away with*
>The robbers made off **with** a huge sum of money.

PUT UP WITH: *tolerate*
>I don't think I can put up **with** all this noise much longer.

Some set combinations of verb and object also take prepositional objects.

>What has given rise **to** his sudden desire for great wealth?
>
>Stop that clowning. Don't make such a fool **of** yourself before others.
>
>Her husband was just hurt in a car accident. It will be hard to break the news **to** her.

A few idioms consisting of verb plus prepositional phrase take prepositional objects.

>He fell in love **with** a beautiful girl.
>
>The gangster lay in wait **for** his victim.

### Verbs with Two Objects

Many verbs take two objects, one or both of which may be prepositional.

## Direct Object
## and Prepositional Object

The direct object usually denotes a person, a group of persons, or a unit consisting of persons.

(In the list that follows, verbs that may also be used without the direct object are marked *also no* **DO**.)

#### PREPOSITIONAL OBJECT WITH *OF*

accuse
acquit
convict
cure
deprive
persuade
rob
suspect

>He accused his bookkeeper of falsifying the records.
>
>We must persuade him of the importance of attending all meetings.
>
>We will not allow any dictator to deprive our people of their basic civil rights.

#### PREPOSITIONAL OBJECT WITH *OF* OR *ABOUT*

advise
convince
remind
warn

*We will advise you of* (or *about*) *the time of the meeting.*

*Please remind me of* (or *about*) *the time of the meeting.* (meaning, *help me to remember*) but:

*He reminds me of my brother* (meaning, *he brings to mind memories of my brother*). **About** is not used in this sense.

## PREPOSITIONAL OBJECT WITH *ABOUT*

> ask (*also no* **DO**)
> consult (*or* **with—on**)
> question

*I have consulted* (*with*) *my lawyer about the will.*

*He asked some questions about the meeting.* (**Ask** may also have *three* objects—*He asked me some questions about the meeting.*)

## PREPOSITIONAL OBJECTS WITH *FROM*

> absolve
> abstract
> borrow (*also no* **DO**)
> buy
> collect (*also no* **DO**)
> conceal
> deduce
> defend
> deter (**from** *only with the gerund*)
> discourage (**from** *only with the gerund*)
> dismiss
> distinguish
> divert
> eliminate
> exclude
> hide
> hinder (**from** *only with the gerund*)
> import (*also no* **DO**)
> keep
> preserve
> prevent (**from** *only with the gerund*)
> prohibit (**from** *only with the gerund*)
> protect
> remove
> rescue
> request (or **of**)
> save
> shield
> stop (**from** *only with the gerund*)

*He concealed the money from his wife.*

*Nothing can discourage him from going ahead with his plans.*

*I would like to buy that ring from you.*

With some of these verbs, the **from** phrase may precede the direct object, especially if the direct object has some modification, or if the reference of the phrase will be ambiguous otherwise.

*He concealed from his wife the money he had won at Las Vegas.*

*Dismiss from the company anyone who takes bribes.*

### PREPOSITIONAL OBJECT WITH *FOR*

ask (*also no* **DO**; *also,* ask something of someone)
beg (*also no* **DO**; *also* beg something of someone)
blame
charge
compensate (*also no* **DO**)
condemn
forgive[7]
pardon[7]
prepare
purchase
reprimand
reproach
scold
search (*also no* **DO**)
substitute (*also no* **DO**)

*May I ask you for a favor (or May I ask a favor of you)?*

*He blames everyone for his failure except himself.*

*The police searched the house for the missing jewels but they found nothing.*

### PREPOSITIONAL OBJECT WITH *ON*

base
bestow
inflict
stick
paste

*The government has bestowed many honors on that general.*

*On what do you base such a belief?*

With **bestow, inflict,** a short **on** phrase may precede the direct object—
**The government bestowed on him many honors.**

---

[7] Sometimes **for** is omitted, especially in older English:

*Our Father who art in Heaven,*

*Forgive us our debts, as we forgive our debtors.*

burden
confuse
connect
entrust (*or* entrust someone—something to someone)
exchange (*or* with someone for something, *or* exchange something for
    something)
furnish (*or* furnish something to someone)
help (*also no* **DO**)
present (*or* present something to)
provide (*or* provide something to)
supply (*or* supply something to)

> *When he retired, his company presented him with many gifts* (or *presented
> many gifts to him*).
>
> *May I exchange this newspaper with you?* (or *May I exchange this newspaper
> for another one?*)
>
> *I can furnish you with everything* (or *I can furnish everything to you*).

With some verbs that take two objects, the first object is a reflexive
pronoun, the second is a prepositional object.

> absent oneself from
> ally oneself with *or* to
> defend onself against
> familiarize oneself with
> free oneself from (*or* of)
> pride oneself on
> separate oneself from

## Two Prepositional Objects

> (dis)agree (*also* with—on)
> argue (*also* with—over)
> confer (*also* with—regarding)
> consult (*also* with—regarding)
> contend (*also* with—against)
> converse (*also* with—on)
> correspond (*also* with—regarding)
> differ (*also* with—on *or* concerning)
> dispute (*also* with—over)
> fight (*also* with—over)
> gossip
> jest
> joke
> quarrel (*also* with—over)

quibble
reason
speak (*also* to—about *or* regarding)
talk (*also* to—about *or* regarding)

*He likes to joke with his wife about everything.*

*He quarreled with his neighbor about* (or *over*) *a parcel of land they both claimed.*

*I'll speak with* (or *to*) *him about* (or *concerning*) *the money he owes me.*

If the object of **about** is short, it may be used informally before the **with** phrase.

*He likes to joke about everything with his wife.*

*She was gossiping about the new neighbor with her friend.*

OF (ABOUT)—TO  (Less commonly with the TO phrase first. The object of TO usually denotes a person.)

boast
brag
complain
talk

*The patient complained about the food to the nurse.*

*He bragged about his son to everyone.*

Less commonly:
*The patient complained to the nurse about the food.*

*He bragged to everyone about his son.*

FROM—TO

referring to a change in form:

alter
change (*also* from—into)
transform (*also* from—into)
translate (*also* from—into, *or sometimes* into—from)
turn (*also* from—into)

These verbs may also have direct objects.

*She translates novels from French* (in)*to German.*

*They changed the color of the walls from beige to white.*

referring to a range in variation :

drop
range
rise
vary

*The temperature dropped from 75 degrees to 55 degrees within a few hours.*

These **from**—**to** phrases might also be considered adverbial.
With some of these verbs the **from** phrase may be omitted.

*He has changed (in)to an old man overnight.*

*He will rise to even greater heights.*

WITH—FOR  (the object of WITH is usually a person)

compete
fight
intercede
vie

*He fought (with) many rivals for the girl he loved.*

*He competed with many other students for the scholarships.*

TO—FOR

account
appeal
attend
tend

*The accountant will (at)tend to that matter for you.*

## Verbs with Direct, Indirect Objects

Indirect objects usually refer to human beings.

INDIRECT OBJECT USED WITH OR WITHOUT *TO*

| | |
|---|---|
| bring | refuse |
| deny | remit |
| give | sell |
| guarantee | send |
| hand | show |
| lend | teach |
| offer | telegraph |
| owe | telephone |
| pay | tell[8] |
| promise | throw[9] |
| refund | write |

*Please bring me that box.*

or *Please bring that box to me.*

*He wrote his wife a long letter.*

or *He wrote a long letter to his wife.*

Generally, the **to** phrase places more emphasis on the indirect object.

[8] With **tell**, the **to** phrase is not common—**He told us the whole story**; or, occasionally,
**He told the whole story to us.**

[9] **At** may be used with **throw** when the intention of striking is implied—**The boy threw a
stone** *at* **the bird. To** used with **throw** implies that the object is thrown with the intention
of being caught.

With many of these verbs the purpose of the action involved is stated in a **for** prepositional phrase.

> *The company paid the inventor a large sum of money **for** the rights to his invention.*
>
> *He sent some money to his daughter **for** her tuition.*

### INDIRECT OBJECT USED WITH OR WITHOUT *FOR*

> buy
> find
> make

> *He bought his wife a new car.*
> or  *He bought a new car for his wife.*
>
> *She made her daughter a dress.*
> or  *She made a dress for her daughter.*

A **to** or **for** phrase will be preferred if an indirect object has much modification—**They gave a generous reward to the boy who found their dog.**

A **to** or **for** indirect object may precede a long direct object.

> *Einstein gave to the world an understanding of atomic energy.*
>
> *He bought for his wife the most expensive car on the market.*

### INDIRECT OBJECT USED ONLY WITH *TO*

Although grammarians often classify the TO phrases after the following verbs as indirect objects, these phrases could with equal justification be called merely prepositional objects.

(Verbs that may also be used without a direct object are marked *also no* **DO**.)

| | |
|---|---|
| adapt (*also no* **DO**) | demonstrate |
| adjust (*also no* **DO**) | describe |
| admit | devote |
| affix | dispense |
| allot | distribute |
| apply (no **DO** in the sense of *make an application*) | entrust |
| | explain |
| appoint | formulate |
| appropriate (something to someone for something) | furnish (*or* with) |
| | hint |
| assign (sometimes also without **to**) | import |
| attribute | impute |
| bequeath | introduce |
| cede | lease (*also no* **DO**) |
| confide (*also*, confide **in**) | limit |
| consecrate | mention |
| contribute (*also no* **DO**) (**for** gives the purpose) | picture |
| | point out |
| dedicate | preach (*also no* **DO**) |

| prefer | reveal |
|---|---|
| propose | speak |
| recommend | say |
| refer (*also no* **DO**) | state |
| relate | submit (*no* **DO** *in the sense of yield*) |
| remember | suggest |
| restore | yield (*also no* **DO**) |

*The foreign student described his home town to the class.*
*Their teacher explained the new vocabulary to them.*
*The broker recommended a good stock to his client.*
*I will suggest some good books to him.*

When these verbs are used in the passive voice, the **to** is usually required (unlike the verbs in the preceding groups where the **to** is optional in the passive).

*The new vocabulary was explained to the class.*
vs. *A new assignment was given (to) the class.*

With these verbs also the **to** phrase may come first, especially if the direct object is long.

*I will suggest to him some books which I am sure he will like.*

The **to** phrase must come first if the direct object is a noun clause after the verbs **demonstrate, explain, hint, mention, preach, propose, recommend, reveal, relate, say, state, suggest**.

*The doctor explained to the patient that pneumonia was an inflammation of the lungs.*
*The police revealed to the newspapers why they had arrested that man.*

A **to** phrase used as an indirect object sometimes appears in initial position for emphasis.

*To his children he willed (or gave, sent, mailed) whatever money they needed.*
*To the many people who came to his lecture he explained how cigarette smoking caused cancer.*

## Other Nominal Functions Than Prepositional Object

| Subjective complement | She was *in tears*.[10] |
|---|---|
| | That case is *out of our jurisdiction*. |
| Objective complement | We found her *in tears*. |
| | We consider that case *out of our jurisdiction*. |
| Object of preposition | I cannot see you until *after the Christmas holidays*. |
| | The dog emerged from *under the* porch. |

[10] Note the contrast in function—In **She was in tears, in tears** is a subjective complement. In **She was in the house, in the house** is an adverbial prepositional phrase of place.

Occasionally, in informal usage, a prepositional phrase may function as a subject.

> **Over the fence** *is out.*
>
> **From ten to two** *is a good time to find me in the office.*

Adverbial Function
of Prepositional Phrases

MODIFYING A VERB.    Such prepositional phrases usually express one of the semantic relationships listed under types of prepositions.

> *I can see you* **at noon.**
>
> *Put the flowers* **in the vase.**
>
> *He was walking* **with his friend**.

MODIFYING AN ADJECTIVE.    Certain adjectives may be followed by prepositional phrases. Such phrases may be interpreted not only as modifiers but as "complements" of the adjectives.

Prepositional phrases that modify adjectives are generally used after:

| | |
|---|---|
| subjective complements | The train is **bound** for Rome. |
| appositive adjectives | The train **bound** for Rome was derailed near Frankfurt. |
| or | **Bound** for Rome, the train was derailed near Frankfurt. |

Occasionally such prepositional phrases follow adjectives used attributively with nouns.

> *He has* **enough** (or **sufficient**) *money for his trip.*
>
> *This is a* **good** (or **suitable**) *location for a restaurant.*

In the list below the adjectives that are followed by prepositional phrases are given under the preposition they require. The symbol *non-attrib.* marks those adjectives that are never (or rarely) used before nouns.

FROM

absent (non-attrib.)
different[11]
distinct
free
immune
remote
safe
separate

---

[11] In informal usage the conjunction **than** is frequently interchangeable with the preposition **from**—**He is different *than* his brother. Different to** is also used in informal British English.

## AT

angry (at, with *someone;* about *something*)
expert (*also* in)
good (at *a skill,* for *a purpose*)
present (*non-attrib.*)
quick (*also* in)
slow (*also* in)
swift (*also* in)

## FOR

(in)adequate
anxious (for *in the sense of desirous;* about *in the sense of worried*)
appropriate (*also* to *for an occasion*)
bound (*referring to destination* [*non-attrib.*])
conspicuous
eager
eligible
enough
famous
(un)fit
good
(un)grateful (to *someone* for *something*)
homesick
necessary
notorious
proper
responsible (to *someone* for *something*)
sorry
sufficient
suitable or suited (to *a person,* for *a purpose*)

## IN

deficient
efficient
proficient
rich
successful

## WITH

commensurate
comparable (to *when used metaphorically*)
compatible
complete
content
(in)consistent
(dis)contented

(un)familiar (I'm not familiar with that *but* that isn't familiar to me.)
gentle
identical (*also* to)
indignant (with *a person;* about *a thing;* at *usually with a gerund*)
(im)patient
replete (*non-attrib.*)

### (UP)ON

dependent
drunk
intent

### ABOUT (or OVER)

careful
careless
enthusiastic
happy

### OF

| | |
|---|---|
| abreast | glad (*non-attrib.*) |
| (un)afraid (*non-attrib.*) | guilty |
| (un)aware | heedful, heedless |
| boastful | hopeful |
| (in)capable | ignorant |
| careful, careless | illustrative |
| (un)certain | innocent |
| characteristic | jealous |
| cognizant (*non-attrib.*) | (un)mindful |
| (un)conscious | neglectful |
| (un)critical | negligent |
| (un)deserving | positive |
| (un)desirous (*non-attrib.*) | proud |
| destitute | rid (*non-attrib.*) |
| destructive | sure (*also* about) |
| devoid (*non-attrib.*) | thoughtful, thoughtless |
| envious | (in)tolerant |
| fearful, fearless | void (*non-attrib.*) |
| fond | weary |
| forgetful | (un)worthy |
| full | |

### TO

| | |
|---|---|
| abhorrent | (in)appropriate |
| (un)acceptable | (in)attentive |
| adjacent | averse (*non-attrib.*) |
| amenable (*non-attrib.*) | beneficial |
| (in)applicable | (un)conducive (*non-attrib.*) |

| | |
|---|---|
| detrimental | pertinent |
| distasteful | (un)pleasant |
| essential | (dis)pleasing |
| (un)faithful | (im)polite |
| fatal | preferable |
| (un)friendly | preparatory |
| generous | prone (*meaning having a* |
| hateful | *natural disposition—non-attrib.*) |
| hostile | (ir)relevant |
| indebted (*non-attrib.*) | repugnant |
| inferior | rude |
| injurious | sacred |
| (un)kind | similar |
| (un)known | strange |
| (dis)loyal | subject (*non-attrib.*) |
| natural | superior |
| (dis)obedient | susceptible |
| painful, painless | tantamount (*non-attrib.*) |
| (im)partial | (un)true |
| peculiar | |

A number of adjectives derived from verbs that occur in idiomatic constructions of the form **be** + *adjective* + **of** or **to** have transitive verb equivalents.

BE ENVIOUS OF:  *envy*
> *He is envious of his brother.*
or  *He envies his brother.*

BE PAINFUL TO:  *pain*
> *This is painful to me.*
or  *This pains me.*

BE PREFERABLE TO:  *prefer*
> *This is preferable to me.*
or  *I prefer this.*

**-Ed** participial adjectives may also require certain prepositions before nouns. These participial adjectives are given in the following list, along with possible alternate forms with reflexive objects. The forms with **-ed** participles usually represent states, while the reflexive verbs represent transitive actions that precede the states.

> absorbed in (*also* absorb oneself in)
> (un)acquainted with (*also* acquaint onself with)
> (un)accustomed to (*also* accustom oneself to)
> adapted to (*a situation;* for *a purpose*) (*also* adapt oneself to)
> afflicted by

alarmed at, by
amazed at, by
annoyed at, by
(un)ashamed of
associated with (*also* associate oneself with)
astonished at, by
(un)attached to (*also* attach oneself to)
blessed with
bored with
burdened with, by (*also* burden oneself with)
clothed in (*also* clothe oneself in)
committed to (*also* commit oneself to)
composed of
concerned about, over (*also* concern oneself with)
confined to (*also* confine oneself to)
confused at, by
covered with (*also* cover oneself with)
dedicated to (*also* dedicate oneself to)
delighted at, by
deprived of (*also* deprive oneself of)
disappointed in, with
disgusted at, by, with
drunk on
embarrassed at, by
employed at (*a place*), by (*a company*)
endowed with
gifted with
hurt at, by
imbued with
(un)impressed by
indebted to
infested with
(un)inhibited by
interested in, by (*also* interest onself in)
irritated at, by, with
(un)known for (*something*), to (*someone*)
loaded with (*also* load oneself with)
married to
occupied with (*also* occupy oneself with)
overcome by, with
perplexed about, at, by
(dis)pleased with, by, at
puzzled at, by
qualified for (*also* qualify oneself for)
(un)related to (*also* relate oneself to)
(dis)satisfied with (*also* satisfy oneself with)
shocked by, at

startled at, by
(un)suited to (*a person*), for (*an occasion*)
surprised by, at
tired from (*involves physical fatigue*), of (*meaning* bored with)
troubled by, about

Note that many of the verbs of feelings given in the preceding list may be followed by either **by** or **at**—**amazed, irritated, shocked, startled, surprised.** The use of **by** after **-ed** participial adjectives strengthens the passive force of these participial forms.

Adjectival Function
of Prepositional Phrases

Many prepositional phrases in noun phrases indicate a function in an original subject-verb-complement core. The head of the noun phrase is often a noun form from a verb—either an abstract noun with a derivational ending, or an **-ing** gerund. The following prepositions introduce phrases involved in the subject-verb-complement core:

---

**of**

With the original *subject* in a simple sentence (traditionally called the subjective genitive)

the recovery *of his son* from pneumonia
*from:* **His son** recovered from pneumonia.

With the original *direct object* in a simple sentence (traditionally called the objective genitive)

the recovery *of the money* from the thieves
*from:* They recovered *the money* from the thieves.

After some nouns derived from transitive verbs, the original direct object is used with the preposition *to* or *for* rather than of

his injury *to* his knee
*from* He injured his knee.
our admiration *for* the doctor
*from* We admired the doctor.
his respect *for* law and order
*from* He respected law and order.

**about, from, with,** etc.

With an original *prepositional object* in a simple sentence

the President's speech *about Hawaii*
*from:* The President spoke *about Hawaii*.
her atonement *for her sins*
*from:* She atoned *for her sins*.
her disagreement *with her brother*
*from:* She disagreed *with her brother*.

**by**

With the agent in a passive construction

Many speeches *by Churchill* are very eloquent.
All the books *by that author* have become famous.

---

Adjectival prepositional phrases may also function as simple modifiers that express the kind of semantic relationships listed under types of prepositions.

| | |
|---|---|
| Time | the class *at ten o'clock* |
| Place | the class *in Johnson Hall* |
| Source | the student *from Paris* |

### POSITION OF PREPOSITIONS

A preposition usually initiates the prepositional phrase. However, in certain informal usages, the object of the preposition may appear in initial position in the clause, and the preposition in final position.

| | |
|---|---|
| Question (independent clause) | Which house does he live *in*? |
| | What is this dress made *of*? |
| Adjective clause | There is the house (which) he lives *in*. |
| | I like the material (which) this dress is made *of*. |
| Noun clause | We don't know which house he lives *in*. |
| | We don't know what material this dress is made *of*. |

Such prepositions in final position are quite acceptable in informal usage, in spite of the old rule that a sentence should not end with a preposition. That this rule is unrealistic can be further proved by the many other constructions we have already given in which the preposition may appropriately appear at the end of the sentence: for example, (1) prepositional forms used adverbially with verbs (**He wants to go** *in*); (2) prepositional forms completing two-part verbs (**I must look this word** *up*); (3) prepositional forms with passive verbs (**He was well thought** *of*); (4) prepositional forms with verbals (**This is not worth worrying** *about*).

### POSITION OF PREPOSITIONAL PHRASES

Position of Prepositional Phrases
in Adjectival Function

One or more prepositional phrases may follow the noun head, with no commas between them. These prepositional phrases (1) may all modify the noun head, (2) may successively modify the noun in the preceding phrase, or (3) may be a combination of (1) and (2).

(1) succession of prepositional phrases *modifying the noun head*

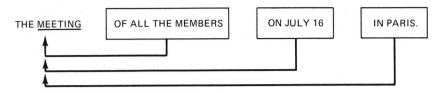

(2) succession of prepositional phrases *modifying the noun in the preceding prepositional phrase*

(3) succession of prepositional phrases representing a *combination of (1) and (2)*

Sometimes in a succession of adjectival prepositional phrases ambiguity may result if the reference back to a preceding noun is not clear. For example, in **his request to his superior for money at the end of the month, at the end of the month** may refer to **request** or to **money.**

Several adjectival prepositional phrases used consecutively in a noun phrase (perhaps with other adjectival constructions) may be awkward or may interfere with comprehension.

> *He mentioned the resignation of the bookkeeper from the company at the beginning of the year because of his inability to get along with the new president.*

This kind of "over-nominalization" can be avoided by putting some of the prepositional phrases into the full subject-predicate form of clauses.

> *He mentioned that the bookkeeper had resigned from the company at the beginning of the year because he was unable to get along with the new president.*

Generally, in a succession of adjectival prepositional phrases, the **of** phrases or phrases representing prepositional objects come before other types of phrases.

 1.  **of** phrases
      a.  **of** as a partitive genitive

*Some*
*Two dozen* } *of the eggs on the table will be used for the wedding cake.*
*One half*

      b.  **of** as a subjective or objective genitive

*The love **of a mother** (original subject) for her children.*

*The devastation **of the land** (original obiect) by the Northern army during the Civil War*

> If this kind of genitive **of** phrase has long modification, it may be preceded by one or more shorter prepositional phrases—**The devastation during the Civil War** *of the land that had been cultivated for two centuries.*
> This genitive **of** phrase may also appear last when it is to be emphasized—**The appearance in such an out-of-the-way place** *of two charming lady tourists.*

 2.  Phrases representing original prepositional objects

*His wife's dependence **on him** in every way*

*His strong rule **over the country** for many years*

### Position of Prepositional Phrases in Adverbial Function

Adverbial prepositional phrases may be used in three positions.

| | |
|---|---|
| Initial position | **Because of his aggressiveness,** the new student could not make many friends. |
| Mid-position | The new student, **because of his aggressiveness,** could not make many friends. |
| Final position | The new student could not make many friends **because of his aggressiveness.** |

Not all adverbial prepositional phrases can fill all three positions. See the chapter on adverbs for additional information about the position and punctuation of prepositional phrases functioning as adverbials.

### FORM OF PREPOSITIONS

Prepositions do not have any special inflectional or derivational endings. They must be learned from a closed list. Although no new prepositions are being coined, as in the case of other parts of speech, some adverbs and participles have been drawn upon for further use as prepositions.

Most prepositions are short words, usually consisting of one or two syllables. Sometimes two short prepositions are joined into a one-word compound (**into, within, upon**); or two or more separate words function together as a phrasal preposition.

### ONE-WORD PREPOSITIONS

aboard

about

across

after

against

alongside

amid (or **amidst**—both are literary)

among (**amongst** preferred in British usage)

around (**round** is informal)

at

atop (U.S. journalistic use—**on top of** is more common)

before

behind

below

beneath

beside

between

beyond

but (in the sense of *except*)

by

despite

down

during

except (for)

for

from

in

inside

less

like

minus

near

of

on

opposite

out (of)

outside

over

past

per (meaning *for each*)

plus

re (or **in re**—meaning *with reference to*—chiefly legal or commercial)

since

through

throughout

till

to

toward(s)

under

underneath

until

up

versus (meaning *against*)

via (meaning *by way of*)

within

without

*Archaic or Poetic*

betwixt

ere

### -*ING PARTICIPLES* USED AS ONE-WORD PREPOSITIONS

barring

concerning

considering
during
excepting
excluding
including
notwithstanding
pending
regarding
respecting
saving
touching

Some of the **-ing** prepositions have phrasal equivalents—**in consideration of = considering, with the exception of = excepting** (also **except**), **to the exclusion of** or **exclusive of = excluding, with regard to = regarding, with respect to = respecting**.

## TWO-WORD PREPOSITIONS

*OF as the Second Element*

ahead of
apropos of (meaning *with reference to*)
because of
east (*or* west, south, north) of
exclusive of
inclusive of
instead of
irrespective of
regardless of
short of

*TO as the Second Element*

according to
antecedent to
as to
contrary to
counter to
due to (informal when used as a preposition)
next to
on to (*also* onto)
owing to
previous(ly) to
prior to
pursuant to
relative to
subject to
subsequent(ly) to
thanks to
up to

Some of the combinations with **of** or **to** that have just been given might be construed as simple adjectives plus prepositions—for example, **exclusive of, irrespective of, antecedent to, pursuant to.**

*WITH as the Second Element*

> along with
> concurrently with
> together with

*FOR as the Second Element*

> as for
> but (for)
> except (for)
> save (for)

*FROM as the Second Element*

> apart from
> aside from
> away from

*UP as the First Element*

> up against
> up at
> up till
> up until
> up to

Actually, **up** in these combinations might be regarded as an intensifier that can be omitted.

> *Place this ladder (up) against the tree.*
> *(Up) until New Year's Day I shall be very busy.*

Some grammar books also consider combinations of **from** plus prepositions of place as phrasal prepositions—**from above, from among, from behind, from below, from beneath, from between, from beyond, from over, from under.**

### THREE OR FOUR-WORD PREPOSITIONS

These are classified here according to the initial prepositional form, with further subclassification according to whether an article is used in the phrasal preposition.

by $\begin{cases} \text{dint} \\ \text{means} \\ \text{order} \\ \text{reason} \\ \text{virtue} \\ \text{way} \end{cases}$ of $\qquad$ at the $\begin{cases} \text{cost} \\ \text{hands} \\ \text{point} \\ \text{risk} \end{cases}$ of

with { reference / regard / respect } to          as a { consequence / result } of

with the { exception / purpose } of

with { an eye / a view } to

for { fear / lack / want } of

for the { benefit / purpose / sake } of

on { account / behalf / pain } of

on the (the) { face / occasion / part / point / strength / top } of

in { accordance — with / addition — to / advance — of / back — of (*or* back of— both are informal) / care — of / case — of / comparison — with / connection — with / contrast — with / favor — of / front — of / lieu — of / proportion — to / regard — to / respect — to / return — for / spite — of }

in (the) { course / event / face / light / process } of (**the** may be omitted)

in the middle (*or* midst) of

Strictly speaking, these 3-4 word prepositions initiate a succession of two prepositional phrases—**in accordance with our agreement.** The list of these phrasal prepositions could be expanded to include such phrases as **in common with, in compliance with, in search of, in recognition of, in default of, in opposition to,** etc.

A few expressions beginning with **as** are sometimes also considered as phrasal prepositions:

    as far as
    as far back as
    as compared with (*or* to) (**As** may be omitted from this group.)
    as contrasted with
    as opposed to

Some phrasal prepositions have the same meaning as single-word prepositions. Where there is a choice of prepositional forms, the shorter prepositions are generally preferred.

*I am writing **with regard to** your advertisement* (preferably **about** or **regarding** *your advertisement*) *in the Sunday Times.*

*Everyone agreed to the proposal **with the exception of** the president* (preferably **except** *the president*).

However, there are occasions when certain phrasal prepositions are preferable because they either draw more attention to the desired relationship or they define the relationship more sharply.

*You will get good value **in return for** (=for) your money.*

*He would give his life **for the sake of** (=for) his cause.*

INTENSIFIERS
WITH PREPOSITIONAL PHRASES

Adverbial intensifiers may be used with prepositional phrases.

*He did it **just** (or **only, merely**) for you.*

*He works **even** at night.*

*I can see you **right** (or **just**) after dinner.*

Some intensifiers add a secondary lexical meaning.

*I can see you **immediately** (or **soon**) after dinner.*

*He came **exactly** on time.*

*They hiked **way** up the mountain.*

*He worked **far** into the night.*

# *10*

## *Conjunctions*
## *and*
## *Compounding*

Most conjunctions are historically derived from other parts of speech, particularly from prepositions. Like prepositions, the conjunctions are members of a small class that have no characteristic form. They function chiefly as nonmovable structure words that join such units as parts of speech, phrases, or clauses.

There are two types of conjunctions, coordinate and subordinate. Subordinate conjunctions will be taken up in detail later under the syntactic structures each one introduces. This chapter will therefore devote more attention to coordinate conjunctions and their role in compounding grammatical units.

COORDINATE CONJUNCTIONS

The coordinate conjunction joins structural units that are equal grammatically. The conjunction comes before the last unit and is grammatically independent of this unit.

Units joined by a coordinate conjunction are labeled *compound*.[1] Com-

---

[1] The term *compound* means consisting of two or more independent elements that have been joined together to form a larger unit. This term is a source of difficulty in grammar because it is applied not only to separate grammatical items joined by a coordinate conjunction (**men and women**), but to word groups combined into a single vocabulary unit (**blackbird, apple pie, son-in-law**). (In this text we are referring to a compound like **men and women** as a *compound noun* and to a compound like **blackbird** as a *noun compound*.) In addition, the term *compound* sometimes also refers to phrasal prepositions (**in accordance with**), phrasal conjunctions (**inasmuch as**), or verb phrases (**has been going**).

pound units may be classified according to the *formal structure* of the units (parts of speech, phrases, clauses) or according to the *function* of the units (subject, predicate, modifier, object).

Structural Units Joined
by Coordinate Conjunctions

## Parts of Speech (Single Words)—
## Conjunctions *And, Or*

> *The old woman **slipped and fell** on the pavement.* (compound verb)
> *The thief moved **quickly and quietly**.* (compound adverb)
> *I'll inform you **if and when** he comes.* (compound conjunction)

**But, yet** are less common conjunctions that join coordinate parts of speech.

> *She is beautiful **but** dumb.*
> *A man who has money **but** (or **yet**) does not share it, is not worthy of respect.*

After a negative, **but** may be interpreted as a preposition meaning *except*:

> *No one **but** him could have done that.*
> *None **but** the brave deserves the fair.*

A pronoun and a noun may be joined by coordinate conjunctions—
**My husband and I love to go to the movies.**
**And, or** are sometimes used interchangeably.

> *This hair cream may be used by men **and** women.*
>    or *This hair cream may be used by men **or** women.*

Auxiliaries may also be joined by coordinate conjunctions.

> *We can and will succeed.*
> *Mistakes have been, and will continue to be, made in that office.*

A comma after the last coordinate auxiliary is optional, depending on whether the user would pause in speech.

Mistakes are sometimes made when the first coordinate auxiliary requires a different form of the lexical verb than the last auxiliary does. In **He always has, and always will, contribute to that cause**—**contribute** can accompany **will**, but **has** requires **contributed**.

## Phrases

Compound Prepositional Phrases.    Conjunctions **and, or**.

> *He walked into the house and up the stairs.*
> *I can see you before two o'clock or after five.*

Often the conjunction joins only the objects of the same preposition—
**after** *dinner* **and a long** *nap*; **his** *love* **and** *respect* **for his king**. However, if

different prepositions are required after the nouns in the compound construction, both prepositions must be used—**His love *for* and allegiance *to* his king**.

COMPOUND VERBAL PHRASES.    Conjunctions **and, or**; less frequently **but, yet**.

> *After eating dinner and taking a long nap, he felt much better.* (gerund phrases joined)
>
> *To be or not to be, that is the question.* (infinitive phrases joined)
>
> *Feeling hungry, but* (or *yet*) *not wanting to wake his wife, he tiptoed down to the kitchen.* (participial phrases joined)

## Clauses

DEPENDENT CLAUSES.    Conjunctions **and, or**; less commonly **but, yet**.

> *Because he didn't care for the country, and because the beach had no appeal to him, he decided to travel during his vacation.* (adverbial clauses joined)
>
> *He married a woman who was very intelligent and charming, but who couldn't cook at all.* (adjectives clauses joined)
>
> *I don't know when he left town or why he wanted to do so.* (noun clauses joined)

INDEPENDENT CLAUSES.    Conjunctions **and, or, nor, but, yet, so, for**[2].

> *I'll pick you up at eight and I'll get you back home by midnight.*
>
> *He decided to withdraw from his physics class, for he kept failing the examinations.*
>
> *Give me liberty or give me death.*

Functional Units Joined
by Coordinate Conjunctions

Coordinate units consisting of parts of speech, phrases or clauses may also be classified according to their function in the sentence.

| | |
|---|---|
| Compound subjects | **Dogs** and **cats** often do not get along. (subject consists of nouns) |
| | **How much she pays for her clothes** or **where she buys them** does not interest her husband. (subject consists of noun clauses) |
| Compound predicates | **They went out for dinner** but **returned in time for their favorite television program**. (predicate consists of verbs and modifiers) |
| Compound objects | He looked everywhere for **his keys** and **wallet**. (object of preposition consists of nouns) |
| | He said **that he was tired** and **that he was going to bed**. (direct object consists of noun clauses) |

[2] Since **for** is a synonym for **because**, its inclusion among the coordinate conjunctions might be questioned. The justification for such a classification is that **for** cannot be moved with its clause to any other adverbial position in the same way as a **because** clause can.

| | |
|---|---|
| Compound modifiers | He was **tired** but **happy**. (modifier consists of adjectives) |
| | The violinist played **brilliantly** but **dispassionately**. (modifier consists of adverbs) |
| | Anyone **who doesn't like the new policy of this company** and **who would like to resign** is free to do so. (modifier consists of adjective clauses) |

A compound subject joined by **and** requires a plural verb—**Mr. Johnson and his wife *are* mistaken**. However, if the compound parts of a subject are thought of as one unit, a singular verb is used.

> *Bread and butter is fattening.*
>
> *The modern housewife and mother wants to know about the chemicals used in foods.*

For a compound subject joined by **or,** formal English requires a singular verb if the coordinate items are singular—**Mr. Johnson or his wife *is* mistaken**. Informally, however, the plural verb is often heard—**Mr. Johnson or his wife *are* mistaken**. Where there is a difference in number or person between the items in a compound subject joined by **or**, the verb agrees with the last item in formal English.

> *Mr. Johnson or his employees are mistaken.*
>
> *Mr. Johnson or I am mistaken.* (In this sentence, the form of the verb seems awkward to native speakers. Usually the sentence is recast—*Mr. Johnson is mistaken or I am.*)

A plural verb accompanies subjects such as **one or two, one or both, one or more**—**One or two exceptions do not invalidate a rule**.

**Or** may be used with parts of speech, phrases, clauses in order to rename, clarify or rectify a preceding item. Commas set off the constructions introduced by **or**.

> *He was afflicted with Hansen's disease, or, as it is more commonly known, leprosy.*
>
> *Most dictionaries give the etymology, or the origin, of each word.*

**Rather, at least, better still** may follow **or**.

> *I fell in love, or rather I thought I was in love, with the girl next door.*
>
> *Why don't you write us before you come here, or, better still, send us a telegram.*

Compounding is most effective for two or three items only. If more than three larger structures are compounded, the reader or listener may lose the thread of the ideas. If more than three units of the same part of speech are compounded, the compounding may have the effect of a mere statistical list of items.

PARALLEL STRUCTURE

When coordinate conjunctions are used, the expectation is that each of the items joined will have the same grammatical form. Faulty parallelism occurs when different grammatical structures are used coordinately for the same grammatical function. Such faulty parallelism is especially common in noun or adjective functions.

---

*Nominal function*

| | |
|---|---|
| Faulty parallelism | I'm reading about the origin of the violin and how it developed through the ages. |
| Corrected to | I'm reading about the origin and development of the violin. |
| Faulty parallelism | Swimming in the lake and to walk through the woods are his favorite pastimes. |
| Corrected to: | Swimming in the lake and walking through the woods are his favorite pastimes. |
| or | To swim in the lake and to walk through the woods are his favorite pastimes. |

*Adjectival function*

| | |
|---|---|
| Faulty parallelism | Mary is tall, with blond hair, and who has blue eyes. |
| Corrected to | Mary is tall, blond, and blue-eyed. |

---

A few words other than coordinate conjunctions also require parallel construction. These words have the force of **and not**.

---

| | |
|---|---|
| not | It was his personality, **not** his talent, that helped him advance professionally. |
| than | He was more pleased **than** annoyed at her remark. |
| rather than | A highly cooperative scientist **rather than** a brilliant one is required for this project. |

---

In formal English, such structural signals as articles (and other determiners), auxiliaries, prepositions and conjunctions are often repeated to make the parallelism clear, especially if the parallel items are long.

> *In Columbus' Day, people believed **that** the earth was square and **that** a person could fall off the edges.*

> *A huge celebration dinner was given **for** all the office holders in the party, **for** all those who had contributed sizable amounts of money to their campaign, and **for** all the party workers who had helped bring about their victory at the polls.*

Items that are grammatically parallel should also be logically parallel. Not logically parallel—**The boy was tall, dark, and very methodical.** (The first two items refer to the boy's appearance, the last item to one of his habits.)

Logical parallelism is required even with independent clauses that are joined coordinately.

---

| | |
|---|---|
| Clauses not logically parallel | Mr. Jones is our neighbor and he has a large house. |
| | The title of this book is *Moby Dick* and it is a story about a whale. |

---

One way to eliminate such faulty coordination is to reduce one of the independent clauses.

> *Mr. Jones, our neighbor, has a large house.*
> *Moby Dick is a story about a whale.*

At times items in a coordinate series can be listed in random order— **We wish to order some paper, pencils, file folders**. At other times, the order is fixed by usage, especially in common phrases—**men, women and children; tall, dark and handsome; safe and sound**. Often, however, the coordinate items must be arranged according to some logical principle. Thus we might have a climactic order (such as from less important to more important), a spacial order (such as from near to far, from left to right), an order according to size (such as from small to large), or a temporal order (such as from earlier to later).

> *Some books are to be tasted, others to be swallowed, and some few to be chewed and digested.* (Francis Bacon) (climactic order)
> *As a small boy, a grown man, and a senile invalid, he had always looked at the gloomy side of life.* (temporal order)

An awareness of parallelism is important not only for the negative purpose of eliminating errors but for the positive purpose of lining up related ideas in similar grammatical forms. Such a use of "positive parallelism" is especially important in formal English; the parallel structures help the reader or listener to see the relationship between the many complexities of thought that are being expressed.

> *It is because nations tend to stupidity and baseness that mankind moves so slowly; it is because individuals have a capacity for better things that it moves at all.* (George Gissling)
> *It is with narrow-souled people as with narrow-necked bottles; the less they have in them the more noise they make in pouring out.* (Alexander Pope)

Positive parallelism not only achieves greater clarity and economy of expression, but it often makes a statement more eloquent because of the rhythmic repetition of the grammatical structures. The more parallel a sentence is, the more esthetically pleasing it often is. For this reason, balanced sentences, that is, sentences that are completely parallel, are more memorable than are other types of sentences.

> *Prosperity is not without many fears and distastes; and adversity is not without comforts and hopes.* (Alexander Pope)
> *For want of a nail the shoe was lost; for want of a shoe the horse was lost; and for want of a horse the rider was lost.* (Benjamin Franklin)

When clauses are used in parallel construction, the verb, and possibly part of the structure around it, may be omitted.

> *Reading maketh a full man, conference a ready man, and writing an exact man.* (Francis Bacon) (***Maketh*** is omitted in the second and third items.)

Such an omission may be indicated by a comma.

> *Their first aim was accomplished by persuasion, their second, by force.* (A comma replaces the omitted **aim was accomplished**)

### Correlative Conjunctions

When **and, or, but** join coordinate elements, the first item may also be preceded by a conjunction. Such paired conjunctions, called correlative conjunctions, serve to intensify the coordination.

---

both—and  Both Helen and I will go to the party.
 She is both beautiful and intelligent.
 They enjoy both going on a vacation and coming back home.

---

**Both** may follow the coordinate elements—**She is older sister and mother both**.

The coordination may be further intensified by **alike** or **as well** after the last item. In such a case **both** may be omitted.

> *Gifts were distributed to* (*both*) *rich and poor alike* (or *as well*).

---

not only—but (also)  Not only the women but (also) the men loved this strange little
 man.

 Not only did he give everyone gifts but he (also) invited them
 to a dinner party.

---

This correlative pair expresses addition, with greater emphasis placed on the second element.

When this correlative joins two independent clauses, **also** may be omitted; or it may be separated from **but** and placed in one of the adverbial positions.

> *Not only the women but the men also loved this strange little man.* (**also** in adverbial position with the verb)
> *Not only did he give everyone gifts but he invited them to a dinner party also.* (**also** in adverbial position at the end of the clause)

**But** may set up a contrast with other negatives than **not only**.

> *It **never** rains but it pours.*
> *I have **no** choice but to listen to the doctor.*
> *It's **not** what you say but what you do that counts.*

**So much as** may replace but—**It's not what you say so much as what you do that counts.** (or **It's not so much what you say as what you do that counts**)

**But also** may be omitted as a second correlative with independent clauses—**Not only did he bring wine, he brought flowers.** (or, informally, **He not only brought wine, he brought flowers**)

---

either—or   Either Sally or Evelyn can drive you home.
She will either pay for the ring or return it.

---

**Whether—or** is sometimes used instead of **either—or.**

*Whether out of avarice or out of need, he asked for a much higher price for his property than it was worth.*

---

neither—nor[3]   Neither money nor power has made him arrogant.
She is neither beautiful nor intelligent.

---

Instead of **neither,** a negative adjective or a negative adverb may function with the first item. In such a case, **or** or **nor** may appear with the last item.

Negative adjective with first item is **no**:

*Although she's very rich, she owns no jewelry (n)or furs.*

Negative adverb with first item is **never, seldom** or **rarely:**

*When the children brought home a flea-ridden dog, their mother didn't scold (n)or punish them.*

*He has never (or seldom, rarely) spoken an unkind word to his wife (n)or to anyone else.*

The use of **nor** in these sentences reinforces the negation.

In the sense of *and not,* only **nor** occurs between negative independent clauses.

*I have never seen her since then, nor do I expect to see her again.*

*He hasn't been invited to the party, nor does he care to go there.*

The second clause with **nor** is often abridged—**He said he will not disappoint us, nor will he.**

**Nor** meaning *and not* may appear not only after a negative clause but after a positive clause.

*Suddenly she stopped speaking, nor could he coax her to say more.*

*They spent the day fasting. Nor did they eat anything the next day.*

Usually **either—or** and **neither—nor** are used for two items, but sometimes they appear with three.

*Neither duty nor honor nor gratitude means anything to him.*

*Neither snow nor rain nor heat nor gloom of night stays these couriers from the swift completion of their appointed rounds.* (motto of U.S. Post Office)

---

[3] An older form for this correlative was **nor—nor**:

*Nor sun nor wind will ever strive to kiss you.* (Shakespeare)

When correlative conjunctions are used in formal English, care must be taken that the first correlative is placed before the proper item. Both parts of the coordination must be grammatically parallel. In **She will either pay for the ring or she will return it**, the correlatives are joining a *predicate* (**pay for the ring**) and an *independent clause* (**she will return it**). While informal English permits this kind of non-parallelism, formal usage requires that the sentence just given be changed to **She will either pay for the ring or return it,** or to **Either she will pay for the ring or she will return it**.

Punctuation
with Coordinate Conjunctions

Commas used with coordinate conjunctions appear only before the conjunctions. Commas may separate items representing the same part of speech, the same type of phrase, or the same type of clause.

If only two words, two phrases, or two dependent clauses are joined by a coordinate conjunction, no comma is used before the coordinate conjunction.

> *Men and women are welcome.*
> *The doctor warned him not to smoke or drink.*
> *He said that he was very tired and that he was going home to rest.*

Sometimes, however, a comma may separate long dependent clauses.

> *Because he didn't like to work in a tropical climate, and because he felt his abilities were not recognized by the company he worked for, he decided to look for a job in a colder climate.*

If three or more items are coordinated, commas separate the items. However, a comma before the conjunction preceding the last item is optional.

> *Men, women (,) and children are welcome.*
> *The doctor warned him not to smoke, drink (,) or eat highly spiced foods.*

Two or more independent clauses are usually separated by a comma before the coordinate conjunction.

| | |
|---|---|
| Two clauses | They had hoped to take a trip around the world, but they were unable to leave because of the sudden illness of their son. |

The comma may be omitted in such sentences if both clauses are short.

> *The band played and the crowd cheered.*

| | |
|---|---|
| Three clauses | In the evening, some people like to watch television, others enjoy a game of cards, and still others prefer to take a nap. |

Here, too, the comma before the coordinate conjunction may be omitted if the clauses are short.

See the chapter on Sentences and Clauses for further information about the punctuation of independent clauses.

OMISSION OF COORDINATE CONJUNCTIONS. For two or more items, **and** or **or** may be omitted before the last item and a comma used instead.

> *A newspaper contains three kinds of news—international, national, local.*

REPETITION OF COORDINATE CONJUNCTIONS. For three or more items, **and** or **or** may be used with each item after the first one. Such repetition of the conjunction reinforces the coordination.

> *Unsanitary conditions (,) or certain insects (,) or nutritional deficiencies may cause disease.*

### SUBORDINATE CONJUNCTIONS

A subordinate conjunction introduces a clause that depends on a main, or independent clause. The subordinate conjunction is grammatically part of the clause it introduces; it is never separated from its clause by a comma.

Broadly speaking, all the introductory words in the three subordinate clauses, even pronouns or adverbs, may be classified as subordinate conjunctions. In a more limited sense, the term is restricted to (1) the words introducing adverbial clauses—**when, until, if, although,** etc.—and (2) **that, whether** introducing noun clauses.

Subordinate conjunctions range in meaning from those having strong semantic content—time, place, cause, etc.—to those having purely structural meaning—**that, than, as, whether**.

Some subordinate conjunctions have the same form as prepositions, especially the conjunctions of time—**before, after, until, since, as**. Some of these forms may also be used alone with verbs as adverbs.

| | |
|---|---|
| **Before**—conjunction | I had never seen him **before** he arrived in town. |
| **Before**—preposition | I had never seen him **before** his arrival in town. |
| **Before**—adverb | I had never seen him **before**. |

Subordinate conjunctions may have **-ing** or **-ed** participial form—**provided** or **providing (that), notwithstanding (that), supposing (that)**. Actually, in some cases, it is hard to draw the line between an **-ing** or an **-ed** form used as a participle or as a conjunction. In this text, with a few exceptions, we are being guided by dictionary classification of such forms.

Some subordinate conjunctions are phrasal—**as soon as, so that, in order that**. Other conjunctions consist of prepositions that have been turned into conjunctions by the addition of **the fact that**—**on account of the fact that, in spite of the fact that.**

Subordinate conjunctions may be preceded by intensifiers—*just* **because,** *only* **when,** *right* **after**—or negatives—*not* **because,** *never* **because.**

By far the greatest number of subordinate conjunctions introduce adverbial clauses. These conjunctions are listed below. We have classified them by form—single-word conjunctions, two-word conjunctions, conjunctions with three or more words. We have also indicated the adverbial relationship that each conjunction expresses.

---

**Single-Word Subordinate Conjunctions**

| | | |
|---|---|---|
| after | time | She never saw him again after he left town. |
| although | contrast (concessive) | Although he had never liked mathematics, he decided to take a course in statistics. |
| as | time | As she was leaving the house, the mailman arrived with a package. |
| | cause | They left the party at 11 P.M., as they had to get up early the next day. |
| | manner | He always does as he pleases. |
| because | cause | He was fined because he was speeding. |
| before | time | She always has a chat with her neighbor before she begins her morning chores. |
| if | condition | If the temperature drops tonight, the lake will freeze over. |
| lest | purpose (negative) | Lest their young son get into further trouble with the police, they decided to send him to a strict military academy. |
| once | time | Once the news about the merger becomes known, the price of the company's stock will rise sharply. |
| | condition | Once you have made a mistake, you cannot correct it. |
| since | time | He has been very ill since he had his accident. |
| | cause | Since the weather is so bad outside, why don't you stay with us overnight? |
| that | purpose | That they might better protect their belongings, they had an elaborate burglar alarm system installed in their home. |
| though | contrast (concessive) | Though he still felt ill, he decided to go back to work. |
| till | time | Let's sit out here till the sun sets. |
| unless | condition (=if not) | He never goes to any social function unless his wife can come with him. |
| until | time | We'll wait inside until the rain stops. |
| when(ever) | time | We can leave when(ever) you are ready. |
| | condition | The roof leaks when(ever) it rains. |
| where(ver) | place | You will find poverty wherever you go. |

| whereas | cause | Whereas the rent for this property has not been paid for four months, the tenant is required to vacate the premises immediately. |
|---|---|---|
| | contrast (adversative) | He was very generous, whereas his brother was quite stingy. |
| while | time | Please watch my baggage while I purchase my train ticket. |
| | contrast: concessive | While he disliked cats, he permitted his wife to have one. (*informal*) |
| | adversative | He would like to have a dog, while his wife would prefer a cat. |

*Archaic Conjunctions*

| ere | time | We will die ere we surrender. |
|---|---|---|
| albeit | contrast (concessive) | Albeit his ordeal was almost beyond human endurance, he held steadfast to his goal. |

**Two-Word Conjunctions**

*Ending in As*

| inasmuch as | cause | Inasmuch as no offer has been made to pay for the damage, our company will have to take this case to court. |
|---|---|---|
| insofar as (*also* in so far as) | degree (extent) | Our firm will do whatever is necessary insofar as we are able to. |

*Ending in That*

| beyond that | condition (exception) | I have no complaint about my job beyond that it is boring. |
|---|---|---|
| but that | condition (exception) | But that he needed money desperately, he would never have turned to his brother for help. |
| except *or* excepting } that | condition (exception) | That house is just what we want, except that it is too expensive. |
| in that | cause or manner | Both girls are similar in that they love expensive clothes. |
| now (that) | time | Now that we are ready to leave, we must say goodbye to all our friends. |
| | cause | Now that it has started to rain, the crops will be saved. |
| only (that) | condition (exception) | I have no complaint about the hotel, only that it is dull here. |
| provided *or* providing } (that) | condition | We should be able to do the job for you quickly, provided (that) you give us all the necessary information. |
| save *or* saving } that | condition (exception) | The plan would have gone off very well, save that one of the officials became very greedy. |
| so (that) | purpose | He traveled through half the world so (that) he might see her once more. |
| | result | The furniture arrived damaged, so (that) we had to send it back. |

To this group might be added some **-ed** and **-ing** participles that function as the first part of subordinate conjunctions:

| | | |
|---|---|---|
| granted (that) | contrast (concessive) | Granted that he was dealt with unjustly, he still should not have killed the man. |
| conceded that | contrast (concessive) | Conceded that a few of his arguments are convincing, the majority of them are not. |
| assuming that | contrast (concessive) | Assuming that we consent to the marriage, what can you offer our daughter? |

*Others*

| | | |
|---|---|---|
| as if | manner | He looks as if he's very tired. |
| as though | manner | They're spending money as though there's no tomorrow. |
| if only | condition | I could get more work done if only there weren't so much noise. |
| in case | condition | In case you leave the house, please close the windows. |
| only if | condition | We will manufacture these handbags only if we can obtain the right leather. |

### Subordinate Conjunctions Beginning with Prepositional Phrases

*Prepositional Phrase + As*

| | | |
|---|---|---|
| as far as | degree (extent) | As far as I am concerned, he can do whatever he likes with the money. |
| as (*or* so) long as | time | I'll remember you as long as I live. |
| | condition | So long as we have no trouble with the car, we should arrive at our destination in four hours. |
| | cause | As long as you're going to the kitchen, get me a ginger ale. |

*Prepositional Phrase + That*

| | | |
|---|---|---|
| for fear that | purpose (negative) | He studied night and day for fear that he might not pass the bar examination. |
| for the purpose that | purpose | For the purpose that justice might be better served, a special committee was appointed. |
| in order that | purpose | They left very early in order that they might arrive before dark. |
| in the event that | condition | In the event that he doesn't call by noon, I'll have to call him. |
| in the hope that | purpose | Radium treatments were given him in the hope that the cancer cells might be destroyed. |
| on condition (that) | condition | We can take care of this matter on condition that payment is made in advance. |
| on the ground(s) that | cause | She's suing for divorce on the grounds that he deserted her and the children. |
| to the end that | purpose | All the efforts of the United Nations are directed to the end that peace may finally prevail all over the world. |

*Preposition or Prepositional Phrase +* **The Fact That**

| | | |
|---|---|---|
| because of the fact that | cause | Because of the fact that they had made their reservation too late, they couldn't get on the plane they wanted. |
| but for the fact that | condition (exception) | Everything would have gone well with the play but for the fact that one of the props caught on fire. |
| despite the fact that | contrast (concessive) | Despite the fact that he was well known all over the world, he was an extremely modest man. |
| due to the fact that (*informal—not yet regarded as acceptable*) | cause | Due to the fact that all trains were delayed, the station was crowded with people. |
| except for the fact that | condition (exception) | Except for the fact that her nose was a little long, she would be very beautiful. |
| in spite of the fact that | contrast (concessive) | He does a full day's work in spite of the fact that he is eighty years old. |
| in view of the fact that | cause | In view of the fact that all the able-bodied men were fighting at the front, the women had to do all the work. |
| notwithstanding (the fact) that | contrast (concessive) | She lived to a ripe old age, notwithstanding the fact that she had a weak heart. |
| on account of the fact that | cause | He was fired on account of the fact that he had stolen money from the company. |
| owing to the fact that | cause | Owing to the fact that not enough members are present to call our meeting to order, we will have to cancel the meeting. |
| regardless of the fact that | contrast (concessive) | She insisted on accompanying her husband through the fields regardless of the fact that the rain was ruining her dress. |

## "Split" Conjunctions

Split conjunctions consist of two parts that "split" around an adjective, adverb, noun or pronoun. Some grammarians consider the first part as an adverb and only the second part as the conjunction.

| | | |
|---|---|---|
| so . . . that | result | He was injured so badly that he had to go to the hospital. (**That** may be omitted in informal speech.) |
| such (a) . . . that | result | It was such a rainy night that they decided to stay home. (**That** may be omitted in informal speech.) |
| as or so } . . . as | degree (comparison) | He works as hard as his brother does. |
| -er more } . . . than less | degree (comparison) | We are having a colder winter this year than we had last year. He is a more (*or* less) diligent student than his cousin is. |

# 11

## Sentences and Clauses

Traditional grammar defines a sentence in one of two ways.

BY MEANING. According to this definition, a sentence is a "complete thought." Such a definition is inadequate, however, because of the vagueness of the term "complete thought." By seeing or hearing a statement, how do we know it is a "thought," and what makes it "complete"?

BY FUNCTION. According to this definition, a sentence consists of a subject and a predicate. This definition is more satisfactory because it is actually possible to identify the structural functions of subject and predicate in a sentence.

The definition we should like to offer here includes both functional and formal characteristics of a sentence: *A sentence is a full predication containing a subject plus a predicate with a finite verb.* Its arrangement may be symbolized by such formulas as S V O (subject + verb + object), $N_1$ V $N_2$ (noun + verb + noun), or NP + VP (noun phrase + verb phrase).

## CLASSIFICATION OF SENTENCES

Sentences are generally classified in two ways, one by *types* and one by the *number of formal predications.*

### Classification of Sentences by Types

#### Declarative Sentences (Statements)

> *The child ate his dinner.*

In a declarative sentence the subject and predicate have normal word order. The sentence ends with a period[1] in writing and a drop in pitch in speech.

### Interrogative Sentences (Questions)

*Did the child eat his dinner?*

In an interrogative sentence the subject and auxiliary are often reversed. The sentence ends with a question mark (or, interrogation point) in writing. In the spoken language, most yes-no questions end with a rise in pitch; most interrogative-word questions end with a fall in pitch. (Further information about questions may be found in the chapter on verbs.)

### Imperative Sentences (Commands, Requests)

*Eat your dinner.*

In an imperative sentence, only the predicate is expressed. The simple form of the verb is used, regardless of person or tense. The imperative sentence ends with a period in writing and a drop in pitch in speech. (The chapter on verbs has more detailed information about imperative sentences.)

### Exclamatory Sentences (Exclamations)

*What a good dinner that was!*

Such sentences begin with an exclamatory phrase consisting of **what** or **how** plus a part of the predicate. The exclamatory phrase is followed by the subject and the balance of the predicate.

In writing, the exclamatory sentence ends with an exclamation mark (or, exclamation point). Sometimes a period is used to lessen the force of the exclamation. In speech, the most important word in the exclamatory phrase may receive a stronger degree of stress and be accompanied by a rise in pitch.

Because exclamatory sentences are not taken up elsewhere, they will be described in some detail here.

**What** (**a**) is used when a *noun* terminates the exclamatory phrase.

> *What beautiful **hair**    she has!*
> *What beautiful **eyes**    she has!*
> *What a beautiful **figure** she has!*    (**What a** with a singular countable noun only)

**How** is used when an *adjective* or an *adverb* terminates the exclamatory phrase.

> *How **beautiful**    she is!*
> *How **beautifully**    she behaves!*

The exclamatory phrase may stand alone when it ends with a noun or an adjective.

[1] Called a full stop in British English.

*What beautiful hair!*
*How beautiful!*

Sometimes an infinitive is used as the verb in an exclamation.

*What a high price to pay for one night's folly!*
*How thoughtful of him to send flowers!*

A preposition that is part of the exclamatory phrase usually appears in final position (**What terrible trouble he is in!**), but it sometimes remains in initial position (***By* what strange fears he is possessed!**).

Sentences that are declarative in form may also be spoken and written as exclamations.

*There's the plane now!*

Occasionally, in literary or poetic style, the subject and verb of an exclamatory sentence are reversed. Such a reverse is felt as archaic.

*How green was my valley!*
*How softly glides the moon.*
*What a fool is an old king who gives away everything to his daughters.*

A sentence with **such (a)** instead of **what (a)** may have the effect of an exclamatory sentence.

*She has **such** beautiful hair!*
*She has **such** beautiful eyes!*
*She has **such a** beautiful figure!*

Declarative and interrogative sentences may take the passive and negative form. Exclamatory sentences are not usually negative. Sometimes, however, they are passive—**What a sight was seen last night**!

Imperative sentences may be negative—**Don't close the door.** On occasion they may be passive—**Don't be fooled by his mild manner.**

In all four types of sentences, any sentence part may be compounded. (See chapter on conjunctions and compounding.)

Classification of Sentences
by Number of Full Predications

This classification is based on the number and kind of clauses within a sentence. A clause may be defined in the same way as a sentence: It is a full predication that contains a subject and a predicate with a finite verb. There are two kinds of clauses, independent and dependent. The independent clause is a full predication that may stand alone as a sentence; the dependent clause has a special introductory word that makes the predication "depend" on an independent clause.

1. *simple sentences*

*The man stole the jewelry.*

Such sentences have only one full predication in the form of an independent clause.

2. *compound sentences*

*The man stole the jewelry and he hid it in his home.*

Such sentences have two or more full predications in the form of independent clauses.

3. *complex sentences*

*The man who stole the jewelry hid it in his home.*

Such sentences also have two or more full predications. One of these is an independent clause (or, main clause) that is similar to the form of the simple sentence, and one or more of these are dependent clauses (or, subordinate clauses).

4. *compound-complex sentences*

*The man stole the jewelry and he hid it in his home until he could safely get out of town.*

Compound-complex sentences contain two or more independent clauses and one or more dependent clauses.

The independent clause in all four classes of sentences may take the form of a statement, question, request, exclamation.

CLAUSES

From the point of view of usage, little needs to be said about the independent clauses used alone in a simple sentence. It is when clauses are combined because a relationship exists between them that questions of usage arise. The balance of this chapter will be concerned with the independent and dependent clauses resulting from the combination of two or more full predications into a single sentence.

Independent Clauses
(in compound sentences)

Full predications may be joined coordinately by punctuation alone, by coordinate conjunctions, or by conjunctive adverbs.

*John was sick; he didn't come to school.* (independent clauses joined merely by *punctuation*)

*John was sick, so he didn't come to school.* (independent clauses joined by a *coordinate conjunction*)

*John was sick; therefore, he didn't come to school.* (independent clauses joined by a *conjunctive adverb*)

## Independent Clauses
## Joined by Punctuation Alone

A semicolon replaces the period that separated the independent clauses. The first word in the clause after the semicolon begins with a small letter. Usually no more than two independent clauses are joined with a semicolon unless the clauses are parallel.

In most cases the use of a comma between such clauses (or no punctuation at all) would be a serious sentence fault. Sometimes, however, short, parallel clauses may be joined by a comma, especially when the second clause is abridged.

| | |
|---|---|
| two clauses joined | Part of the search party went to the right, the rest (went) to the left. |
| three clauses joined | I came, I saw, I conquered. |

In formal English, a colon sometimes replaces a semicolon when the second clause explains or illustrates the first.

> *Because we are so greatly outnumbered, there is only one way we can avoid total destruction by the enemy: we must make a surprise attack at once.*

In such sentences the colon serves an anticipatory function.

Sometimes the first word after the colon is capitalized, especially if it begins a question.

> *The questions being raised are these: How should the balance of the appropriations be spent, and to whom should they be given?*

## Independent Clauses
## Joined by Coordinate Conjunctions
## *And, Or, Nor, But, Yet, So, For*

Coordinate conjunctions are less formal than the equivalent conjunctive adverbs, but all such conjunctions are acceptable in formal discourse except **so**. Informal conversation is full of the loose coordination expressed by **and**, but careful writing requires more exact connectives or a reduction in the form of some of the predications.

A comma usually appears before the coordinate conjunction, especially if the clauses are long. However, it is not obligatory. The writer is often guided by whether he would pause in speech. For example, the contrast set up by **but** or **yet** is usually reflected by a pause in speech and a comma in writing.

Generally, it is advisable to use a comma before the coordinate conjunction **for**, in order to prevent misreading it as a preposition—**The girl did all the shopping and cooking, for her mother was in the hospital.**

A semicolon may appear before a coordinate conjunction joining clauses if there is already internal punctuation within one or more of the clauses.

> *The French Revolution was fought for the abstract ideals of liberty, equality, and fraternity; but the Russian Revolution was fought for the more concrete goals of peace, bread, and land.*

Each clause in a compound sentence may be preceded by correlative conjunctions.

> *Not only did he give his wife a new fur coat, but he bought her an expensive car.*

**But** may set up a complete contrast of positive-negative opposition, or a partial contrast of concession.

| | |
|---|---|
| Positive-negative contrast | His wife likes the mountains, **but** he doesn't. |
| Concession | He was aware of the danger of the mission, **but** he insisted on undertaking it. |

**Yet** is interchangeable with **but** in its concessive use (**He was aware of the danger of the mission, yet he insisted on undertaking it**) but not in its use for positive-negative contrast.

**Only** joining independent clauses is an informal equivalent of **but** in its sense of *except that*.

> *They wanted to continue traveling, only they ran out of money.*

When independent clauses are joined by **but**, the verb in the first clause may have conditional form.

> *I would go to the party tonight, but I have too much work to do.*
>
> *I would have gone to the party last night, but I had too much work to do.*

In such sentences, **but** may also be considered an alternative of **except that**.

The coordinate conjunction **or** (with or without **else**) may express a condition. It is an informal equivalent of the conjunctive adverb **otherwise**.

After a positive statement, **or** means *if not*:

| | |
|---|---|
| After an imperative verb | Get off this property or (else) I'll call the police. |
| After a modal auxiliary | You must (*or* should) do your homework or you'll fail the course. |

After a negative statement, **or** means *if so*:

| | |
|---|---|
| After an imperative verb | Don't take too long in dressing or you'll be late for the theater. |
| After a modal auxiliary | I can't stay longer or I'll miss my bus. |

Abridgment
of Second Independent Clause

In general, clauses are abridged in two ways. One is through *omission* of words necessary for the full subject-predicate structure. This kind of abridgment of "understood" words is often called *ellipsis*. Another kind of abridgment is through *substitution*. In this type of abridgment, one word is allowed to stand for an entire structure.

Independent clauses are abridged mainly through substitution; dependent clauses are abridged either through substitution or through the omission of words.

In independent clauses, several types of substitution are possible if the predicate of the second clause parallels the predicate of the first clause.

1. An *auxiliary* may represent the second predicate.

> He says he will finish the work on time (,) and he **will**.
>
> He says he will finish the work on time (,) but he **won't**.
>
> John caught a cold (,) and I **did** too.
>
> John caught a cold (,) and so **did** I.

2. **To** may represent the balance of the second predicate after verbs taking the infinitive.

> I will do it for him (,) but I don't want **to**.

3. **So, not** may substitute for the balance of the second predicate after verbs like **think, believe, hope.**

> My wife thinks that there will be a war soon, but I don't think **so** (or but I think **not**).

In another type of abridgment with independent clauses, the second verb may be omitted if two short clauses are parallel.

> Some went to the left, others to the right.
>
> To err is human, to forgive divine.

**Independent Clauses**
**Joined by Conjunctive Adverbs**

A semicolon replaces the period that separated the two sentences.

The conjunctive adverbs which join independent clauses behave both as conjunctions and as adverbs. As conjunctions, they have the function of connecting grammatical structures. As adverbs they both provide transitional adverbial meanings and have the ability of filling adverbial positions. Conjunctive adverbs are more likely to be found in formal writing than in informal conversation.

The more common conjunctive adverbs are listed below under the relationship they show.

| | Conjunctive Adverb | Corresponding coordinate conjunction |
|---|---|---|
| Addition | besides, likewise, moreover | and |
| Condition | otherwise | or |
| Result | accordingly, consequently, hence, then, therefore | so |
| Time | then | |
| Concession (contrast) | however, nevertheless, still | but, yet |

A conjunctive adverb has a more specific meaning than the corresponding coordinate conjunction.

Some grammarians also classify **indeed, also, anyhow, henceforth, meanwhile, too** among the conjunctive adverbs. In fact, the list of conjunctive adverbs is often extended to include certain adverbial word groups, especially those showing the same relationship as the ones given above—**in addition, as a result, for this reason, in spite of this fact**, etc.

Conjunctive adverbs may be used correlatively with subordinate conjunctions—***If* we miss the bus, *then* we'll have to take a taxi**. Other adverbs and adverbial word groups may function as conjunctive coordinates.

| | |
|---|---|
| Addition | for one thing—for another (thing); partly . . . partly |
| Time | at one moment . . . at the next; sometimes . . . sometimes; now . . . then |
| Contrast | on the one hand . . . on the other (hand) |

Conjunctive adverbs occupy the three possible positions of adverbs.

| | |
|---|---|
| Initial position | The boy is sick; therefore, he didn't come to school. |
| Mid-position | The boy is sick; he therefore didn't come to school. |
| Final position | The boy is sick; he didn't come to school, therefore. (final position only in a short clause) |

Conjunctive adverbs joining clauses are punctuated in the same way as other adverbs. The writer is guided by whether he would pause in speech. However, it is customary, although not obligatory, to use a comma after a conjunctive adverb in initial position.

A coordinate conjunction may be followed by another coordinate conjunction or by a conjunctive adverb. In such a use, the principal meaning is in the second word.

| | |
|---|---|
| *but* | *still* |
| *and* | *yet* |
| *and* | *so* |
| *and* | *therefore* |

| and | thus |
|-----|------|
| or | otherwise |
| or | else[2] |

*The doctor has warned him many times about the dangers of heavy smoking,* ***and so*** *he has decided to give up this habit (or* ***and*** *he has* ***therefore*** *decided to give up this habit).*

Such combinations are used not only with independent clauses but with words, phrases, and dependent clauses.

If a strong break is desired between clauses ordinarily joined by either a coordinate conjunction or a conjunctive adverb, the clauses may be written as two separate sentences. Textbooks warn against starting a sentence with one of these connectives, especially the coordinate conjunction, a chief reason being that young writers have a tendency to break up short sentences into still shorter ones. However, the works of the best authors contain ample evidence of sentences beginning with such connectives. This usage is in line with the modern tendency, even in formal writing, toward shorter sentences.

## Dependent Clauses
## (in Complex Sentences)

In a dependent clause, the full predication is altered in such a way that the clause must be attached to another clause, an independent clause. The alteration may be an added introductory word (**I'll go straight home *after* I finish my work.**) or a change in the form of the subject or object (**They want to hire a woman *who* can cook French food.**).

There are three types of dependent clauses, named according to their function in the sentence.

| | |
|---|---|
| Adverbial clause | The concert was canceled *because the soloist became ill*. (**Because the soloist became ill** modifies the verb **canceled**.) |
| Adjective clause | The student *who gets the highest grades* will receive an award. (**Who gets the highest grades** modifies the noun **student**.) |
| Noun clause | I don't know *whether they still live there*. (**Whether they still live there** functions as the object of **know**.) |

## Sequence of Tenses
## in Dependent Clauses

A main verb in any tense but the past does not require any special verb form in the dependent clause. A past main verb, however, often "attracts" a past verb form in the dependent clause.

---

[2] The combinations **but yet, but nevertheless** are sometimes found, but are generally not considered acceptable in formal writing.

| | *Present Main Verb* | *Past Main Verb* |
|---|---|---|
| Adverbial clause | The child *is staying* home from school because he *is* ill. | The child *stayed* home from school because he *was* ill. |
| Adjective clause | The teacher *is* worried about the boy who *has been* ill for a week. | The teacher *was* worried about the boy who *had been* ill for a week. |
| Noun clause | The child's mother *says* that he *may go* back to school soon. | The child's mother *said* that he *might go* back to school soon. |

This kind of sequence of tenses is especially applicable in noun clause objects after past main verbs. More details about sequence of tenses in such clauses will be given in the chapter on noun clauses.

Abridgment
of Dependent Clauses

Dependent clauses may be abridged through substitution in the same way as independent clauses are.

> She visits her parents whenever she **can**.
>
> I'm going on this trip because I have **to**, not because I want **to**.

In addition, the entire predicate may be omitted from a dependent clause (usually a clause of comparison).

> She isn't as pretty as her sister.
>
> The new secretary did the work much faster than the old one.

In certain adverbial clauses, the subject and a form of **be** may be omitted. The principal word in the predicate may be:

| | |
|---|---|
| an adjective | When (you are) *angry*, think before you speak. |
| a noun | While (he was) *a student*, he began to play in the band. |
| a prepositional phrase | Although (she was) *in a hurry*, she stopped to help the old lady. |
| a participle | When (he was) *talking* to women, he was very sentimental. (present participle from a progressive form) |
| | If (you are) *arrested* for demonstrating, call your lawyer at once. (past participle from a passive form) |

Usually such abridgment occurs in an adverbial clause with a single-word conjunction and with a subject that is the same as the subject of the main clause.

In informal usage, certain introductory words may be omitted from dependent clauses.

Adjective clauses      **whom, that, which** used as objects in restrictive clauses
Here's a list of the books (which) you'll need for this course.

Noun clauses          **that** introducing noun clauses used as objects
He said (that) he would be leaving soon.

Adverbial clauses    **that**
He took a taxi so (that) he wouldn't miss his plane.
The moment (that) he saw her, he fell in love with her.

Reference should also be made here to another type of abridgment than substitution of one word for part of a structure or omission of a part of the structure. In this kind of abridgment, the introductory word of the clause is retained, but the verb is reduced to infinitive form and the subject is omitted.

Adverbial clause    He won't be *so* foolish *as to resign from the company now.*
Adjective clause    He had to borrow money *with which to buy food.*
Noun clause         I don't know *whether to do it.*

The chapter on infinitive phrases gives a fuller explanation of this kind of abridgment of dependent clauses through reduction of the verb forms.

# 12

## Introduction to
## Complex Syntactic Structures

In modern grammar two approaches to the analysis of syntactic structures have contributed to an understanding of how such structures are used to build up sentences. Both are based on different conceptions of what the sentence is. According to one view, the sentence represents an expansion of the subject-verb-complement core. Thus, in the sentence **The boy's arrest for murder shocked his parents**, the subject **arrest** is expanded by the preceding modifier **the boy's** and the following modifier **for murder**. This kind of emphasis on physical arrangement of elements within a sentence is known as structural grammar.

In the second view, the sentence represents a changed form of a simple, basic sentence, or a combination of such changed forms. According to this interpretation, the sentence **The boy's arrest for murder shocked his parents** consists of two simple sentences, the first of which—**The boy was arrested for murder**—has been changed so that it can become the subject of the second. This kind of grammar, which is concerned with the process by which basic sentences are changed to fit into larger sentences, is called transformational grammar.

Both interpretations—the structural and the transformational—offer insights into the way complex structures are used in sentences. In this text, the structural arrangement of words has already been considered to some extent in connection with the parts of speech that function as the central core of a sentence and those that function as their modifiers. It is now important to analyze syntactic structures in terms of the predications contained within them and to see what kinds of changes have been made from simple sentences to permit them to combine into larger sentences. It is through the use of these structures of predication that the complex strands of a line of thought may be put into their proper perspective.

The subject-predicate structures that will be presented in the following chapters are listed below. We are beginning with those that are least changed from full subject-predicate form and are ending with those that are most changed.

---

*Dependent clauses* (full subject and predicate)
Adverbial clauses
**Because he was sick,** the boy didn't go to school.
Adjective clauses
The boy, **who was sick,** didn't go to school.
Noun clauses
We were told **that the boy was sick.**

*Verbal constructions* (verb of predicate is reduced)
*Subject omitted*
Participial phrases
**Being sick,** the boy didn't go to school.
*Subject reduced or omitted*
Gerund phrases
**His being sick** was unfortunate.
Infinitive phrases
**For him to be sick** is unusual.
*Subject retained*
Absolute constructions
**The boy being sick,** his mother called a doctor.

*Abstract noun phrases* (verb reduced or omitted, subject reduced or omitted)
**The boy's sickness** disturbed his mother.

*Appositive phrases* (subject and a form of **be** omitted)
Appositive noun phrases
**A very sick boy that day,** he didn't go to school.
Appositive adjective phrases
**Very sick that day,** the boy didn't go to school.

---

Because a consideration of these syntactic structures which function as grammatical shapes for predications takes us into the larger area of communication, we now need to broaden our analysis to include not only those aspects that make for correct sentences but those that make for effective sentences. For this reason we will examine next not only the grammatical dimensions of each structure, but the stylistic and semantic dimensions as well. The presentation of each structure will therefore include: (1) an analysis of the changes from full subject-predicate form, especially changes from the original subject, verb and complement of the simple sentence from which the structure is derived; (2) types of the structure, and any special grammatical usages connected with these types; (3) position and punctuation of the structure; (4) stylistic matters related to the use of the structure—for example, its rhetorical function (economy, continuity, emphasis, etc.), its degree of formality, its level of abstraction; (5) possible abridgments of the structure; (6) possible meanings of the structure. In addition, the first structures presented, the dependent clauses, will contain a summing up of all subject-predicate structures that alternate with them, either in meaning or in function.

# *13*

## *Adverbial Clauses*

In an adverbial clause, a special introductory word is added to a full subject-predicate structure. This introductory word requires the clause to be attached to another full predication, the main clause—**I could not come last night** *because* **I had to work**.

Most types of adverbial clauses are considered as modifying the verb of the main clause, some more loosely than others. A few types, such as clauses of time or clauses of place, are sometimes interpreted as modifiers of the entire sentence.

Like the adverb, the adverbial clause has three possible positions.

INITIAL POSITION.   Here the adverbial clause adds one means of variety to a sentence opening. An introductory adverbial clause is usually set off by commas, especially if the clause is long. (However, there are variations in usage, sometimes even by the same writer.) This position gives more emphasis to the adverbial clause; it may also relate the clause more closely to the preceding sentence. Generally, a long adverbial clause before a short main clause should be avoided to prevent the sentence from appearing "topheavy."

Mid-Position (often after the subject of the main clause). Here the adverbial clause must be set off by commas, since it acts as an interrupting element. An adverbial clause in mid-position helps to vary the rhythm of the sentence.

Final Position. This is the most usual place for the adverbial clause (as it is for most adverbial expressions). Clauses of time and place (often also result, purpose, degree) in final position are generally not set off by commas. For the other clauses, the writer uses a comma if he would pause before one of them in speech, especially if the clause is long or is added as an afterthought.

(Where it is considered useful, further information about the position and punctuation of adverbial clauses will be given under the individual type of clause.)

TYPES
OF ADVERBIAL CLAUSES

Adverbial clauses are usually classified according to the meaning of the conjunctions that introduce them. In the pages that follow, detailed descriptions will be given for each type of adverbial clause. Further information about special usages connected with each type of clause may be found in the chapters on verbs (the uses of the tenses), auxiliaries, adverbs (intensifiers), and conjunctions (subordinate).

## Clauses of Time

*Conjunctions*

| | |
|---|---|
| when(ever) | You may begin when(ever) you are ready. |
| while | While he was walking home, he saw an accident. |
| whilst—British | |
| since | They have become very snobbish since they moved into their expensive apartment. |
| before | Shut all the windows before you go out. |
| after | After she finished dinner, she went right to bed. |
| until | Until Mr. Smith got a promotion in our company, I had never noticed him. |
| till | We'll do nothing further in the matter till we hear from you. |
| as | As he was walking in the park, he noticed a very pretty girl. |
| as soon as | I'll go to the post office as soon as I wrap this package. |
| as long as | You may keep my book as long as you need it. |
| now (that) | Now (that) the time has arrived for his vacation, he doesn't want to leave. |
| once | Once she makes up her mind, she never changes it. |

**Whenever** has a greater generalizing force than **when**. It is equivalent to *at any time that.*

**Till**, a synonym for **until**, is probably less common in the written language than **until** is. **Till** often has a literary or poetic effect—**I will love you till the seas run dry.**

Sometimes **as long as** is preceded by **for**—**You may keep my book for as long as you need it.**

**Now (that)** may also express cause, or both time and cause simultaneously —**Now that my replacement has come, I can leave.**

**Once** is synonomous with **after**—**Once you have been to Europe, you will always want to go back.** A conditional relationship is also implied in this use of **once.**

Most single-word conjunctions of time may be preceded by intensifiers, by **not,** or by both.

|     |      |        |
|-----|------|--------|
|     |      | *as*   |
|     | *just* | *until* |
|     |      | *when* |
| *not* | *only* | *before* |
|     |      | *after* |
|     | *even* | *since* |

An introductory adverbial clause beginning with **only** or **not** requires a reversal of subject and verb in the main clause.

*Not until* (or *only when*) *the plane landed did she feel secure.*

Other special intensifiers of conjunctions of time are:

| | |
|---|---|
| *ever* | *since* |
| *right* | *until* |
|  | *when* |
|  | *before* |
|  | *after* |
| *long* | *before* |
| *half an hour* | *after* |
| (or other | |
| quantities) | |
| *immediately* | |
| *directly* | |

**Not** may also precede these intensifiers (except **ever**)—**not right after, not long before.**

Certain adverbial expressions of time may serve as conjunctions, with or without **that.**

| | |
|---|---|
| Prepositional phrases | (at) the moment (that) |
|  | by the time (that) |
|  | (at) the same time (that) |
|  | during the time (that) |
| Nouns | the year (that) |
|  | the month (that) |
|  | every time (that) |
|  | (the) next time (that) |

|                          |                   |
|--------------------------|-------------------|
| Adverbs (British usage)  | directly (that)   |
|                          | immediately (that)|
|                          | instantly (that)  |

---

The conjunctions of time **whereat, whereupon** are older forms that are now found mainly in literary prose.

*The court jester began to imitate the royal gestures of the king, whereupon (or whereat) the king began to laugh uproariously.*

**Ere** is an archaic equivalent for **before.**

*I will be betrayed thrice ere I die.*

**As** signifies time in its broadest sense. Because the conjunction **as** can express several relationships besides time, it should be used sparingly, especially at the beginning of a sentence.

In its use as a conjunction of time, **as** is sometimes a synonym for **when, while.**

$\left.\begin{array}{l} As \\ When \\ While \end{array}\right\}$ *I was walking in the park, I saw two men fighting.*

**As** may also be synonomous with **as soon as.**

$\left.\begin{array}{l} As \\ As\ soon\ as \end{array}\right\}$ *he stepped into the house, his children rushed over to greet him.*

**When** and **while** are often synonomous, **when** connoting time in a broad sense, **while** connoting time that has duration.

$\left.\begin{array}{l} When \\ While \end{array}\right\}$ *I was in Japan, I bought some beautiful pearls.*

A **when** clause introducing a definition after a form of **be** should be avoided in formal usage—**Automation is when certain processes are operated by machines alone.** Such a definition should be reworded so that a true nominal appears in the predicate—**Automation is the operation of certain processes by machines alone.**

### CORRELATIVES OF TIME

| | |
|---|---|
| when) . . . then<br>after) | When (or after) all the day's chores were done and the children had been put to bed, then she sat down with her husband to plan their summer vacation. |
| no sooner . . . than | No sooner had he finished one task than he was asked to do another one.<br>*or*<br>He had no sooner finished one task than he was asked to do another one. |

(**When,** which is often used here in place of **than,** is not acceptable to all grammarians.)

scarcely (or hardly) . . . when     Scarcely had the words escaped from his lips when
he realized he had committed a blunder.

*or*

The words had scarcely escaped from his lips when
he realized he had committed a blunder.

(**Before** may be interchangeable with **when** in such sentences. **Than,** which is
often used here in place of **when,** is not acceptable to all grammarians.)

---

### SPECIAL VERB FORMS IN TIME CLAUSES

| *Time Expressed* | *Verb in Main Clause* | *Verb in Time Clause* | *Sentences* |
|---|---|---|---|
| Future | Future tense (or future-equivalent) | Present tense | He will go (*or* is going) straight home after he *closes* his store. |
|  | *or* | | |
|  | Future tense (or future-equivalent) | Present Perfect tense | He will go (*or* is going) straight home after he *has closed* his store. |
|  | Future Perfect tense | Present tense | We will have finished all the adverbial clauses by the time the semester *ends*. |
|  | *or* | | |
|  | Future Perfect tense | Present Perfect tense | We will have finished all the adverbial clauses by the time the semester *has ended*. |
|  | (emphasis on one future time before another) | | |
| Past | Past Progressive tense | Simple Past tense | She was ironing when the telephone *rang*. |
|  | *or* | | |
|  | Simple Past tense | Past Progressive tense | The telephone rang while she *was ironing*. |
|  | (one past action in progress interrupted by another past action) | | |
|  | Past Progressive tense (or Simple Past tense) | Past Progressive tense (or Simple Past tense) | I *was watching* (*or watched*) television while my wife *was preparing* (*or prepared*) dinner. |
|  | (two past continuous actions going on simultaneously | | |
|  | Past Perfect tense | Simple Past tense | I had just dozed off when the telephone *rang*. |
|  | (one past action completed just before another past action) | | |

**Will** or **shall** sometimes appears in the time clause as well as in the main
clause—**It will be a long time before we will** (or **shall**) **see him again.**

The present subjunctive in the time clause is sometimes met with in older usage and in poetry.

> *I shall wait till he send for me.*
>
> *The tree will wither long before it fall.*

Abridgment
of Clauses of Time[1]

The subject and a form of **be** may be omitted from a time clause. The retained portion of the predicate may be:

| | |
|---|---|
| A predicate noun | When (I was) *a boy*, I went to the lake every summer. |
| A predicate adjective | When (we are) *young*, we are full of hopes and anxieties. |
| A prepositional phrase | When (you are) *in the army*, you must obey all commands. |
| A participle | |
|   present participle | She turns on the radio when (she is) *doing* the housework.[2] |
|   past participle | War, when (it is) *waged* for a long time, can destroy the morale of a country. |

Many of the other types of adverbial clauses that follow may also be abridged by the omission of the subject and a form of **be**. With this type of abridgment, the subject of the main clause serves also as the "subject" of the abridged clause. If the subject of the main clause cannot do so, the abridged clause is considered as "dangling," as in the sentence **While (*he* was) still a boy, *his ambition* was to become a doctor.** Such a sentence should be corrected to **While still a boy, he had the ambition to become a doctor.**

Alternate Subject-Predicate Structures
Expressing Time

The alternate structures illustrated here are based on the adverbial clause in the sentence **After we finished breakfast, we went for a walk.**

| | |
|---|---|
| Coordinate clause | *We finished breakfast; then* we went for a walk. (The relationship of time is established by the coordinating word.) |
| Prepositional phrase with gerund | *After finishing breakfast,* we went for a walk. |
| Participial phrase | *Having finished breakfast,* we went for a walk. |
| Absolute construction | *Breakfast finished,* we went for a walk. |

[1] The information under abridgment of each type of adverbial clause will be chiefly confined to abridgment through omission of part of the structure (or in some clauses, reduction of the verbs to infinitive form). Abridgment through substitution, because it is so widespread among all the adverbial clauses, will not be given except when it seems useful to do so.

[2] A present participle appearing after an introductory word that may also function as a preposition is interpreted as a gerund object of the preposition rather than as part of an abridged clause—**after (or before, since, until) doing the housework.**

Clauses of Place

*Conjunctions*

---

where(ver)     She lives where the Johnsons used to live.
               Only fools rush in where angels fear to tread.
               They sat down wherever they could find empty seats.

---

**Where(ver)** may be preceded by intensifiers, by **not**, or by both.

| not | *just* | |
|-----|*only*| *where(ver)* |
|     |*even*| |
|     |*right*| |

*He sat, not right where he always sits, but a short distance away.*

A conjunction of place may consist of an adverbial compound ending in **-where** or **-place**, with or without **that** following it.

> anywhere (that)
> nowhere (that)
> everywhere (that)
> any place (or anyplace) (that)
> no place (that)
> every place (that)
> (These forms with **place** are U.S. informal)

*He goes everywhere (that) she goes.*

**Wherever** has a greater generalizing force than **where**. It is synonomous with **anywhere that**—**He goes wherever she goes. Where(ver)** and **when(ever)** may be interchangeable in some general statements—**He believes that wherever** (or **whenever**) **there's trouble, a woman is involved.**

**Where(ver) . . . there** are correlatives of place.

> *Where there is poverty, **there** we find discontent and unrest.*

> *Where there was trouble, **there** he was sure to be.*

If the main clause is short, **there** may appear at the end of the clause—
*Wherever* **there was trouble, he was sure to be** *there*.

Abridgment
of Clauses of Place

The subject and a form of **be** may be omitted from a clause of place. The retained portion of the predicate may be:

---

*A predicate adjective*     Repairs will be made wherever (they are) ***necessary***.
*A participle*              He will work wherever (he is) ***sent by his company***.

---

Alternate Subject-Predicate Structures
Expressing Place

The alternate structures illustrated here are based on the adverbial clause in the sentence **Accidents frequently happen** *where several roads intersect.*

| | |
|---|---|
| Prepositional phrase with abstract noun | Accidents frequently happen *at the intersection of several roads.* |
| with gerund | Accidents frequently happen *at the intersecting of several roads.* |

Clauses of Contrast

There are two types of clauses of contrast, concessive and adversative. The concessive clause offers a partial contrast—it states a reservation that does not invalidate the truth of the main clause. The adversative clause makes a stronger contrast that may range all the way to complete opposition.

## Concessive Clauses

*Conjunctions*

| | |
|---|---|
| although | We couldn't meet the deadline, although we worked day and night. |
| though[3] | Though he had always preferred blondes, he married a brunette. |
| even though | Even though she disliked the movies, she went with her husband to please him. |

These three conjunctions have practically the same meaning. **Though** is a little less formal than **although**; **even though** adds the most force to the concession.

Some concessive clauses are reversible—**Although he married a brunette, he had always preferred blondes**. In such cases, the predication that is to receive greater emphasis is put in the main clause.

Prepositions of concession may function as conjunctions by the addition of **the fact that**.

in spite of the fact that
despite the fact that
regardless of the fact that
notwithstanding (the fact) that (*literary*)

**While** is frequently used as a concessive conjunction, especially in informal English.

[3] When not used in initial position in its clause, **though** is an informal equivalent of **however** —**The meat is very good; it is tough, though.**

*While he admitted stealing the money, he denied doing any harm to the owner.*

*While I don't like that artist personally, I admire his work.*

**While** concessive clauses appear in initial position only; they are more likely to be reversible than those clauses beginning with **although**.

*While he denied doing any harm to the owner, he admitted stealing the money.*

*While I admire that artist's work, I don't like him personally.*

**Albeit (that)** is a formal conjunction of concession with an archaic flavor—**Albeit that he was sorely wounded, he remained cheerful in spirit.** It is probably used most often today in abridged clauses—**He chose a satisfying, albeit ill-paid profession.**

In **even if**, a concessive meaning may merge with the conditional meaning.

*Even if he's unreliable at times, he's still the best man for the job.*

*Even if you (will) punish me, I'll do it.*

In such sentences the idea of concession may be reinforced by the correlative **still**. Many sentences with **even if** can convert to predications joined by **but**—**He may be unreliable at times, but he's still the best man for the job.**

**If** is sometimes used alone to express this kind of concessive-conditional meaning.

*The house is very comfortable (even) if (it is) a little small. (=The house is very comfortable but [it is] a little small.)*

*He is very friendly, (even) if he is an aristocrat.*

Such **if** clauses are usually in final position, with the verb stressed. Occasionally, however, they are found in initial position—**If they are poor, they are at any rate happy.**

**For all (that)** is an informal conjunction of concession.

*For all that she was a heavy woman, she danced with unusual grace and ease.*[4]

In formal English, certain participles combining with **that** function as conjunctions of concession.

---

| | |
|---|---|
| granted (that) *or* granting | Granted (that) he has always provided for his children, still he has never given them any real affection. |
| conceded that | Conceded that his testimony is unimpeachable, still it might be merely circumstantial evidence. |
| admitted that (less common) | Admitted that what you say is true, still there is much to be said for the other side. |

---

[4] **For all (that)** is also used idiomatically with **know** or **care** to imply a lack of knowing or caring—**For all (that) I know, (=I don't know; I'm not sure), he may have already arrived at his destination.**

Certain interrogative words function as concessive conjunctions.

1. Interrogative words compounded with **-ever**

*Whatever he has done, he is still your friend and needs help.*

*She will not leave her husband, however cruel he is.*

The older forms with **-soever** are still met with today—**Wheresoever she may be, he will find her.**

2. Interrogative words preceded by **no matter**

*No matter what he has done, he is still your friend and needs help.*

*She will not leave her husband, no matter how cruel he is.*

Note that each of these two constructions may convert to the other (**whatever he has done**, or **no matter what he has done**). Both constructions may also convert to a noun clause used as the object of **regardless of** or **in spite of**— **regardless of how cruel her husband is; in spite of what he has done.**

In formal style, part of the predicate of the concessive clause may precede the conjunction **though** or **as**. Such structures are the equivalent of clauses beginning with **no matter though.**

| | |
|---|---|
| Predicate noun precedes | Fool though (*or* as) he was, he knew how to make money. (=No matter though he was a fool, he knew how to make money.) |
| Predicate adjective precedes | Foolish though (*or* as) he was, he knew how to make money. |
| Participle precedes | Badly damaged as (*or* though) it was, the ship managed to reach port. |
| Adverb precedes | Rashly as (*or, less commonly,* though) he had behaved, he didn't deserve the punishment he received. |
| Verb precedes | Detest him as (*or* though) we may, we must admire what he has accomplished. |

Occasionally this structure has the **as** . . . **as** form of a clause of degree.

*(As) quickly as he worked, he couldn't finish the job on time.* (compare with degree—*As quickly as each piece was finished, it was sold.*)

*(As) much as they wanted to, they couldn't get to see their new grandson.*

**Whether . . . or (whether)** is often classified as a concessive construction. We have chosen, however, to consider such a construction as conditional and will take it up under clauses of condition.

Correlatives Expressing Concession

Adverbs like **nevertheless, still, at any rate, anyhow** (informal) and the coordinate conjunction **yet** may co-occur with subordinate conjunctions of concession.

> **Although** it may seem incredible, it is **nevertheless** true.
>
> **Even though** he felt he might not succeed in his new business, **still** (or **yet**) he decided to take a chance.
>
> **Though** he (*had*) studied very hard for the examination, he failed **anyhow**.

Such co-occurrence is especially common with the participial conjunctions that denote concession—***Granted that* he stole the money under extenuating circumstances, *still* he must be punished for this theft.**

Verb Forms
in Concessive Clauses

Usually the indicative form of the verb is used, but special verb forms may also be found in concessive clauses.

1. *Present subjunctive* (older style):

> Though this be madness, yet there is method in't. (Shakespeare)
>
> Whoever he be, he cannot succeed.

The conjunction may be omitted, and the subject and the subjunctive verb inverted—**Be it ever so humble, there's no place like home.**

2. *Modal auxiliary*

| | |
|---|---|
| may—might | Whoever he may (*or* might) be, he cannot succeed. |
| | No matter who he may (*or* might) be, he cannot succeed. |
| | Cost what it may, I must have that ring. |
| should | I'll come to you by moonlight though hell should bar the way. (Alfred Noyes) |

## Adversative Clauses

*Conjunctions*

| | |
|---|---|
| while[5] | While Robert is friendly with everyone, his brother makes very few friends. |
| where[5] | Where the former governor had tried to get the cooperation of the local chiefs, the new governor aroused their hostility by his disregard for their opinions. |
| whereas | Soccer is a popular spectator sport in England, whereas in the United States it is football that attracts large audiences. |
| when | He claims to be a member of the royal family when in fact his family were immigrants. |

**But** may substitute for these adversative conjunctions that introduce

---

[5] In spite of the fact that many reputable writers use **while** and **where** as adversative conjunctions, some authorities consider such usage unacceptable in formal English.

clauses in final position. Like **but**, adversative conjunctions often set up a complete contrast.

| | |
|---|---|
| Positive-negative contrast | Some newspapers carry many advertisements, whereas others have none at all. |
| Semantic contrast | Some people delight in doing good, while others take pleasure in doing evil. |

The clauses in such sentences are often reversible.

> *Some newspapers have no advertising at all, whereas others carry many advertisements.*
>
> *Some people take pleasure in doing evil, while others delight in doing good.*

## Abridgment of Clauses of Contrast

The subject and a form of **be** may be omitted from a clause of contrast. The retained portion of the predicate may be:

| | |
|---|---|
| A predicate noun | Although (he is) *only a child*, he works as hard as an adult. |
| A predicate adjective | Although (he is) *very young*, he works as hard as an adult. |
| A prepositional phrase | Although (he was) *in a hurry*, he stopped to help the blind man cross the street. |
| | I'll come and visit you soon, if (it is) *only for a day*. |
| A participle | |
| present participle | Although (he is) *working long hours*, he manages to find time for relaxation. |
| past participle | Although (she was) *hired as a bookkeeper*, she also does secretarial work. |

## Alternate Subject-Predicate Structures Expressing Contrast

The alternate structures illustrated here are based on the adverbial clause in the sentence *Although he was ill*, **he managed to look cheerful**.

| | |
|---|---|
| coordinate clause: (The relationship of contrast is established by the coordinating word.) | |
| with coordinate conjunction | *He was ill but* (or *yet*) he managed to look cheerful. |
| with conjunctive adverb | *He was ill*; *however*, he managed to look cheerful. |
| prepositional phrase: | |
| with abstract noun | *In spite of* (or *regardless of*) *his illness*, he managed to look cheerful. |
| with gerund | *In spite of being ill*, he managed to look cheerful. |

Clauses of Cause

*Conjunctions*

| | |
|---|---|
| because | They had to move because their building was to be torn down. |
| since | Since he couldn't take his wife with him, he decided not to go to the conference. |
| as | As he was in a hurry, he hailed the nearest cab. |
| now (that) | Now (that) he's inherited his father's money, he doesn't have to work any more. |
| whereas *(formal)* | (for arguments, decrees, preambles, resolutions) Whereas a number of the conditions in the contract have not been met, our company has decided to cancel the contract. |
| inasmuch as *(formal)* | Inasmuch as every effort is being made to improve the financial condition of this company, the term of the loan will be extended. |
| as (*or* so) long as | As long as it's raining, I won't go out tonight. |
| on the ground(s) that | His application for the job was rejected on the ground that he had falsified some of the information. |

**Because** may be preceded by intensifiers:

$$\left. \begin{array}{l} only \\ just \end{array} \right\} \ because$$

A **because** clause is the only possible answer to a question beginning with **why**.

*Why did you do it? —Because I wanted to help him.*

Some phrasal prepositions may be changed to conjunctions by the addition of **the fact that**.

> on account of the fact that
> owing to the fact that
> in view of the fact that
> due to the fact that (*informal—not accepted by all*)

**In that** combines the meaning of extent with that of cause—**He is like his father in that he is very susceptible to feminine charms.** It is closely related to **in the respect that** or **to the extent that**. **In that** often appears after verbs or adjectives expressing similarity or difference.

Another conjunction that denotes both cause and extent is **(all) the more that**—**Those arguments moved him (all) the more that they came from a man of great authority.** **That** may be separated from the first part of the conjunction—**The arguments are (all) the more weighty (in) that they come from a man of great authority.**

Certain participles plus **that** may serve as conjunctions of cause:

| | |
|---|---|
| seeing that (*informal*) | Seeing that no one wants to go out tonight, we'll stay home and watch television. |

| taking into consideration (the fact) that | Taking into consideration (the fact) that he began his business with almost no capital, he has done remarkably well. |
| --- | --- |

**Being that** used as a conjunction of cause is regarded as substandard.

**As long as** is a synonym for **since**, but not for **because**. It is a more casual conjunction, often suggesting the feeling of **anyhow**.

> *As long as you're here (anyhow), let's have dinner.*
>
> *As long as you're going to the store (anyhow), get me a quart of milk.*

Since **as long as** also expresses time, its use may result in ambiguity—**He'll take care of her as long as she's his wife.** In speech the intended meaning would be clearer, because the word **long** would receive greater stress for time than for cause.

If emphasis on *reason* is desired, **for the (simple) reason (that)** may introduce the causal clause—**He cannot be accused of that crime for the simple reason that he was out of town when the crime was committed.**

Certain structures in which part of the predicate precedes the conjunction **as** may function as clauses of cause.

> *Knowing him as I do, I can tell you that he'll never pay you the money he owes you.*
>
> *The house was very quiet, isolated as it was on the side of a mountain.*
>
> *Coward as he was,* he ran back as soon as the enemy attacked. *That* may alternate with *as* after the predicate noun *coward.* The *as* or *that* clause here may also be interpreted as an adjective clause modifying the noun *coward.*

Note that this kind of structure is parallel to the one that expresses concession with **though** or **as**—**Coward though he was, he ran forward at the signal to attack.**

**That** may substitute for **because** in a contrast with **not . . . but**—**He came to very few of the meetings, not that (=not because) he thought they were unimportant, but because he had too much work to do.**

**Because** may have the sense of **if only because**. The main verb in a sentence with **because** used thus requires the conditional **would** form.

> *You would like her because she is so charming and warm.*
>
> *I would have lent the money to him, because he has done many favors for me.*

**Because** clauses used as nominals are not acceptable in formal English:

1. *Because clause as subjective complement*—**The reason the car broke down is *because* we drove too fast.** While this construction with **the reason . . . is because** is very common, formal usage requires **the reason . . . is that**.

2. *Because clause as subject*—**Because he doesn't like her is no reason to treat her so badly.** This construction is found only in very informal English.

Formal English requires the sentence to be reworded so that the **because** clause functions as an adverbial—**He shouldn't treat her so badly just because he doesn't like her.**

Punctuation
of Clauses of Cause
in Final Position

The terms restrictive or nonrestrictive often distinguish final clauses of cause that are closely or loosely related to the main verb. Restrictive causal clauses are generally not preceded by a pause in speech or a comma in writing.

Unpunctuated restrictive clauses are introduced mainly by the conjunction **because**—**The boy was severely punished** *because he was insolent.* The nonrestrictive clauses that are preceded by commas may be introduced by **because, since** or **as**—**The insolent boy was severely punished,** *because* (or *since, as*) *his father wanted to teach him a lesson.* Such nonrestrictive clauses often give an explanation or justification. A second type of nonrestrictive clause, used only with **because**, gives the reason for an inference—**The insolent boy must have been severely punished,** *because we saw him crying bitterly.*

A test for a comma before a causal clause is to see whether **for** can be substituted for the introductory conjunction. If it can, then the clause is nonrestrictive and a comma is advisable. At times, however, the comma is necessary to establish a difference in meaning, especially after a negative main verb.

> *He didn't kill his wife because he loved her.* (but for some other reason)
>
> *He didn't kill his wife, because he loved her.* (The ***because*** clause gives the reason why he would not have killed her.)

Abridgment
of Clauses of Cause

The subject and a form of **be** may be omitted from a clause of cause. The retained portion of the predicate may be:

| | |
|---|---|
| A predicate adjective | Her nasty remarks are all the more insulting since (they are) *intentional.* |
| A participle | Since (it was) *agreed on by the majority*, this measure will be carried out. |

Alternate Subject-Predicate Structures
Expressing Cause

The alternate structures illustrated here are based on the adverbial clause in the sentence ***Because Mr. Black was an extremely timid person*, he did not try to advance himself professionally.**

| | |
|---|---|
| Coordinate clause | Mr. Black did not try to advance himself professionally, *for he was an extremely timid person.* |
| Prepositional phrase | |
| with abstract noun | *On account of his extreme timidity*, Mr. Black did not try to advance himself professionally. |
| with gerund | *On account of his being extremely timid*, Mr. Black did not try to advance himself professionally. |
| Participial phrase | *Being extremely timid*, Mr. Black did not try to advance himself professionally. |
| Absolute construction | *Mr. Black being an extremely timid person*, he did not try to advance himself professionally. |
| Adjective clause | Mr. Black, *who was an extremely timid person*, did not try to advance himself professionally. |
| Appositive noun phrase | *An extremely timid person*, Mr. Black did not try to advance himself professionally. |
| Appositive adjective phrase | *Extremely timid*, Mr. Black did not try to advance himself professionally. |

Occasionally a gerund phrase or an abstract noun phrase functioning as subject may express cause.

(Examples from sentence with adverbial clause—*Because he selflessly devoted himself to his patients*, **he won the respect of all**.)

| | |
|---|---|
| Gerund phrase | *His devoting himself selflessly to his patients* won him the respect of all. |
| Abstract noun phrase | *His selfless devotion to his patients* won him the respect of all. |

## Clauses of Result

*Conjunctions*

| | |
|---|---|
| so . . . that | |
| so + *adjective* + that | She is so *emotional* that every little thing upsets her. |
| so + *adverb* + that | She behaved so *emotionally* that we knew something terrible had upset her.   , |
| such (a) . . . that | |
| such a + *singular countable noun* | This is such an ugly *chair* that I am going to give it away. |
| such + *plural countable noun* | These are such ugly *chairs* that I am going to give them away. |
| such + *noncountable noun* | This is such ugly *furniture* that I am going to give it away. |
| so (that) | They spent their vacation at the seashore, so (that) when they came home they were quite tan. |

**With the result that** places strong emphasis on the idea of result—**He made some very bad investments in the stock market, with the result that he lost his entire fortune.**

The same cause-effect relationship can often be established in either the cause clause or the result clause.

---

| | |
|---|---|
| Cause clause | *Because* the children had rehearsed many times, their school play was very successful. |
| Result clause | The children had rehearsed many times, *so that* their school play was very successful. |

---

The "split" conjunctions **so . . . that** and **such (a) . . . that** combine the result relationship with that of degree.

In a **such (a) . . . that** clause, the noun that comes between the two parts of the conjunction may be used alone or with adjective modification. Often the meaning of the result clause hinges on the adjective modifier rather than on the noun—**It was such a *terrible* experience that I will never forget it.** This sentence is the equivalent of **The experience was so *terrible* that I will never forget it.**

**Such** may be used as a pronoun (usually after a form of **be**) in a clause of result.

> *The experience was such that I will never forget it.*
>
> *Conditions were such that I could not get my money at the time.*

In very informal English, **that** may be omitted from **so . . . that** and **such (a) that** clauses. In such cases **that** is replaced by a pause in speech or a comma in writing.

> *She is so emotional, every little thing upsets her.*
>
> *This is such an ugly chair, I'm going to give it away.*

When **so** is used alone, it may be indistinguishable from a coordinate conjunction, as in **He sat in the front of the room, so he heard every word of the lecture.** We might say arbitrarily that if we can replace **so** by **so that**, then **so** is a subordinate conjunction introducing a clause of result. If we cannot, then **so** is a coordinate conjunction, as in **He was sick, so he couldn't go to school.**

Sometimes **so that** is separated in such a way that **so** begins the main clause; in these cases a reversal of word order in the main clause is required.

> *So powerful was he that none dared resist him.*
>
> or *So powerful was he, none dared resist him.*

The structure beginning with **so** may also appear in final position—**None dared resist him, so powerful was he** (also, informally, **so powerful he was**). This **so** construction is sometimes interpreted as a cause clause.

The clause with **so** may be used in mid-position, with or without a reversal in word order.

> *Many people do not realize, so great is the hold of tradition (or the hold of tradition is so great), that the primary form of a language is its speech, not its writing system.*

After a negative statement or a question, a negative clause introduced by **that** or **but (that)** is sometimes considered a result clause.

*A day never went by that (or but that, but) he didn't bring his wife a little gift.*

In popular speech **but what** is also heard—**Things are not so bad but what they might be worse.**

**So much so that,** which sometimes functions as an emphatic conjunction of result, also denotes an element of degree.

*He hates his work, so much so that he is thinking of resigning.* (compare with *He hates his work so much that he is thinking of resigning*)

*His cold kept getting worse, so much so that he had to go home.*

**So much so that** is preceded by a pause in speech or a comma in writing. Certain **that** clauses may be interpreted as result clauses.

*Something is wrong that she hasn't arrived yet.*

*I must have been blind that I couldn't see what a hypocrite he was.*

*What has the child done that he should be reprimanded so harshly?*

*Have you finished all your homework, that you are now reading the comics?*

Position and Punctuation
of Result Clauses

Outside of the few exceptions already noted, a result clause is in final position only. Commas often appear before **so (that)** clauses. No commas are used with clauses introduced by split conjunctions.

Abridgment
of Clauses of Result

| | |
|---|---|
| Infinitive phrase | He won't be so foolish as *to reject that offer.* |
| | *or* He won't be such a foolish person as *to reject that offer.* |

Alternate Subject-Predicate Structures
Expressing Result

The alternate structures illustrated here are based on the adverbial clause in the sentence **Mr. Black was *such* a timid person *that he did not try to advance himself professionally.***

| *Coordinate clause* | |
|---|---|
| With coordinate conjunction | Mr. Black was a timid person, *so he did not try to advance himself professionally.* |
| With conjunctive adverb | Mr. Black was a timid person; *therefore, he did not try to advance himself professionally.* |
| *Infinitive phrase* | Mr. Black was too timid *to try to advance himself professionally.* |

In addition, subjectless participial phrases in final position may express the result of what is stated in the first part of a sentence.

> *My train arrived two hours late,* **thus causing me to miss my train connection.**

## Clauses of Purpose

*Conjunctions*

| | |
|---|---|
| (in order) that | He decided to take a trip around the world (in order) that he might learn about different people and their customs. |
| so (that) | The flowers will be delivered as late in the evening as possible so (that) they will be fresh for the party. |
| in the hope that | They are working night and day in the hope that they can finish the building at the scheduled time. |
| to the end that (*formal*) | To the end that justice may be served, the defendant will be offered every opportunity to establish his innocence. |

The time denoted by the purpose clause is generally future in relation to the time represented by the main clause.

Sequence of tenses is required in purpose clauses.

| | |
|---|---|
| Present time | He is saving his money so that he may (*or* can) take a long vacation. |
| Past time | He was saving his money so that he might (*or* could) take a long vacation. |

A purpose clause, especially one introduced by **so (that)** often resembles a clause of result.

| | |
|---|---|
| Purpose | He's sitting in the front row so (that) he may hear every word of the lecture. |
| Result | He sat in the front row, so (that) he heard every word of the lecture. |

However, certain physical features distinguish the two constructions: (1) the auxiliary **may, can** or **will** usually appears in the purpose clause; (2) the purpose clause may be moved to initial position; (3) there is a greater pause in speech before the result clause, and usually a comma in writing.

*Negative Purpose*

| | |
|---|---|
| lest (*formal*) | He told his wife as little as possible, lest she spread (*or* should spread) the news all over town. |
| for fear that | For fear that any of the children might (*or* should) get lost, the camp forbade them to go beyond a certain point. |

Such clauses may be closely related to clauses of cause—**He told his wife as little as possible, because she might spread the news all over town.**

The verbs in clauses of negative purpose are either in present subjunctive form or are accompanied by auxiliaries such as **might, should** or **would**.

## Position and Punctuation
## of Purpose Clauses

A purpose clause generally appears in final position, with no comma preceding it. Sometimes it is placed in initial position for greater emphasis— **In order that he might learn about different people and their customs, he decided to take a trip around the world.**

A clause of negative purpose with **lest** and **for fear that** may appear in either initial or final position.

## Alternate Subject-Predicate Structures
## Expressing Purpose

The alternate structures illustrated here are based on the adverbial clause in the sentence **They went to the box office early so that they might buy the best seats.**

| | |
|---|---|
| Infinitive phrase | They went to the box office early (*in order*) *to buy the best seats*. |
| Prepositional phrase with gerund | They went to the box office early *for the purpose of buying the best seats*. |

## Clauses of Condition

*Conjunctions*

| | |
|---|---|
| if | If I see him, I'll invite him to our party tomorrow. |
| | If it doesn't rain, we'll go to the beach tomorrow. |
| even if | Even if I had known about the meeting I couldn't have come. |
| unless (=if . . . not) | Unless it rains, we'll go to the beach tomorrow. |
| in the event (that) *or* in event that (*formal*) | In the event (that) the performance is called off, I'll let you know at once. |
| in case | In case a robbery occurs in the hotel, the management must be notified at once. |
| provided (that) *or* providing (that) | We will be glad to go with you to the theater tonight provided (that) we can get a baby-sitter. |
| on condition (that) (*formal*) | The company will agree to arbitration on condition (that) the strike is called off at once. |
| as (*or* so) long as | As (*or* so) long as someone was willing to treat her, she would go to the movies. |
| if only | She would forgive her husband everything, if only he would come back to her. |
| suppose (that) *or* supposing (that) | Suppose (that) your house burns down. Do you have enough insurance to cover such a loss? |
| whether . . . or (whether) | Whether she is at home or whether she visits others, she always has her knitting with her. |

In older style, **so (that)** also occurs as a conjunction of condition—**We forgive much ill-treatment, so (that) it is secret.** In this use **so (that)** is the equivalent of **so long as.**

Most of the conjunctions of condition may be preceded by the intensifier **only**:

|  |  |
|---|---|
| *only* | *if* |
|  | *unless* |
|  | *so long as* |
|  | *on condition (that)* |
|  | *provided (that)* |
|  | *in the event (that)* |
|  | *in case* |

*He will give his wife more money only on condition that she use it for household expenses.*

*Only in the event (that) war breaks out will our government prohibit travel outside the country.*

A few conjunctions of condition may be preceded by **just**:

|  |  |
|---|---|
| *just* | *so long as* |
|  | *in the event (that)* |
|  | *in case* |

*She was perfectly content just so long as she could stay home and take care of the house.*

**Not** may precede some conjunctions of condition:

|  |  |
|---|---|
| *not* | *if* |
|  | *unless* |
|  | *so long as* |
|  | *even if* |

**If** may be used with the correlative **then**—**If you have paid your rent regularly, then the landlord will not ask you to move.**

The conjunction **if** (or **even if**) may combine other meanings with those of condition.

---

| | |
|---|---|
| time | |
| **if** (=when, whenever) | If (*or* whenever) the child cries, she gets what she wants. |
| contrast | |
| **even if** | We'll leave for our automobile trip tomorrow even if it rains. |
| **if** (=although *or* whereas) | If I disliked him before, I now loathe him. |
| | If he is not a dynamic administrator, he is at least a conscientious and hard-working one. |
| Correlatives of contrast may be used in such sentences. | *If* private opinions may not be openly expressed in a totalitarian state, the current official view, *on the other hand,* must be loudly and enthusiastically professed. |

degree
| if (=just as ... so) | If the play is true to life, it is also as absurd as life. |
| | If he was unable to handle his business problems, still less was he able to cope with his marital problems. |
| The correlative **so** may appear in the main clause. | *If* he was disappointed, *so* was she. |

---

**If** used in the sense of **although,** or **just as ... so** may be considered as setting up "pseudo-conditions" which operate differently from normal **if ... then** conditions.

A cause-effect relationship may also be expressed with an **if** clause plus indefinite **it** in the main clause—**If I am being critical, it is because I want you to improve.** This is a loose construction for **I am being critical because I want you to improve.**

Meanings of Statements
Containing Conditional Clauses

In statements with true conditions, the main clause gives the *result* of a condition. If there is some possibility that such a result may be accomplished, the forms for a *real* condition are used; if the result is impossible or uncertain of realization, the forms for an *unreal* condition are used.

**Statements with Real Conditions**

In most statements with real conditions, there are only two possible results —if the condition is realized, then the result stated in the main clause will take place; if the condition is not realized, then the result will not take place.

Statements with real conditions may express various kinds of conditional meaning.

EVENTUALITY.   **If, in the event (that), in case.**

1. *Possibility* The realization of the condition is open to chance; the condition may or may not be realized. In such statements, the main clause may signify:

---

| Intention | If he bothers you, what will you do? |
| Prediction | In the event (that) the dam breaks, there will be great loss of life and property. |
| Conjecture | If Mr. Smith is not in his office now, he is (*or* must be) out for lunch. |
| Instructions | In case you need anything else, please let me know. |

---

2. *Necessity* The realization of the condition is not open to chance. If a certain condition exists, a certain conclusion inevitably follows. The use of such conditions is common in mathematics and logic.

> *If a figure is a square, it has four right angles.*
> *If this creature is a man, he is mortal.*

PROVISIONALITY.   **If, provided (that), on condition that, only if, as long as.**
The condition is a stipulation, a requirement, or a demand that is expected
to be met.

> *You will have no trouble with these plants provided that you water them
> regularly.*
>
> *The strikers will go back to work if* (or *only if*) *they get the raise they are
> asking for.*
>
> *As* (or *so*) *long as they are back in the dormitory by midnight, students may
> go wherever they like.*

SUPPOSITION.   **If, suppose (that), supposing (that).**
The conjunctions in these conditions may be considered the equivalent of
**if we suppose (that)** or **let us suppose (that).**

> *Suppose (that) you are elected. What will you do for your constituents?*
>
> or *Supposing (that) you are elected, what will you do for your constituents?*

Such conditional clauses are usually in initial position, but occasionally in
informal speech they follow short main clauses—**What will you do for your
constituents, supposing you are elected?**

**Statements with Unreal Conditions[6]**

Some statements with unreal conditions are impossible to realize at any
time in the present or future.

> *If I were you, I would get more rest.* (The speaker can never be the other
> person.)

Other statements with unreal conditions apply only to the impossibility
of realization in the present.

> *If I had enough money, I would take a vacation.* (This statement indicates
> that the speaker does not have enough money *now*. The situation may
> change in the future, but the statement is not concerned with this.)

A statement with a past unreal condition indicates that the condition was
not realized, and therefore the result given in the main clause did not take
place.

> *If I had had enough money last year, I would have taken a vacation.* (This
> statement reveals that the speaker did not have enough money last year.
> He therefore did not take a vacation.)

Still other statements with unreal conditions merely express doubt, uncertainty, improbability about a given situation.

> *If he really needed money, I would give him some.* (This statement sug-
> gests doubt that he needs the money.)

---

[6] Unreal conditions are also called *contrary-to-fact* conditions.

vs. a real condition: *If he needs money, I'll give him some.* (Implied in this statement is its opposite alternative—*If he doesn't need money, I won't give him any.*

Verb Forms in Sentences
Containing Conditional Clauses

## Statements with Real Conditions

The forms of the verbs depend on whether the conditional statement involves one event or repeated events.

STATEMENT REFERRING TO ONE EVENT. The present tense appears in the conditional clause, and the future tense in the main clause.

| Conditional Clause (*present* tense) | Main Clause (*future* tense) |
|---|---|
| If John *studies* hard, | he *will pass* the test. |
| If the roads *are* good, | we*'ll take* the bus. |
| If he *leaves*, | I*'ll be leaving* too. |

The verb in the main clause may also be one of the future tense equivalents.

*If John studies hard, he's going to pass the test.*
*If the roads are good, we're taking the bus.*
*If he leaves, I leave too.*

The verb in the main clause may be in imperative form.

*If it rains, close the windows.*
*Unless it rains, please water the lawn.*

If the conditional clause is stressing a *relationship to present time*, the present progressive form may occur in the conditional clause.

*If he is bothering you (now), I'll call the police.* (time of condition is present)
vs. *If he bothers you, I'll call the police.* (time of condition is future)
*If he is studying hard, he will pass the test.*
*If it is raining, close the windows.*

If the conditional clause is stressing a *relationship to future time*, the future tense or a future tense equivalent may be used in the conditional clause.

*If he will get* (more commonly *gets*) *the money, he will give it to charity.*
*If you will be sleeping* (or *are sleeping*) *when I get home, I won't disturb you.*
*If he's going to get angry, I won't do it.*

If the conditional clause is stressing a *relationship to past time*, the present perfect tense is often used in the conditional clause.

*If he has made a mistake, he will try to correct it.*

> *If he has lost his keys, he will be in trouble.*
>
> *If he has worked hard (or if he has been working hard), he will succeed.*

Sometimes the past tense is used informally in such conditional clauses.

> *If he made a mistake, he'll try to correct it.*
>
> *If he lost his keys, he'll be in trouble.*
>
> *If he worked hard, he'll succeed.*

In some real conditions referring to one event, the main verb may express *time other than the future.* Most of these non-future conditions are introduced by **if** and are contained within statements that denote eventuality (especially conjecture or opinion). These other tense forms are given below. The first tense in each heading is for the conditional clause, the second tense is for the main clause.

1. *Present—Past*

> *If he **has** a tape recorder, he probably **borrowed** it.*
>
> *If rumor **is** to be trusted, both men **were** in love with the same woman.*

2. *Present—Present Perfect*

> *If he **has** a tape recorder, he **has** probably **borrowed** it.*
>
> *If she **is** not at home, she **has** probably **gone** to the market.*

3. *Past—Present*

> *If she **went** to the office today, she **is** probably **catching up** on her correspondence.*
>
> *If they **finished** dinner early tonight, they're probably watching television now.*

4. *Past—Past*

> *If he **was** at the meeting last night, I **didn't see** him.*
>
> *If she **did** what you say, she **was** wrong.*

5. *Past—Present Perfect*

> *If she **did** what you say, she **has done** wrong.*
>
> *If he deliberately **broke** the street light, he **has committed** a misdemeanor.*

6. *Present Perfect—Present Perfect*

> *If she **has done** what you say, she **has done** wrong.*
>
> *If she **has bought** a new coat, then she **has bought** a hat too.*

STATEMENTS REFERRING TO REPEATED EVENTS.    Real conditions may be contained within generalizations that range from general truths to customary actions. The conjunction **if** (or its negative **unless**) is most common in such conditions. The conjunction of time **when(ever)** alternates with this generalizing **if**.

Generalizations with conditional clauses may denote "timeless" time or past time. Those generalizations that express "timeless" time require the *present tense* in both clauses; those that refer to past time require the *past tense* in both clauses.

| Repetition Involves: | Conditional Clause | Main clause |
|---|---|---|
| Past, present, and future ("timeless time") | If (*or* when) the weather *is* good, If (*or* when) lightning *flashes*, | I usually *go* to the beach. thunder *follows*. |
| past time only | If (*or* when) the weather *was* good last summer, If (*or* when) an epidemic **broke out** in the Middle Ages, | I *went* to the beach. it *spread* with amazing speed. |

The future tense is sometimes also used in the main clause for generalizations.

> *If this is true, (then) that **will be** true.*
> *If lightning flashes, thunder **will follow**.*
> *If a man doesn't eat, he **will die**.*

With customary action, however, the future tense in the main clause can refer to only one event—**If the weather is good, I will go to the beach**.

SUBJUNCTIVE FORM USED IN REAL CONDITIONS.    This form represents an archaic usage. It occurs chiefly with **if** (or **unless**).

1. *Present subjunctive*

> *If gold rust, what shall iron do?*
> *If the Lord keep not the city, the keepers watch in vain.*

The present subjunctive of **be** in real conditions still occurs in modern English. Its use is formal or literary.

> *If this be treason, make the most of it.* (Patrick Henry)
> *The slight, if there be one, is unintentional.*
> *If this be the case, then we must help him at once.*

The present subjunctive may also still be found after **provided (that), as long as, on condition (that)**, as a formal alternative of the indicative.

> *He will do the work provided that he do* (or *gets*) *union wages.*
> *I will help him on condition that he do* (or *does*) *as I say.*

2. *Past subjunctive* (only occasionally found in modern English, mostly the form **were**).

> *If it were so, it was a grievous fault.* (William Shakespeare)
>
> *We do not recommend that the same theory of teaching be used throughout the world, if indeed that **were** possible.*

### Statements with Unreal Conditions

In statements with unreal conditions, subjunctive forms are used in the conditional clause, **would** or **would have** forms in the main clause.

| | Conditional Clause | Main Clause |
|---|---|---|
| *Present* time (starting from now and extending to the future) | If he *tried* harder (in general), If the weather *were* good (now),  Verb is in *past subjunctive* form (same form as past indicative)[7] | he *would succeed.* I *would go* to the beach. (verb phrase consists of *would + the simple form of the verb*) |
| *Past* time | If he *had tried* harder (last week), If the weather *had been* good (last week),  Verb is in *past perfect subjunctive* form (same form as past perfect indicative) | he *would have succeeded.* I *would have gone* to the beach. (Verb phrase consists of *would have + the past participle*) |

For those who observe the **shall—will** distinction, **should** is used for the first person in statements with unreal conditions—**If the weather were good now, I should go to the beach.**

Most unreal conditions begin with the conjunction **if**, but other conjunctions may also introduce unreal conditions.

> ***Suppose* (*that*)** *you had seen her. What would you have done?*
>
> *I would help **provided that** he did his part too.*
>
> ***In the event that*** *a robbery had occurred, the management would have called the police immediately.*
>
> ***Even if*** *he weren't so insolent, I still wouldn't like him.*

**If only** clauses generally require unreal conditional forms.

> *If only I had known about his coming, I would have met him at the station.*
>
> *If he were only here now, I would be very happy.*

**If only** clauses expressing wishes also have the form of unreal conditions.

> *If only he were here now! or If he were only here now!*
>
> *If only I had known! or If I had only known!*

Such wishes may also be expressed as—**Were he only here now! Had I only known!**

---

[7] The one exception is the verb **be**. It has only one past subjunctive form, **were**, which is used for all three persons.

Unreal conditional forms are also used after **would that**, a literary alternative for an **if only** wish.

*Would that he were here now!*

*Would that I had known!*

Past forms of modal auxiliaries may appear in either the conditional clause or the main clause.

*If I **might** (or **could**) see him once more, I would be happy.*

*If he were here, he **might** (or **could**) help us.*

**Would** or **would have** sometimes also occurs in both clauses, especially in informal speech.

| | |
|---|---|
| would | If he would (only) do his homework, he would pass his tests. |
| | You would get over your cold if you would (only) stay in bed. |
| would have | If the weather would have been good, I would have gone to the beach. |
| | If he would have consented, everything would have been all right. |

The use of **would have** forms in conditional clauses is unacceptable to some authorities even in informal English.

**Will** or **would** may be used in both clauses to stress willingness.

*If you will make the beds, I will wash the dishes.*

or *If you would make the beds, I would wash the dishes.*

**Will** or **would** may also appear in conditional clauses that are little more than polite requests—**If you will** (or **would**) **pardon me for a moment** (=**please pardon me for a moment**), **I'll check on that matter.**

**Should** may be used in both real and unreal conditional clauses as an equivalent of **happen to—If you should see him, what will** (or **would**) **you do?**

In unreal conditions, **if** may be omitted and the subject and verb reversed.

*Were I in your position, I would call the police.*

*Might (or could) I (but) see him once more, I would be content.*

*Should you see him, what would (or will) you do?*

*Had he gone to the doctor right away, he might still be alive today.*

*Even had he been there, he (still) wouldn't have helped her.*

Contractions with **not** do not occur in such constructions—**Should he not be there, I would be disappointed.**

Conditional statements that refer to past time may be a blend of the real and the unreal. A real clause expressing some doubt or uncertainty may combine with a main clause that indicates lack of reality through a **would have** form.

*If he **was** there (i.e., perhaps he was there), I would have seen him.*

vs. *If he **had been** there (i.e., he was *not* there), I would have seen him.*

*If you **mailed** the letter last week* (i.e., perhaps you mailed the letter), *I would have received it by now.*

vs. *If you **had mailed** the letter last week* (i.e., you did *not* mail the letter), *I would have received it by now.*

In formal speech, the past perfect forms are more likely to be chosen for past unreal conditions.

It is possible for the two different times of unreal conditional statements to be combined. A past unreal conditional clause may be used with a present unreal main clause.

*If the boy **had listened** to his parents last year, he **wouldn't be** in trouble now.*

*"There is a concatenation of events in this best of all possible worlds: for, if you **had** not **been kicked** out of a magnificent castle for the love of Miss Cunegonde: if you **had** not **lost** all your sheep from the fine country of El Dorado: you **would** not **be** here eating preserved citrons and pistachio nuts."* (Voltaire, from the conclusion of *Candide*)

The verb forms for statements with unreal conditions often appear in sentences with **if** clauses after adjectives expressing feeling, especially contentment or discontent.

*I would* (or *should*) *be*
| happy |
| glad |
| delighted |
| distressed |
| sad |
| sorry |
*if he came* (or *should come or comes*) *now.*

*I would have been happy (glad, etc.) if he had come yesterday.*

But—*I will be glad if he comes.* (Future time requires a real condition.)

Unreal conditional forms are also used in sentences with **if** clauses that follow certain adjectives of advisability in impersonal **it** constructions.

*It would be*
| wise |
| advisable |
| desirable |
| good (better, best) |
*if you saw the president of the company first.*

The adjectives in these constructions may be accompanied by nouns—**It would be a good thing** (or **a wise move**) **if you finished as soon as possible.**

These **if** constructions after adjectives of advisability alternate with infinitive constructions.

*It would be wise* (or *advisable, desirable, good*) *for you to see the president of the company first.*

## Coordinate Conditions
## with WHETHER . . . OR (WHETHER)

These coordinates contrast two opposing conditions.
positive-negative opposites:

*Whether true or not, the story is interesting.*

*Whether they have help or not* (or *whether they have help or they don't*), *they plan to go ahead with the project.*

semantic opposites:

*Whether true or false, the story is interesting.*

*The show will go on whether the theater is full or whether there are only a few people in the audience.*

**Whether . . . or (whether)** coordinates may be used with two full clauses, or with one or both clauses abridged. The second **whether** is more likely to be retained if the clauses are full.

| | |
|---|---|
| Two full clauses | Whether the story was true or whether a false rumor was circulated, he should not have repeated the story. |
| One clause abridged | Whether the story was true or false, he should not have repeated it. |
| Both clauses abridged | Whether true or false, the story should not have been repeated. |

In **whether** conditional clauses, **or not** is usually placed directly after **whether**—**I'll go whether** *or not* **he goes**. If the conditional clause is short, **or not** may come at the end of the clause—**I'll go whether he goes** *or not*. In older style, **or no** also occurs here—**I'll go whether he goes** *or no*.

Certain structures in which **or** joins positive and negative items are the equivalent of **whether . . . or** clauses.

*They plan to continue their project,* **government help or no government help**.

*They plan to continue their project,* **with or without government help.**

The preceding positive-negative structures are alternatives for **whether they have government help or not**.

In formal style, the subjunctive form **be** may appear in **whether . . . or (whether)** constructions.

*A story for children, whether it* **be** *written or spoken, should have a great deal of action.*

The first **whether** may be omitted and the subject and **be** reversed.

*Be it written or spoken, a story for children should have a great deal of action.*

Conditional **if** or **whether** clauses should not be confused with noun clauses.

| | |
|---|---|
| Conditional clause | If he goes to the party, I will go. |
| | Whether he goes to the party or not, I'll go. |
| Noun clause | I don't know if he is going to the party. |
| | I don't know whether (or not) he is going to the party. |

The **if** or **whether** noun clause is the object of the verb **know. If** and **whether** are equivalents in a noun clause.

Certain sayings that consist of short, parallel parts may be considered as equivalent to statements with introductory conditional clauses.

| | |
|---|---|
| With verb | Nothing ventured, nothing gained. (=If you don't take risks, you won't gain anything.)<br>Love me, love my dog.<br>Easy come, easy go.<br>Forewarned is forearmed. |
| Verbless | Once a farmer, always a farmer. |

Some grammarians claim that the construction **the** + *comparative,* **the** + *comparative* (the more, the merrier) denotes a conditional relationship, but we prefer to interpret the relationship as proportion and will say more about this construction in the section on clauses of proportion and extent.

### Abridgment of Clauses of Condition

The subject and a form of **be** may be omitted from a clause of condition. The retained portion of the predicate may be:

| | |
|---|---|
| A predicate noun | If (it is) *a success,* the experiment could lead the way to many others. |
| A predicate adjective | If (he is) *still alive,* he must be at least ninety years. |
| A prepositional phrase | If (it is) *out of the question,* please let me know. |
| A participle | |
| present participle | If (he is) *meeting with too many unexpected difficulties,* he will abandon the project. |
| past participle | If (it is) *carefully done,* the experiment should be very successful. |

Certain **if only** clauses may be abridged by the omission of **it is.** The retained portion of the predicate may be:

| | |
|---|---|
| A prepositional phrase | I will go if (it is) only *for a few moments.* |
| An infinitive phrase | She will apologize if (it is) only *to avoid bad feeling.* |
| An adverbial clause | He would do it if (it is) only *because he loves her.* |

Some of these abridged **if only** clauses may be preceded by **even—even if only for a moments; even if only to avoid bad feeling.**

**If so** and **if not** are abridgments through substitution: **so** or **not** stand for an entire subject and predicate.

*The rumor may be true; if so* (=if the rumor is true), *he will be in trouble with the government.*

*We must pay our taxes; if not* (=if we do not pay our taxes), *we will be in trouble with the government.*

Alternate Subject-Predicate Structures
Expressing Condition

The alternate structures illustrated here are based on the adverbial clause in the sentence *If we do not have food,* **we cannot survive.**

---

*Coordinate clause* (The conditional relationship is established by the coordinating word.)

| | |
|---|---|
| with coordinate conjunction | *We must have food, or* we cannot survive. |
| with conjunctive adverb | *We must have food; otherwise* we cannot survive. |
| *Participial phrase* | |
| with present participle | *Not having food,* we cannot survive. |
| with past participle | *Deprived of food,* we cannot survive. |
| *Prepositional phrase* | *Without food,* we cannot survive. |
| *Infinitive phrase* | *To survive,* we must have food. |

---

Clauses of Exception
(Negative Condition)

A clause of exception is introduced by a conjunction that is equivalent to **if it were not (for the fact) that** and therefore may be interpreted as a kind of negative condition.

*Conjunctions*

---

| | |
|---|---|
| except that (*occasionally* excepting that) | The building would have already been finished except that a trucking strike had delayed delivery of some materials. |
| but that (*formal*) | But that his assailant's pistol failed to fire, he would surely be dead now. |
| save that (*formal*) (*occasionally* saving that) | Save that he lapsed into vulgarity every now and then, he had great appeal to his genteel women readers. |
| only (that) | This antique vase is in very good condition, only that there is a little crack near the top. |
| beyond that | The police could get nothing out of the boy beyond that he had become separated from his mother in the crowd. |
| other than (the fact) that | Other than (the fact) that he is now in good financial condition, I have no news to report. |

---

Note that by the addition of **that** to the prepositions **but, except, save, beyond,** these words become conjunctions. The addition of **the fact that** may also turn some prepositions into conjunctions of exception—**but for the fact** that, except for the fact that, beyond the fact that, aside from the fact that, apart from the fact that.

**Only (that)** usually occurs in final position. **Only** without **that** is informal—**This antique vase is in very good condition, only there is a little crack near the top**. Used thus, **only** is hardly distinguishable from a coordinate conjunction.

In many sentences containing clauses of exception, the verb in the main clause takes conditional form with **would, would have**—He *would have gone* **except that he was tired** (=if he had not been tired). In such sentences the coordinate conjunction **but** may be used instead of **except that**—He *would have gone* **but he was tired**.

Abridgment
of Clauses of Exception

The construction **but, except, save** plus a noun or pronoun may be considered either as an abridged clause of exception or as a prepositional phrase. Those grammarians who feel that such a construction is an abridged clause insist on a subject-object distinction in pronouns.

> *She loves no one but (she loves)* **him.**
>
> *No one can do it but* **he** *(can do it).*

Most speakers, however, find it more natural to use the object form in both cases, perhaps because the construction is felt as a prepositional phrase —**No one can do it but** *him.*

The following abridgments with **except** are not typical abridgments since no "missing" words can be supplied. These structures, too, might be considered as prepositional phrases of time or place rather than as abridged clauses.

| | |
|---|---|
| Abridgment with adverbial clause only | She is never cross *except when she is tired.*[8] |
| Abridgment with prepositional phrase only | The dog is permitted everywhere in the house *except in the living room.* |
| Abridgment with adverb only | Put the package down anywhere *except over there.* |

(See clauses of comparison for similar "abridgment" of **as** and **than** clauses.)

Clauses of Manner

*Conjunctions*

| | |
|---|---|
| as if | They all treat him as if he were a king. |
| as though | He walked around as though he was in a daze. |
| as | She always does as her husband tells her. |

---

[8] This kind of construction can be abridged still further—**She is never cross except when (she is) tired.**

These conjunctions of manner may be preceded by the intensifiers **just, exactly**.

> *They all treat him **just** as if he were a king.*
>
> *She always does **exactly** as her husband tells her.*

In clauses beginning with **as if, as though**, two verb forms are possible: the indicative form if the speaker is certain about the statement, the past subjunctive form if the speaker is more doubtful about the statement.

| | |
|---|---|
| Indicative | He looks as if he **needs** sleep. |
| Subjunctive ("timeless") | He looks (*or* looked, has always looked) as if he **needed** sleep. |

These two choices are also possible if the manner clause refers to time that is past in relation to the time of the main verb.

| | |
|---|---|
| Indicative | He looks as if he **hasn't slept** for a week. |
| Subjunctive | He looks (*or* looked, has always looked) as if he **hadn't slept** for a week. |

**Like** may occur as an informal alternative for the conjunction **as—Winstons taste good like (=as) a cigarette should; He looks like (=as if) he needs more sleep.** Although condemned by some, this use of **like** as a conjunction is common even among educated speakers.

**How(ever)** may also introduce a clause of manner—**He wants the right to spend his allowance how(ever) he pleases.** In this use **how(ever)** is the equivalent of **in any way that** or **in whatever way that.**

**As** manner clauses may include the idea of comparison—**They behave toward him as they would (behave) toward a king.**

Position
of Clauses of Manner

Like adverbs of manner, adverbial clauses of manner usually appear in end position. Occasionally, however, they occupy initial position (especially clauses beginning with **as** and **as though**).

> *As though he were an enraged bull, he sprang forward to attack the man who was taunting him.*

Some **as** clauses merely indicate the manner in which a statement is made and thus modify the entire sentence. These clauses may appear in any of the three positions of sentence adverbs.

| | |
|---|---|
| Initial position | As I think back on it, we made a mistake in telling him about our plans. |
| Mid-position | He was, as we remember him, a very honest man. |
| Final position | It is ten miles from here, as the crow flies. |

Abridgment
of Clauses of Manner

The subject and a form of **be** may be omitted from a clause of manner. The retained portion of the predicate may be:

| | |
|---|---|
| A predicate noun | As though (he were) *still the king*, Lear demanded all the privileges of majesty. |
| A predicate adjective | He left the room as though (he were) *angry*. |
| A participle | Everything went off just as (it was) *planned*. |
| An infinitive | He opened his mouth as if (he were) *to speak*. |
| A prepositional phrase | His illness disappeared as if (it was) *by magic*. |

Manner clauses with transitive verbs are sometimes abridged.

> She plays with him as **a cat** (*plays*) **with a mouse**.

> He treats his wife as (*he would treat*) **a child**.

This **as** may be interpreted as a preposition, a synonym for **like**—**He treats his wife like a child.**

Sometimes only the subject is omitted from an **as** manner clause. This omitted subject may be interpreted as **it.**

> As (*it*) usually happens, I can't find my glasses.

> As (*it*) was expected, his speech was full of fancy talk that amounted to nothing.

When a manner clause is abridged through substitution of a verb form for a predicate, the verb and subject may be reversed.

> This text will be concerned, as was classical rhetoric (=as classical rhetoric was concerned), with persuasive discourse.

> The word maize comes from the American Indian, as do many other words which describe American flora and fauna.

Clauses of Degree

**Comparison**

| Conjunctions | |
|---|---|
| *Equal comparison of two units* | |
| $\left.\begin{array}{l}\textbf{as}\\\textbf{so}\end{array}\right\}$ + *adj. or adv.* . . . **as** | The new machine is just as efficient as the old one (was). |
| | The new machine works just as efficiently as the old one (did). |
| *Unequal comparison of two units* | |
| $\left.\begin{array}{l}\textit{adj. or adv.} + \textbf{-er}\\ \text{or}\\ \textbf{more} + \textit{adj. or adv.}\end{array}\right\}$ . . . **than** | The new machine is more efficient than the old one (was). |
| | The new machine works more efficiently than the old one (did). |
| **less** + *adj. or adv.* . . . . **than** | The new machine is less expensive than the old one (was). |

**So . . . as** is used after a negative—**The new machine is not** *so* **efficient as the old one. As . . . as** is also common in such negative sentences—**The new machine is not** *as* **efficient as the old one.**

Sometimes **so . . . as** occurs in a positive sentence for emphasis—**In a country** *so* **large as the United States, we find great diversity of opinion.**

Clauses of comparison may follow certain pronouns or adjectives of indefinite quantity.

> *More, less—This house cost **more** (money) than I had expected.*
>
> *Much, many, little, few—Take as **much** (money) as you need.*

A **than** clause after **different** and **other(wise)** is often treated as a clause of comparison—**He was different (or other) than I had expected.** Those conservative grammarians who insist that only a preposition may follow **different** would require the more awkward **from** plus a noun clause here—**He is different from what I had expected,** or even **He is different from that which I had expected.**

An **as** clause after **the same** may be classified as a clause of comparison.

> *The new machine works the same as the old one (does).*
>
> *He charged me the same as (he did) last year.*

If a noun follows **the same,** the **as** clause might better be interpreted as an adjective clause—**She is wearing the same hat as (=that) her friend is.**

**Rather than** and **sooner than** have the form of conjunctions of comparison, but they actually express choice or preference—**Rather than (or sooner than) give up his car, he would give up his house.** Such clauses do not include subjects, and they contain only the simple form of the verb. In their negative form, **not** precedes the verb—**Rather than (or sooner than) not have his car, he would give up his house.** When such clauses are in final position, **rather** or **sooner** may be separated from **than** and placed with the verb—**He would rather (or sooner) give up his home than (give up) his car.**[9]

Position and Punctuation
of Clauses of Comparison

Clauses of comparison are usually in final position, with no commas preceding them. Occasionally a clause of comparison appears in initial position for emphasis or for a particular stylistic effect.

> *As well as she can sing, I can also sing.*
>
> *More efficient than my supervisor I can never become.*

---

[9] **Before** sometimes functions as a synonym of **rather than** or **sooner than** in the sense of preference—**Before he would give up his car, he would give up his house.** Such **before** clauses occur only with the auxiliary **would**; they are not used with past time, or with a negative.

Abridgment
of Clauses of Comparison

Abridgment through ellipsis is very common in clauses of comparison. Such abridged clauses are usually in parallel construction.

| | |
|---|---|
| Subject retained | She works as hard as *her husband* (works). When the subject is retained, an auxiliary may also substitute for the entire predicate—**She works as hard as her husband does.** |
| Object retained | She desires happiness more than (she desires) *wealth.* |
| Predicate adjective retained | She is more shy than (she is) *unsocial.* |

In most cases a noun appearing after **as** or **than** is the subject of the abridged clause. Strict grammarians insist that personal pronouns functioning thus as subjects must be in subject form—**He is as tall as I (am tall)**. However, in conversational usage, educated speakers frequently use the object form—**He is as tall as me**—possibly because the two parts of the structure are felt as a prepositional phrase rather than as an abridged clause.

An elliptical clause of comparison may be ambiguous after a transitive verb—**He likes Tom better than John**. In such cases the speaker must carry the construction further—**He likes Tom better than John does** or **He likes Tom better than he does John**.

The subject that is retained in an abridged clause of comparison may also be one of the larger nominal structures.

| *Nothing is* | *so (or as) hard as* | *getting up in the morning* (*is*). *Gerund phrase.* |
|---|---|---|
| | *harder than* | *to get up in the morning* (*is*). *Infinitive phrase* (Less likely after *as*). |
| | | *what I am doing now* (*is*). *Noun clause.* |

If one of these nominal structures appears in the main clause, strict parallelism requires that the same nominal structure be used in the abridged clause of comparison.

*Getting up in the morning* is harder than *going to bed at night.*
*To get up in the morning* is harder than *to go to bed at night.*
*What I am doing now* is harder than *what I used to do.*

On the surface, sentences like

*John is as stubborn as his brother.*
*John is as stubborn as a mule.*

might seem to contain the same type of abridged structure. Actually, however, it is probably better to interpret only **as stubborn as his brother** as an abridged clause of comparison, and to regard **as stubborn as a mule** merely as an idiomatic expression in which **as a mule** serves as a lively intensifier of the adjective **stubborn**. In fact, because the first **as** is frequently omitted in such idioms of comparison (**John is stubborn as a mule**) in informal usage, **as a mule** may be classified simply as a prepositional phrase.

An impersonal **it** may be interpreted as an omitted subject in certain clauses of comparison containing passive verbs.

> *The volcano erupted much more violently than (it) was foreseen.*
>
> *He never reads as much as (it) is required of the class.*
>
> *He will not do other(wise) than (it) is expected of him.*

**As** and **than** plus certain adverbials signifying time or place may be considered as a special kind of abridgment.

| | |
|---|---|
| Abridgment with adverbial clause only | She is never so beautiful as (she is) *when she is angry*. |
| Abridgment with prepositional phrase only | His mind is never so sharp as (it is) *in the morning*. |
| Abridgment with adverb only | You could not put the plant in a better location than (you can) *right here*. |

This type of abridgment is parallel to the abridgment with **except**—**She is never beautiful except when she is angry**.

**Proportion or Extent**

*Conjunctions*

| | |
|---|---|
| as | As he acquires more power, he becomes more unscrupulous. |
| as . . . so | As you sow, so shall you reap. (*proverb*) |
| in proportion as . . . (so) | In proportion as the value of land increased, so too did taxes become higher. |
| to the extent that | The project will succeed only to the extent that each of us puts his best efforts into it. |
| according as | We can earn more or less according as the company can give us overtime work. |
| as (*or* so) far as | As (*or* so) far as we can see, he appears satisfied with this arrangement. |
| insofar as (*also* in so far as) | Insofar as I understand modern art, I find it very exciting. |
| to the degree that | You will succeed to the degree that you apply yourself diligently. |

The intensifier **just** or **only** may precede a few of these conjunctions.

> *just* } *as . . . so*
> *in proportion . . . so*
>
> *Just as his love for her grew stronger, so did his need to see her more frequently.*
> (note the reversal of word order after **so**)

| only | as |
| | to the extent that |
| | according as |
| | to the degree that |

*Only as he grew older did he realize the truth of what his father had told him.*

**Also** or **too** may accompany the **so** correlative—**(Just) as she began to see her employer's many good points, so too** (or **also**) **did she become aware of some of his weaknesses.**

An unabridged clause of comparison that is fully parallel with the main clause may denote proportion or extent.

*She is as handsome as her husband is ugly.*

*She is as wise as she is beautiful.*

An **as** or **as that** clause after **so much** may also be considered a clause of proportion or extent.

*He was not so much tired as he was bored.*

or *It was not so much that he was tired as that he was bored.*

An older type of correlative of proportion or extent takes the form **the** + *comparative*, **the** + *comparative*. The comparative may be an adjective, adverb or pronoun.

**The sooner** *he leaves,* **the happier** *I will feel.*

**The more difficult** *the job is,* **the better** *he likes it.*

**The more** *(money) he makes,* **the less** *(money) he spends.*

Each part of this correlative construction may consist of no more than **the** and the comparative. This form is found especially in certain aphorisms or set expressions.

*The more, the merrier.*

*The sooner, the better.*

*The more haste, the less speed.*

Sometimes only the second part of this construction is abbreviated, especially if the comparative in this part is **the better**.

*The more guests that come, the better.*

*The sooner you can arrive, the better.*

**That** may be inserted before a clause following the first comparative in a **the . . . the** construction.

*The sooner (that) a man begins to enjoy his wealth the better.*

*The more (that) life disappointed him, the more he sought refuge in books.*

The second part of a **the . . . the** construction may have inverted order.

*The more people that sign up for the trip, the cheaper will be the price.*

*The noisier the children were, the better was he pleased.*

What would ordinarily be the second part of a **the . . . the** construction is sometimes placed first. This part of the construction then takes normal subject-verb-complement form.

*He became more cynical the older he grew.* (compare with *The older he grew the more cynical he became*).

*He gets more and more restless the longer he stays in the same place.*

*THAT* CLAUSES

AFTER ADJECTIVES

**That** clauses after certain adjectives, as in the sentence **I am happy that you came**, are particularly hard to classify. These clauses cannot be classified by meaning, as most of the other adverbial clauses can, because the introductory **that** merely serves as a structural connector. In this text we are interpreting such **that** clauses as adverbials on the basis of *function* rather than meaning—we are considering them as modifiers of the preceding adjectives. However, we must add that, because many of these clauses developed historically out of causal clauses, they still retain some shade of this adverbial meaning—**I am happy that** (=**because**) **you came.**

Another common interpretation of **that** clauses after certain adjectives is also by function. Some grammarians feel that such **that** clauses are the "complements" of the adjectives. Others consider that these clauses are the "complements" of the combination of the verb **be** plus the adjective; thus, **that** clauses in the construction **he is sorry that . . .** or **he is happy that . . .** function in the same way as **that** noun clause objects ⁓of verbs—**he regrets that . . .** or **he rejoices that . . . .** As a matter of fact, we will have occasion later on, in the chapter on noun clauses, to group these **that** clauses with noun clause objects when certain generalizations about grammatical behavior can apply to both types of clauses.

The adjectives that may be followed by **that** clauses are listed below. These adjectives generally occur in the predicate after a form of the verb **be** (or another linking verb). Most of the adjectives listed express emotion; for this reason a person-denoting subject of the main verb is required.

| | |
|---|---|
| afraid | content |
| angry | desirous |
| aware | discontented |
| (un)certain | eager |
| cognizant | envious |
| conscious | fearful |

glad            mindful
hopeful         positive
ignorant        proud
indignant       sorry
jealous         sure

### -ED PARTICIPIAL ADJECTIVES

amazed          irritated
annoyed         perplexed
ashamed         satisfied
astonished      shocked
concerned       startled
contented       surprised
determined      pleased
disappointed    troubled
disgusted       worried
impressed

Informal usage permits the omission of **that** after some of the adjectives just listed.

> *We're glad you're feeling better today.*
>
> *I'm afraid we've come too late.*

**That** is less likely to be omitted after the **-ed** participial adjectives. The verb in a **that** clause after **eager, desirous, determined** may be in the present subjunctive form.

> *We are desirous that he get* (or *should get*) *here on time.*
>
> *We are determined that it be finished at once.*

In literary English, **lest** may replace **that** after **afraid, fearful**. The subjunctive form of the verb may be used in such a **lest** clause.

> *She was fearful lest the child be* (or *should be, might be*) *hurt.*

The noun forms from some of these adjectives may also be followed by **that** clauses.

> *His awareness that Mrs. Brown disliked him made him uneasy in her presence.*
>
> *He could barely conceal his satisfaction that his plan had succeeded so well.*
>
> *His disappointment that he had not been promoted made him bitter.*

Such noun clauses may be considered as appositive noun clauses.

**That** clauses after many of the adjectives given above, especially the **-ed** participial adjectives, may alternate with infinitive constructions.

| I am | happy | that I live in this country. |
|------|-------|------------------------------|
|      | grateful | or |
|      | sorry | to live in this country. |
|      | satisfied | |
|      | pleased | |

**That** clauses after the adjectives of emotion that have just been discussed need to be distinguished from **that** clauses appearing after predicate adjectives, of an impersonal nature. **That** clauses after impersonal adjectives like **necessary important, inevitable** are the actual subjects in anticipatory **it** constructions—**It is important that he come; It is inevitable that he will succeed.** These clauses, unlike **that** clauses after **sorry, happy, annoyed,** etc., have the option of being moved to regular subject position—**That he come is important; That he will succeed is inevitable.**

# *14*

## *Adjective Clauses*

In an adjective clause[1], a full subject and predicate is changed by means of a special introductory word which has the same referent as the preceding noun or pronoun. The form and position of this introductory word subordinates the adjective clause to a main clause. The introductory word also performs one of three functions in the adjective clause itself: (1) nominal function—the boy *who* gave me the book; The boy from *whom* I received the book; (2) adjectival function—the boy *whose* book I borrowed; (3) adverbial function—the store *where* the boy bought the book.

The adjective clause modifies a preceding noun or a pronoun. The noun or pronoun being modified is called the *antecedent*.

An adjective clause may be classified according to the antecedent that the introductory word refers to.

---

[1] The adjective clause is also called a *relative* clause.

276

| *Noun Antecedent Meaning:* | *Introductory Word* | *Illustrative Sentences* |
|---|---|---|
| | (1) *relative pronoun:* | *Introductory word functioning as:* |
| a person | who (whom or whose) or that | *Subject*—He paid the money to the man *who* (or *that*) had done the work. |
| | | *Object of verb*—He paid the man *whom* (or *that*) he had hired. |
| | | *Object of preposition*—He paid the man from *whom* he had borrowed the money. |
| | | *Possessive adjective*—This is the girl *whose* picture you saw. |
| a thing | which or that | *Subject*—Here is a book *which* (or *that*) describes animals. |
| | | *Object of verb*—The chair *which* (or *that*) he broke is being repaired. |
| | | *Object of preposition*—She was wearing the coat for *which* she had paid $2,000. |
| | (2) *relative adverb:* | |
| a time | when | This is the year *when* the Olympic Games are held. |
| a place | where | Here is the house *where* I live. |
| a reason | why | Give me one good reason *why* you did that. |

INTRODUCTORY WORDS
OF ADJECTIVE CLAUSES

The relative pronoun **who** (**whom** for object, **whose** for possessive) refers to persons (also pets); **which** refers to things. **That** may refer to persons or things.

**That** does not appear after a preposition—**He is the man about** *whom* **I spoke.** Neither does it start a nonrestrictive clause—**You must write to Mr. Jones, who represents us in Europe**. (See section on punctuation for explanation of restrictive, nonrestrictive clauses.)

**That** is preferred in an adjective clause after a superlative—**He is the best student that has ever studied here.** Occasionally, **who** or **which** occurs here—**This is the best book which** (more commonly, **that**) **I have ever read**.

Some authorities claim that **that** should refer only to things, and that in formal prose only **which** is appropriate to denote things. However, these "rules" are largely ignored in the United States. It would probably be more in accord with actual usage in this country to say that, with nonrestrictive clauses referring to things, the choice between **that** and **which** is merely one of style; **that** is chosen if a "lighter" structure word is desired, and **which** if a "heavier" one is preferred.

We have already seen that conversational English permits several other usages of the relative pronoun than the ones given in the preceding chart.

1. The preposition governing the relative pronoun is placed at the end of the clause.

> *There's the man **whom** (or **that**) I was telling you **about**.*
>
> *He paid the man **whom** (or **that**) he had borrowed money **from**.*

2. **Who** often alternates with **whom** for a pronoun object of a verb or of a preposition placed at the end of the clause.

> *He paid the man **who**(**m**) he had hired.*
>
> *He paid the man **who**(**m**) he had borrowed the money **from**.*

3. Relative pronouns functioning as objects of verbs or prepositions may be omitted from restrictive clauses.

> *He paid the man **he had hired**.*
>
> *He paid the man **he had borrowed the money from**.*

However, the pronoun object must be retained in nonrestrictive clauses.

> *He paid Mr. Jones, **whom** he had hired yesterday.*
>
> *There is Mr. Jones, **whom** I was telling you about.*

A noun or pronoun functioning as part of an adjective clause may precede a relative pronoun used in a prepositional phrase. The preposition in such a phrase is usually **of**.

> *Rembrandt's "Windmill," **the original of which** is at the Metropolitan Museum, is one of my favorite paintings.*
>
> *He asked many questions, **the answers to which** were impossible to give.*

Such a construction is especially common with pronouns of quantity or number.

> *The students, **some of whom** had already started to leave the classroom, were called back by the professor.*

This construction is sometimes a more formal alternative for a **whose** construction that refers to things.

> *The mountain, **the peak of which** (or **whose peak**), was barely discernible, was an impressive sight.*

However, many writers avoid this **of which** choice because of its awkwardness.

An **of which** or **of whom** phrase may also be preceded by a superlative adjective which is part of the adjective clause.

> *She owns several diamond rings, **the least expensive of which** is worth a small fortune.*
>
> *The agency sent us several applicants, **the most qualified of whom** was the first one.*

A parenthetic expression such as **I remember, we suppose,** etc., does not influence the form of the relative pronoun—**John, who I remember was good in high school, didn't do so well in college. (Who** is the subject of **was.)**

A **which** clause that refers back to an entire statement instead of to one particular antecedent, although commonly used, is not considered acceptable formal usage by some authorities—**He is a graduate of one of the Ivy League universities, *which should open many doors to him.*** This indefinite **which** construction often expresses result when in final position. Indefinite **which** may occur in a prepositional phrase—**They may refuse to pay, *in which case* we shall have to take more drastic action.** In such sentences indefinite **this** may be interchangeable with indefinite **which**; indefinite **this**, however, requires a semicolon or period to separate the clauses.

> *He is a graduate of one of the Ivy League universities. **This** should open many doors to him.*
>
> *They may refuse to pay; **in this case** we shall have to take more drastic action.*

After the word **reason, why** may be interchangeable with **that** or it may be omitted—**The reason (that) I came should be obvious to you.** Some grammarians consider such a clause as a noun clause in apposition with the word **reason.**

**When** or **where** may be interchangeable with a preposition of place plus **which.**

> *The small town **in which** (=**where**) I was born has grown to a large metropolis. (or **the small town I was born in.** . . .)*
>
> *The day **on which** (=**when**) they were to leave finally arrived.*

Sometimes **that** replaces **where** or **when.**

> *The day that (or **when, on which**) the trial was to take place was a stormy one.*
>
> *Please suggest a good place **that** (or **where**) we can meet.*

In informal style, **that** may be omitted from both sentences—**the day the trial was to take place; a good place we can meet.**

The relative **where** is sometimes found after an abstract noun that does not really denote place—**a system where, a condition where, a plan where. Whereby** is also used here—**a plan whereby everyone could prosper.** This loose use of relative **where**, in spite of objections to it, often fills the need for a simple prepositionless connector of an adjective clause after nouns like those illustrated here.

Other words that may introduce adjective clauses are:

| | |
|---|---|
| **before** or **after** | He became sick the day **before** he was to leave for his vacation. |
| **as** (after **the same**) | She made the same mistakes as (=**that**) her sister did. |
| **but** (literary usage—appears after a negative verb and is itself negative) | There is not one of us **but** would (=**who would not**) find the work difficult. |

The verb of the adjective clause agrees with the antecedent in number (**A *man* who *runs* away is a coward**) and in person (**It is *I* who *am* to blame**).

Formal usage requires a plural verb in an adjective clause following **one of the** (**That is one of the best films that have** [informal **has**] **appeared in a long time**), and a singular verb after **the only one of the** (**That is the only one of the films that *has* pleased me**).

After a collective noun representing a group of persons, relative **which** may be used when the word is felt as referring to a single unit rather than to the individual members of the group—**He spoke to the crowd *which* was following him.**

The normal position of an adjective clause is immediately after the noun or pronoun to which it refers. However, sometimes a prepositional phrase or a participial phrase may intervene—**He greeted all his old friends *from Paris*, who were delighted to see him again.** Where such a phrase intervenes, the antecedent of the adjective clause may be ambiguous. For example, in the sentence **The dean wrote to the parents of the students who had helped with the annual carnival**, it is not clear whether the antecedent of **who** is **the parents** or **the students**.

Occasionally an adjective clause referring to the subject comes after the verb, especially when the antecedent is a pronoun—**Everyone came *who could afford the price of the ticket*.** Such a construction may have a literary or even an archaic flavor:

>All's well ***that ends well***. (Shakespeare)
>He prayeth best ***who loveth best***. (Coleridge)

If the adjective clause serves to narrow down the reference of the noun it modifies, no commas are used for the clause. Thus, in **The boy *who lives next door* is my best friend**, the adjective clause limits the reference of the class word **boy** to the one **boy-who-lives-next-door**. In speech there would be no pause after **boy**. These clauses that limit, or "restrict" nouns further are called restrictive clauses.

Most clauses which modify pronouns are restrictive.

> He resists **anyone** who tries to help him.
>
> The next **one** who disturbs the class will be punished.

If, however, the clause does *not* serve to narrow down the reference of the noun, especially when the noun is already restricted in itself (e.g., a proper noun), commas are frequently used *both before and after the clause*—**John Blair,** *who lives next door,* **is my best friend.** In speech there would be a pause after the antecedent of the clause, **John Blair.** These clauses that do not limit the reference of a noun but merely add more information about the noun are called nonrestrictive clauses.

The use of commas with adjective clauses is summed up in the following chart.

| *Use Commas (Nonrestrictive Clauses)* | | *Do Not Use Commas (Restrictive Clauses)* |
|---|---|---|
| 1. *When the antecedent is restricted in itself* | | 1. *When the antecedent is restricted by the adjective clause:* |
| Antecedent a proper noun | Many people congratulated **William Faulkner,** who had just won the Nobel Prize for literature. | Many people congratulated **the man** who had just won the Nobel Prize for literature. |
| Antecedent one of a kind | **The boy's mother,** who loves him very much, has made many sacrifices for his happiness. | **A mother** who loves her son very much will make many sacrifices for his happiness. |
| | **His aunt,** who lives in California, came to visit him recently. (The adjective clause does not single out one aunt from others. He may have only one aunt.) | **His aunt** who lives in **California** came to visit him recently. (He has more than one aunt. The adjective clause designates which one is meant.) |
| Antecedent identified by the preceding context | Late in the evening they sent out for some coffee. **The coffee,** which had been boiling for a long time, tasted rancid. | **Coffee** which has been boiling for a long time will taste rancid. |
| 2. *When the antecedent refers to **all** of a class* | | 2. *When the antecedent is limited by the adjective clause to **some** of a class* |
| | **The chairs,** which were in bad condition, were sent out to be repaired and refinished. (All the chairs were in bad condition.) | **The chairs** which were in bad condition were sent out to be repaired and refinished. (Some chairs were in bad condition; the others were not.) |

The most usual abridgment of an adjective clause is through the use of an auxiliary that substitutes for a part of the predicate of the main clause—**Most people don't work hard, but a person who *does* gets ahead**.

A **to** or **so** substitute may also abridge an adjective clause.

> *Do you think there will be another war?*
> *—No, I don't, but I know people who think **so**.*
> *Anyone who wants **to** may enter the contest.*

Abridgment through reduction of the clause to infinitive form may also occur in an adjective clause.

> *He borrowed some money with which to buy food.*

| | | |
|---|---|---|
| 1. | *Cause* | **The man who had stolen the money** was sought by the police. |
| 2. | *Time* | The day **when he could leave prison** finally arrived. |
| 3. | *Place* | There's the house **where I used to live**. |
| 4. | *Contrast* | Our teacher, **who is very strict with us in class**, is very kind to us outside class. |

The alternate structures illustrated here are based on the adjective clauses in sentences 1 to 3 below.

1.  The church **which is located in the square nearby** is very beautiful.

    Participial phrase — The church **located *in the square nearby*** is very beautiful.

    Prepositional phrase — The church ***in the square nearby*** is very beautiful.

    Adverbial expression — The church ***nearby*** is very beautiful.

2.  Mrs. Hamilton, **who was always a kind and generous woman**, felt she had to take care of her sick old uncle.

    Appositive noun phrase — Mrs. Hamilton, ***always a kind and generous woman***, felt she had to take care of her sick old uncle.

    Appositive adjective phrase — Mrs. Hamilton, ***always kind and generous***, felt she had to take care of her sick old uncle.

3.  The only thing **which you can do now** is hope for the best.

    Infinitive phrase — The only thing ***to do now*** is hope for the best.

# 15

# Noun Clauses

In a noun clause, the full subject and predicate are retained, but the structure is changed by the addition of a special introductory word, by a special word order, or by both. These changes permit the noun clause to fill the same positions and to serve the same functions as nouns.

Noun clauses may be classified according to the kinds of sentences from which they are derived—statements, questions, requests, exclamations. The following chart illustrates these four types of noun clauses, with examples of their uses in different nominal functions.

| Noun Clause Derived From: | Introductory Conjunction | Function of Clause | Examples |
|---|---|---|---|
| 1. *a statement* Coffee grows in Brazil. | **that** | subject | *That coffee grows in Brazil* is well known to all. |
| | | subject after **it** | It is well known *that coffee grows in Brazil*. |
| | | subjective complement | My understanding is *that coffee grows in Brazil*. |

| Noun Clause Derived From: | Introductory Conjunction | Function of Clause | Examples |
|---|---|---|---|
| | | object of verb | I know *that coffee grows in Brazil.* |
| | | appositive | His belief *that coffee grows in Brazil* is correct. |
| 2. *a question* | | | |
| a. expecting *yes* or *no* answer *Will he get the money?* | **whether (or not)** also **if** | subject | *Whether (or not) he gets the money* doesn't concern me. |
| | | subjective complement | The question is *whether he will get the money.* |
| | | object of verb | Do you know *whether* (or *if*) *he will get the money?* |
| | | object of preposition | We were concerned about *whether he would get the money.* |
| b. interrogative word question *How will he get the money?* | **who; what; which; when; where; why; how** | subject | *How he gets the money* is his own affair. |
| | | subjective complement | The question is *how he will get the money.* |
| | | object of verb | I don't know *how he will get the money.* |
| | | object of preposition | We were concerned about *how he would get the money.* |
| 3. *a request* *Write the letter soon.* | **that** | object of verb | He suggested *that I write the letter soon.* |
| 4. *an exclamation* *What a pretty girl she is!* | **what; how** | object of verb | I hadn't realized *what a pretty girl she was.* |
| | | object of preposition | We talked about *what a pretty girl she was.* |

**That, whether, if** introducing noun clauses are classified as "particles" in some grammar books. The chief meaning of these words is structural—they function merely as connectors.

The generalizing forms of the interrogative words may also appear in noun clauses— **whoever, whatever, whichever, whenever, wherever, however.**

Sentences in direct speech that are accompanied by verbs of saying or asking may be regarded as noun clause objects of these verbs.

> *"There will be no school tomorrow,"* the teacher announced.
> *"Who knows where the Aleutian Islands are?"* the teacher asked.

In connection with types of noun clauses, we might again refer to **that** clauses after predicate adjectives denoting feeling and perception. While we have interpreted such clauses as adverbial modifiers of the adjectives they follow, we have already pointed out that they can also be classified as nouns— either as "complements" of the adjectives, or as "complements" of the combined verb and predicate adjective (thus **I *am sorry* that** = **I *regret* that**). In this chapter, it will be useful to include this type with the others listed here when certain generalizations about **that** clauses can apply equally to both.

Another kind of **that** clause which might be mentioned here under types of noun clauses actually almost defies classification. It occurs in the sentence pattern: *it* + *an adverbial* + *a **that** clause*.

| *It was* | *thus*<br>*then*<br>*there*<br>*under these circumstances*<br>*not without trepidation*<br>*to save them from destruction*<br>*when he was a lad* | *that he did it.* |

Such a construction enables the speaker or writer to place greater emphasis on the modifier after the form of **be**. The sentences just given often have alternate forms without the **that** clauses—**He did it thus** (or **then, under these circumstances,** etc.).

Because of the similarity of some of their introductory words, noun clauses and adjective clauses are sometimes confused. There are two important differences between these two clauses.

1. The adjective clause is preceded by a noun or pronoun antecedent.

| *Adjective Clause* | *Noun Clause* |
|---|---|
| I know the house *where he lives*. (Where he lives has an antecedent the house, which is the object of know.) | I know *where he lives*. (Where he lives is the object of know.) |

2. A preposition that precedes the introductory word belongs to the adjective clause, but usually does not belong to the noun clause.

| The woman *to whom he has been giving money* is a poor relative of his. (The adjective clause begins with to, which forms a prepositional phrase with whom within the adjective clause. To may be moved to the end of the adjective clause.) | He gives money to *whoever needs it*. (The noun clause begins with whoever. The entire clause is the object of to, which may not be moved. Also, the -ever forms appear with noun clauses only.) |

A noun clause subject requires a singular main verb.

*What their names are **doesn't matter** to me.*

*That big hotels should now be lining these streets **was undreamed of** ten years ago.*

Occasionally a plural verb occurs with a plural complement—**What we need** **are** more *housing units* **for married students**. However, it is best to avoid such a construction in formal usage.

Noun clauses from statements are introduce by the conjunction **that**. They may have any nominal function except that of object of a preposition.

**That** noun clauses are used as subjects of sentences only with certain verbs. The most common of these verbs are the linking verbs, especially **be**.

*That the child's fever has gone down is very encouraging.*

*That the water has become polluted is a matter of grave concern.*

*That he should disappear so suddenly seems very strange.*

Other common types of verbs occurring with **that** noun clause subjects are:

1. *Causative verbs*

   *That her husband left her made her very melancholy.*

   *That the two nations cannot find an area of agreement may result in the failure of the peace talks.*

2. *Verbs expressing emotion*

   *That she was called upon to speak flattered her greatly.*

   *That he was not consulted in the matter angered him.*

**That** clauses may also function as subjects of verbs like **mean, matter, make a difference**.

*That they are very rich means nothing to me.*

*That there were extenuating circumstances for the murder should make a big difference to the jury.*

**That** noun clause subjects occur less frequently in subject position than in predicate position after anticipatory **it**.

*It is very encouraging that the child's fever has gone down.*

*It made her melancholy that her husband left her without any explanation.*

*It flattered her greatly that she was called upon to speak.*

The auxiliary **should** often appears in ˋthat noun clause subjects of sentences containing verbs or predicate adjectives that express emotion.

*It is surprising that you should say that.*

*That she should be called upon to speak flattered her greatly.*

Verbs Followed
by THAT Noun Clauses

**That** noun clauses occur most frequently as objects of verbs. Such verbs usually have subjects that refer to human beings. They are chiefly verbs of *indirect speech* and verbs expressing *mental activities*.

VERBS OF INDIRECT SPEECH

| | | |
|---|---|---|
| admit | declare | promise |
| (dis)agree | deny | relate |
| allege | explain | remark |
| announce | foretell | remind |
| argue | hint | report |
| assert | inform | say |
| assure | insist[1] | state |
| aver | maintain | swear |
| boast | notify | teach |
| claim | persuade | tell |
| complain | pray | threaten |
| confess | predict | warn |
| convince | proclaim | |

With some of these verbs, indirect objects may precede the **that** clauses— **assure, convince, inform, notify, persuade, promise, remind, teach, tell, warn.**

*The company notified **their employees** that a pay raise would go into effect the following month.*

*She taught **her son** that he must be honest and fair with everyone.*

With many of the other verbs, **to** phrases may come before the **that** clauses. These **to** phrases may be regarded as the equivalent of indirect objects.

*He complained **to his friend** that his wife couldn't cook.*

*She disagreed **with her husband** that the children should be spanked when they misbehaved.*

---

[1] In the sense of *state strongly* (**He insists that there is a mistake**), not in the sense of *make a strong request* (**He insists that she be there**). See p. 279 for verbs of requesting.

## VERBS OF MENTAL ACTIVITY

| | | |
|---|---|---|
| ascertain | grant | question |
| assume | guess | realize |
| believe | hear | recall |
| calculate | hold (*an opinion*) | reckon |
| care (*often in negative* | hope | recollect |
|    *or interrogative*) | imagine | reflect |
| conceive | indicate[2] | regret |
| conclude | know | rejoice |
| consider | judge | remember |
| convince | learn | reveal[2] |
| decide | mean[2] | see |
| discover | mind (*often in negative* | show[2] |
| doubt |    *or interrogative*) | suppose |
| dream | notice | surmise |
| expect | perceive | think |
| fancy | presume | trust |
| feel | pretend | understand |
| find out | prove[2] | wish |
| forget | | |

Some of the verbs in the lists just given may be used in the passive with
**that** clauses as their grammatical subjects.

> *That one race is more inherently intelligent than another race has never been proven.*
>
> *That the world would be destroyed in the year 2000 was predicted by Nostradamus.*

With anticipatory **it**:

> *It has been said that women generally learn a new language faster than men do.*
>
> *It was thought for a while that he might not recover from his illness.*

To the verbs of mental activity followed by **that** clauses might be added
verbs expressing preference—**prefer, would** (or **had**) **rather, would** (or **had**)
**sooner.** Such **that** clauses occur after these verbs only if their subjects are
different from the subjects of the main verbs—**I prefer that he leaves now**
(compare with **I prefer to leave now**, or **I prefer leaving now**). Subjunctive forms
also occur in such clauses, especially if **would** accompanies the verbs expressing preference—**I would prefer that he leave** (or **left**) **now.**

After certain verbs of thinking and judging, a **that** clause containing a
form of **be** may be interchangeable with an infinitive phrase. Examples of
such verbs are **assume, believe, consider, feel, imagine, judge, presume, sup-**

---

[2] **That** clauses may be used after these verbs even when their subjects denote things rather
than persons.

**pose, think**. (A more extensive list will be found in the chapter on infinitive phrases.)

> *I believe him (to be) innocent.* (vs. *I believe that he is innocent.*)
>
> *We consider him (to be) a fair person.* (vs. *We consider that he is a fair person.*)
>
> *I suppose him to be still there.* (vs. *I suppose that he is still there.*)

Note that after some of these verbs **to be** may be omitted.

After some verbs of indirect speech **that** clauses may be interchangeable with prepositional gerund phrases.

> *He boasted about having killed a bear* (or *that he had killed a bear*).
>
> *She confessed to having told a lie* (or *that she had told a lie*).
>
> *They hinted at having lost a great deal of money* (or *that they had lost a great deal of money*).

Some grammarians believe that a **that** clause may be the object of such combinations as:

| | |
|---|---|
| a verb + object | have an idea (*or* notion) that (*compare with* believe that) |
| | express the view (*or* opinion) that |
| | give proof that |
| | take care that |
| a verb + prepositional phrase | have (*or* bear) in mind that (*compare with* remember that) |
| | be in terror that |
| | be of the opinion that |

The more common view however is that such **that** clauses are in apposition with the nouns that precede them.

Certain verbs are followed by an **it** construction + a **that** clause. The **that** clause may be considered in apposition with **it**.

> answer for it that
> consider it awkward that
> depend (*or* rely, count) upon it that
> have it on authority that
> hear it said that
> make it a condition that
> make (it) clear that
> make it possible that
> regard it (as) an honor that
> see to it that
> take it for granted that
> take it that
> think it probable that

**That** clauses used in apposition with nouns may be either restrictive or nonrestrictive.

RESTRICTIVE CLAUSES.    Such clauses are in apposition with nouns derived from verbs or adjectives that normally take **that** clauses.

> The announcement **that all flights were canceled because of bad weather** greatly distressed the waiting passengers.
>
> He carefully concealed his indignation **that he was not given the appointment he had asked for.**

A few nouns followed by **that** appositive clauses are not derived from such verbs or adjectives—**axiom, circumstance, fact, hypothesis, idea, news, notion, principle, reason, theory, thesis.**

> His notion **that whatever he does is right** is very irritating to his wife.
>
> All his friends congratulated him on hearing the news **that he had won the award.**

NONRESTRICTIVE CLAUSES.    Such clauses are often in apposition with **this** or **that.**

> Things may yet come to **this—that no place will be safe** from nuclear attack.

THE FACT THAT vs. THAT

When **the fact** appears before a **that** clause, technically the clause is in apposition with **fact.**

Some verbs must be followed by **the fact that** rather than by **that** alone—**accept, conceal, discuss, disregard, hide, overlook.**

> We must accept the fact that we live in a world of great political tension.
>
> He cannot conceal the fact that he dislikes his employer.

After some verbs of mental activity, either **that** or **the fact that** may be used.

> He always regretted that (or the fact that) he had not continued his schooling.
>
> He can never forget that (or the fact that) none of his friends helped him while he was penniless.

Almost all subject **that** clauses in subject position may be preceded by **the fact.**

> The fact that the company is almost bankrupt is not generally known.
> but It is not generally known that the company is almost bankrupt.

A **that** clause may be used after a preposition only if **the fact** precedes the clause.

> He is constantly boasting about the fact that his son is an excellent athlete.

*The police are suspicious of the fact that the safe was not locked at the time of the robbery.*

*He was irritated by the fact that his wife spent so much money on clothes.*

## Omission of THAT

In informal speech, **that** is frequently omitted from object clauses if the meaning is clear without it.

*He says (that) they plan to come to the dance.*

*We thought (that) you had already left for Europe.*

A sentence may contain a succession of object clause from which **that** is omitted.

*He says (that) someone told him (that) the old lady believes (that) she is very rich.*

A subject clause retains **that** when the clause is in subject position. When the subject clause appears after anticipatory **it**, however, **that** may be omitted.

*It is a pity (that) she is so narrow-minded.* (Compare with *That she is so narrow-minded is a pity.*)

*It is believed (that) the escaped convicts are in hiding nearby.*

**That** may also be omitted from clauses after predicate adjectives.

*I'm sorry (that) I couldn't meet you at the station.*

*It's not certain (that) she can help us.*

**That** is sometimes omitted informally from clauses functioning as predicate nouns.

*The truth is, (that) I don't remember where I met him.*

*The reason we returned so early is, (that) one of the children got sick.*

Care must be taken that when a **that** clause has a long introductory modifier, the word **that** is not repeated before the subject of the clause. In the sentence **the doctor told his patient that when she had another attack of asthma, that she was to call him immediately**, for example, the second **that** is superfluous.

A verb of indirect speech or of mental activity may be inserted parenthetically without **that** in what would normally be its noun clause object.

*This, **he tells me**, is the only solution.* (=*He tells me [that] this is the only solution.*)

*Mr. Jones, **I understand**, is a multimillionaire.* (=*I understand [that] Mr. Jones is a multimillionaire.*)

Such a verb may also be placed at the end of this type of noun clause equivalent.

> *They can leave at once, **he says**. (=He says [that] they can leave at once.)*
> *He is an honest man, **I believe**. (=I believe [that] he is an honest man.)*

## Alternatives for THAT

In an older style that is still met with today, **but** or **but that** may replace **that** after verbs like **doubt, know, wonder,** especially when they are negative.

> *I don't doubt but (that) the story is true.*
> *We didn't know but (that) he might have missed his train.*

**Lest** is a literary equivalent of **that** after expressions of fear or apprehension—**fear, beware, be in terror, there is danger.** The present subjunctive form of the verb or a modal auxiliary is used in noun clauses after such expressions.

> *We feared lest he take (or should take) his life. (=We feared that he would [or might] take his life.)*

**Lest** may also be the equivalent of **that not.**

> *Beware lest he take advantage of your kindness. (=Beware that he doesn't take advantage of your kindness.)*

## THAT Clauses after WISH

**That** clauses after the verb **wish** often contain subjunctive forms similar to those in unreal conditions. These forms are used when the wish is impossible to realize.

The wish refers to present time (past subjunctive form):

> *I wish (that) I **were** at the beach now.*

The wish refers to past time (past perfect form):

> *I wish (or wished) (that) I **had been** at the beach yesterday.*

Several older, literary forms express such wishes without the verb **wish.**

> *Would that I had known.*
> *That I had but known.*
> *If I had only known.*
> *Had I but known.*

If there is some possibility that the wish can be realized in the present or future, a past form of an auxiliary is used in the **that** clause.

> *I wish (that) it **would stop** raining.*
> *I wish (that) I **could go** to the beach.*
> *I wish (that) I **might see** him once more. (or If I might but see him once more, or Might I but see him once more.)*

**I wish you would** is a formulaic equivalent of **please** in sentences such **I wish you would stop making so much noise.**

## NOUN CLAUSES
## FROM QUESTIONS

In noun clauses derived from questions beginning with an auxiliary verb (yes-no questions), the introductory word **whether** or **if** is added to the question. In noun clauses from questions beginning with interrogative words like **who(ever)**, **when(ever)**, the interrogative word itself serves as the introductory connector.

Noun clauses derived from questions are capable of performing any function that a noun can fulfill, including object of a preposition.

Subject noun clauses derived from questions appear with many of the same main verbs as do clauses derived from statements.

> *How the fire started **is** a mystery to me.*
>
> *Whatever he did **enraged** her.*
>
> *Where he got the money from **doesn't matter** to her.*

Noun clauses from questions may also be the subject of passive verbs.

> *Whatever the witness said was written down by the court stenographer.*
>
> *Whoever caused the damage will be punished.*
>
> *What the negotiators decided on was not revealed to the press.*

After verbs that take double objects, noun clauses from questions may function as one or both objects.

|  | Indirect Object | Direct Object |
|---|---|---|
| Give | the man | *what is in this envelope.* |
| Give | *whoever comes to the door* | the money in this envelope. |
| Give | *whoever comes to the door* | *what is in this envelope.* |
|  | Direct object | Objective complement |
| I consider | *what you have said* | a great insult. |
| He named | his cat | *whatever came to his mind first.* |

Noun clauses from questions may serve as objects of prepositions after adjectives, verbs, or nouns.

| After adjectives | We were astonished at **how old she looked.** |
|---|---|
| After verbs | The children stare at **whoever passes by their house.** |
| After nouns | The boy could hardly contain his curiosity about **what was in the box.** |

Sometimes prepositions governing noun clauses from questions are omitted in informal English.

> *She hesitated (about) whether she should send the money.*

*They were uncertain (of) how they were to proceed.*

A noun clause begins with a preposition only when the question it is derived from also begins this way. Thus the noun clause in the sentence **I don't know** *about what he is talking* is derived from **about what is he talking**. Generally, this form of noun clause is awkward; it is even more so if the noun clause is itself the object of a preposition—**It is now only a question of** *to whom the money should be sent*. Normally, the form with the preposition at the end of the noun clause would be preferred, especially in informal English—**I don't know what he is talking** *about*; **It is only a question of who(m) the money should be sent** *to*.

A noun clause derived from a question may be in loose apposition with an anticipatory **it**.

> *It matters very little to us* **whether he goes or not**. (=*Whether he goes or not matters very little to us.*)
>
> *It is wonderful* **what you have done for her**. (=*What you have done for her is wonderful.*) (This use of a **what** clause is informal.)

Some grammarians consider a **why** clause after **reason** a noun clause in apposition—**The reason** *why he did it* **is not clear**. (We have listed this kind of clause under adjective clauses.)

In popular speech, a **where** clause is sometimes used as the object of **see, hear, read**.

> *I see* (or *read, hear*) *where our property taxes are going to be raised again.*

Introductory Words
in Noun Clauses from Questions

*Whether*

Since **whether** introduces a noun clause from a yes-no question, it is not unnatural that it should denote a positive or a negative choice. The negative choice may be explicitly expressed by the addition of **or not**.

> *I don't know whether or not he plans to come to the meeting tomorrow night.*
>
> *Whether or not he will come tomorrow is still uncertain.*
>
> or *It is still uncertain whether or not he will come tomorrow.*

The **or not** may come at the end of a short noun clause—**It is still uncertain whether he will come tomorrow or not**.

**If** is an informal alternative for **whether** in noun clause objects only.

> *Please see if our guests need anything else.*
>
> *I wonder if their train has arrived.*

**Or not** may be used with **if** only at the end of a short noun clause object— **Let me know if you are coming or not**.

Certain verbs that take **that** clause object may also take **whether** clause objects. These verbs are often in negative, interrogative or imperative form.

1. Verbs of *indirect speech*—**announce, ask, debate, explain, indicate, inquire, mention, reveal, say, state, suggest, tell**

> *Did they say whether they were bringing the children?*
>
> *She never indicated whether she was pleased by the party given for her.*

2. Verbs of *mental activity*—**care, choose, consider, decide, determine, doubt, find out, hear, judge, know, learn, notice, observe, see, wonder**

> *Please see whether the children are ready to go to school.*
>
> *I didn't notice whether she was wearing her watch.*
>
> *I wonder whether a heart transplant from one person to another will ever be successful.*

**That** clauses after these verbs merely state a fact, whereas **whether** clauses indicate yes-no alternatives.

> *I doubt* (or *don't know*) **that** *he'll go.* (there is doubt about the fact itself of his going)
>
> *I doubt* (or *don't know*) **whether** *he'll go.* (there is doubt about the choice of his going or not going)

A **whether** clause may also function as the *grammatical subject* of the passive form of the verbs given above.

> *Whether the non-scheduled flight leaves next week or the week after will be announced soon.*
>
> *Whether he was a spy for one side or both will never be known.*

### Interrogative Words

Noun clauses from questions may begin with interrogative words functioning as:

| | |
|---|---|
| pronouns | who(ever), what(ever), which(ever) |
| adjectives | whose, what(ever), which(ever) |
| adverbs | how(ever), when(ever), where(ver), why |

As in direct questions, the forms of **who** and **whoever** in noun clauses are determined by the function of these pronouns.

| | |
|---|---|
| who | We don't know *who* will be coming from the employment agency. (**Who** is the subject of **will be coming**.) |
| | We don't know *whom* the employment agency will send. (**Whom** is the object of **will send**. Informally **who** also occurs here.) |
| whoever | We will interview **whoever** comes from the employment agency. (**Whoever** is the subject of **comes**.) |
| | We will interview *whomever* the employment agency sends. (**Whomever** is the object of **sends**. Informally **whoever** also occurs here.) |

Phrases like **you think, he remembers** that appear in noun clauses are considered parenthetical and do not influence the form of **who** or **whoever**.

*I know who you think did it. (**Who** is the subject of **did**.)*

## *Who* vs. *Whoever*

The use of the pronoun **who** in noun clauses is more limited than that of **whoever**. **Who** does not appear in noun clause subjects. **Who** in noun clause objects occurs chiefly after some verbs of indirect speech or mental activity.

| | |
|---|---|
| who | Please tell me who is in charge here. |
| (=*the* person that) | I don't know whom he is referring to. |
| | It's a question of who would be willing to do it. |
| whoever | Whoever broke the window must pay for it. |
| (=*any* person that) | He will employ whoever is willing to work hard. |
| | He tells the same story to whomever he meets. |
| | Give this to one of the boys, whoever comes to the door first. |

## *What* vs. *Whatever*

Introductory **what** or **whatever** may appear in all noun functions. The **-ever** forms are often interchangeable with **what**, depending on the degree of generality desired.

| | |
|---|---|
| what *only* | What the insolent child needs is a good spanking. |
| (=*the* thing that) | He told us what he had done. |
| | He gave us what we asked for. |
| | After what he has done, he doesn't deserve any pity. |
| | We are shocked at what has happened. |
| | The full story of what really happened will never be known. |
| what (=*the* thing that) *or* | What (ever) you need will be supplied. |
| | What(ever) is worth doing at all is worth doing well. |
| whatever | Take what(ever) you want. |
| (=*any* thing that) | Throw away what(ever) is left over. |
| | He always makes fun of what(ever) she says. |

In older style, the pronoun **who** was used in sentences that today would require **whoever**.

*Who (=whoever) steals my purse steals trash.* (Shakespeare)

*Whom (=whomever) the gods would destroy they first make mad.*

**Whosoever, whatsoever** are older forms for introductory **whoever, whatever**.

*Whosoever would be a man, must be a non-conformist.*

*Whatsoever thy heart desires shall be given you.*

Word Order
in Noun Clauses from Questions

In noun clauses from questions, the subject and verb have normal word order after the introductory word rather than question order.

|  | **Noun Clause** |  |  | **Original Question** |
|---|---|---|---|---|
|  | *Introductory Word* | *Subject* | *Verb* |  |
| I don't know | whether | he | did it. | Did he do it? |
|  | when | they | are coming. | When are they coming? |
|  | who | she | is. | Who is she? |
|  | what | her name | is. | What is her name? |

Note that a single form of the independent verb **be** is placed last in the noun clause object. However, if the subject in such a clause has much modification, informal usage permits the verb to be placed before the subject.

> *He asked me what **was** the name of the blond lady who had just applied for a job.*

## NOUN CLAUSES FROM REQUESTS

Like noun clauses from statements, noun clauses from requests are introduced by **that**. Such clauses occur most frequently as objects of verbs that often combine with the idea of requesting some degree of urgency, advisability or desirability.

| | |
|---|---|
| advise | move |
| ask | propose |
| beg | recommend |
| command | request |
| demand | require |
| desire | stipulate |
| forbid | suggest |
| insist | urge |

The verbs in noun clauses from requests usually take present subjunctive form.

> *He is requesting that a company car **be placed** at his disposal.*
> *The doctor recommended that he **take** a vacation.*
> *The lawyer of the accused will ask that a re-trial **be granted**.*

In such sentences, the auxiliary **should** may be an informal alternate form for the present subjunctive, especially if the request is not of a strongly imperative nature.

> *The doctor recommended* (or *advised, suggested*) *that he should take a vacation.*

Infinitive constructions are less formal alternatives for **that** clauses after some of these verbs of requesting.

| | | |
|---|---|---|
| *I* | *advise*<br>*ask*<br>*beg*<br>*command*<br>*desire*<br>*forbid*<br>*order*<br>*request*<br>*require*<br>*urge* | *him to leave soon.*<br><br>or<br><br>*that he leave soon.* |

A gerund phrase is also possible after some of these verbs of requesting—**I advised** (or **forbid, recommended, requested, urged**) **his leaving soon.**

**That** clauses after nouns derived from verbs of requesting also require verbs in subjunctive form or with the auxiliary **should.**

> *He ignored his doctor's advice that he take* (or *should take*) *a vacation.*

**That** clause subjects often appear after passive verbs of requesting in anticipatory **it** constructions.

> *It is requested that all gentlemen wear coats and ties.* (=*That all gentlemen wear coats and ties is requested.*)
> *It has been suggested that each member contribute some money for the renovation of the clubhouse.*

Related to **that** clauses after verbs of requesting are **that** clauses after adjectives denoting advisability or urgency—**advisable, desirable, essential, good** (or **better, best**), **imperative, important, mandatory, necessary, requisite, urgent, vital.** Appearing after anticipatory **it,** such **that** clauses also contain subjunctive verbs or the auxiliary **should.**

> *It is advisable that he stay for the entire conference.*
> *It is essential that a guard be on duty at all hours of the day.*

This construction also has a less formal alternate form with **for . . . to.**

> *It is advisable* (*desirable, essential, etc.*) *for him to stay for the entire conference.*

After verbs like **believe, consider, find, think,** these adjectives of advisability or urgency may come between **it** and an appositive **that** clause.

> *I think it advisable that he leave soon.*

## NOUN CLAUSES
## FROM EXCLAMATIONS

Noun clauses from exclamations are introduced by the same words that introduce exclamations—**what (a), how**. The word order of exclamations is preserved in these noun clauses.

---

| | |
|---|---|
| Exclamation | How beautiful his wife is! |
| Noun clause | I am amazed at **how beautiful his wife is**. |
| Exclamation | What a beautiful figure his wife has! |
| Noun clause | He is always boasting about **what a beautiful figure his wife has**. |

---

Noun clauses from exclamations occur chiefly as objects of verbs or prepositions. As objects of verbs these noun clauses occur after a limited number of verbs denoting mental activity such as **realize, notice, see, remember, understand**.

*Did you notice how large that diamond was?*

*I still remember what a wonderful cook his mother is.*

As objects of prepositions, these clauses may occur after certain verbs of indirect speech that take prepositional objects—**boast (about), complain (about), talk (about), remark (about)**—and after the noun forms of these verbs.

*She is always boasting about what good children she has.*

*The company is investigating his complaint about how badly the new bus driver treats his passengers.*

Noun clauses from exclamations also appear after such **-ed** participial adjectives of emotion as **amazed, astonished, disappointed, disgusted, surprised**. The noun clauses are the objects of the prepositions that follow the **-ed** adjectives, usually **at**.

*I was astonished at how small their house was.*

*The candidates were disappointed at how small a crowd showed up for the political rally.*

## SEQUENCE OF TENSES
## IN NOUN CLAUSES

A past main verb often requires a past form in a noun clause. This special requirement is known as "sequence of tenses." Sequence of tenses occurs most frequently with noun clause objects.

| Present Main Verb (No Sequence of Tenses) | Past Main Verb (Sequence of Tenses) |
|---|---|
| He *says* (that): | He *said* (that): |
| the train always arrives late. | the train always arrived late. |
| the train is arriving. | the train was arriving. |
| the train has arrived late. | the train had arrived late. |
| the train just arrived. | the train had just arrived. |
| the train will arrive soon. | the train would arrive soon. |
| the train may be arriving soon. | the train might be arriving soon. |

Informally, the past tense is frequently used instead of the past perfect in noun clauses after past main verbs—**He said that the train arrived late**.

If a noun clause object refers to a general truth or to a customary action, the present "timeless" form is also possible in the noun clause.

> He said that the train always arrives late.
>
> She said that she gets up at seven o'clock every morning.
>
> The professor explained that water consists of two parts hydrogen and one part oxygen.

However, even in noun clause objects containing generalizations, the past tense is probably more common because of the pressure of sequence of tenses.

Sequence of tenses may also be required for noun clause subjects, or objects of prepositions.

| | *Present Main Verb* | *Past Main Verb* |
|---|---|---|
| Subject | It *seems* strange that he *hasn't come* to the meeting. | It *seemed* strange that he *hadn't come* to the meeting. |
| | Whether he *comes* or not *doesn't interest* me. | Whether he *came* or not *didn't interest* me. |
| Object of preposition | He *listens* only to whoever *flatters* him. | He *listened* only to whoever *flattered* him. |
| | We *are* astonished at how long it *will take* to publish the book. | We *were* astonished at how long it *would take* to publish the book. |

BLEND OF DIRECT
AND INDIRECT SPEECH

In informal English, we often find a blend of direct and indirect speech. In such a blend, the word order of direct questions is frequently retained. Also, the pronouns of direct questions may be used.

> I wonder will they finish on time. (or Will they finish on time, I wonder?)
>
> He asked me what was my name?

Usage varies as to the end punctuation of such blends.

A rhetorical question, with or without quotation marks, may function as a noun clause in a sentence.

> *We may ask, What were the chief causes of World War Two?*
>
> *An analysis of the problem comes down to the question: Who are the culprits, and how shall they be punished?"*
>
> *Can he do the job quickly? is the question.*

The questions within these sentences may begin with a capital letter even when they do not initiate the sentence.

Because of the influence of direct speech, the sequence of tenses after past main verbs is not always observed in noun clause objects. In such cases the verb forms used in direct speech may be unchanged in the noun clause objects.

> *He said that he **will come**.* (vs. *He said that he **would come**.*)
>
> *She said that she **must go**.* (vs. *She said that she **had to go**.*)

Another even more common type of informal blend involves the use of certain expressions of time and place in noun clause objects. In direct speech, such adverbial expressions are tied to a specific situation. For indirect speech, formal English requires that these expressions be changed to have a more remote or more general designation. The blend results from the retention in indirect speech of these adverbial expressions that are characteristic of direct speech.

| **Direct Speech** | **Indirect Speech** | |
| --- | --- | --- |
| | *Formal* | *Informal Blend* |
| Are the boys **here**? | He asked whether the boys were **there**. | He asked whether the boys were **here**. |
| I saw her **three days ago**. | He said that he had seen her **three days before** (or **earlier**). | He said that he had seen her **three days ago**. |
| They will arrive **tomorrow**. | She said that they would arrive **the next day**. | She said that they would arrive **tomorrow**. |
| They arrived **yesterday**. | She said that they had arrived **the day before**. | She said that they (had) arrived **yesterday**. |

## POSITION OF NOUN CLAUSES

Noun clauses appear in the same position as nouns, that is, subjects appear before the verb, objects after the verb, etc.

Like nouns, noun clause objects may occupy initial position for greater emphasis.

> ***Why he had to buy three suits instead of one** I'll never understand.*

*That a flying machine would be transporting people by air no one would have believed a hundred years ago.*

Noun clauses in direct speech may appear at the beginning or end of the sentence.

| | |
|---|---|
| Initial position | "If you want, we can buy a new car," he said to his wife. |
| Final position | He said to his wife, "If you want, we can buy a new car." |

The verb of saying or asking may also be used in mid-position with a noun clause in direct speech.

*"If you want," he said to his wife, "we can buy a new car."*

## PUNCTUATION OF NOUN CLAUSES

Just as no punctuation sets off nouns as subjects or objects, so no punctuation sets off noun clauses in these functions.

*He said that he had lost his wallet.*

*He asked why she had done that.*

*That he would never amount to anything was obvious to us all.*

Question marks or exclamation marks are dropped from noun clauses made from questions or exclamations.

Noun clauses in direct speech have quotation marks placed at the beginning and end of the clause. The first word of the direct quotation is capitalized. The phrase with the verb of saying or asking is cut off by a comma.

*She said, "Today is a good day to have a picnic."*

*"Today," she said, "is a good day to have a picnic."*

Note that both the comma and the period are placed inside the quotation mark.

A question mark used with a direct question is also placed within the quotation mark—**"Why must you be so unreasonable?" she asked**.

## ABRIDGMENT OF NOUN CLAUSES

1. *Auxiliary verb* (substitution)

   *Most people feel that she won't succeed in that job, but I know **that she will**.*

2. *Infinitive* (with noun clauses from questions)

   *I don't know **how to do it**.*

   *I don't know **whether to go or not**.*

This kind of abridged clause has as its "subject" either (1) the subject of the main clause, as in the above examples, or (2) the object of the main verb— **He told me** *when to go*.

Abridgment of noun clauses with infinitives is very common, especially with noun clause objects. However, it is also possible to use such abridgment with noun clauses in other functions.

| | |
|---|---|
| Subject | *How to do it* is the question. |
| Subjective Complement | The question is *how to do it*. |
| Object of Preposition | We talked about *how to do it*. |

## ALTERNATE SUBJECT-PREDICATE STRUCTURES FOR NOUN CLAUSES

The alternate structures illustrated here are based on the noun clause in the sentence *That he is behaving so rashly at this time* **is incredible**.

| | |
|---|---|
| *infinitive phrase* | **For him to behave so rashly at this time** is incredible. |
| *gerund phrase* | **His behaving so rashly at this time** is incredible. |
| *abstract noun phrase* | **His rash behavior at this time** is incredible. |

# 16

## Participial Phrases

With the participial phrases we begin the description of the verbal constructions. Other verbal constructions that will be taken up in the following chapters are gerund phrases, infinitive phrases, and absolute constructions.

Verbal constructions function as parts of speech other than verbs, usually as nouns, adjectives, or adverbs. In these constructions the elements of simple sentences are more changed in form than they are in dependent clauses. The verbs are generally reduced to participial **-ing** or **-ed** form, or to **to** infinitive form. However, these verbal forms, like the finite verbs in full sentences, can take complements or adverbial modifiers.

In verbal constructions, the subjects and objects from original simple sentences may remain unchanged in form, or they may be reduced to possessive, objective or prepositional form. Also, they may not occur in the verbal construction at all but may be found elsewhere in the sentence or be implied from the general context.

Because we are stressing derivation from a simple sentence in all the structures that follow, we are using the term *"subject"* to refer to an original subject, and the term *"object"* to refer to an original object. Occasionally, also, we will find it convenient to use the term *agent* for an original subject of a simple sentence.

All verbal constructions are made negative by the use of **not** before the verbs.

| | |
|---|---|
| Participial phrase | *Not knowing anyone in town,* he felt very lonesome. |
| Gerund phrase | *Not having an education* is a handicap. |
| Infinitive phrase | He advised me *not to invest money at this time.* |
| Absolute construction | *The children not wanting to leave the beach,* their mother decided to stay a little longer. |

When functioning as a subject, a verbal construction, like a noun clause, requires a singular main verb.

| | |
|---|---|
| Gerund phrase | Their leaving the children alone at night **is** very dangerous. |
| Infinitive phrase | For them to leave the children along at night **is** very dangerous. |

A participle, gerund or infinitive may function alone in the same way as it would if it were used in a phrase. Such single verbals will therefore be included among the examples of the various types of verbal phrases that follow.

## PARTICIPIAL PHRASES
### *CHANGE FROM*
### *FULL SUBJECT-PREDICATE FORM*

The participial phrase represents the predicate part of a sentence beginning with the verb in reduced **-ing** or **-ed** form. The "subject" of a participial phrase is usually a noun or pronoun in the main clause (or in a dependent clause)—*Anyone* **applying to that school must take a difficult entrance examination.**

### Form of Verb in Participial Phrases

The participle in a participial phrase cannot indicate differences in person or number. It has only two forms for time. One is a "general" form which is neutral with respect to time; the time that is intended is established by the main verb. The other form, the perfect, indicates time which precedes that expressed by the main verb.

| | Active Voice | | Passive Voice | |
|---|---|---|---|---|
| | | *Progressive* | | *Progressive* |
| General form | **offering** (present participle) | | **offered** (past participle) | **being offered** |
| Perfect form | **having offered** | **having been offering** | **having been offered** | |

Depending on the main verb, the present participle can indicate:

| | |
|---|---|
| Present time | The man *addressing the audience now* is a famous scientist. |
| Past time | The trapped miners, *hoping to be rescued soon*, told stories to keep up their morale. |
| Future time | A person *traveling in foreign countries* will need to take the required documents. |

Although the general passive form (**offered**) is traditionally called the past participle, this form can actually show time that occurs:

At the same time as that of the main verb:

*He dislikes driving along a road (which is)* **covered with mud.**

*We drove along a road (which was)* **covered with mud.**

Before the time of the main verb:

*We drove along a road (which had been)* **partially destroyed by the flood of the week before.**

With intransitive verbs, the past participle may represent the active perfect tenses—**The boys, (who have)** *now grown to manhood,* **have taken over their father's business.**

The present perfect participle indicates time that corresponds to:

The present perfect tense: with a present or future main verb

*A person having had dealings* (=**who has had dealings**) *with him will never forget him.*

*Having made up his mind* (=**after he has made up his mind**), *he does not change it.*

*Never having lived away from home* (=**because they have never lived away from home**), *the new students will probably get homesick.*

The past perfect tense: with a past main verb

*Having made up his mind* (=**after he had made up his mind**), *he did not change it.*

*Having finished all his work* (=**after he had finished all his work**), *he left the office.*

The present participle may be a less formal variant in such constructions—**Finishing all his work, he left the office.** (Compare the choice between the past perfect tense or the past tense in **after** clauses—**After he [had] finished his work, he left the office.**)

An archaic form of the present participle contains the prefix **a-**: **With his giant mausoleum abuilding, go ahunting, set the bells aringing.**[1]

---

[1] In the speech of the uneducated, the present participle with **a-** also occurs with progressive verbs—**I'm not agoing.**

FUNCTION
OF PARTICIPIAL PHRASES

Most participial phrases have adjectival function. Such phrases, like the adjective clauses which alternate with them, may be restrictive or nonrestrictive.

---

| | |
|---|---|
| Restrictive | Students *arriving late* will not be permitted to enter the lecture hall. (**Arriving late** limits the reference of **students**.) |
| Nonrestrictive | Henry, *arriving late*, was not permitted to enter the lecture hall. (**Arriving late** does not limit the reference of **Henry**.) |

---

Some grammarians classify nonrestrictive participial phrases as adverbials because of their ability to occupy the three adverbial positions and to denote some of the adverbial meanings. In such an interpretation, the nonrestrictive phrases are regarded as modifying either the verb or the entire sentence.

A few participial phrases that have general reference are considered as sentence modifiers—**generally speaking, considering everything**.

There are some constructions having participial form whose function is particularly hard to define. These participial constructions appear in final position; some of them refer back to the *subject* of the main verb, others to the *object* of the verb. They are usually not set off from the rest of the sentence by a pause in speech or a comma in writing.

THE SUBJECT OF THE MAIN VERB IS THE "SUBJECT" OF THE PARTICIPIAL CONSTRUCTION. Such structures appear more often with the **-ing** participle. They may be considered as having a function intermediate between adverbial and adjectival.

1. Constructions showing a loose adverbial relation to the rest of the sentence (often manner or attendant circumstances)

*They spend their leisure time playing cards.*

*She was very busy packing for her trip.*

*The women do all the work in the factory sitting down.*

If the main verb is passive, the participial construction refers to the agent of the action rather than to the grammatical subject.

*Their leisure time is spent playing cards.*

*All the work in the factory is done sitting down.*

Many of these participial constructions may be preceded by the prepositions **in** or **by**, in which cases the constructions would be interpreted as gerund objects of the prepositions. The entire prepositional phrase then functions as an adverbial modifier of the verb.

*He wore himself out by trying to work at two jobs.*

*They have some difficulty in getting domestic help.*

2. Constructions that correspond to adjective clauses

*No one looks important wearing shabby clothes.* (Compare **No one looks important who is wearing shabby clothes.**)

*Books have been written trying to prove that flying saucers come from outer space.*

*Laws were passed requiring all aliens to register with the government.*

3. Constructions with a form of **be** + an intervening element + the **-ing** participle

    a.   the subject intervenes. Such constructions occur after the expletive **there.**

*There is someone knocking at the door.*

*There were some guests in the garden being served refreshments.*

    b.   an adverbial expression of place intervenes

*They are in England visiting relatives.*

*He is at the library looking up some information.*

These **-ing** constructions stress the duration of an action. They may be interpreted as alternate ways of expressing progressive verbs by means of "splitting" the two parts of the verb between the subject or the adverbial expression. Thus **there** *is* **someone** *knocking* **at the door** corresponds to **Someone** *is knocking* **at the door**[2]; **They are in England** *visiting* **relatives** corresponds to **They** *are visiting* **relatives in England.**

4. Constructions after **sit, stand, lie**

*She sat there staring at the wall.*

*He lay gasping for breath.*

*He's standing at the corner watching the girls go by.*

A comma may be used if the participial construction is felt as less closely connected with the preceding part of the sentence.

*She just stood there, wondering what to do next.*

*She's sitting at her desk, writing a long letter to her mother.*

In such cases, however, the participial construction might better be interpreted as a nonrestrictive modifier of the subject.

5. Constructions after **come, go**

*His daughter came running to the door.*

*His papers went flying in all directions.*

---

[2] We have a similar choice after **there** + a form of **be** used without the participle—**There is someone at the door** is interchangeable with **Someone is at the door.**

As used here, **come** and **go** might be considered as having auxiliary-like function.

THE OBJECT OF THE MAIN VERB IS THE "SUBJECT" OF THE PARTICIPIAL CONSTRUCTION. The function of these participial constructions might be regarded as intermediate between nominal and adjectival. Some grammarians refer to such participial constructions as "objective complements," functioning in the same way as **president** in **The members elected him president**. Actually, it might be better to consider these participial constructions as the second part of a two-part object, the two parts standing in the relationship of subject-predicate to each other.

1. After verbs of perception—**behold, feel, hear, listen to, notice, observe, perceive, see, watch, witness**.

> *We heard the children crying.*
> *I saw them running across the street.*
> *We watched a kitten trying to climb a tree.*
> *I saw him being attacked.*

After these verbs of perception the **to**-less infinitive alternates with the participle—**We heard the children cry; I saw them run across the street.** The participial form stresses the duration of an action, often its lack of completion; the infinitive stresses an action as a whole.

These verbs of perception may be passive—**He was seen going into the store; He was heard talking to himself.** The infinitive is not usual in such a passive; if it is used, it cannot appear without **to**—**He was heard to say it.**

2. After **have**

a. with present participle:

> *He had his wife's portrait hanging in his office.*
> *They may have starvation facing them.*
> *I will not have* (meaning **allow**) *anyone smoking cigars in my living room.*

b. with past participle:

> *They had a large sum of money allocated to them for the project.*
> *You'll have your jewelry stolen if you don't put it in a safe place.* (informal)
> *We will not have* (meaning **allow**) *him made fun of.*

c. Often in the sense of *cause to be*:

> *He had his wife's portrait hung in his office.*
> *They'll have you arrested if you don't pay your taxes.*
> *Please have these dresses cleaned.*

These constructions that follow the pattern *have something done* represent the passive form of the active pattern *have someone do something*.

3. After **get** + present or past participle (informal—often meaning *achieve, succeed in doing*)

*He got the program moving in the right direction.*

*He got all the work done last night.*

*We finally got our policy changed.*

4. After **catch, find, keep, leave, send,** + present or past participle

*The police caught the young boy stealing a car.*

*My savings will keep me going for a while.*

*The singer's superb performance left the audience begging for encores.*

*The wind sent his papers flying.*

*They found (or discovered) the horse tied to a tree.*

If one of these verbs is passive, the agent of the participial construction is the original object of the active verb.

*Their rowboat was found drifting in the lake. (Active—They found their rowboat drifting in the lake.*

*He was left stranded in the desert. (Active—They left him stranded in the desert.)*

After **make** and a few verbs of *ordering* and *wishing*, a past participle may also be considered as the second part of the object.

*He is now making his power felt.*

*We desire the work done immediately.*

*It was ordered completed.*

It is possible to interpret these participles as elliptical forms of the passive infinitive, especially after the verbs of ordering and wishing, which normally take infinititives.

*We desire the work (to be) done immediately.*

*It was ordered (to be) completed.*

As with objective complements, a participial construction functioning as the second part of an object may be preceded by **as.**

*We consider this agreement as legally binding to both parties.*

*The dictator justified his repressive measures as being the only ones possible at the time.*

In such a construction, **being** may be expressed or understood. In a passive sentence the participal construction with **as** is retained after the verb—**This agreement is considered as legally binding to both parties.**

POSITION OF ADVERBS
IN PARTICIPIAL PHRASES

Adverbs are generally in initial or final position in participial phrases, depending on where they would appear with a finite verb.

> *Quickly* clearing the table (or *clearing the table* **quickly**), she went into the kitchen to bring out the coffee.
>
> *The boy,* **now** *wearing a beard* (or *wearing a beard* **now**), *looked very mature.*
>
> **Always** *thinking of others* **first**, *he allowed everyone else to precede him in line.*

An adverb takes the same position with an auxiliary of a participle as it does with an auxiliary of a finite verb.

> *Being* **completely** *absorbed in his experiment, he was unaware of the passage of time.*
>
> *Having* **recently** *been late to work because his alarm failed to go off, he decided to buy a new clock.*

Some adverbs of frequency may appear either before or after the first auxiliary.

> *Having* **never** *learned to drive properly* (or **never** *having learned to drive properly*), *she was afraid to go on the highway.*

POSITION AND PUNCTUATION
OF PARTICIPIAL PHRASES

Those participial phrases that are alternate constructions for adjective clauses usually appear after the nouns they modify.

---

| | |
|---|---|
| Restrictive | A student *hoping to finish college in three years* must work very hard. |
| Nonrestrictive | Robert, *hoping to finish college in three years*, worked very hard. |

---

For such participial phrases, the punctuation is the same as for adjective clauses; that is, commas cut off only nonrestrictive phrases.

Nonrestrictive phrases referring to the subject of the main verb are movable and may be found in the two other positions for nonrestrictive elements.

1. At the beginning of the sentence—***Hoping to finish college in three years*, Robert worked very hard**. Here a comma sets off the phrase from the rest of the sentence.

When a participial phrase occurs in initial position, the expectation is that its "subject" will appear immediately after it as the subject of the main verb—***Looking out of the window, she* saw a breath-taking view**. If this expectation is not fulfilled, the construction is considered an undesirable "dangling" element—***Looking out of the window,* a breath-taking view was seen**. Only an initial participial expression that has general reference does not require a "subject" to follow it—**taking everything into consideration, speaking about that matter, etc.**

2. At the end of the sentence—**Robert worked very hard**, *hoping to finish*

*college in three years*. A comma is usually required here. However, if the participial phrase is felt to be tightly connected with the rest of the sentence (especially when there is no pause in speech), the comma may be omitted— **We drove around the block** *looking for a place to park*. In such instances, if the agent of a participial phrase is not clear, as in **I met him coming home**, the end position should be avoided.

Where there are two nouns that might be interpreted as the agent of a participial phrase in end position, the punctuation alone may indicate which noun is the agent.

> *The manager reprimanded the man* **pounding on the table**. (Nonmovable restrictive phrase—the noun being modified is *man*)
>
> *The manager reprimanded the man,* **pounding on the table**. (Movable non-restrictive phrase—The noun being modified is *manager*. The comma corresponds to a pause in speech.)

STYLISTIC MATTERS
RELATED TO PARTICIPIAL PHRASES

By providing an alternate construction for an adjective clause, the participial phrase enables a speaker or writer to avoid a succession of adjective clauses—**He showed me a book** *describing* (for **which described**) *children's literature* **which he had taken from the library**. Normally, the participial phrase precedes the adjective clause, as in the example just given.

Greater complexity of sentence structure may also be achieved by including within a sentence a nonrestrictive participial phrase that might otherwise have been put in a following sentence—**Thousands of people filled the station, waiting anxiously for the trains that had been delayed because of an accident.**

Since the participial phrase begins immediately with the action expressed by a verb, this construction often adds a note of liveliness to descriptive details —**At the sound of the gong, the children burst forth into the schoolyard,** *jostling* **each other furiously and** *splitting* **the air with their screams.**

POSSIBLE MEANINGS
OF PARTICIPIAL PHRASES

1. *Time*:

   a. = *after*—**Having finished all her housework,** *she sat down to watch television.*

   b. = *while* or *when*—**Walking along the street,** *I met a friend whom I had not seen for a long time.*

2. *Cause*:

   **Having worked hard all his life,** *he decided to take a long vacation.*

Often *time* and *cause* are simultaneously implied in a participial phrase. In **Having eaten too much, he became sleepy**, the participial phrase signifies both **because** and **after**.

Other less common relationships that may be expressed by participial phrases are:

3. *Manner*:

> He came to the party *looking like a bum*.

4. *Result*:

> He contributed a large sum to the library, (*thus*) *making possible the purchase of some badly needed books*.

The participial phrase of result may begin with **thus** or **thereby**. Appearing in end position only, this kind of phrase refers back to the entire statement, not to a single noun. Although frequently used, such a participial phrase is not acceptable to all authorities.

# 17

## Gerund Phrases

The verb in a gerund phrase is reduced to participial form. All participial forms may function as gerunds except the **-ed** past participle; the most common form, however, is the **-ing** present participle.

The "subject" of a gerund may be found in another part of the sentence or it may be understood. A "subject" that is contained within the gerund phrase takes inflected possessive form, prepositional form, or unchanged form. The "object" of a gerund is unchanged or is contained within an **of** phrase. By means of such changes in the nominal elements of a simple sentence, these elements may be strung along after the verb as prepositional phrases. Thus, the simple sentence **The hunters shot the birds** can become the gerund phrase **the shooting of the birds** (original object) **by the hunters** (original subject).

These changes from subject-predicate form also permit the gerund phrase to be embedded as a noun within another predication—**The shooting of the birds by the hunters caused her great distress.** The gerund functions as noun head of the gerund phrase, the transformed "subject" and "object" as adjectival modifiers.

Gerund phrases may perform all the functions that nouns are capable of fulfilling.

| | |
|---|---|
| Subject of verb | *Her cleaning the house every day* is not necessary. |
| Object of verb | Her husband appreciates *her cleaning the house every day*. |
| Object of preposition: | |
|   In prepositional object | Her husbands insists on *her cleaning the house every day*. |
|   In adverbial phrase | By *cleaning the house every day* she is pleasing her husband. |
| Subjective complement<br>  (predicate noun) | What her husband insists on is *her cleaning the house every day*. |
| Appositive | Her husband insists on one thing—*her cleaning the house every day*. |

## KINDS OF TIME
## EXPRESSED BY THE GERUND

The participial forms used in gerund phrases indicate the same kind of time as they do in participial phrases. The **-ing** form is neutral with respect to time; the time that is intended often depends on the tense or the meaning of the main verb.

| | |
|---|---|
| Present time | By repairing the TV set himself, he is saving a lot of money. |
| Past time | By repairing the TV set himself, he saved a lot of money. |
| Future time | By repairing the TV set himself, he will save a lot of money. |

The perfect form expresses time that precedes that of the main verb. If the main verb is *present or future*, the perfect form corresponds to the *present perfect* tense:

> *His having worked in a factory is no disgrace.* (=**That** he **has worked** in a factory is no disgrace.)
>
> *He will never admit having done it.* (=He will never admit that he **has done** it.)

If the main verb is *past*, the perfect gerund corresponds to the *past perfect* tense:

> *He denied having taken any money from the cash register.* (=He denied that he **had taken** any money from the cash register.)
>
> *The refugee grieved at having left his wife and children behind.* (=The refugee grieved that he **had left** his wife and children behind.)

The **-ing** general form is often used loosely instead of the perfect form for gerund objects of verbs—**He denied taking any money from the cash register**. Here there is no desire to emphasize time that precedes that of the main verb. In formal writing, the perfect gerund, like the past perfect tense in a **that** clause object, would be preferred because of its ability to make a finer distinction in time.

"SUBJECTS"
IN GERUND PHRASES

The "subject" of a gerund usually denotes a live being, but sometimes it designates a lifeless thing or an abstract idea.

In the majority of gerund phrases, especially those functioning as objects of verbs or prepositions, the "subject" is either understood or is found in another part of the sentence.

THE "SUBJECT" IS UNDERSTOOD.    a. The "subject" is understood as a generic person (**everyone, anyone, people, etc.**). Such a subjectless gerund phrase is common in general statements, especially with a form of **be** as the main verb.

> *Playing with guns is dangerous.*
> *Fishing in this lake is forbidden.*
> *Working in a factory is no disgrace.*

b. The "subject" is understood from the general context

> *He suggested eating dinner at the airport.*
> *Bringing up that subject will only cause trouble.*
> *Going there today isn't wise.*

THE "SUBJECT" IS IN ANOTHER PART OF THE SENTENCE.

> *On seeing the damage he had done, the child felt ashamed.* (the "subject" of **seeing** is **child**, the *subject* of the main verb)
> *We thanked them for making such a generous contribution.* (the "subject" of **making** is **them**, the *object* of the main verb)

If a "subject" is included in the gerund phrase, it may be used: (1) in possessive or unchanged form  (2) in an **of** phrase  (3) in a **by** phrase.

**"Subject of Gerund
in Possessive or Unchanged Form**

"SUBJECT" A WORD DENOTING A LIVE BEING.    The choice of possessive or non-possessive form often depends on whether formal or informal usage is being observed.

In *formal usage*, possessive forms of nouns and pronouns are required.

> *The girl resents **her sister's** getting more attention than she does.*
> *The idea of **Harold's** getting a job as a traveling salesman doesn't appeal to his wife.*

If the gerund phrase is the *subject of the sentence*, the possessive form is obligatory in both formal and informal usage—*His* **undertaking such a difficult task is to be commended.**

In *informal usage*, the unchanged forms of nouns, as well as the object forms of personal pronouns, may be used for "subjects" of gerunds. These forms establish a closer relationship with the verb or preposition after which they commonly apear. They are more emphatic than the possessive forms; in speech they receive greater stress and are followed by a longer pause.

*Gerund phrase after a main verb:* especially such verbs as **(dis)like, not mind, miss, remember, understand.**

> *We can't understand **them** doing a thing like that.*
>
> *I remember **my father** being very strict with us.*
>
> *Can you imagine **him** being elected president!*

Such a gerund phrase may be considered as the second part of a two-part object.

*Gerund phrase after a preposition:*

> *I don't approve of **a woman** walking by herself late at night.*
>
> *She was proud of **her son** winning first prize.*
>
> *She went there without **him** knowing about it.*

The non-possessive forms are probably more common with noun "subjects" than with pronoun "subjects." Conservative textbooks claim that the use of object forms of personal pronouns in some of the sentences just given is highly informal, or even unacceptable.

"SUBJECT" A WORD DENOTING A LIFELESS THING OR AN ABSTRACT IDEA. Much less frequent than a "subject" that represents a human being, such a "subject" of a gerund is usually in non-possessive form.

> *They told us a story of **a pirate ship** having been sunk in these waters.*
>
> *The doctors are afraid of **a relapse** occurring in a few months.*
>
> *Instead of **her health** improving after the operation, it got worse.*

This type of "subject" is sometimes also found with '*s* possessive endings.

> *I can't understand **the door's** not being open.*
>
> *There is a real danger of **a war's** destroying the world.*
>
> *Who could imagine **a thing's** seeming so different from what it is?*

"Subjects" with modifiers, especially modifiers that follow them, generally do not occur in possessive form even in formal English.

> *There is no need of **the president of the company** attending the meeting.*
>
> *I marvel at **anything of such small importance** standing in his way.*
>
> *I cannot bear the thought of **my best friend, once so rich and powerful,** being almost destitute now.*

A long gerund phrase functioning as subject of a verb or as object of a preposition is generally awkward, especially if the "subject" of the gerund has non-possessive form. Most experts suggest avoiding such sentences as the following:

> *The government inspector walking into the factory without any previous warning disconcerted the plant superintendent.*
>
> *Because of the money not being where he had put it, he was afraid it had been stolen.*

In gerund phrases derived from sentences beginning with expletives, **it** or **its** may be used; **there** remains unchanged.

> *In spite of its* (informal, *it*) *being a rainy night, he went out for a long walk.*
>
> *We were mistaken about there being a meeting tonight.*

### "Subject" of Gerund
### an OF Phrase

An **of** phrase "subject" of a gerund may denote a live being or an inanimate thing. This kind of "subject" is used mostly with intransitive verbs. **The** (occasionally another determiner) initiates the phrase.

> *The plotting and intriguing **of the ambassador** for his own ends finally caused his dismissal.*
>
> *The shouting **of the children** disturbed his sleep.*

Personal pronouns are not used as "subjects" in **of** phrases—**\*the shouting of them**.

A "subject" representing a live being may sometimes be put either in an **of** phrase or in *s'* possessive form—**the shouting of the children** or **the children's shouting**. The gerund with the possessive "subject" has greater force as a verb; the gerund with the **of** phrase "subject" has greater force as a noun.

### "Subject" of Gerund
### a *By* Phrase

A **by** phrase "subject" marks the passive voice of a transitive verb in a gerund phrase.

> *The broadcasting by that station comes from the top of a skyscraper.*
>
> *He resents being nagged by his wife.*

"OBJECTS"
IN GERUND PHRASES

The form of an "object" in a gerund phrase may depend on what precedes the gerund.

If **the** *introduces the gerund*, the "object" of the gerund is in an **of** phrase.

> *The shooting **of those rare birds** appalled us.*
>
> *The storing **of merchandise** became a problem after the warehouse burned down.*

Determiners other than **the**—for example **a, this, some, any**—occasionally initiate a gerund phrase containing an **of** phrase "object."

> *We must put an end to this killing **of innocent people.***

*Some cutting **of taxes** will result from this law.*

In the construction *the . . . -ing* **+** *of phrase "object,"* only the **-ing** ending is used for the gerund: the gerund cannot have perfect or passive form, nor can it be made negative.[1]

If there is *no **the** or possessive "subject" preceding the gerund*, the "object" of the gerund remains unchanged.

*Repairing **that lamp** will not be expensive.*

*They plan on setting aside **some money** each month for their old age.*

If *a possessive "subject" precedes the gerund*
a. the "object" may remain unchanged

*Their returning **the money** was a surprise.*

*I can't understand her losing **the ring**.*

b. the "object" may be in an **of** phrase (less frequent)

*His reporting **of the war** won him an award for good journalism.*

*The dictator was hated by many people for his silencing **of all opposition**.*

Sometimes choices of "objects" with or without **of** are possible—**shooting those rare birds** or **the shooting of those rare birds, the government's suppressing the news** or **the government's suppressing of the news**. Generally, the construction with the **of** phrase has stronger nominal force.

**Of** phrase "objects" are not used at all with gerunds that represent non-action—*the remembering of, *the thinking of, *the needing of. (But, compare with abstract noun phrases—**the remembrance of, the thought of, the need of**.)

Personal pronoun "objects" of gerund phrases (as well as "subjects") cannot be put in **of** phrases—*the launching of it, *their finding of it.

In a gerund construction that is given passive force only by a **by** phrase, an **of** phrase expresses the original object.

*The sailor told us a story about the sinking of a ship by pirates.*

*They complained about the shooting of the birds by the hunters.*

This kind of gerund construction with passive force competes with the construction containing the passive form of the gerund itself.

*The sailor told us a story about a ship having been sunk by pirates.*

*They complained about the birds being shot by the hunters.*

Without a **by** phrase, a gerund construction containing an **of** phrase may sometimes be interpreted as either active or passive. Thus, in **The shooting of the birds disturbed him**, the gerund phrase may be considered as being derived from either **Someone shot the birds** or **The birds were shot by someone**.

After verbs that have both a transitive and an intransitive sense, an **of** phrase may cause ambiguity, since it functions either as "subject" or "object" of the gerund.

---

[1] The same restrictions apply if the **of** phrase is a "subject" in a gerund phrase introduced by **the**.

*The ringing of the bells* (may be derived from **The bells are ringing,** or **Someone is ringing the bells**)

*The sinking of the ship* (may be derived from **The ship is sinking** or **Someone sank the ship**)

Generally, however, in such phrases the presumption with **of** is in favor of the "object" rather than the "subject."

ADVERBS
IN GERUND PHRASES

In a gerund phrase, a word used as an adverb may remain unchanged or it may take adjective form.

### Adverbs in Unchanged Form

Such adverbs may be used in final position, or, less commonly, in initial position.

1. *Final position*

> *The company appreciated his handling the affair* **discreetly.**
>
> *Eating and drinking* **intemperately** *may ruin one's health.*
>
> *He received a reward for returning the lost money* **promptly.**

An unchanged adverb is rare in a *the . . . -ing* **+** *of phrase* construction, but occasionally such a form appears in final position—**The administering of artificial respiration** *immediately* **may save a person's life.**

Adverbs in final position in gerund phrase subjects are sometimes ambiguous in written English—**His leaving the country** *immediately* **made the police suspicious of him.** In this sentence, it is not clear whether **immediately** refers to the gerund subject **leaving** or to the main verb **made.** In the spoken language, the slight pause before or after **immediately** would signal which construction the word belonged to.

2. *Initial position*

> *He received a reward for* **promptly** *returning the money.*
>
> *His employer was irritated at his* **never** *getting to work on time.*
>
> **Needlessly** *criticizing other people is cruel.*

Gerunds are usually preceded by the same types of adverbs as those that precede finite verbs—usually manner or frequency adverbs.

### Adverbs Changed to Adjective Form

In gerund phrases, adverbs from simple sentences are often transformed to adjectives that precede the gerund.

*His wife was shocked at his **reckless** breaking of the law.*

*The company appreciated his **discreet** handling of the affair.*

*Her mother's **constant** meddling in her affairs was a source of great annoyance to her.*

It is this adjective-from-adverb form that is most common in the ***the . . .
-ing + of*** *phrase* construction.

*The **constant** dripping of the water irritated her.*

*The **unexpected** closing of the hotel left the tourists with no place to stay.*

The use of such an adjective-from-adverb reinforces the nominal effect of the gerund phrase.

The negative adjective **no** is used instead of the adverb **not** with certain types of gerund phrases.

1. after **there** + a form of **be**

*There is no stopping him.*

*There is no denying that she is very efficient.*

2. prohibitions against certain activities

*No smoking is allowed in this classroom.*

*No trespassing on these premises will be permitted.*

### GERUND PHRASES
### AS SUBJECTS OF VERBS

A gerund phrase does not occur frequently as a subject. One of its common uses as a subject is in general statements with **be** as the main verb.

*Eating a good breakfast is very wise.*

*Taking a long walk every day is good exercise.*

The gerund phrase may also function as the subject of a verb expressing:

1. *Cause-effect relationship*

*Seeing her every day made him realize how wonderful she was.*

*His finding the error quickly saved him (=caused him to save) many hours of extra work.*

A gerund phrase subject with such a verb may have conditional meaning.

*Doing such a thing now (=If you do such a thing now, it) will cause you much trouble later on.*

2. *Emotion*

*Being overcharged for anything enrages her.*

*Seeing her so thin and pale shocked him.*

It should be noted that such verbs of emotion often also denote some degree of cause; thus **enrages her, shocked him** in the above sentences may be interpreted as *causes her to become enraged, caused him to be shocked.*

Gerund phrases may also function as subjects of passive verbs.

> *His keeping accurate records has never been questioned.*
>
> *Their accepting the money will be considered unwise.*

A gerund phrase subject sometimes appears after anticipatory **it** + an adjective. Such a construction usually represents informal usage.

> *It's very embarrassing (,) not remembering your name.*
>
> *It's incredible (,) meeting an old schoolmate so far from home.*
>
> *It's not worthwhile taking that trip for only one day.*

A comma is required if the "subject" is included in the gerund phrase—**It's strange,** *his* **doing that**.

Sometimes a noun is used rather than an adjective in this construction after anticipatory **it**.

> *It will be a sad thing, not seeing her any more.*
>
> *It's been a pleasure meeting you.*
>
> *It's no use* (or *no good*) *crying over spilled milk.*

**No use** and **no need** may also be preceded by expletive **there**—**There's no use** (or **no need**) **crying over spilled milk**.

Gerund phrase subjects after anticipatory **it** often have alternate forms with infinitive phrases.

> *It's very embarrassing not to remember your name.*
>
> *It's been a pleasure to meet you.*
>
> *It's no use to cry over spilled milk.*

### GERUND PHRASES
### AS OBJECTS OF VERBS

Certain verbs in English are followed by verbals—either gerunds or infinitives—which are considered as the objects of these verbs. Most of these verbs denote mental activity or indirect speech and therefore require subjects that refer to human beings. Others have little semantic content outside of indicating aspect—the beginning, duration, end or repetition of an action; these verbs may or may not be used with subjects denoting persons. There is less agreement that a verbal following one of these aspect-denoting verbs is its object; actually, there is some justification for considering a verb that expresses aspect as a quasi-auxiliary rather than as a verb that takes an object.

### VERBS FOLLOWED BY GERUND OBJECTS[2]

| | | |
|---|---|---|
| acknowledge | evade | quit (=stop, informal) |
| admit | facilitate* | recommend |
| advocate | fancy (=imagine) | relinguish |
| anticipate | finish | relish |
| appreciate | give up (=stop) | renounce |
| avoid | (be)grudge | report |
| cannot help | imagine | resent |
| consider | involve** | resist |
| contemplate | justify* | risk |
| defer | keep* | sanction |
| delay | keep on* | shirk |
| deny | leave off* | stop* |
| detest | mean* | suggest |
| disclaim | mention | tolerate |
| drop (=stop) | miss | try (=make an experiment with) |
| encourage | necessitate** | understand |
| enjoy | postpone | urge |
| entail** | practice | withhold |
| escape | put off | |

\* *These verbs can also have subjects that do not designate human beings.*
\*\* *These verbs usually have subjects that denote lifeless things.*

> *We have considered selling our home.*
> *He mentioned meeting the governor at the reception.*
> *I cannot tolerate his constant complaining about everything.*

Some verbs on this list, because of their semantic nature, cannot refer to events happening in the past—for example, **avoid, defer, give up, miss, risk, urge**. After such verbs only the **-ing** gerund is used.

> *He risked losing the money.*
> *He missed being teased by his younger sister.*

### VERBS FOLLOWED BY GERUND OR INFINITIVE OBJECTS

| | |
|---|---|
| abhor | continue* |
| attempt | decline |
| begin* | disdain |
| cannot bear | dread |
| cannot stand | endure |
| cease* | hate |
| commence* | hesitate |

---

[2] In referring to a list such as this, the reader must keep in mind that with verbals as well as with prepositions, there may be some difference between British and American usage.

| | |
|---|---|
| intend | propose |
| (dis)like | regret** |
| love | remember** |
| neglect | scorn |
| plan | start* |
| prefer | try |

\* *These verbs may also have subjects which do not designate human beings.*
\*\* *After these verbs, the gerund represents past time; the infinitive represents future time.*

*I remember taking care of that matter.* (past time)

vs.   *I must remember to take care of that matter.* (future time)

*He began attending classes regularly.*

or   *He began to attend classes regularly.*

*I intend doing that tomorrow.*

or   *I intend to do that tomorrow.*

*You mustn't neglect making the reservation right away.*

or   *You mustn't neglect to make the reservation right away.*

**Try** + a gerund has the special meaning of *make an experiment with*—**Try going to bed earlier; you'll feel better.** In this sense the infinitive may also be used. **Try** meaning *make an attempt to* requires the infinitive—**He is trying to enter a good university.**

After a non-human subject, **need** and **want** in the sense of *require* will take an -ing gerund—**This lamp needs repairing.** (Such a gerund may alternate with a passive infinitive—**This lamp needs *to be repaired*.**) **Bear** may also be used in some contexts in the same way as **need**—**These new developments will bear watching.**

GERUND PHRASES
AS OBJECTS OF PREPOSITIONS

Any verb used as the object in a prepositional phrase takes the form of a gerund. Most gerund phrases after prepositions are subjectless, especially those in adverbial prepositional phrases.

**Nominal Function
of Prepositional Gerund Phrases**

Such gerund phrases function as prepositional objects of verbs. A great many of the verbs listed under prepositional objects in the chapter on prepositions take such gerund objects.

*He insisted on paying the entire bill for dinner.*

*She often dreams about having a lot of money to spend on luxuries.*

Some verbs are followed by either gerund phrase prepositional objects or infinitive phrase objects.

agree in (or on) going, agree to go
care about going, care to go
caution (someone) against going, caution someone to go (*opposite meanings*)
decide on going, decide to go
forget about going, forget to go
grieve (or rejoice, exult) at going, grieve (or rejoice, exult) to go
help (someone) in going, help (someone to) go
plan on going, plan to go
serve for going, serve to go
suffice for going, suffice to go
warn (someone) against going, warn someone to go (*opposite meanings*)

The word **to** after the following verbs is a preposition rather than the sign of the infinitive and therefore requires a gerund after it—**accustom oneself, allude, confess, confine oneself, dedicate oneself, limit oneself, look forward, object, plead guilty, reconcile oneself, resign oneself, resort, revert**.

> *He objected to their entering the factory without permission.*
>
> *We look forward to seeing you again.*

### Adjectival Function
### of Prepositional Gerund Phrases

These adjectival constructions appearing after nouns begin mostly with **of** or **for**. There are two main types.

a. Those prepositional gerund phrases that follow nouns derived from verbs or adjectives.

> *His pretense of being rich didn't fool anyone.*
>
> *Their preparations for traveling abroad were very time-consuming.*
>
> *He spoke of the necessity of hiring more men.*

b. Those prepositional gerund phrases appearing after nouns that are nonderivational. Such adjectival constructions are mostly adjective clause equivalents.[3]

> *The money for traveling around the country* (=**with which they could travel around the country**) *was soon used up.*
>
> *This is not a good way of doing it* (=**in which you can do it**).
>
> *The time for making excuses* (=**in which you can make excuses**) *is past.*

Both types of prepositional gerund phrases may have alternate infinitive forms.

> *He spoke of the necessity to hire more men.*
>
> *This is not a good way to do it.*
>
> *The time to make excuses is past.*

---

[3] These phrases are sometimes interpreted as appositives to the nouns that precede them.

### Adverbial Function
### of Prepositional Gerund Phrases

PREPOSITIONAL GERUND PHRASES MODIFYING VERBS. These phrases may express almost all adverbial relationships except place.

> *After listening to the news, she started to prepare dinner.*
>
> *He earned the money for his tuition by working as a waiter during the summer months.*
>
> *I passed him in the street without his recognizing me.*
>
> *In spite of traveling alone, she enjoyed her vacation very much.*

A prepositional gerund phrase may appear in all three adverbial positions, but most frequently in initial or final position. In initial position the "subject" of the phrase is rarely expressed, since it is understood as the subject of the sentence. If the agent of an introductory gerund phrase is other than the subject of the sentence, the phrase is considered an unacceptable "dangling" element—**On looking out the window, a beautiful scene met his eyes.**

PREPOSITIONAL GERUND PHRASES MODIFYING ADJECTIVES. **At** introduces most prepositional gerund phrases after adjectives, especially **-ed** participial adjectives.

> *He was embarrassed at hearing himself praised.*
>
> *I'm disappointed at your doing such a thing.*
>
> *He's very quick at adding figures.*

Other prepositions introducing gerund phrases after adjectives are:

---

| | |
|---|---|
| about | He's very careless about keeping appointments. |
| for | Their funds are adequate for meeting their moderate needs. |
| of | He's afraid of displeasing his parents. |
| with | They must be content with seeing each other at infrequent intervals. |
| by | I was annoyed by the dog's barking all night. (This prepositional gerund phrase may also be interpreted as a modifier of the passive verb **be annoyed.**) |

---

Many of these prepositional gerund phrases after adjectives have alternate forms with infinitive phrases or **that** clauses.

1. *Infinitive phrases*

> *He was embarrassed to hear himself praised.*
>
> *He's afraid to displease his parents.*

2. **that** *clauses*

> *He was embarrassed that people were praising him.*
>
> *He's afraid that he will displease his parents.*

The word **to** after some adjectives, especially certain **-ed** participial adjectives, is a preposition rather than the sign of the infinitive and therefore requires the gerund form as its object—**accustomed[4], addicted, averse, dedicated, disposed, given, opposed, used[4].**

> *I have never become accustomed* (or *used*) *to American food.*
>
> *Some government officials are not averse to accepting bribes.*

## POSITION AND PUNCTUATION
## OF GERUND PHRASES

The gerund phrase appears in all positions occupied by the noun. Like the noun, it is not set off by punctuation except when it is used in apposition, in which case a comma, a colon or a dash precedes it.

> *He has devoted his life to one cause: fighting against all political and social injustice.*
>
> *Only one problem still remains—the storing of the grain.*

## STYLISTIC MATTERS
## RELATED TO GERUND PHRASES

In general, the gerund phrase retains a stronger verbal force than do the other nominals (noun clauses, infinitive phrases, abstract noun phrases). However, its varying forms offer choices that range from emphasis on the action of a verb to emphasis on the abstract idea of a noun.

> *The teacher's indoctrinating the children* *disturbed their parents.* (emphasis on an action)
>
> *The teacher's indoctrinating of the children* *disturbed their parents.* (emphasis intermediate between an action and an idea)
>
> *The indoctrinating of the children* (*by the teacher*) *disturbed their parents.* (emphasis on an idea)

In this last choice, **the indoctrinating of the children,** there is less concern for the "subject" as agent. This choice is closest to the nominal form used for the highest level of abstraction, the abstract noun phrase—**the indoctrination of the children (by the teacher).** As a matter of fact, however, if an abstract noun form of the verb exists, this form is generally preferred in a *the . . . of phrase* construction.

---

[4] Sometimes in older style, or in British usage, **accustomed to** or **used to** may be followed by the infinitive form rather than the gerund form.

# 18

## Infinitive Phrases

In this type of verbal construction, the verb is reduced to **to** infinitive form. The "subject" of the infinitive phrase may be implied or it may be found elsewhere in the sentence, often in a preceding prepositional phrase. The "object" is also sometimes found in a structure before the infinitive phrase.

By means of these changes in the subject-verb-complement core, the infinitive phrase may function, not as the main verb of a clause, but as another part of speech—either as a noun, adjective or adverb.

In most cases, the "subject" of an infinitive phrase denotes an animate being, especially a person. In some sentences, however, the "subject" may represent a thing or an idea.

> *For the clothes to dry properly, they must be hung out in the sun.*
>
> *You shouldn't allow such trifles to worry you.*

A "subject" denoting an idea or thing is often likely to be a passive "subject."

> *I don't want this news to be made public yet.*
>
> *The courses to be taught are listed in the catalog.*

IMPLIED "SUBJECT". a. The "subject" is a generic person. Such a subjectless infinitive phrase is common in a general statement, especially with a form of **be** as the main verb.

*It's not good (for anyone) to know too much.*
*It's more blessed (for people) to give than to receive.*
*(For everyone) to eat certain foods is a necessity.*

b. The "subject" is understood from the general context.

*To do such a thing will only cause trouble.*
*The doctor left instructions to change the bandages every day.*
*It was dreadful to witness that spectacle.*

"SUBJECT" IN ANOTHER PART OF THE SENTENCE. The "subject" is the *subject* of the main verb:

**We** *are happy to see you again.*
*To learn English,* **you** *must practice every day.*

The "subject" is the *object* of the main verb:

*She told* **him** *to write more often.*
*It amuses* **her** *to sing.*

"SUBJECT" IN A PRECEDING PREPOSITIONAL PHRASE.

**For you** *to do such a thing will only cause trouble.*
*His appeal* **to the crowd** *to go home was completely ignored.*
*It was foolish* **of you** *to have done that.*

The expletive "subject fillers" **it** and **there** may be used with infinitive phrases containing **to be**.

*I don't want there to be any trouble.*
*They wish it to be known that they cannot make any exceptions to this rule.*

The construction with **there** is usually avoided in formal prose.

### FORM OF THE INFINITIVE

Like the participle, the infinitive makes no distinctions for person or number. Also like the participle, the infinitive has only two forms for indicating time. One is a general form called the "present" infinitive, which expresses time simultaneous with or future from that of the main verb. The other is a perfect form, which expresses time *preceding* that of the main verb.

|  | **Active Voice** | **Passive Voice** | |
|---|---|---|---|
|  |  | *Progressive* | |
| General form (present infinitive) | to offer | to be offering | to be offered |
| Perfect form | to have offered | to have been offering | to have been offered |

The general form (**to offer**) is often given as the "name" of the verb. The form without **to** (**offer**) is called either the *simple form* of the verb, or the verb *stem* (sometimes the *bare* infinitive, or the *plain* infinitive).

Examples of the kind of time the present infinitive can express are:

| | |
|---|---|
| Present time | I *am* happy to meet you. |
| Past time | I *was* happy to meet you. |
| Future time | I *will be* happy to meet you. |

The present infinitive, while depending on the main verb to establish the time in general, often has future reference with respect to the main verb.

*I had hoped to see him soon.*

*The man for you to consult on that matter is out of town now.*

*We are eager to begin the work.*

Examples of past time denoted by the perfect infinitive are:

*He is lucky to have found such a wonderful wife.*

*The poison was strong enough to have killed ten people.*

*It's better to have loved and lost than never to have loved at all.*

The present infinitive is also possible in these sentences (**to find, to kill, to love**); the perfect infinitive merely provides additional stress on past time. In other sentences, however, only the perfect infinitive may indicate time prior to that of the main verb.

*I seem to have made a mistake in the address.*

*He was found to have lied about his business experience.*

Occasionally the perfect form represents future time before another future time, and thus corresponds to the future perfect tense—**She expects to have finished the next chapter by tomorrow**. This form is probably less common than the form in—**She expects to have the next chapter finished by tomorrow**.

The use of the perfect infinitive after **would like** is sometimes troublesome. The following verb forms are possible.

*I would like to give them some money.* Both verbs express present time.

*I would like to have given them some money.* The main verb indicates present time; the infinitive, past time.

*I would have liked to give them some money.* Both verbs express past time.

Occasionally the perfect forms of both verbs are heard (**I would have liked to have given them some money**), but such usage is considered unacceptable.

FUNCTION
OF INFINITIVE PHRASES

Infinitive phrases may function as nouns, adjectives or adverbs in many instances.

*Illustrative Sentences*

| | |
|---|---|
| *Nominal function:* | |
| Subject | *For her to clean the house every day* is absolutely necessary. |
| | *or* |
| | It is absolutely necessary *for her to clean the house every day*. |
| Object of verb | Her husband wants *her to clean the house every day*. |
| Subjective complement (Predicate noun) | The regulation is *for boys and girls to live in separate dormitories*. |
| Appositive | He had only one desire—*for his family to be in good health*. |
| *Adjectival function:* | He is a good man *for you to know*. |
| *Adverbial function:* | |
| Modifier of a sentence | *To tell the truth*, I don't understand him at all. |
| Modifier of a verb | (*In order*) *for me to buy a car*, I'll have to take a loan from the bank. |
| Modifier of an adjective | I'm sorry *to see you leave*. |
| | This music is too hard *for me to play correctly*. |

## NOMINAL FUNCTIONS
## OF INFINITIVE PHRASES

Infinitive phrases functioning as nouns differ from gerund phrases in that they cannot be preceded by determiners nor can they serve as objects of prepositions.

### Infinitive Phrases as Subjects

Infinitive phrase subjects occur chiefly with the same type of verbs as do other nominals: **be**, causative verbs, verbs expressing emotion, and a few other verbs like **require, take, mean**.

> *To ask for more money would be wrong.*
> *To see his children again will make him very happy.*
> *To see a fine play exhilarates him.*

Such infinitive phrase subjects appear more commonly after anticipatory **it**.

> *It would be wrong to ask for more money.*
> *It will make him very happy to see his children again.*
> *It exhilarates him to see a fine play.*

After a predicate adjective in an anticipatory **it** construction, the "subject" of the infinitive phrase may be in a **for** phrase, an **of** phrase, or either.

> *It's difficult for me to do that.*
> or *It's impolite of (or **for**) you to keep avoiding him.*
> *It was kind of you to help him.*

Predicate adjectives that may be followed by infinitives in anticipatory **it** constructions are listed below. These adjectives are classified according to the type of prepositional "subjects" that accompany them.

| Adjectives Followed by FOR Phrases Only | Adjectives Followed by FOR Phrases or OF Phrases | Adjectives Followed by OF Phrases Only |
|---|---|---|
| (dis)advantageous | (dis)courteous | generous |
| ádvisable | foolish | good (=*kind*) |
| beneficial | impertinent | intelligent |
| delightful | (un)natural | kind |
| difficult | noble | (dis)loyal |
| easy | (im)polite | magnanimous |
| essential | (im)proper | magnificent |
| fatal | rash | malicious |
| good (=*beneficial*) | right | nice (informal) |
| hard | rude | unworthy |
| hopeless | strange | |
| important | stupid | |
| necessary | wicked | |
| pertinent (=*relevant*) | (un)wise | |
| (un)pleasant | wrong | |
| (im)possible | | |
| preferable | | |
| (ir)relevant | | |
| satisfactory | | |
| useful | | |
| useless | | |
| worthwhile | | |

Note that most of these adjectives represent a judgment or an opinion.

A **for** phrase "subject" after a predicate adjective has two possible grammatical interpretations. The most common one is that it belongs with the infinitive phrase that follows it. The justification for this interpretation is that the **for** phrase can be moved with the infinitive to subject position. Thus, a sentence like **It is easy for me to do that** is interchangeable with **For me to do that is easy.** Another possible interpretation is that the **for** phrase in such a construction belongs with the predicate adjective that precedes it. This view is justified by the fact that, even when the infinitive is in subject position, the **for** phrase may remain in the predicate—**To do that is easy for me.** In a parallel sentence with a gerund phrase—**Doing that is easy for me**—the **for** phrase is also considered a modifier of the predicate adjective.

The **of** phrase after a predicate adjective in an **it** construction seems more obviously to belong with the adjective than with infinitive. The pause in speech that often marks the terminal point of a grammatical structure is after the **of** phrase—**It was foolish of you | to do that.** The pause in the sentence with a **for** phrase, on the other hand, is after the predicate adjective— **It was foolish | for you to do that.**

If the infinitive occurs in subject position with any of the predicate adjectives from the second column, only the **of** phrase is used.

> *To do that was foolish of you.*
>
> vs. *It was foolish of (or **for**) you to do that.*

A sentence with an **of** phrase "subject" of an infinitive may alternate with one in which the subject of the sentence is the "subject" of the infinitive.

> *You are foolish (or wise, wrong, kind) to do that.*
>
> vs. *It is foolish (or wise, wrong, kind) of you to do that.*

A number of **-ing** participial adjectives expressing emotional states also enable infinitive subjects to be used after anticipatory **it**.

| | | |
|---|---|---|
| alarming | disturbing | puzzling |
| amazing | embarrassing | satisfying |
| amusing | entertaining | shocking |
| annoying | exhilarating | startling |
| astonishing | fascinating | surprising |
| astounding | interesting | terrifying |
| disappointing | intriguing | troubling |
| disgusting | irritating | |
| distressing | pleasing | |

> *It is alarming to see how thin he has become.*
>
> *Not to have won first prize was disappointing.*
>
> *It would be embarrassing to give a speech in public.*

If a "subject" is used with the infinitive phrase after one of these participial adjectives, it is usually in a **to** phrase, which in some instances alternates with a **for** phrase.

> *It is alarming to me to see how thin he has become.*
>
> *Not to have won first prize was disappointing to the young violinist.*
>
> *It would be embarrassing to (or **for**) him to give a speech in public.*

Infinitive phrases may be used with other complements than predicate adjectives.

| Nouns | To build such a bridge will be *a difficult task*. |
|---|---|
| | It's *a pleasure* to serve you. |
| | To have him on our side will be *a great advantage* to us. |
| | It's *our policy* to hire people only on the basis of competence and reliability. |
| Prepositional phrases | It was *to our interest* to pay them at once. |
| | To hire an inexperienced person is *against our policy*. |

### Infinitive Phrases as Objects of Verbs

Infinitive objects of verbs need to be distinguished from post-verb infinitives that have other functions. At one extreme, for example, are the infinitives after verbs that are so closely related to the verb as to form a single unit with it, the first part being considered merely an auxiliary—for example, **have to, have got to, ought to, used to**, and perhaps **need to** and **dare to**. At the other extreme are infinitives that have only a loose adverbial connection with the verb, so much so that the infinitive phrase may be transferred to one of the two other adverbial positions. The infinitive phrase object might be considered intermediate between the two extremes. It participates in the subject-verb-complement relationship in much the same way as a noun object does; in fact, many of the verbs taking infinitive objects also take noun objects. However, it is difficult to draw a clearcut line between all three types of post-verb infinitives. Some of the verbs we are listing here under infinitive objects are on the borderline of auxiliaries like **ought to** because of their modal or future meaning; other verbs listed take infinitives that shade off into adverbial meanings.

Most infinitive objects have future reference in relation to the time of the main verb. For this reason, the perfect form is rarely used for infinitive objects.

Infinitive objects may be divided into two groups according to what functions as the "subject" of the infinitive.

THE SUBJECT OF THE MAIN VERB IS THE "SUBJECT" OF THE INFINITIVE. The subjects of the main verbs listed in this group usually denote human beings.

| | | | |
|---|---|---|---|
| *abhor | *commence | *hesitate | refuse |
| afford | condescend | hope | *regret |
| arrange | consent | *intend | resolve |
| ask | *continue | learn | *scorn |
| *attempt | decide | *(dis)like | seek |
| beg | *decline | *love | *start |
| *begin | deserve | manage | strive |
| bother | desire | mean | struggle |
| *cannot bear | determine | *neglect | swear |
| (also interrog.) | *disdain | *plan | tend |
| *cannot stand (also | *dread | *prefer | threaten |
| interrogative) | endeavor | prepare | *try |
| care (negative or | *endure | pretend | undertake |
| interrogative) | expect | proceed | venture |
| *cease | fail | promise | volunteer |
| choose (=*prefer*) | forget | profess | want |
| claim[1] | *hate | *propose | wish |

\* *These verbs may also be followed by gerunds.*

[1] The perfect infinitive may be used after **claim**—**She claims to have been the victim of threats.**

THE OBJECT OF THE MAIN VERB IS THE "SUBJECT" OF THE INFINITIVE. Some infinitives are the second element of a two-part object after a verb, the first part being a noun or a pronoun. The two parts of the object—the (pro)noun and the infinitive—stand in the relationship of subject-predicate to each other. The infinitives in such two-part objects are sometimes classified as objective complements.

The subjects of sentences containing these two-part objects usually denote human beings, as do the (pro)nouns that function as the "subjects" of the infinitives.

| | | | |
|---|---|---|---|
| advise | defy | incite | *prepare |
| allow | *desire | induce | *promise |
| *ask | direct | instruct | provoke |
| *beg | empower | invite | remind |
| beseech | enable | *(dis)like (may | request |
| cause | encourage | also take a gerund) | require |
| caution | entitle | *love (may also | teach |
| challenge | entreat | take a gerund) | tell |
| command | *expect | motivate | tempt |
| condemn | forbid | obligate | urge |
| coerce | force | oblige | *want |
| compel | get (=*cause*) | order | warn |
| convince | impel | permit | *wish |
| dare (=*challenge*) | implore | persuade | |

 * *These verbs, which have also been given in the preceding list, may be used with or without (pro)noun objects.*

Note that many of the verbs in this second list involve a communication or a desiring; or they have causative, compelling, or motivating force.

A sentence containing a (pro)noun plus infinitive object may be changed to passive voice.

---

| | |
|---|---|
| Active | His wife persuaded him to buy a new car. |
| Passive | He was persuaded by his wife to buy a new car. (*less commonly*, He was persuaded to buy a new car by his wife.) |
| Active | Her teacher has encouraged the girl to write short stories. |
| Passive | The girl has been encouraged by her teacher to write short stories. |

---

This kind of passive probably occurs more often without any agent expressed.

> *He has been warned not to do that again.*
>
> *They will not be permitted to enter the building without a pass.*

After some verbs the first part of a two-part infinitive object may be a

**for** phrase—**arrange, not care, hope, intend, mean, pray, plan, prepare, cannot stand, wish.**

> *The store arranged for us to pay the money in three installments.*
> *We had intended for the children to come to church with us.*
> *She didn't care for him to see her while she was sick.*

Without the **for** phrase, such an infinitive would normally refer back to the subject of the sentence.

In colloquial speech, a **for** phrase is sometimes added extraneously before the (pro)noun that precedes an infinitive in a two-part object of a verb. This usage is especially common after the verbs **hate, (dis)like, love, prefer, want.**

> *I hate (for) anyone to be late for an appointment.*
> *We would like (for) you to come to the office tomorrow.*

The **for** construction sometimes also occurs informally after the verb **say** in the sense of *give instructions*—**He said (for you) to go in.**

The use of a **for** phrase with **suggest** and **recommend** is of doubtful acceptability—**They suggested (or recommended) for us to return the next day.**

Some verbs are followed by a two-part object with the **to**-less infinitive.

1.  The causative verbs **make** (=*compel*), **have**

    > *She made the children clean up their own rooms.*
    > *She had the maid clean all the rooms.*

2.  **let** (=*allow*), **bid** (=*request*)

    > *They let the children stay up late on weekends.*
    > *She bid the children be quiet.*

3.  **Help** (the omission of **to** is optional)

    > *He helped the old woman (to) cross the street.*

4.  verbs of physical perception—**feel, hear, listen to, look at, notice, observe, overhear, see, watch.**

    > *I heard the whistle blow a few minutes ago.*
    > *She watched the passengers get off the bus.*

We have already pointed out that the **to**-less infinitive alternates with the participial form in this construction after a verb of perception.

There are a number of other verbs taking infinitive objects that need to be put in a special category. Unlike the verbs already given, these verbs may be used with perfect infinitives—**She seems to have made a mistake; We supposed him to have left by now.** In addition, the infinitive **to be** is very common in the objects after such verbs. This infinitive is often optional; if it is omitted, only a subjective complement or an objective complement remains.

| | | |
|---|---|---|
| He seems to be happy. | *vs.* | He seems happy. |
| (**To be happy** is an infinitive object of the verb **seems**.) | | (**Happy** is a subjective complement referring back to the subject **he**.) |
| We supposed him to be happy. | | We supposed him happy. |
| (**Him to be happy** is a two-part object of the verb **supposed**.) | | (**Happy** is an objective complement referring back to the object **him**.) |

In this special group of verbs, there are only two that take infinitives referring back to the subject—**seem** and **appear**.

With the infinitive **to be**:

> *He appears (to be) angry.*
>
> *She seems (to be) a very intelligent woman.*
>
> *They appeared (to be) in a hurry.*

but   *—They seem **to have been** rich once.*

The perfect infinitive of **be** cannot be omitted.

With other infinitives:

> *He seems to enjoy himself wherever he goes.*
>
> *She appears to be telling the truth.*

Infinitive objects in these sentences are interchangeable with **that** clause subjects after anticipatory **it**.

> *It seems that he enjoys himself wherever he goes.*
>
> *It appears that she is telling the truth.*

In sentences containing **seem** or **appear** plus an infinitive, either the main verb or the infinitive may be made negative without changing the meaning.

> *He doesn't seem to have understood the instructions.*

or

> *He seems not to have understood the instructions.*

The first form is probably more common; the second form places stronger emphasis on the negative force of the infinitive.

Verbs in this special group that refer back to the *object* of the verb are more numerous—**acknowledge, assume, believe, consider, declare, discover, fancy** (=*imagine*), **feel, find, imagine, judge, know, picture, presume, prove, report, represent, reveal, show, suppose, take** (=*suppose*), **think, understand**.

With the infinitive **to be**:

> *We found her (to be) a very dull person.*
>
> *The court declared him (to be) insane when he committed the murder.*
>
> *The company considers her (to be) a competent worker.*

but   *—We believe there **to have been** an accident.*

With other infinitives:

> *The police found him to be driving a stolen car.*
> *The investigation revealed him to have acted honestly.*
> *We believe her to be dominated by her mother.*

Except for the infinitive form **to be**, infinitives after verbs like **acknowledge** occur much less frequently than **that** clauses do.

> *We believe that there has been an accident.*
> *The police found that he was driving a stolen car.*
> *The investigation revealed that he had acted honestly.*

Most of the verbs in the **acknowledge** group can be followed by anticipatory **it** plus an optional **to be**. **It** points ahead to either another infinitive phrase or to a **that** clause.

> *I find it (to be) difficult to pay my bills now.*
> *We believed it (to be) possible that he would be successful.*
> *Your friends think it (to be) a mistake for you to leave now.*

Without **to be**, these infinitive phrases or **that** clauses can be considered in apposition to **it**.

Like the first group of verbs taking two-part infinitive objects, the verbs in the **acknowledge** group are often used in the passive voice, the original (pro)noun object becoming the subject of the sentence.

> *The thief is assumed to be hiding in the woods.*
> *She was thought by many to have married for money.*
> *Her husband was believed to have done her a terrible injustice.*

The verbs **rumor** and **say**, while not followed by a (pro)noun plus infinitive object in the active voice, may be made passive in the same way as the verbs in the **acknowledge** group.

> *He is rumored to be dying.*
> *She is said to have an immense fortune.*

In these passive constructions, infinitive objects are interchangeable with **that** clause subjects after anticipatory **it**.

> *It is assumed that the thief is hiding in the woods.*
> *It was thought by many that she had married for money.*
> *It is rumored that he is dying.*

**To be** is sometimes omitted from the progressive or passive infinitives after some of the verbs like **acknowledge**. In such cases the resulting structures may also be regarded as participial phrases.

> *We found him (to be) living a life of luxury on the Riviera.*

*The newspapers reported the soldier (to be) missing in action.*

*I imagined the author (to be) surrounded by his many admirers.*

A few verbs of *ordering* or *wanting* function like the verbs in the **acknowledge** group in that the **to be** of a following passive infinitive may be omitted.

*He wants all the newspapers (to be) delivered right away.*

*Their commander ordered all the bridges (to be) destroyed as they retreated.*

Many of the verbs like **acknowledge** may also be followed by alternate participal constructions introduced by **as.**

*She was revealed as having (or **to have**) acted honestly.*

*We considered him as being (or **to be**) first rate.*

*He was reported as having (or **to have**) led the guerrilla attack.*

To the verbs like **acknowledge** we might add the small group of verbs that normally take objective complements with an optional **to be**—**appoint, choose, christen, elect, name, nominate, select.**

*The president appointed him (to be) head of the new committee.*

*The students elected her (to be) their representative.*

After the verbs like **appoint,** and after some of the verbs in the **acknowledge** group, **as** may be an alternative for **to be** used as an infinitive object.

*They chose him as (=**to be**) their leader.*

*He was known as (=**to be**) a man of great integrity.*

*We consider your suggestion as (=**to be**) worthy of serious thought.*

## Infinitive Phrases
## as Subjective Complements

The infinitive phrase frequently functions as a predicate noun after a form of the verb **be.**

*The only thing we can do is to call the police.*

*A good way to prepare liver is to broil it.*

*To see her is to love her.*

Without **to**:

*The only thing we can do is call the police.*

*All he does now is sit at a big desk and look important.*

## Infinitive Phrases
## as Appositive Nouns

*He asked for only one thing—to be left in peace.*

*I am aware that a heavy responsibility rests on you, to help support your aging parents.*

Without **to**:

*There is one thing I will never do—refuse money to a beggar.*

ADJECTIVAL FUNCTION
OF INFINITIVE PHRASES

There are several types of nouns or pronouns that infinitive phrases may modify. The most common are (1) noun forms of verbs or adjectives normally followed by infinitives, and (2) (pro)nouns also functioning as "subjects" or "objects" of the infinitives. Infinitives after such nouns often have future reference with respect to the time of the main verb.

Noun Derivational Forms

NOUN FORMS OF VERBS FOLLOWED BY INFINITIVES

| | | | |
|---|---|---|---|
| advice | *determination | *motivation | reminder |
| arrangement | encouragement | order | request |
| attempt | *endeavor | permission | requirement |
| *challenge | expectation | plan | *resolution |
| *choice | *failure | preference | *struggle |
| *claim | *fight | preparation | suggestion |
| command | *hesitation | *pretense | temptation |
| *compulsion | hope | *promise | tendency |
| consent | inducement | proposal | warning |
| *decision | instruction | recommendation | wish |
| desire | intention | *refusal | |

\* *Infinitives after these nouns are not generally used with* **for** *phrases.*

> *His decision to move to the West Coast was made a long time ago.*
> *I admire her resolution not to be intimidated by any threats.*

The infinitive after any of these nouns may also be viewed as the "object" of the noun (**his desire to go**) just as it is after the verb (**he desired to go**) or it may even be viewed as an appositive, like the **that** clause in **his desire that I go**.

NOUN FORMS OF ADJECTIVES FOLLOWED BY INFINITIVES

*ability
advantage
anxiety
*certainty
*competence
impatience
necessity
pleasure
*readiness
reluctance

\* *Infinitives after these nouns are not generally used with* **for** *phrases.*

*His impatience to leave right away was very noticeable.*

*We were surprised at her reluctance to accept any money for her work.*

Infinitive phrases may also modify the noun forms of some participial adjectives that are normally followed by infinitives—**His astonishment** (or **amazement, disappointment, satisfaction, surprise**) **to learn the news was quite obvious**.

(Pro)nouns Functioning
as "Subjects" or Objects" of the Infinitives

The infinitive modifiers of these (pro)nouns are adjective clause equivalents, often with the added force of such modals as **can—could, would** or **should**.

## The (Pro)noun Is the "Subject" of the Infinitive

*She has no one to help her.* (=**no one who can help her**)

*He was the first to arrive and the last to leave.* (=**the first who arrived and the last who left.**

*He is not a person to let little things disturb him.* (=**a person who would let little things disturb him**)

*In years to come* (=**in years that are to come**), *he will regret having left his native land.*

Numerals and pronoun compounds with **-one, -body, -thing** are especially common as "subjects" of such adjectival infinitive phrases.

## The (Pro)noun Is the "Object" of the Infinitive

Only an *active* infinitive follows its (pro)noun "object." This infinitive modifier, however, may also be interpreted as having passive force.

*The best man to see is Mr. Jones.*

*To see* = active   **whom** you should see
         passive   **who** should be seen

This is probably one of the most common types of adjectival infinitive. Additional examples are:

*The next question to consider was the crucial one.*

*I have two more chores to do.*

*"Honesty is the best policy" is a good rule to follow.*

*There was nothing more to say about that matter.*

Most of the infinitive phrases in these examples may also be stated with passive forms of the infinitive—**the next question to be considered, two more chores to be done**, etc. With these passive forms, the nouns being modified are the grammatical "subjects" of the infinitives.

**The (Pro)noun Is the**
**"Object" of a Preposition**
**in the Infinitive Phrase**

*He has nothing to complain about.* (*Nothing* is the "object" of *about*.)

*I can find little to laugh at in that movie.* (*Little* is the "object" of *at*.)

*Please tell me the person to show my samples to.* (*The person* is the "object" of *to*.)

Some nouns which do not have any of the functions just mentioned may also be modified by infinitive phrases. These phrases are often classified as appositives to the nouns they follow.

*Will you do us the honor to dine with us?*

*I don't have the courage to ask my employer for a raise in pay.*

*She will have the chance* (or *opportunity, occasion*) *to use her French when she goes to Europe this summer.*

*The power to help others depends on the power to help oneself.*

Included in this group are nouns denoting time, place, reason. The infinitive phrases after these words may be considered the equivalent of adjective clauses introduced by the relative adverbs **when, where, why.**

*There is a time to be born and a time to die.* (Infinitives = *when we are to be born, when we are to die.*)

*The best place to put the piano is in the living room.* (Infinitive = *where you should put the piano.*)

*He had a good reason to be angry.* (Infinitive = *why he should be angry.*)

ADVERBIAL FUNCTION
OF INFINITIVE PHRASES

Like other adverbials, an adverbial infinitive phrase may modify the entire sentence, the verb, an adjective or an adverb.

Infinitive Phrases
Modifying the Entire Sentence

Such sentence modifiers commonly represent a speaker's parenthetic remarks. These parenthetic infinitive phrases may take the form of:

1. A speaker's side comments on the subject under discussion—**to tell the truth, to speak strictly, strange to say, to be honest, to make things worse, to use a common expression, to coin a term.** An element of condition is contained within these infinitive phrases. Some of these phrases have corresponding -ly sentence adverbs—**truthfully, strangely, honestly.**

2. A transitional expression in the development of a narration or discussion—**to change the subject, to return to our subject, to begin with, to conclude, to cut a long story short, to take a simple example, to mention a few examples.**

Infinitive Phrases
Modifying the Verb

Many adverbial infinitive phrases that occur in final position are tightly connected with the main verb. These *restrictive* modifiers are not usually set off with commas, nor can they be moved to other adverbial positions. Other adverbial infinitive phrases in final position are only loosely related to the verb. These *nonrestrictive* modifiers also occur in the two other adverbial positions; they usually require commas in all three positions.

**Types of
Adverbial Infinitive Phrases
Modifying the Verb**

These infinitive phrases are being classified by meaning. In some instances the phrases may signify more than one adverbial relationship. Where it seems useful, we will make distinctions between restrictive and nonrestrictive phrases.

1. *Infinitive phrases of purpose*

With this type of infinitive, the adverbial relationship of purpose may be strengthened by the special forms **in order to** or **so as to**.

a. *Restrictive phrases*

> *He moved his chair to be closer to her.*
> *We eat to live; we should not live to eat.*
> *He came to New York in order to look for a job.*

It is sometimes difficult to distinguish between this type of restrictive adverbial in final position and other infinitive phrases in this position. For example, an infinitive after a verb like **appoint, bribe, hire, pay, summon** may be interpreted as either a restrictive adverbial of purpose or as the second part of an infinitive object.

> *They hired their neighbor's son to take care of their lawn.*
> *He was summoned to testify in court.*
> *They bribed him not to tell what he knew.*

These constructions are like infinitive objects in that **for** phrases are not generally used with them, and in that they can be made negative with **not** alone. However, they are also like adverbial infinitives of purpose in that they may be preceded by **in order to**.

Other final infinitive phrases may be interpreted as restrictive adverbials of purpose or as adjectivals after some nouns.

> *She bought a toy to give her daughter.*
> *They lent me a book to read.*
> *The teacher dictated some sentences for the children to write down.*

Like adjectival infinitives, these infinitives may be changed to adjective clauses—**which she might give her daughter, which I might read, which the children might write down.** Like adverbials, these infinitives may be preceded by **in order to—in order to give it to her daughter, in order for me to read it, in order for the children to write them down.**

　b. *Nonrestrictive phrases*

> *He moved to New York with his family, (in order) to have a better opportunity to find a good position.*
>
> *The lecturer, (in order) to make his talk more interesting, used colored slides.*
>
> *(In order) to make room for his new merchandise, the owner of the store decided to have a big sale.*

If a **for** phrase "subject" is used with **in order to**, the infinitive cannot draw upon the preceding part of the sentence for its "object."

> *She brought her fiancé to the club in order for her friends to meet **him**.*
>
> vs.　*She brought her fiancé to the club for her friends to meet.*

　2. *Infinitive phrases of condition*
　a. *Restrictive phrases*

> *He will do anything to have the chance to see her again.* (Infinitive = **if he may have the chance to see her again.**)
>
> *I would have given my life to have saved hers.* (Infinitive = **if I could have saved hers.**)

　b. *Nonrestrictive phrases*

> *To judge by her reaction, she must have deeply resented his remarks.* ((Infinitive = **if we are to judge by her reaction.**)
>
> *One would suppose, to look at him, that he has never had a care in his life.* (Infinitive = **if one looks at him.**)

Some infinitive phrases express both condition and purpose simultaneously. This is true of the first two sentences given under restrictive phrases of condition. It is also true of the following nonrestrictive infinitive phrases.

> *(In order) to get to work on time, I must take the early bus.*
>
> *They will have to blast through the mountains (in order) to build the highway.*

In sentences with infinitive phrases that denote both condition and purpose, the main verb refers to either *present* or *future* time. However, if the main verb indicates *past* time, the infinitive phrase expresses purpose only.

> *In order to get to work on time, I had to take the early bus.*
>
> *They had to blast through the mountains in order to build the highway.*

The next two types of infinitive phrases appear in final position only. They are written with or without commas, depending on whether a pause occurs before them in speech.

　3. *Infinitive phrases of result*

> *He finally won his lawsuit (,) only to find that his lawyers would get most of the money.*
>
> *He left his native country, never to return.*
>
> *He returned home (,) to find his wife ill in bed.*
>
> *What crime have I committed (,) to be treated this way?*
>
> *He must have been blind (,) not to have seen that.*

4. *Infinitive phrases of cause*

> *He rejoiced to see his old friends again.*
>
> *She blushed to hear herself praised by the teacher.*

Infinitive Phrases
Modifying Predicate Adjectives

The predicate adjectives followed by infinitive subjects in **it** constructions (**It would be wise to do that**) have already been mentioned. The predicate adjectives given here are modified by the infinitive phrases.

| | | |
|---|---|---|
| *afraid | *eager | lucky |
| *anxious | eligible | proud |
| apt | *(un)fit | ready |
| bound | fortunate | sorry |
| careful | *glad | *suitable |
| certain | *happy | sure |
| *content | *impatient | (un)worthy |
| deserving | likely | |

\* *Infinitives may occur with* **for** *phrases after these adjectives.*

> *I am anxious to see my lawyer at once.*
>
> *We are fortunate to have such a good teacher.*
>
> *The audience was impatient for the concert to begin.*

A person-denoting subject is required in sentences with all the adjectives that express emotional states. With the adjectives signifying judgment or a degree of possibility, a person-denoting subject may or may not be used.

Unless the "subject" is given in a **for** phrase, the subject of the main verb is the "subject" of the infinitive. **For** phrase "subjects" are used chiefly with adjectives that express feeling.

While the **-ing** participial forms of many verbs expressing emotion take infinitive subjects in anticipatory **it** constructions (**It was embarrassing for him to speak in public**)[2], the **-ed** participial forms from these same verbs are followed by infinitive phrase modifiers (**He was embarrassed to give a speech in public**). Sentences used with such infinitives require person-denoting subjects.

---

[2] See p. 333 for a list of these verbs.

After a few predicate adjectives—mainly **easy, hard, difficult**—the subject of the main verb is the "object" of the infinitive.

> *John is **easy** to please.* (***John*** is the "object" of ***please***)
>
> vs.   *John is **eager** to please.* (***John*** is the "subject" of ***please***)

Actually an infinitive after an adjective like **easy** may be interpreted as having active or passive meaning. Thus, the sentence **John is easy to please** may be understood as:

> *It is easy (for anyone) to please John.* (active interpretation)
>
> *It is easy for John to be pleased.* (passive interpretation)

Infinitive Phrases
Modifying Adjectives or Adverbs
Used with TOO or ENOUGH

### 1. *Modifying adjectives*

> *She's too intelligent to be deceived by such a lie.*
>
> *The canoe is large enough to hold four people.*

### 2. *Modifying adverbs*

> *It's raining too hard for me to go out.*
>
> *We can't get to the theater quickly enough to see the play from the beginning.*

Note that the word **enough** follows the adjective or adverb it modifies.

An infinitive phrase may also follow a *noun* modified by **enough, too much** or **too many.**

> *He doesn't have **enough** money to buy a house.* (or, less commonly, *He doesn't have money **enough** to buy a house.*)
>
> *She has **too many** students in the class to give them individual attention.*

### *TO* SUBSTITUTION

To substitution occurs after many words that are normally followed by infinitives. Such substitution is used to avoid repetition of a part of a predicate that has already been mentioned.

### 1. **To** substitution after modal auxiliaries

> *She doesn't live in the country now, but she used to.*
>
> *We had better fix the car now or we will have to later on during our trip.*

### 2. **To** substitution after verbs taking infinitive objects

> *He expects to fail his course, and he deserves to.*
>
> *We didn't ask him to pay, but he wanted to.*
>
> *The men were reluctant to move forward, but their commander ordered them to.*

3. **To** substitution after predicate adjectives

> *Please bring your children with you. —I'll be glad to.*
> *He'd like to go into the jungle, but he's afraid to.*

4. **To** substitution after nouns

> *She goes to the beach every time she has the opportunity to.*
> *I'd like to do it, but I don't have the courage to.*
> *I haven't gone to that exhibit yet, nor do I have any intention to.*

Although the **to** substitute usually occurs after the predicate it stands for, it may also precede this predicate.

> *A person who wants to can find a way.*
> *Although he really would like to, he's ashamed to ask a girl to dance.*

The negative of the **to** substitute is **not to**.

> *The guests got up to leave, but their hostess begged them not to.*
> *We're going to the meeting, although we would prefer not to.*
> *You may go there if you wish, but it would be advisable not to.*

The substitute for infinitives preceded by **how** is **how to**.

> *I would like to help you but I don't know how to.*
> *The children will make the decorations if we show them how to.*

**How** may stand alone as the substitute in such sentences.

> *I would like to help you but I don't know how.*
> *The children will make the decorations if we show them how.*

In informal English the **to** substitute is sometimes omitted.

> *His wife asked him to mail the letter, but he forgot (to).*
> *He wanted to ask her to dance but he hesitated (to).*

INFINITIVES PLUS
PREPOSITIONAL PARTICLES

In some sentences, prepositional particles are inseparable from infinitives. The "objects" of such prepositions are usually in the preceding part of the sentence.

Prepositional Particles
in Infinitive Phrases
Used as Nominals

The infinitives in such phrases are usually passive.
1. *In infinitive objects*

| He expected | to be | taken care of. |
| | | provided for. |
| | | laughed at. |
| | | interfered with. |
| | | listened to. |
| | | imposed upon. |
| | | discriminated against. |
| | | looked down on. |

The "objects" of such prepositional particles are the subjects of the main verbs.

2. *In infinitive subjects*

    *It disturbs him to be imposed upon.*

or  *To be imposed upon disturbs him.*

    The object of the verb is the "object" of the preposition.

    *To be laughed at is not pleasant.*

or  *It is not pleasant to be laughed at.*

    The "object" of the preposition is an understood generic person.

Prepositional Particles
in Infinitive Phrases
Used as Adjectivals

We have already seen that the noun being modified is the "object" of the preposition.

    *We need more money to live on.*

    *They have much furniture to be disposed of.*

The particle may follow **to be** + an adjective.

    *We have many blessings to be grateful for.*

    *You are a son to be proud of.*

The particle may be part of an idiom consisting of a verb + noun + preposition.

    *We have some important business to take care of.*

    *He is not the kind of person to be made fun of.*

The particle may express a relationship such as place, agent, manner.

    *I would like a more comfortable chair to sit on.*

    *She advertised for a companion to travel with.*

    *Most religions provide some moral principles to live by.*

Sometimes the particle is omitted after an adjectival infinitive, especially in informal speech.

    *The best place to go (to) for dinner is the little restaurant around the corner.*

    *She has no money to buy food (with).*

    *You may have an hour to do it (in).*

Prepositional Particles
in Infinitive Phrases
Used as Adverbials

> *He told no one about his plans, in order not to be interfered with.*
>
> *So as to be well thought of, the politician gave a large donation to the university.*
>
> *To be cared for properly, the plants should be watered every day.*

The "objects" of these particles in adverbial infinitive phrases are the subjects of the main verb. The infinitives in such phrases are usually passive.

INFINITIVES USED

FOR ABRIDGMENT OF DEPENDENT CLAUSES

Since much of this information has already been given under each of the dependent clauses, we will merely summarize it here. In the kind of abridgment we are considering, the subordinate conjunction is retained, but the finite verb of the clause is reduced to an infinitive, usually the present active infinitive.

In abridged noun and adjective clauses, the infinitives generally have modal force; **can—could, should** often accompany the verb when the clause is expanded to full subject-predicate form.

With the few exceptions noted below, the subject of the main verb is the "subject" of the infinitive in abridged dependent clauses.

Abridgment in Noun Clauses

1. Abridgment in subject:

> *How to do it*
> *Whether (or not) to buy it* } *is the question.*

2. Abridgment in subjective complement:

> *The problem is* { *where to get the money.*
> *whether to pay now (or not).*

3. Abridgment in object of verb:

| | |
|---|---|
| *Clauses from yes-no questions* | They are wondering whether (or not) to do it. We can't decide whether to go (or not). |
| *Clauses from interrogative word questions* | I don't know {when to leave. how to get there. |
| | Please tell me {what to do. whom to see. what to look for. |

Abridged noun clauses with infinitives are very common after certain verbs—**ask, consider, decide, explain, find out, forget, guess, hear, inquire, know, learn, observe, perceive, remember, show, teach, tell, understand, wonder**.

After the verbs **ask, explain, show, teach, tell**, person-denoting objects may precede the abridged infinitive objects.

> *He asked **his doctor** whether (or not) to take sleeping pills.*
>
> *They will tell **us** when to come.*

The preposition **to** is used before the first object of **explain**—**The foreman will explain to you how to do the work**. Except for the verb **ask**, the person-denoting objects that precede these abridged infinitives act as the "subjects" of the infinitives.

4. Abridgment in prepositional phrases:

> *He consulted his stockbroker on how to invest his money.*
>
> *She saw her lawyer about whether to file for a divorce.*
>
> *He was always having discussions with his friends about how to bring up children.*

## Abridgment in Adjective Clauses

This kind of abridgment occurs in clauses containing prepositional phrases.

> *He needs more money with which to travel.* (=**with which he can travel.**)
>
> *She found a pretty vase in which to put the flowers.* (=**in which she could put the flowers.**)
>
> *We all have some sins for which to atone.* (=**for which we must atone.**)

The less formal structures, with the prepositions in final position—**money to travel with, a pretty vase to put the flowers in, some sins to atone for**—are parallel to the alternate adjective clauses with prepositions in final position—**money (which) he can travel with, a good vase (which) she can put the flowers in, some sins (which) we must atone for.**

## Abridgment in Adverbial Clauses

> *He won't be so foolish as to resign from the company now.*
>
> *It rained with such great force as to flood the town.*
>
> *I will do it if only (or **if but**) to save my honor.*

We might also consider infinitives after **than** as abridged adverbial clauses in sentences like the following:

> *He knows better than to come to work late.*
>
> *You cannot do more (or less, better, worse) than to accept that offer.*

## POSITION OF ADVERBS
## IN INFINITIVE PHRASES

The adverb in the infinitive phrase may occur in any of the three adverbial positions—initial, mid, or final. The actual position chosen often parallels that used for an adverb with a finite verb.

Initial Position
(Preceding TO)

In this position the adverb is felt as modifying the entire infinitive phrase. Emphasizing adverbs such as **even, only** are often found here.

> *He did it only* (or *just, merely*) *to annoy her.*
>
> *It was rude of her even to suggest such a thing.*

The position before **to** is required especially for the negative adverb **not**.

> *Not to have met him while he was in town was a great disappointment to me.*
>
> *It's very embarrassing not to remember your name.*

Occasionally, other types of adverbs such as manner, time, degree appear in initial position for emphasis.

> *It was wrong of you deliberately to make fun of her.*
>
> *She didn't follow her mother's advice always to tell the truth.*
>
> *I don't want ever again to work with such an unpleasant person.*

When such adverbs occur between the main verb and the **to** of the infinitive, it is sometimes difficult in the written language to determine which verb the adverb really modifies.

> *He chose deliberately to ignore my wishes.*
>
> *They desire wholeheartedly to be my friends.*
>
> *He failed entirely to comprehend it.*

Since initial position is not common for such adverbs with infinitives, especially manner adverbs, the tendency is to feel that the adverbs in these sentences belong with the main verbs. Ambiguity may be avoided in writing by moving the adverb to a position that clearly indicates which verb is being modified.

> *He deliberately chose to ignore my wishes.*
>
> or *He chose to deliberately ignore my wishes.*

Mid-Position
(Between TO and the Verb)

An adverb placed between **to** and the verb of an infinitive has long been condemned by purists on the grounds that the adverb "splits" the infinitive.

However, in spite of such objections, this position of an adverb has often been favored for two reasons: (1) it is a natural position for adverbs with finite verbs (2) it is a position that clearly indicates which word the adverb is modifying.

As evidence that the best writers have not hesitated to use this position of adverbs with infinitives, we cite here many examples of "split" infinitives taken from the works of reputable authors of the nineteenth and twentieth centuries.[3]

> *to still further limit the hours, without permitting himself to actually mention the name, in order to fully appreciate Lord Holland, to half surmise the truth, things which few except parents can be expected to really understand, I wish the reader to clearly understand, to so arrange it, I was once more to calmly review my chances of escape, to basely desert his friend, to thoroughly understand life, to further complicate our problem*

Mid-position is generally avoided if the adverb consists of a word-group, but sometimes it is possible to produce acceptable sentences with more than one word in this position.

> *He seems to more or less suspect that his business partner is dishonest.*
> *We plan to, if possible, be away for a whole month.*
> *We are happy to once again announce the winners of this contest.*

Final Position

This position is used only if the infinitive phrase is short.

> *The doctor instructed the nurse to change the bandage immediately.*
> *He was determined to restore order quickly.*
> *It's advisable to define the problem accurately.*

Position with Auxiliaries
of Infinitives

Adverbs occupy the same positions with auxiliaries of infinitives as they do with auxiliaries of finite verbs.

> *I'm happy to have **finally** met you.*
> *To be **genuinely** loved is a wonderful thing.*
> *She seems to have been **greatly** admired in her youth.*

The position of some adverbs of frequency is flexible with infinitives having auxiliaries.

> *She seemed always to be falling asleep.*
> or *She seemed to always be falling asleep.*
> or *She seemed to be always falling asleep.*

---

[3] The examples quoted are from George O. Curme's *Syntax,* pp. 461–65.

*Never to have sinned is impossible.*

or *To never have sinned is impossible* (least common position).

or *To have never sinned is impossible.*

Infinitive phrases appear in the same position as do nominals, adjectivals and adverbials. Commas are usually required for adverbial infinitive phrases that are movable, particularly those that express purpose or condition.

## Infinitive Phrases
## in Initial Position

*(In order) to see better, we moved our chairs closer to the light.*

*To get the best results, you should take this medicine before meals.*

*To tell the truth, the Watsons never did like their neighbors.*

When a sentence begins with a subjectless adverbial infinitive (except for sentence modifiers like **to tell the truth**), the expectation is that the subject of the main verb will function as the "subject" of the introductory infinitive. If this does not happen, then the infinitive is considered to be "dangling," as in:

*(In order) to make his talk more interesting, colored slides were used by the lecturer.*

*To get the best results, this medicine should be taken before meals.*

This kind of "dangling" verbal is not always as strongly condemned as an initial "dangling" participle is; indeed, it often passes uncriticized when used in a final position where, to a lesser extent, the verbal is also expected to be tied to a "subject" within the sentence—**This medicine should be taken before meals to get the best results.**

## Infinitive Phrases
## in Mid-position

*Poetry, to be effective, should be written with strong feeling.*

*The Watsons, to tell the truth, never did like their neighbors.*

*Mrs. Black, to do her justice, was always scrupulously honest.*

## Infinitive Phrases
## in Final Position

*Poetry should be written with strong feeling (,) to be effective.*

*The Watsons never did like their neighbors, to tell the truth.*

*You should take this medicine before meals (,) to get the best results.*

Sentence modifiers are used in final position only if the sentence is short.

As with other nonrestrictive modifiers in final position, commas may be omitted before nonrestrictive infinitive phrases at the end of a sentence.

The infinitive phrase is more economical than the dependent clause it may replace, but it is less exact in its ability to show time, person and number. Like the gerund phrase, the infinitive phrase is often preferred to the clause if there is no need to express a subject.

Subject position for infinitive phrases, as for all complex noun constructions, lends a formal tone to a sentence—**To try to minimize the mistakes we are constantly making is quite natural**. The alternate *it* construction for the infinitive phrase subject is usually more casual—**It is quite natural to try to minimize the mistakes we are constantly making**. Generally it is best to avoid any long nominal in subject position, especially if the predicate of the sentence is short.

Choices are often possible between the infinitive phrase and the gerund phrase. Where such choices exist, the infinitive usually has stronger verbal force, the gerund greater nominal force. Also, the infinitive generally represents an act or state as a whole, whereas the gerund represents an act or state in progress.

The greatest choice between an infinitive or a gerund is in subject function, especially if the main verb is present or future.

> *To learn* (or *learning*) *a new language is difficult.*
>
> *To give up* (or *giving up*) *now would be disastrous.*
>
> *For us to back out* (or *our backing out*) *of the agreement would create much resentment.*
>
> *To hear* (or *hearing*) *such praise will embarrass him.*

If the main verb indicates a past single action, or if the verb is in the passive voice, the gerund is usually required.

| | |
|---|---|
| Past main verb | Her changing her mind at the last minute caused everyone a great deal of inconvenience. |
| | Finding the answers presented a problem. |
| | His opposing the bill did not make any difference. |
| Passive main verb | His accepting such a large gift is being investigated by the committee. |
| | Our spending the money without authorization will be criticized. |
| | Her stealing merchandise from the store will eventually be noticed. |

Such gerund phrases are usually short. Often an alternate abstract noun phrase is preferred—**His opposition to the bill did not make any difference.**

# 19

## *Absolute Constructions*

The absolute construction does not occur as often as the other verbal constructions, but its use is common enough to warrant more attention than it has received in most grammar books. Although many grammarians claim that the absolute construction is found chiefly in literary English, actually it occurs just as frequently in conversational English.

An absolute construction contains a "subject" that is unchanged from the form it has in a full sentence. (For this reason, it is sometimes called a *nominative* absolute.) In the predicate, the finite verb is changed to a participle, or, if the verb is **be**, it may be omitted entirely.

Absolute Construction
with Participle

> *The elevator being out of order, everyone had to walk.*
> *The rain having already begun, they decided to call off the concert in the park.*

Absolute Construction
without Participle

**Being** is implied before the following complements used as predicates of absolute construction.

| | |
|---|---|
| A predicate noun | His book *now a bestseller*, he felt pleased with the world. |
| A predicate adjective | His book *now famous*, he felt pleased with the world. |
| An adverb | His long work *finally over*, he felt pleased with the world. |
| A prepositional phrase | His book *now on sale at all bookstores*, he felt pleased with the world. |

Occasionally the complement precedes the subject in absolute constructions without participles.

> *She came running toward him, in her hands the letter they had been waiting for so eagerly.*
>
> *All day long, people were thronging the streets, conspicuous among them the many men in uniform.*

The participial forms of **be**—**being** and **having been**—tend to be omitted in absolute constructions that give descriptive details.

> *She sat despondently in a corner, her hands over her eyes.*
>
> *The candidate for mayor addressed the audience, his tone confident, forceful, cajoling.*
>
> *The boy came running into the room, his face and hands covered with mud.*

Infinitives may also function as the verbs in absolute constructions. These infinitives might be viewed as the second part of the idiom **be to**, used in the sense of *part of a future plan, arrangement, or requirement.*

> *They decided to row all night, all the men to take turns.* (The absolute construction is the equivalent of the sentence *All the men* **were to** *take turns.*)
>
> *He is leaving for the conference next week, all expenses to be paid by his company.*
>
> *All his money was left to his children, each to receive an equal share.*

The infinitives in such absolute constructions may alternate with **-ing** participles if there is no desire to stress future action—**They decided to row all night, all the men taking turns.**

The word **with** (or its negative **without**) may initiate an absolute construction, making the construction technically a prepositional phrase and thereby relating it grammatically to the rest of the sentence. Such **with** absolutes generally have the same kinds of predicates as absolutes without **with**.

> *The ocean looks very beautiful with the moonlight glimmering on its surface.*
>
> *With half the work still unfinished, she became frantic about the lack of time.*
>
> *With the police on all sides of them and ready to shoot, the bank robbers finally surrendered.*

These **with** absolutes sometimes differ from simple prepositional phrases merely by the position of the participle.

| *With Absolute Construction* | *Prepositional Phrase* |
|---|---|
| with arms outstretched | with outstretched arms |
| with a sneer barely suppressed | with a barely suppressed sneer |

## FUNCTION OF ABSOLUTE CONSTRUCTIONS

The absolute construction has a semantic or logical connection with the rest of the sentence, but, except when it is introduced by **with**, it has no grammatical link with the sentence.[1] It may be interpreted as a modifier of the entire sentence.

## KINDS OF TIME EXPRESSED BY PARTICIPLES IN ABSOLUTE CONSTRUCTIONS

The participle used in an absolute construction generally expresses the same kind of time as it does in a participial phrase. The present participle and the past participle indicate time that is determined by the context; the perfect participle points to time that precedes that of the main verb.[2]

1. *Present participle:*

| | |
|---|---|
| Present time | Her mother being away, she has to do all the housework. |
| Past time | Her mother being away, she had to do all the housework. |
| Future time | Dinner will be served outdoors, weather permitting. |

2. *Past participle:*

| | |
|---|---|
| Present time | She is walking along slowly, the infant held tightly in her arms. |
| Past time | She walked along slowly, the infant held tightly in her arms. |
| Future time | His books once published, he will never have to worry about money again. |

3. *Perfect participle:*

*More vaccine had to be sent for, the epidemic having spread at an alarming rate.*

*The rebels having been defeated, the dictator began to rebuild the towns that were destroyed in the fighting.*

*All flights having been canceled because of the storm, they decided to take the train.*

---

[1] The term *absolute* refers to a free grammatical element within a sentence.

[2] See the chapter on participial phrases for the forms of the participles.

If there is no desire to emphasize past time before another past time, the present participle may be used instead of the perfect participle, especially if the construction is in initial position.

> *The epidemic spreading at an alarming rate, more vaccine had to be sent for.*
>
> *The rebels being defeated, the dictator began to rebuild the towns that were destroyed in the fighting.*

With a present or future main verb, the perfect participle in an absolute construction may also be the equivalent of the present perfect tense.

> *All her fears of the dark having been overcome, the child **is sleeping** more peacefully now.* (The absolute construction is the equivalent of *because all her fears of the dark **have been overcome.***)

"SUBJECTS"
IN ABSOLUTE CONSTRUCTIONS

The "subject" in an absolute construction generally does not have the same referent as the subject of the main verb. If the agent of both is the same, a participial phrase is preferred. Thus, a sentence like **The children having eaten very late, they became sleepy right after dinner** is better recast with a participial phrase—**Having eaten very late, the children became sleepy right after dinner**. Occasionally, however, an object-turned-subject of a passive main verb may also have the same referent as the "subject" of the absolute construction—**The children having eaten very late, they were put to bed immediately**.

Personal pronoun "subjects" of absolute constructions are more likely to occur in conversational English than in formal English.

> *We divided the work, she taking one half and I the rest.*
>
> *He being sick, we'll have to do his work.*

In popular speech, the object form of the "subject" of an absolute construction is sometimes heard—**Him being sick, we'll have to do his work.** This object form reflects an older usage which we still find in poetry of an earlier period—**Him destroyed for whom all this was made, all this will soon follow.** (Milton, *Paradise Lost*)

If a personal pronoun "subject" is used informally in a **with** absolute construction, the pronoun must be in object form—**With him being sick, we'll have to do his work.**

The expletives **it** and **there** may fill subject position in an absolute construction.

> *It being Sunday, the stores were not open.*
>
> *There having been some question about the bookkeeper's honesty, the company asked him to resign.*

POSSIBLE MEANINGS
OF ABSOLUTE CONSTRUCTIONS

Since there is no word in the absolute construction that signals a specific meaning, the "meaning" of such a construction must be inferred from the context. Some of the meanings given below may be stronger in some absolutes than in others; also, some of these meanings may be intermingled with others.

1. *Time*

   a. in the sense of *after*

> *Dinner (being) ready, the hostess asked her guests to be seated.*
>
> *Day finally breaking, we resumed our long automobile trip across the country.*

   b. in the sense of *while*

> *The anthropologist questioned many of the natives in that remote area, his host acting as interpreter.*
>
> *Cleopatra sat resplendent on her throne, her ladies-in-waiting grouped all around her.*

2. *Cause*

> *The table not having been constructed properly, one of the legs became loose.*
>
> *With his wife sick in the hospital, he is taking care of the children alone.*

Often an absolute construction, like a participial phrase, may signify both time (in the sense of **after**) and cause at once.

> *The children having been fed, their mother put them to bed.*

The inclusion of **being** or **having been** within the absolute construction tends to reinforce the idea of cause.

3. *Condition*

> *A riot once begun, our small police force will be unable to handle it.*

Some stereotyped phrases in absolute form have conditional meaning— **weather permitting, God willing, everything considered, all things being equal, present company excepted**.

Absolute constructions may also convey some shade of the meaning of *having*.

> *He entered the room quickly, a smile on his lips and a handshake for everyone.*

This meaning of *having* is signaled even more strongly in **with** constructions.

> *Today's students, with many opportunities to support themselves through college, are far more fortunate than the students of a hundred years ago.*
>
> *She walked out into the street without a hat and coat on.*

Absolute constructions may appear in all three of the adverbial positions, but more often they occur in initial or final position. Initial position is preferred for absolute constructions that indicate cause, final position for constructions that are logically coordinate with the main clause.

Being nonrestrictive, absolute constructions are usually set off with commas no matter where they occur. An exception is the **with** construction in final position, which may be written without a preceding comma. Occasionally dashes or parentheses are used with absolute constructions; examples of such punctuation may be found throughout this chapter.

Absolute constructions that appear in mid-position are often equivalents of nonrestrictive adjective clauses.

> *The children, many of them only infants (=**many of whom were only infants**), were left with nothing to eat.*
>
> *A few of the committee members—among them the chairman—(=**among whom was the chairman**), wanted to investigate the matter immediately.*
>
> *The old house—its roof sagging and its windows broken—(=**whose roof was sagging and whose windows were broken**) was finally put up for sale.*

A common error in the punctuation of absolute constructions in final position is the use of a period instead of a comma:

> *The members of the jury could not come to a unanimous decision about the guilt of the accused. The reason being that the evidence against the defendant was inconclusive.*

Since the absolute construction does not contain a finite verb, it should not be cut off from the rest of the sentence. A colon or a semicolon is generally also inappropriate before an absolute construction in final position.

The absolute construction is especially useful as a grammatical device that permits the addition of a logically coordinate idea to a sentence that might otherwise be written separately. Such a coordinate absolute usually appears in final position, but sometimes it occurs at the beginning of the sentence.

A second coordinate sentence might be changed to an absolute construction in the following circumstances.

1. The second sentence gives a further explanation of the first sentence.

*She looks almost like her twin sister, the only difference being that she is a little taller.*

*The absolute construction has no grammatical connection with the rest of the sentence (the term* **absolute** *referring to a free element within a sentence).*

2. The second sentence represents a "partitioning" of one of the referents in the first sentence. This type of absolute construction appears only in final position, and frequently has two or more parts. It may be used in both formal and informal English.

*The men work in two shifts, the first starting at 8: 00 a.m., the second at 4: 00 p.m.*

*The students walked into the classroom, some in pairs, others alone.*

*He left his wife well provided for, with half her income to come* (or **coming**) *from stocks, the other half from mutual funds.*

The "subjects" in these absolute constructions are usually words of quantity, often indefinite; sometimes, however, other types of words may function as "subjects" in such absolutes—**As the couples came up to the building they separated, the women going to the door at the right, the men to the door at the left.**

3. The second sentence gives descriptive details that represent one or more aspects or component elements of a broader subject mentioned in the main clause. Although this type of coordinate absolute may be found in informal English, it is particularly characteristic of literary or formal style.

*We could see the mountain from our hotel, its steep slopes bare of vegetation, its snow-capped peak disappearing into the clouds.*

*Her face white and drawn, and her hands trembling, the patient could barely tell the doctor what was ailing her.*

Because absolute constructions in final position permit an open-ended listing of descriptive details about a subject, a writer can sketch a loose succession of vignettes without having to impose on them a tight grammatical control. The following well-known quotation illustrates the use of absolutes to give a series of pictures.

*After all these years I can still picture that old time to myself now, just as it was then: the town drowsing in the sunshine on a summer's morning; the streets empty, or pretty nearly so; one or two clerks sitting in front of the Water Street stores with their splint-bottomed chairs tilted back against the walls, chins on breasts, hats slouched over their faces, asleep . . .; two or three wood flats at the head of the wharf, but nobody to listen to the peaceful lapping of the wavelets against them; the great Mississippi, the majestic, the magnificent Mississippi, rolling its mile-wide tide along, shining in the sun; the dense forest away on the other side; the point above the town and the point below, bounding the river-glimpse and burning it into a sort of sea, and withal a very still and brilliant and lonely one.* (Mark Twain, *Life on the Mississippi*)

4. The second sentence refers to events that occur simultaneously with the events denoted in the main clause. Some degree of the meaning of **while** is therefore included without them. Such absolutes are often also used for descriptive details.

> *For a long time he lay ill in bed, the days blending into the nights in one mass of oblivion.*

> *The commander arranged to move his men to the next town, (with) his scouts going on ahead to warn them of any danger.*

# 20

## *Abstract Noun Phrases*

Not all abstract nouns serve to form abstract noun phrases. The term *abstract noun* as it is being used for this construction does not include class nouns for concrete objects, but only those nouns representing changed forms of important elements of simple sentences.

In abstract noun phrases, verbs and predicate adjectives are changed to nouns that function as the grammatical center of the construction. Other changes are similar to those made in gerund phrases. The "subject" in the abstract noun phrase may or may not be included. If included, the "subject" has inflected possessive form or is contained within an **of** phrase or a **by** phrase. An "object" in an abstract noun phrase is usually in an **of** phrase, but it may also be in possessive form or it may be introduced by a preposition other than **of**.

By means of these changes, the abstract noun phrase, like the gerund phrase, functions as a noun within another sentence. Of all the nominal structures that may be inserted in a main subject-verb-complement core, the abstract noun phrase is embedded most tightly into the main predication, and its own subject-predicate relationship is least apparent.

FORM OF NOUNS
IN ABSTRACT NOUN PHRASES

*Nouns from verbs*

1. nouns with derivational endings—**-tion, -ance, -age, -ment,** etc.

    *He moved slowly* becomes *his slow movement.*
    *She married him* becomes *her marriage to him.*

2. nouns without derivational endings

    *She requested a transfer* becomes *her request for a transfer.*
    *John loved money* becomes *John's love of money.*

*Nouns from predicate adjectives*

1. nouns with derivational endings—**-y, -ance, -ity, -ness,** etc.

    *He was very vigilant* becomes *his great vigilance.*
    *The woman was jealous* becomes *the woman's jealousy.*

2. nouns without derivational endings (usually from **-ous** adjectives)

    *The soldier was courageous* becomes *the soldier's courage.*
    *The writer was famous* becomes *the writer's fame.*

Some nouns in abstract noun phrases represent changes from *predicate nouns.* In these cases **-hood** or **-ship** is often added to the predicate noun.

    *He was a friend of John's* becomes *his friendship for John.*
    *He was a leader of men* becomes *his leadership of men.*

Nouns derived from verbs not only lack the grammatical property of number but also those of person and tense. In addition they are usually neutral with respect to voice. Thus the phrase **the development of the land** may be interpreted as being derived either from an active sentence such as **Someone developed the land** or from a passive sentence such as **The land was developed (by someone).**

Although the noun that heads an abstract noun phrase cannot of itself indicate tense, the time it refers to can be inferred from the tense of the main verb.

| | |
|---|---|
| Present time | The inauguration of the President *is taking place* now. |
| Past time | The inauguration of the President *took place* yesterday. |
| Future time | The inauguration of the President *will take place* tomorrow. |

NOMINAL FUNCTIONS
OF ABSTRACT NOUN PHRASES

Abstract noun phrases may perform all nominal functions in many instances.

| Subject of verb | *His rejection of that good offer* surprises me. |
| Object of verb | I can't understand *his rejection of that good offer*. |
| Object of preposition: | |
| In prepositional object | We talked about *his rejection of that good offer*. |
| In adverbial phrase | By *his rejection of that good offer*, he showed very poor judgment. |
| Subjective complement (predicate noun) | What I can't understand is *his rejection of that good offer*. |
| Appositive | I can't understand one thing—*his rejection of that good offer*. |

An abstract noun phrase used as subject selects the same kind of main verb as a gerund phrase subject or an infinitive phrase subject.

*Main verb*

| **be** | The possession of firearms is a misdemeanor. |
| causative verb | His great love for his wife made him blind to her many faults. |
| verb denoting an emotion | Their separation after twenty years of marriage surprised their friends. |

In addition, since abstract noun phrases have greater noun force than gerund phrases or infinitive phrases, they may occur as subjects of other main verbs, especially those in the passive voice.

*The committee's report to the governor is being prepared now.*

*Congressional approval of the measure is expected soon.*

*His loyalty to the cause has never been questioned.*

An abstract noun phrase functioning as the object of **with** is related to the **with** absolute construction.

| Abstract noun phrase | With the arrest and imprisonment of the prowler, everyone in the neighborhood felt relieved. |
| **With** absolute construction | With the prowler arrested and imprisoned, everyone in the neighborhood felt relieved. |

## "SUBJECTS" IN ABSTRACT NOUN PHRASES

As in the gerund phrase, a "subject" in an abstract noun phrase usually denotes a live being, although it may sometimes refer to a thing or an idea.

A "subject" in an abstract noun phrase may be implied, or it may be included within the phrase.

1. *Implied "subject" a generic person*

   The construction of bridges is a difficult undertaking.

   The drugs now used for the prevention of diseases have saved many lives.

2. *Implied "subject" in another part of the sentence*
   a. *subject* of the main verb:

      He is responsible for the **management** of the office. (The "subject" of **management** is **he**.)

   b. *object* of the main verb:

      He consulted his lawyer for **advice** on how to draw up the contract. (The "subject" of **advice** is **lawyer**.)

3. *"Subject" contained within the abstract noun phrase*
   a. "subject" in *possessive form*:

This "subject" form is generally preferred for personal pronouns and for proper nouns.

   The threatening monetary crisis made **their** departure for Europe unwise.

   All his friends were astounded at **Mr. Smith's** arrest for fraud.

   b. "Subject" in an **of** *phrase*:

   The sudden death **of an old friend** was a great shock to them.

   The police were immediately notified about the disappearance **of the money**.

An **of** phrase is generally avoided for a personal pronoun "subject"—
**\*the arrival of them.** The **of** phrase is required if the "subject" in an abstract noun phrase has much modification, especially if a modifier *follows* the subject.

   They were grateful for the help **of their many kind and generous neighbors**.

   He greatly desires the approval **of everyone involved in the production of the play**.

With the exception of personal pronoun "subjects," short "subjects" referring to live beings may be used in either form.

   The **actors'** arrival at the theater or the arrival **of the actors** at the theater

   **Robert's** dependence on his parents or the dependence **of Robert** on his parents

The **of** phrase is generally preferable for "subjects" that do not denote live beings.

   Some authorities believe in the existence **of flying saucers** (but, **their** existence).

   The absence **of pain** (but, **its** absence) does not mean the disease has been cured.

Occasionally possessive form is used for "subjects" other than those denoting live beings.

> *The plane's arrival with food caused great joy among the flood victims.*
>
> *Hawaii's location in the mid-Pacific makes it a strategic military port.*

c. "Subject" in a **by** *phrase*:

A **by** phrase "subject" is the only formal indication of the passive voice in the abstract noun phrase.

> *The destruction of the bridge **by the retreating army** gave them time to flee to safety.*
>
> *The performance **by the young musicians** was excellent.*
>
> *We wondered about his sudden dismissal **by the company**.*

In some sentences, **by** "subjects" alternate with **of** "subjects"—**these inventions by** or **of Edison,** the performance **by** or **of the young musicians, the decision by** or **of his brother to run for political office.**

"COMPLEMENTS"

IN ABSTRACT NOUN PHRASES

When a simple sentence is transformed into an abstract noun phrase, the original direct object often takes **of** phrase form, or less frequently, possessive form.

> *The execution **of the prisoners** will cause much public disapproval.*
>
> or   *The prisoners' execution will cause much public disapproval.*

The possessive form is more usual with person-denoting "objects," and is obligatory for personal pronoun "objects"—**his murder, their arrest, our education**. The possessive of the personal pronoun is occasionally used also for "objects" that signify things—**its** (referring to **gold**) **discovery, their** (referring to **books) publication.**

Since the possessive form and the **of** phrase may be either a "subject" or an "object," some danger of ambiguity might result if only one of these forms appears in the abstract noun phrase.

Ambiguity with a possessive form—**His murder outraged the people.** Is **his murder** derived from **He murdered someone** or **Someone murdered him**?

Ambiguity with an **of** phrase—**A translation of Jefferson is being published.** Is **a translation of Jefferson** derived from **Jefferson translated someone,** or **Someone translated Jefferson**?

Actually, such instances of ambiguity are rare. Usually the context in which the sentence is used helps to keep the meaning clear.

If an abstract noun phrase contains both a "subject" and an "object," some choice of forms for these elements of predication are more desirable than others. For example, the combination of a possessive "subject" and an **of** phrase "object" is often preferred, perhaps because these forms permit the "subject" and the "object" to remain in the same position as in a full sentence. In addition, when prepositional phrases are used for both the "subject" and the "object," the "subject" is usually in a **by** phrase, the "object" in an **of** phrase.[1] In line with the natural tendency in English to place an object right after its verb, the **of** phrase often precedes the **by** phrase— **government of the people by the people, the discovery of oil by the farmers, the seizure of power by the Bolsheviks, the persecution of the minority by the majority, the possession of heroin by the defendant.**

Sometimes, however, the **by** phrase is put first in order to give it additional emphasis—**the possession by the church of certain lands, the payment by the defeated country of an annual sum, the portrayal by the author of a saintly man.**

The **by** phrase may also precede if it is shorter than the **of** phrase "object" —**the discovery by the farmers of oil on their fields, the purchase by the newly- weds of a modest home near a lake.**

Sometimes a **for** phrase is interchangeable with an **of** phrase as a "direct object" in an abstract noun phrase. This choice usually occurs before a noun that expresses feelings—**her love for** or **of her mother, his admiration for** or **of Shakespeare, his hatred for** or **of all women.**

Some original direct objects of finite verbs require prepositions other than **of** when they follow the abstract noun derived from the verb.

---

| | |
|---|---|
| **for** | *after* demand, desire, pity, preference, request, respect reverence, urge, wish |
| | He demanded money **becomes** his demand for money. |
| | He preferred blondes **becomes** his preference for blondes. |
| **to** | *after* address, answer, assistance, damage, injury, obedience, resemblance, resistance |
| | She answered his letter **becomes** her answer to his letter. |
| | He resembles his father **becomes** his resemblance to his father. |
| **on** | *after* attack |
| | The enemy attacked the town **becomes** the enemy's attack on the town. |
| **in** | *after* trust |
| | We trust him **becomes** our trust in him. |

---

Prepositional complements that follow finite verbs or adjectives also appear after the noun forms of these verbs or adjectives.

Nouns from verbs—**his atonement for; his belief in; his connivance at; his consent to; his cooperation with; his demonstration against.**

Nouns from adjectives—**his absence from, his dependence on, his enthusiasm about** (or **over**), **his familiarity with; his proficiency in, his responsibility for.**

When adjectives that are normally followed by **of** prepositional phrases are converted to abstract nouns, these nouns are used chiefly with possessive "subjects"—*her* **jealousy of her sister;** *his* **envy of his cousin's good fortune,**

---

[1] The use of **of** phrases for both "subject" and "object" is rare—**The donation *of* a well-known philanthropist *of* one million dollars will be used to build a new library for the university.**

*Mary's* **ignorance of the whole matter.** Occasionally the **of** of the original complement is changed after such nouns—**the young man's fondness** *for* **pretty women** (also, **the fondness of the young man for pretty women**), **the natives' pride** *in* **their local customs** (also, **the pride of the natives in their local customs**).

Infinitive phrases or **that** clauses after abstract nouns may be regarded either as "complements" of the nouns or as appositives to these nouns.

> *His suggestion for us to see a lawyer* (or *that we see a lawyer*) *seemed reasonable.*
>
> *In her anxiety for everything to go well* (or *that everything should go well*), *she started to prepare for the party several days in advance.*

Abstract nouns from verbs denoting emotions may be followed by either infinitive phrases or **at** phrases.

|     | astonishment |     |
|-----|--------------|-----|
|     | disgust |     |
| his | irritation | *to learn the truth.* |
|     | satisfaction | or |
|     | surprise | *at learning the truth.* |
|     | embarrassment |     |

### TRANSFORMATION OF ADVERBS IN ABSTRACT NOUN PHRASES

**-Ly** adverbs in simple sentences are usually transformed to adjectives in abstract noun phrases. These **-ly** adverbs appear originally as modifiers of verbs or predicate adjectives.

*Change from* **-ly** *adverbs with verbs* (mostly manner; some time, degree)

> *She was promoted* **rapidly** becomes *her* **rapid** *promotion.*
>
> *He was* **recently** *assassinated* becomes *his* **recent** *assassination.*
>
> *They failed* **completely** becomes *their* **complete** *failure.*

If the adverb in the simple sentence is unmarked by **-ly**, the adjective used with the abstract noun will have the same form as the adverb—thus, **The train arrived late** (or **early**) becomes **the late** (or **early**) **arrival of the train.**

Other adverbs or adverbial word groups from simple sentences are merely placed after the abstract noun—thus, **He arrived there last week** becomes **his arrival there last week.** An **of** "subject" or "object" may precede or follow such an adverbial.

> *The visit last week of the queen* or *the visit of the queen last week.*
>
> *The robbery, late one evening, of a poor government clerk* or *the robbery of a poor government clerk late one evening.*

*Change from* **-ly** *adverbs with predicate adjectives* (time, degree)

> *She is* **frequently** *absent* becomes *her* **frequent** *absence.*
>
> *He is* **extremely** *selfish* becomes *his* **extreme** *selfishness.*

**Very** before a predicate adjective, and **very much** before a verb usually become the adjective **great** before abstract nouns.

*She is very generous* becomes *her great generosity.*

*He loved his children very much* becomes *his great love for his children.*

**Very** before other adverbs in simple sentences remains unchanged in abstract noun phrases—**He was promoted very rapidly** becomes **his very rapid promotion**.

On rare occasions an **-ly** adverb is used in unchanged form in an abstract noun phrase. Such an adverb is set off with commas—**The discussion, honestly and openly, of all matters causing friction between the two countries would be very desirable.**

POSITION AND PUNCTUATION
OF ABSTRACT NOUN PHRASES

The position and punctuation of abstract noun phrases are identical to those of gerund phrases. Abstract noun phrases appear in subject or object position, and like any noun construction in these positions, they are not used with commas. If an abstract noun phrase functions as an appositive, it may be set off by a comma, a colon, or a dash.

*They have one major concern: the proper education of their children.*

*Only one problem still remains—the storage of the grain.*

STYLISTIC MATTERS RELATED
TO ABSTRACT NOUN PHRASES

The compression resulting from the use of the abstract noun phrase, which reduces a predication to a noun that functions on the main subject-verb-complement core, makes this phrase a desirable construction for textbooks, academic papers, technical reports. Its suitability for such prose is further increased by the fact that it does not require distinctions for person, number, tense, or voice.

Sentences that are densely packed with noun-centered structures such as abstract noun phrases and noun compounds often lack the sense of movement generated by the actor-action relationship of a full subject and a full predicate. An overuse of such nominal structures results in a "heavy" or ponderous style that slows down the comprehension of the sentences. Rhetoricians advise a sparing use of such noun-centered structures within sentences; they suggest giving these compressed predications more "space" by expanding them into structures that have stronger verbal force, or into full clauses.

# 21

## *Appositive Noun*
## *and Adjective Phrases*

Grammar books have paid little attention to the appositive phrase as a structure derived from a full sentence, probably because it retains only a single element of a simple sentence. For this reason, too, a speaker or writer might not always think of using an appositive phrase as a reduction of a full sentence. Since it is important that he should have at his command every structure that provides a grammatical shape for his ideas, he should not overlook this additional means of including a subject-predicate idea within a sentence.

CHANGE FROM
FULL SUBJECT-PREDICATE FORM

The appositive phrase may be considered a changed form of an adjective clause. It consists of the complement that remains after the relative pronoun and a form of **be** are omitted. At a deeper level, the appositive phrase, like the adjective clause itself, can be further derived from a simple sentence with a linking verb.[1]

Complements after the main verb **be** that become the grammatical center in appositive phrases are:

---

[1] The reader is probably more familiar with the term *appositive* as it is used for nouns standing after other nouns without a grammatical link. Actually, any nominal structure may be used in the *function* of appositive: noun, pronoun, noun clause, infinitive phrase, etc. However, we are reserving the term *appositive phrase* only for those structures placed alongside nouns that are the equivalent of complements found in the predicate after the verb **be**.

| a predicate noun | He has asked Mr. Wilson, (who is) a prominent *lawyer*, to represent him in court. |
|---|---|
| a predicate adjective | The professor, (who was) *unaware* that many of his students were asleep, kept right on lecturing. |
| an adverb (or adverbial expression) | The gentleman (who is) over *there* by the door is our accountant. |
| a prepositional phrase | Mr. Harris, (who was) *in a hurry* to get home, took a taxi from the airport. |

The noun in an appositive phrase may be concrete or abstract. If it is abstract, the phrase may also be considered an abstract noun phrase—**The students included in their demands an item that is surely justified: the increased *participation* of students in curriculum planning**.

Occasionally a pronoun expressing quantity functions as the grammatical center of an appositive noun phrase—**The last *ones* to get off the stricken ship, the crew members sadly watched the ship go down.**

Although appositive adjectives and nouns are generally used with modifiers, single adjectives and nouns may also function as appositives.

> His parents, *asleep*, did not hear him leave the house that night.
>
> The new manager—*efficient, friendly, fair*—gained the respect of the workers.
>
> The literary influence of Emerson—*poet, essayist, lecturer*—was particularly strong in the mid-nineteenth century.

Adverbs and prepositional phrases serving as the grammatical heads of appositive phrases usually signify place or time. Many (but not all) prepositional idioms after **be** may also function as the grammatical center of appositive phrases.

> The boy's mother, (who was) *at a loss* to know why he was crying, tried to console him.
>
> The young man, (who is) madly *in love with* his employer's daughter, is afraid to ask her to marry him.

The changes from full subject-predicate form that take place in the appositive phrase are similar to some of the changes occurring in participial phrases and in verbless absolute constructions.

SIMILARITIES WITH PARTICIPIAL PHRASES. Appositive phrases and participial phrases are alike in that both represent only predicate parts of simple sentences. In addition, a form of **be** may also be assumed to have been omitted from a participial phrase, not, however, as the main verb, but as an auxiliary of the main verb.

| Appositive phrase | The guests, (who **were**) angry at their hosts' rude behavior, left without saying good-by. |
|---|---|
| Participial phrase | The guests, (who **were**) angered by their hosts' rude behavior, left |

without saying good-by. (omission of a form of **be** with a *passive* verb)

The guests, (who **were**) becoming angry at their hosts' rude behavior, left without saying good-by. (omission of a form of **be** with a *progressive* verb)

---

Sometimes the inclusion of an introductory **being** is the only difference between a participial phrase and an appositive phrase.

---

| | |
|---|---|
| Appositive phrase | Too ill to get out of bed, he asked his wife to call a doctor. |
| | An honest employee, he refused the bribe that was offered him. |
| Participial phrase | Being too ill to get out of bed, he asked his wife to call a doctor. |
| | Being an honest employee, he refused the bribe that was offered him. |

---

**Being** used in such participial phrases usually denotes cause.

Often appositive phrases and participial phrases appear together in a coordinate series.

> One of the major difficulties of an underdeveloped country is the scarcity of able leaders, **knowledgeable** enough to run the government, **skilled** enough to operate its industries, **caring** enough to place the interests of the country above their own personal interests, and **motivated** by the desire to make this a better world to live in.

SIMILARITIES WITH VERBLESS ABSOLUTE CONSTRUCTIONS. Because the main verb that has been omitted in such absolute constructions is **be**, these absolutes contain the same type of complements as do appositive phrases. The only difference between the two structures is that the absolute retains the subject of the original simple sentence.

---

| | |
|---|---|
| Appositive | *Now a bestseller,* his book should make a lot of money for him. (The "subject" of the appositive is outside the construction.) |
| Absolute | *His book now a bestseller,* he should be making a lot of money. (The "subject" of the absolute is inside the construction.) |

---

Since the most common complements that function as grammatical heads of appositive phrases are predicate nouns and predicate adjectives, the rest of this chapter will be concerned mainly with appositive noun phrases and appositive adjective phrases.

"SUBJECTS"
IN APPOSITIVE PHRASES

Any noun or pronoun in another part of the sentence may function as the "subject" of an appositive phrase.

| | |
|---|---|
| subject of verb | *Colonel Williams*, a tough and able leader, was respected by all his men. |
| | *Her hair*—long, thick, dazzlingly blond—immediately attracted his attention. |
| complement (predicate noun) | One officer who is respected by all his men is *Colonel Williams*, a tough and able leader. |
| | Her chief asset is *her hair*—long, thick, dazzlingly blond. |
| object of verb | All his men respect *Colonel Williams*, a tough and able leader. |
| | One immediately notices *her hair*—long, thick, dazzlingly blond. |
| object of preposition | The order to advance was given by *Colonel Williams*, a tough and able leader. |
| | He was immediately attracted by *her hair*—long, thick, dazzlingly blond. |

## MODIFIERS AND "COMPLEMENTS" IN APPOSITIVE PHRASES

Adverbial modifiers of **be** in simple sentences are retained in appositive phrases.

> *New York, **once** a small town (or a small town **once**,) now has eight million people.*
>
> *Mr. Harris, **in his youth** a talented musician (or a talented musician **in his youth**), still gives concerts every now and then.*
>
> *New Yorkers, **not always** patient or polite, are often criticized by people who do not understand the tensions of city life.*

Note that these adverbials keep the same position they would have in the sentences from which they are derived.

Appositive adjectives or nouns are also modified in the same way as the predicate adjectives or predicate nouns in the sentences from which they are derived.

### ADJECTIVAL MODIFIERS OF APPOSITIVE NOUNS

*before* the noun:
New York, a very *large* and *busy* city, has always fascinated me.
*after* the noun:

| | |
|---|---|
| adjective clause | New York, a city *which has eight million people*, has always fascinated me. |
| participial phrase | New York, a city *housing eight million people*, has always fascinated me. |
| prepositional phrase | New York, a city *of eight million people*, has always fascinated me. |

Sometimes an article modifying a singular noun is omitted in an appositive noun phrase—**The book is by Dr. Watson,** *professor of physics at one of the large universities.*

## MODIFIERS OF APPOSITIVE ADJECTIVES

| | |
|---|---|
| Adverbial modifiers | |
| | His mother, *seriously* ill, had to be taken to the hospital at once. |
| | The girl, *too* restless to sit still, asked if she could go outside to play. (This appositive phrase can also be rephrased as an adverbial clause modifier—**so restless that she couldn't sit still.**) |
| | Their son, intelligent *enough* to get into any university, decided to go into the army instead. |
| "Complements" of appositive adjectives | |
| **that** clause | The man, *aware that he had made a mistake*, tried to correct it. |
| infinitive phrase | The man, **eager** *to correct his mistake*, said he would send a revised bill. |
| prepositional phrase | The man, *aware of his mistake*, tried to correct it. |

Structures of comparison may follow appositive adjectives.

> *The girls, as eager **as the boys to play baseball**, asked if they could partici-pate in the game.*

> *His young cousin, prettier **than he had remembered her**, came over to greet him.*

## POSITION AND PUNCTUATION OF APPOSITIVE PHRASES

### Restrictive Phrases

Only appositive adjective phrases may be restrictive. Like the other restrictive adjectivals—adjective clauses and partieipial phrases—such phrases appear only after the nouns they modify, with no commas to set them off.

> *We want to rent a hall **large enough to seat 500 people**.*

> Compare with: *We want to rent a hall **seating 500 people**.* (participial phrase)

> and *We want to rent a hall **which is large enough to seat 500 people**.* (adjective clause)

### Nonrestrictive Phrases

All nonrestrictive appositive phrases require commas. Their most common position is immediately after the nouns which act as their "subjects."

> *His uncle, **a proud and unbending man**, refused all help that was offered him.*

> *Charles, **eager to get ahead in his career**, worked hard day and night.*

Those phrases that refer to the subject of the main verb—as in the sentences just given—may also occupy the two other adverbial positions that nonrestrictive participial phrases do.

Initial position:

> *A proud and unbending man,* his uncle refused all help that was offered him.
>
> *Eager to get ahead in his career,* Charles worked hard day and night.

Final position:

> His uncle refused all help that was offered him, *a proud and unbending man.*
>
> Charles worked hard day and night, *eager to get ahead in his career.*

Such appositive phrases in final position are often avoided because of the danger of ambiguous reference. In some sentences, however, final position is the natural position for appositive phrases.

> His uncle died as he had lived, *a proud and unbending man.*
>
> His uncle is a writer, *the only one in the family with literary talent.*

Some appositive phrases in final position are used without commas, especially if they are felt as closely related not only to the subject but to the verb.

> He died *so poor that his friends had to pay for his funeral.*
>
> They parted *the best of friends.*

Dashes used instead of commas set off appositive phrases more strongly.

> How could they guess that their son—young, handsome strong—would soon become a victim of polio?

### STYLISTIC MATTERS RELATED TO APPOSITIVE PHRASES

The parenthetic nature of the appositive phrase, linked to a noun "subject" in the rest of the sentence only by an implied copula, makes it especially useful for appending details in descriptive and biographic writing.

> The son grew up to be a lazy fellow, *no more eager to work than his father was.*
>
> *A tall, lanky fellow with frightened eyes,* the young boy never seemed to know what to do with his arms.
>
> *One of the most powerful union leaders in the country,* he was born in a small Southern town, *the son of a poor and ignorant miner.*

The ideas expressed in such appositive phrases are actually often coordinate in importance with the ideas in the main clauses.

Where choices exist between an appositive phrase and an adjective clause, the appositive phrase might be preferred for its greater economy of expression, the adjective clause for its ability to distinguish person, number, tense.

An important use of an appositive noun phrase is to characterize a noun further: the appositive noun phrase may identify, classify, define, or explain its noun "subject."

> *This is Mr. Jones, **the editor of our morning newspaper.***
>
> *Astronomy—**the science of the celestial bodies**—is more likely to be taught in a university than astrology—**the study of the influence of the celestial bodies on human affairs.***

Some appositive nouns have narrow reference with respect to their noun "subjects," while others have broad reference. A noun with narrow reference coincides exactly with its "subject" in the main clause. The repetition of the noun not only emphasizes it more strongly, but opens the way for an additional comment about the "subject."

> *Hitler gave a number of guarantees for the concessions he obtained at Munich, **guarantees** he had intention of keeping.*

An appositive noun with broad, or indefinite reference points back to the entire preceding statement, or to a part of it, rather than to any single noun "subject."

> *The leaves are falling from the trees, an **indication** that the summer is over. (**Indication** refers to **the leaves are falling from the trees.**)*

This construction with an appositive noun having indefinite reference is acceptable in formal usage, whereas a **which** clause with indefinite reference is not. For this reason writers are advised to put a word like **fact, idea, thing** before a **which** clause with broad reference, thereby turning the construction into an appositive phrase. Thus the sentence **Mrs. Henderson's ancestors came to America on the Mayflower,** *which makes her feel superior to most people in this country* would be revised to read **Mrs. Henderson's ancestors came to America on the Mayflower,** *a fact which makes her feel superior to most people in this country*.

An appositive noun with broad reference may sum up several nouns that have preceded it. Such a summarizing noun permits an additional statement to be made about all of the nouns.

> *An alternate adjective clause would be chosen only if a writer wished to make distinctions for person, number, tense (**properties** which the appositive phrase does not have).*

Note that the appositive noun **properties** sums up the nouns **person, number, tense.** In this sentence the parenthetic information could also have been put in an adjective clause—**which properties the appositive phrase does not have**.

POSSIBLE MEANINGS
OF APPOSITIVE PHRASES

Appositive phrases frequently denote cause or contrast, especially if used in initial position.

*Cause*

**A rich man,** he could buy anything he desired.

**Curious about their new neighbors,** the Johnsons went to visit them at the first opportunity.

*Contrast*

*Concession:*    **An enemy of strong powers for the federal government,** Jefferson nevertheless pushed these powers to the utmost when he purchased the Louisiana Territory.

*Time:*    The desert, **by day a blazing inferno,** was blessedly cool at night.

**Once calm-tempered and considerate of others,** he became eccentric and self-centered in his old age.

*Place:*    **A tyrant in the office,** at home he was kind and gentle.

# *Appendix*

COLON: *Anticipates what follows* (formal usage)

1. *The second clause explains the first*

There is now only one way for the country to avert financial catastrophe: the government must declare a period of great austerity.

2. *Before a list* (especially if anticipated by **the following**)

Our office would like to requisition the following: 3 dozen stenography notebooks, 5 dozen pencils, 2 reams of typing paper.

3. *Before an appositive* (for greater emphasis)

She has always cared about only one person: herself.

4. *Before a formal or long quotation*

We quote from Lincoln's Gettysburg Address: Fourscore and seven years ago our forefathers brought forth on this continent a new nation, conceived in liberty, and dedicated to the proposition that all men are created equal.

SEMICOLON: *Marks a sharper break in a sentence than a comma does*

1. *Separates independent clauses*
   a. with no connecting conjunction

   The work in the office was quite simple; she had merely to answer the phone and do a little typing.

   Commas may be used if the clauses are short and parallel.

   I came, I saw, I conquered.

   b. with conjunctive adverb (**therefore, however, moreover, otherwise, etc.**)

   The bookkeeper had checked all her figures very carefully the night before;

**379**

however, when the accountant came he
found several mistakes in her records.

c. with coordinate conjunction when
the clauses already contain
commas

Mr. Jones, the owner of the largest factory
in town, is setting up another factory in
the next town; and, for all we know, he
may try to run both of them himself.

2. *Separates items in a list when the
items already contain commas*

The capitals of the South American
countries are: Argentina, Buenos Aires;
Bolivia, Sucre; Brazil, Brazilia; etc.

COMMA: *Separates or cuts off sentence elements*

1. *Separates coordinate elements*
   a. *two items*
      *independent clauses* joined by **and,
      or, but, yet, so, for**

The children were becoming more and
more bored at the theater, and she
knew that soon they would start looking
for some form of mischief.

The comma may be omitted if the
two clauses are short.

The band played and the crowd cheered.

No commas are used if two words,
phrases, or dependent clauses are
joined.

Women and children were put in the
lifeboat first.
She put the milk in the refrigerator and
the canned goods in the cupboard.
They are always arguing about how
bridge should be played and who was
the best player.

Two long phrases or dependent
clauses are sometimes separated by
commas.

Because the children had gone out to play
without permission, and because they
had stayed out far too long, their
parents were very angry with them.

   *contrasting items*—separated by
   **not, but**

It was Mary, not Jane, who baked these
pies.
He's to be pitied, not blamed.
The question is not what to do, but how
to do it.

   b. *three or more items* (The comma
   is often optional before the
   conjunction **and** or **or** that joins
   the last item)
   *words* (nouns, verbs, adjectives,
   adverbs)

Men, women (,) and children were all
seated on long benches in the simple
church.
The room was small, dark (,) and dingy.

   *phrases*

Highly trained in his field, a quick and
intelligent worker (,) and ingratiating to
his superiors, the young man advanced
himself to a position of great responsibility in a very short time.

   *dependent clauses*

The child told the police that he had lost
his mother in the crowd, that he had
been wandering around for a long time
(,) and that he was very frightened.

| | |
|---|---|
| *independent clauses* | The men were all sitting together on the porch drinking beer, the women were in the kitchen preparing dinner, and the children were outside playing in the snow. |
| If there is no conjunction with coordinate items, a comma separates each item. | He was living in a small, dark room. |
| | They want to live where there is peace, where there is freedom, where there is respect for the individual. |

2. *Cuts off sentence elements*

a. *Introductory elements* (especially if long, or if followed by a pause in speech)

| | |
|---|---|
| *adverb or adverbial expression, interjection* | Unfortunately, I cannot come now. |
| *exclamation* | Indeed, the work was well done. |
| *words in direct address* | John, please come here. |
| *prepositional phrase* | Because of the bad condition of the road, we decided to take the train. |
| *adverbial clause* | Because the road was in such bad condition that driving would be dangerous, we decided to take the train. |
| *participial phrase* | Hoping to finish all the typing that had accumulated, the secretary decided to work overtime for several hours. |
| *infinitive phrase* | To finish all the typing that had accumulated, the secretary decided to work overtime for several hours. |
| *absolute construction* | A great deal of typing having accumulated, the secretary decided to work overtime for several hours. |
| *appositive phrase* | Anxious to finish all the typing that had accumulated, the secretary decided to work overtime for several hours. |
| It is especially important to use a comma after an introductory element that might be misread otherwise. | Inside, the old house was still in good condition. |
| | As soon as she entered, the room seemed more cheerful. |

b. *Interrupting elements* (commas must be used on *both sides* of the interrupting element)

| | |
|---|---|
| *parenthetic phrase or clause* | John, some students feel, is the only one in the school who can win the medal for swimming. |
| *nonrestrictive adjective clause* | John, who was wearing the medal he had won for swimming, displayed it very conspicuously. |
| *nonrestrictive participial phrase* | John, wearing the medal he had won for swimming, displayed it very conspicuously. |

| | |
|---|---|
| *appositive phrase* | John, proud of the medal he had won for swimming, displayed it very conspicuously. |
| *adverb or adverbial expression* | John, as a matter of fact, was the only one in the school who had won a medal for swimming. |
| Commas may be omitted if the adverb or adverbial expression is felt to be closely related to the rest of the sentence. | John is actually the only one in the school who had won a medal for swimming. |
| *adverbial clause* | John, as was his custom, was too modest to admit he was proud of the medal he had won for swimming. |

c. *Final elements* (especially if long, or if preceded by a pause in speech)

| | |
|---|---|
| *adverb or adverbial expression* | No one was hurt, fortunately. |
| *adverbial clause*<br>A comma is more likely to occur before **if, although, because, so that** than before **when** or another conjunction of time. | No one was killed in the plane crash, although a few passengers were badly hurt. |
| *participial phrase* | She left the office early that day, hoping to get as much of her Christmas shopping done as possible. |
| *infinitive phrase* | He never did like her, to tell the truth. |
| *absolute construction* | The plane finally landed safely, with all on board frightened but unhurt. |
| *appositive phrase* | She left the office early that day, anxious to get as much of her Christmas shopping done as possible. |

DASH: *Marks an emphatic or abrupt break* (used with an interrupting or a final element)

| | |
|---|---|
| 1. *Represents a sudden shift in sentence structure* | My glasses—where could I have left them? The boy—he had been out playing in the snow—ran into the house crying bitterly about something. |
| 2. *Alternates informally with a colon, a semicolon, or a comma in some of their uses* | |
| a. Alternative for a colon before an enumeration | There are three qualities in people that I hate—deceit, dishonesty, and dullness. |
| b. Alternative for a semicolon between two independent clauses | He claimed that he was too ill to attend the meeting—the truth is, he didn't want to go. |
| c. Alternative for a comma—marks a greater break in continuity than a comma does | |
| (1) with a group of items that already have commas within them | Three books—Shakespeare's *Plays, The Bible*, and Walt Whitman's *Leaves of Grass*—have strongly shaped the poet's work. |

| (2) before an appositive | He is now faced with an important decision—a decision that can affect his entire future. |
|---|---|
| A dash is often preferred before a summarizing pronoun used as an appositive. | Da Vinci, Rembrandt, Cezanne, Picasso—all have the quality of greatness in their paintings. |
| Dashes should be used sparingly, especially as substitutes for other marks of punctuation. | |

Special Note on Punctuation

There are three kinds of punctuation for elements of an interrupting or parenthetic nature:

1. The comma, which sets off elements that represent the smallest break in continuity with the main idea.

2. Parentheses, which set off elements having the least connection with the main idea.

3. The dash, which sets off elements that the writer wishes to emphasize most strongly.

SPELLING RULES

1. ie *and* ei *words*
   A. **When the letters have the sound of** [*i*] **(as in** e*a*t**):**
      **PLACE** *i* **BEFORE** *e*, **EXCEPT AFTER** *c*

| ie Words | | ei After c | Other Exceptions[2] |
|---|---|---|---|
| achievement | siege | receive | weird |
| priest | chief[1] | receipt | seize |
| niece | yield | perceive | leisure |
| belief | relieve | conceive | either |
| piece | reprieve | deceive | neither |
| thief | wield | deceit | protein |
| grief | retrieve | conceit | caffeine |
| field | shield | ceiling | codeine |
| pier | fierce | | sheik |
| besiege | pierce | | |

[1] Derivatives with -**chief** are also spelled with *ie* even though the pronunciation of -**chief** changes—**mischief, mischievous, kerchief, handkerchief.**

[2] In some of these words the [*i*] vowel sound alternates with another sound.

B.  **When the letters have another sound: (especially [eɪ] as in *ate*):**
    **PLACE *e* BEFORE *i***

| Sound of [eɪ] | Other Sounds | |
|---|---|---|
| weigh | foreign | |
| weight | forfeit | |
| neighborhood | counterfeit | |
| eight | sovereign | |
| vein | their | |
| freight | heir | |
| reign | height | |
| veil | stein | |
| deign | but: | friend |
| feign | | sieve |
| sleigh | | |
| heinous | | |

2.  *Doubling of final consonants before vowels*
    **Double the final consonant before an added suffix beginning with a vowel if:**
    1.  THE SYLLABLE BEFORE THE ADDED SUFFIX ENDS IN A *SINGLE* CONSONANT PRECEDED BY A *SINGLE* VOWEL.
                            *and*
    2.  THE *STRESS* IS ON THE *SYLLABLE BEFORE* THE ADDED SUFFIX.

| Nouns | Verbs | Adjectives (includes -y ending) |
|---|---|---|
| occúrrence | plánned | bígger |
| propéller | drópped | hótter |
| góddess | stópping | sáddest |
| admíttance | hítting | thínner |
| wédding | bégging | regréttable |
| wrápper | contróller | rebéllious |
| bátter | permítted | fóggy |
| póttery | begínning | rótten |
| róbbery | forgótten | slíppery |
| bággage | sádden | snóbbish |
| begínner | fátten | uncontróllable |
| drúggist | allótted | unforgéttable |
| commíttee | conférred | intermíttent |
| detérrence | commítted | recúrrent |
| rebéllion | occúrred | súnny |
| reférral | forbídden | mánnish |
| béggar | annúlled | pádded |
| shípper | equípped | spótted |
| recúrrence | | múddy |
| | | fítting |

but   préference          but   cónquered          exceptions:   éxcellent
      réference                 intérpreted                       transférable (*but*
      ínference                 bénefited                              *also* tránsferable)
      cónference                súffered
      déference                 óffered
                                díffered

exceptions:   éxcellence
              càncellátion

---

In British usage, a final *l* (occasionally *p, m, s*) is often doubled before an added suffix beginning with a vowel even if the stress is not on the syllable preceding the added suffix.

|  |  |
|---|---|
| tótal(l)ing | wórship(p)ed |
| quárrel(l)ed | kídnap(p)er |
| cóunsel(l)ed | fócus(s)ed |
| équal(l)ed | bías(s)ed |
| sígnal(l)ed | márvel(l)ous |
| cáncel(l)ed | jewel(l)er |
| bévil(l)ed | díagram(m)ing |
| enámel(l)ed | prógram(m)ed |

3. *Final silent* e

   A. **Drop final silent *e* before a suffix beginning with a vowel**

| Nouns | Verbs | Adjectives (includes -y ending) |
|---|---|---|
| situation | changed | natural |
| sincerity | argued | universal |
| admiration | used | admirable |
| separation | arranging | nervous |
| pleasure | writing (*but* written) | sensible |
| exploration | shining | noisy |
| university | arguing | observant |
| survival | dining | imaginary |
| confusion | losing | receivable |
| imitation | choosing | valuable |
| resemblance | continuing | ridiculous |
| interference | using | becoming |
| treasury | coming | greasy |
| servant | noticing | hasty |
| arrival | arising | juicy |
| scarcity | hoping | shady |
| competition | practicing | smoky |
| confusion | hasten | conceivable |
| guidance | widen | desirable |
| observance | loosen | famous |
| communism |  | commercial |

*Exceptions*

1. *After final* c *and* g, *and before the vowels* a, o, u. The *e* is retained in order to prevent the *c* or *g* from changing to a [k] or [g] sound.

| Final c | Final g |
|---------|---------|
| noticeable | manageable |
| peaceable | courageous |
| serviceable | advantageous |
| replaceable | knowledgeable |
| traceable | outrageous |
| | changeable |
| | exchangeable |

2. *Before* -able. The *e* may be retained when *-able* is added to some one-syllable words. This form represents a less common variant of the adjective with the omitted *e*.

| | |
|---|---|
| us(e)able | sal(e)able |
| lik(e)able | mov(e)able |
| lov(e)able | siz(e)able |
| liv(e)able | |

3. *-ing after* oe. Verbs ending in *oe* keep the *e* before *-ing*—**canoeing, shoeing, tiptoeing, hoeing.**

4. -ing *added to* **tie, die, lie.** Not only is the *e* omitted from these words before *-ing*, but the *i* changes to *y*—**tying, dying, lying.**

5. *Words ending in* ee. Verbs ending in *ee* retain both *e*'s before suffixes beginning with vowels—**agreeing, seeing, freeing, guaranteeing, agreeable.** But, like verbs ending in silent *e*, verbs ending in *ee* form their past tense by the addition of *d* only—**agreed, freed, guaranteed.**

B. **Retain final silent *e* before consonants**

| Nouns | Adjectives | Adverbs |
|-------|------------|---------|
| arrangement | careful | accurately |
| movement | lively | sincerely |
| advertisement | lonely | extremely |
| achievement | graceful | immediately |
| strangeness | tasteless | safely |
| politeness | lifelike | entirely |
| boredom | valueless | fortunately |
| safety | useless | leisurely |
| encouragement | likely | definitely |
| ninety (*but* ninth) | shameful | adequately |
| likeness | noiseless | completely |
| management | hateful | entirely |
| realization | hopeless | |
| excitement | peaceful | |
| measurement | awesome | |
| statement | lonesome | |

Exceptions:  (1)  argument            duly
                  judgment            truly
                  abridgment          wholly
                  acknowledgment      wisdom
                                      awful
             (2)  when adding *-ly* to words ending in *-ple*,
                  *-ble*, *-tle*, drop the *-le* before the *-ly*.
                  simply              reasonably
                  possibly            sensibly
                  subtly              noticeably
                  gently              agreeably
                  terribly            terribly
                  miserably           nobly
                  probably            favorably
                  humbly

---

4. *Changing final* y *to* i

   **Change final *y* to *i* before an added suffix *beginning with a vowel or a consonant*.**

   A.  y *before a vowel*

| Nouns | Verbs | Adjectives |
|-------|-------|------------|
| factories | studies | happier |
| babies | married | loneliest |
| industries | hurries | dirtier |
| marriage | carried | heaviest |
| burial | worried | easiest |
| carrier | empties | friendlier |
| librarian | envied | envious |
| supplier | | industrial |
| variety | | colonial |
| industrialist | | victorious |
| trial | | ceremonial |
| carriage | | mysterious |
| | | undeniable |
| | | twentieth |
| | | bodily |

---

B.  y *before a consonant*

| Nouns | Verbs | Adjectives | Adverbs |
|-------|-------|------------|---------|
| livelihood | glorify | daily | hungrily |
| happiness | beautify | historical | greedily |
| glorification | | beautiful | happily |
| cleanliness | | plentiful | merrily |
| loneliness | | dutiful | angrily |
| manliness | | merciless | speedily |
| likelihood | | pitiless | hastily |
| emptiness | | | heartily |
| merriment | | | luckily |
| multiplication | | | |
| accompaniment | | | |

---

*Exceptions*

  1. Final *y* is unchanged:

    a. When the added suffix begins with *i*—**studying, marrying, hurrying, worrying, babyish, lobbyist.**

    b. When the *y* is preceded by a vowel—**plays, enjoyment, destroyed, employed, monkeys, valleys, delayed, employment, employer, joyous, joyful, annoyance, payment** (but **paid, said, laid**).

    c. Before the suffix **like**—**babylike, ladylike, citylike, countrylike.**

    d. In compounds written as one word—**handyman, laundryman.**

  With some words from one-syllable adjectives (**dry, shy, sly, gay**), *y* or *i* is used—**gaiety** or **gayety, shier** or **shyer, gayly** or **gaily, drier** or **dryer.**

  2. Final *y* is dropped before *-ize*—**apologize, colonize, theorize, agonize, memorize, sympathize.**

5. *-ic, -ical adjectives*

  Some adjectives that end in *-ic* have an alternate form *-ical.* The adverbs formed from these adjectives end in *-ically.*

| | | |
|---|---|---|
| alphabetic | alphabetical | alphabetically |
| geometric | geometrical | geometrically |
| historic | historical | historically |
| geographic | geographical | geographically |
| syntactic | syntactical | syntactically |
| economic | economical (*different meaning*) | economically |
| philosophic | philosophical | philosophically |
| hysteric | hysterical | hysterically |

  Those adjectives that do not have an alternate *-ical* form also take the *-ically* ending for the adverb.

| | | |
|---|---|---|
| basic | basically | Exception: public—adjective |
| hygienic | hygienically | publicly—adverb |
| artistic | artistically | |
| poetic | poetically | |
| sympathetic | sympathetically | |
| emphatic | emphatically | |

6. *Adding* k *to* c *before vowels*

| | | | |
|---|---|---|---|
| panic | panicking | panicked | panicky |
| picnic | picnicking | picnicked | picnickers |
| mimic | mimicking | mimicked | |
| frolic | frolicking | frolicked | |

7. *Differences between American and British spelling*

| American | British |
|---|---|
| *-or* | *-our* |
| glamor | glamour |
| labor | labour |
| neighbor | neighbour |

| American | British |
|---|---|
| (Cont.) | |
| rumor | rumour |
| honor | honour |
| behavior | behaviour |
| *-ize* | *-ise* |
| civilize | civilise |
| industrialize | industrialise |
| criticize | criticise |
| memorize | memorise |
| standardize | standardise |
| fertilize | fertilise |
| *-ization* | *-isation* |
| civilization | civilisation |
| industrialization | industrialisation |
| *-ense* | *-ence* |
| license | licence |
| offense | offence |
| pretense | pretence |
| defense | defence |
| *-ll* | *-l* |
| fulfill | fulfil |
| fulfillment | fulfilment |
| installment | instalment   (but **installation** in both American and British spelling) |
| enrollment | enrolment |
| skillful | skilful |
| dullness | dulness |
| *-ment* | *e-ment* |
| judgment | judgement |
| argument | arguement |
| abridgment | abridgement |
| acknowledgment | acknowledgement |
| *-er* | *-re* |
| center | centre |
| caliber | calibre |
| fiber | fibre |
| meter | metre |
| theater | theatre   (also common in the United States) |
| *l-ed, l-ing* | *ll-ed, ll-ing* |
| traveled | travelled |
| canceled | cancelled |
| equaling | equalling |
| signaling | signalling |
| *e-* | *ae-* |
| esthetic | aesthetic |
| encyclopedia | encyclopaedia |
| medieval | mediaeval |
| anesthesia | anaesthesia |
| *-ection* | *-exion* |
| connection | connexion |

(Cont.)

| American | British |
|---|---|
| reflection | reflexion |
| inflection | inflexion    (but **complexion** in both American and British spelling) |
| *-ed* | *-t* |
| burned | burnt |
| learn | learnt |
| spelled | spelt |
| leaped | lept |
| smell | smelt |
| spilled | spilt |
| spoiled | spoilt |

VOCABULARY

### GREEK AND LATIN PREFIXES

| Prefix | Meaning | English Derivatives |
|---|---|---|
| **a-, an-** | not | amoral, amorphous, anarchy, asymmetrical |
| **ab-** | away from | abnormal, abrupt, abduct, abstain |
| **ambi-** | both | ambidextrous, ambivalence, ambiguous |
| **amphi-** | around, both | amphibious, amphibian, amphitheater |
| **ante-** | before, in front of | anteroom, antecedent, antediluvian, anterior |
| **anti-** | against, opposite, not | antidote, anti-Semitic, antipathy, antiseptic |
| **arch-** | chief, prime | archbishop, archangel, archduke, archenemy |
| **bene-** | well | benefit, benefactor, benevolent, benediction |
| **bi-** | two | bisect, bifocal, bigamy, bilateral |
| **circum-** | around, on all sides | circumference, circumspect, circumlocution, circumnavigate |
| **con-** | with | conversation, concord, concomittant, convoy |
|   **com-** before *m, p, b* | | committee, compact, combat |
|   **col-** before *l* | | colleague, collateral, collapse |
|   **cor-** before *r* | | correlate, correspond, correct |
|   **co-** meaning joint(ly) with | | co-worker, cooperate, co-author, coexist |
| **contra-** | against, opposite | contradict, contraband, contrary, contravene |
| **counter-** | opposite | counterpoint, counteract, counterclockwise, counterespionage |
| **de-** | not, away from, down from, entirely | descend, dehydrate, deviate, decentralize |
| **dia-** | through | diagonal, diaphram, diaphanous, diagnosis |
| **dis-** | apart, away, not | disembark, disintegrate, disinterested, disorder |

(Cont.)

| Prefix | Meaning | English Derivatives |
|---|---|---|
| epi- | upon, at | epidemic, epidermis, epigram, epitaph |
| eu- | good | eugenic, eulogy, euphemism, euphony |
| ex-, e- | out from, former | exit, excavate, ex-governor, exhale, egress |
| extra- | outside, beyond | extraordinary, extrasensory, extracurricular, extravagant |
| hyper- | over, excessive | hyperacidity, hypersensitive, hyperthyroid |
| hypo- | less than, under | hypo-acidity, hypodermic, hypotenuse |
| in- | into, not | inhale, inept, indecent, innocent |
| im- before *m, p, b* | | imbalance, immoral, impolite, impel |
| il- before *l* | | illiterate, illegal, illegible |
| ir- before *r* | | irregular, irresponsible, irresolute |
| inter- | between, at intervals | intersperse, intermittent, intersect, intervene |
| intra- | within | intrastate, intramural, intravenous, intracellular |
| intro- | within | introspection, introvert, introduce, introject |
| mal- | ill, bad, badly, wrong | malfunction, malnutrition, malevolent, malcontent |
| mis- | wrong, wrongly, not | misunderstanding, misuse, mistrust, miscalculate |
| mono- | one, alone | monotone, monopoly, monosyllable, monomania |
| multi- | much, many | multitude, multiply, multimillionaire, multicolored |
| non- | not | nonexistent, nonpayment, nonobjective, nonconformist |
| per- | throughout, completely, very | percussion, persistence, pervasive, perennial |
| peri- | around, about, enclosing | perimeter, periscope, periphery, peripatetic |
| post- | behind, after | posterity, posthumous, postscript, post-impressionism |
| pre- | before, earlier, in front of | preconceive, premonition, prearrange, predict |
| pro- | forward, before | propulsion, prologue, project, progress |
| quad- | four | quadrangle, quadruped, quadruplet, quadrille |
| re- | back, again | reappear, recapture, recede, reclaim |
| retro- | backwards | retrospect, retrogress, retroactive, retroflex |
| se- | aside, apart | seclusion, secede, seduce, sequestered |
| semi- | half, partly | semiannual, semicircle, semiprecious, semiclassical |
| sub- | under, below | submarine, subnormal, subterranean, submerge |
| super- | over, above, extra | superimpose, supernatural, superabundant, superfluous |
| syn-, sym- | together with | synchronize, synthesis, sympathy, symmetry |

(Cont.)

| Prefix | Meaning | English Derivatives |
|--------|---------|---------------------|
| **trans-** | across, over, through, beyond | transition, transcend, transcontinental, transgress |
| **tri-** | three | tristate, triangle, triplicate, trilogy |
| **ultra-** | beyond, excessively | ultraconservative, ultramodern, ultraviolet |
| **uni-** | one | uniform, unilateral, unicameral, unique |
| **vice-** | one who takes the place of another | vice-president, viceroy, vice-consul, vice admiral |

## GREEK ROOTS[1]

| Root | Meaning | English Derivatives |
|------|---------|---------------------|
| *anthrōpos* | man | anthropology, anthropomorphic, anthropoid, misanthropy |
| *astĕr, astron* | star | asteroid, astronomy, astrology, astronaut |
| *autos* | self | automatic, autobiography, autonomy, autocrat |
| *biblion* | book | bibliography, bibliophile, Bible |
| *bios* | life | biography, biology, biochemistry |
| *chrōma* | color | kodachrome, chromatic, chromosome |
| *chronos* | time | chronology, chronicle, chronic |
| *dēmos* | people | epidemic, endemic, democracy, demagogue |
| *derma* | skin | dermatology, epidermis, dermatoid |
| *dynamis* | power | dynamo, dynamic, dynasty |
| *gamos* | marriage | bigamy, monogamy, polygamy |
| *geo-* | earth | geography, geopolitics, geochemistry, geology |
| *glotta* | tongue | epiglottis, glottal, polyglot |
| *gōnia* | angle | pentagon, octogon, hexagon |
| *gramma* | letter, thing written | telegram, epigram, monogram |
| *graphein* | write | telegraph, graphology, monograph, graphic |
| *hēlios* | sun | helium, heliotrope, heliocentric |
| *heteros* | other, different | heterosexual, heterodox, heterogeneous |
| *homos* | same | homogeneous, homosexual, homogenized |
| *hydōr* | water | hydrant, hydraulic, dehydrate, hydrophobia |
| *hypnos* | sleep | hypnotic, hypnotize |
| *isos* | equal, alike | isothermal, isometric, isotope, isosceles |
| *-itēs* | disease, inflammation | bronchitis, appendicitis, laryngitis |
| *kosmos* | order, the world | cosmic, cosmopolitan, cosmos, cosmonaut |
| *kratos* | power, rule | democrat, autocrat, aristocrat, plutocrat |
| *kryptos* | hidden | cryptic, cryptogram, crypt |
| *kyklos* | circle | cycle, cyclone, cyclical, bicycle |
| *lithos* | stone | lithograph, monolith, neolithic |
| *logos* | study of, science of | psychology, biology, theology, astrology |

[1] Some of the Greek or Latin roots listed in this appendix also serve as prefixes or suffixes of English words.

(Cont.)

| Root | Meaning | English derivatives |
|------|---------|---------------------|
| *mania* | madness | mania, maniac, manic-depressive, kleptomaniac |
| *meg*as, *megal*on | great, mighty | megalomania, megaphone, megalith, megalopolis |
| *metro*n | measure | micrometer, metric, metronome, geometry |
| *mikro*s | small | microscope, microbe, microfilm, microphone |
| *morphē* | shape, structure, form | morphology, amorphous, polymorphic (*or* polymorphous) |
| *naut*ēs | sailor | nautical, astronaut, nausea |
| *neo*s | new | neoclassic(al), neologism, neophyte |
| *neuro*n | nerve | neurology, neurotic, neuralgia |
| *nomo*s | law, order, knowledge | economy, agronomy, astronomy |
| *onom*a | name | synonym, antonym, homonym, pseudonym |
| *ortho*s | right, straight | orthodox, orthodontia, orthography |
| *pan* | all, completely | pan-American, panacea, panorama, panhellenic |
| *patho*s | feeling, suffering, disease | pathetic, antipathy, pathology, pathos |
| *philo*s | loving | philosopher, anglophile, philology |
| *phobo*s | fear | phobia, hydrophobia, agorophobia |
| *phōne* | sound, voice | phonetics, telephone, phonics, phonograph |
| phos, *photo*s | light | photograph, photogenic, photoengraving, photoelectric |
| *-polis* | city | metropolis, metropolitan, megalopolis |
| *poly*s | many | polygamy, polyglot, polygon, polytechnic |
| *proto*s | first | protagonist, proton, protoplasm, prototype |
| *pseud*ēs | false | pseudo-intellectual, pseudo-science, pseudonym |
| *psychē* | mind, life, soul | psychic, psychology, psychosomatic |
| pyr, *pyro*s | fire | pyromaniac, pyre, pyrotechnics |
| *scope*in | view, instrument for examining | telescope, microscope, scope |
| *soph*os | clever, wise | philosophy, sophist, sophisticated, sophomoric |
| *tēle* | distant | telegram, telephone, telepathy |
| *theo*s | god | theology, atheist, theocracy, polytheism |
| *thermē* | heat | thermos, thermodynamics, thermometer, thermonuclear |
| *typo*s | image, model | typist, teletype, typical, archetype |
| *zō*ion | animal | zoo, zoology, zodiac |

## LATIN ROOTS

| Root | Meaning | English Derivatives |
|------|---------|---------------------|
| *acer* (*acri-*) | sharp | acrid, acumen, acrimony, acute |
| *aequ*us (*equ-*) | equal, fair | equanimity, equity, equality, adequate |

(Cont.)

| Root | Meaning | English Derivatives |
|------|---------|---------------------|
| *ager* (*agr-*) | field | agriculture, agronomy, agrarian |
| *am*are, *amat*us | love | amatory, enamor, amateur, amour |
| *anim*a | life, breath, soul, mind | animal, animated, magnanimous, unanimous |
| *ann*us | year | annual, anniversary, biennial, perennial |
| *apt*are | fit | aptitude, adapt, inept |
| *aqu*a | water | aqueduct, aquatic, aquarium, aqueous |
| *arbit*er | judge | arbitration, arbitrary, arbitrator |
| *aud*ire | hear | auditorium, auditor, audition, inaudible |
| *bell*um | war | belligerent, bellicose, antebellum |
| *brev*is | short | brief, brevity, abbreviate |
| *cap*ere, *capt*us | take, accept | capture, capacious, capacity, captive |
| caput, *capit*is | head | captain, capital, decapitate |
| caedere (*cid-*) | kill | homicide, germicide, suicidal |
| *carn*is | flesh | carnal, carnival, carnivorous, incarnate |
| *ced*ere, *cess*us | go away, move, yield | antecedent, procedure, accessible, predecessor |
| *celer*are | hasten | celerity, accelerate, decelerate |
| *cent*um | hundred | cent, percent, century, centennial |
| *civ*is ⎱ | citizen | civil, civilian, civics, civilization |
| *civil*is ⎰ | civil | |
| *clam*are | cry out | clamor, acclamation, exclaim, declamation |
| *clar*us | clear | clarify, clarity, declare |
| *claud*ere (*clud-*, *clus-*) | shut, close | include, exclusive, seclusion, occlude |
| *corp*us | body | corporeal, corpse, incorporate, corporation |
| *cred*ere, *credit*us | believe, trust | credulous, creditable, credible, creed |
| *cresc*ere, *cret*us | grow | excrescence, crescent, accretion, increase |
| crux, *cruc*is | cross | crux, crucial, crucify, crucifix |
| *culp*are | blame | culpable, exculpate, culprit |
| *curr*ere, *curs*us | run | cursory, current, discursive, concur |
| dens, *dent*is | tooth | dentifrice, dental, dentist, dentition |
| *de*us | god | deify, deity, deist |
| *dext*er | right | dexterity, ambidextrous |
| *dic*ere, *dict*us | say | malediction, dictaphone, contradict, interdiction |
| *dom*us | house | domicile, domestic, dome |
| *domin*us | master, lord | dominate, dominant, dominion, predominant |
| *don*are, *donat*us | give, present | donor, donate |
| *duc*ere, *duct*us | lead | abduct, viaduct, ductile, conductor |
| *du*o | two | duet, dual, duo |
| *duplic*are | double | duplicate, duplex, duplicity |
| *err*are | wander | erratic, error, erroneous |
| *fac*ere, *fact*us (*-fic*) | do, make | malefactor, manufacture, facsimile, factory |
| *fall*ere | deceive | fallacy, fallacious, infallible |

(Cont.)

| Root | Meaning | English Derivatives |
|------|---------|---------------------|
| *fervere* | boil, glow | fervor, fervent, effervescent |
| *fidere* ⎫ | trust | fidelity, confidence, fiduciary |
| *fidelis* ⎭ | faithful | |
| *flare, flatus* | blow | deflate, inflation, flatulent |
| *flectere, flexus* | bend | flexible, reflection, deflect |
| *fluere, fluctus* | flow | affluent, influx, fluent, fluctuation |
| *fortis* | strong, brave | fortify, fortitude, fortress |
| *frater* | brother | fraternize, fraternity, fratricide |
| *fundere, fusus* | pour, melt | diffuse, refund, confound, effusive |
| *genus* | kind, sort, race | degenerate, generic, genealogy, genesis |
| *gratus* | pleasing, thankful | gratitude, grateful, gratuitous, congratulate |
| *gradi, gressus* | go, step | progressive, gradual, gradation, digress |
| *ire, itus* | go | transit, exit, transient |
| *judicium* | judgment | adjudicate, judicious, judicial, judiciary |
| *lapsus* | a fall | lapse, elapse, collapse |
| *latus* ⎫ | side | unilateral, collateral, lateral |
| *lateralis* ⎭ | lateral | |
| *legere, lectus* | choose, gather, read | electorate, colleague, predilection, lecturn |
| *lex, legis* | law, rule | legislate, legislature, legal |
| *liber* | free | liberate, liberal, liberty, libertine |
| *lingua* | tongue, language | bilingual, lingo, linguistics, lingua franca |
| *litera* | letter (of the alphabet) | literate, literal, obliterate, literature |
| *locus* | place | local, locomotive, locus |
| *loqui* | speak | eloquent, elocution, loquacious, colloquial |
| *lumen, luminis* | light | illuminate, luminous, luminary |
| *magnus* | great | magnify, magnitude, magnet, magnificent |
| *mandare, mandatus* | entrust, command | commandant, mandate, mandatory, demand |
| *manus* | hand | manicure, manacle, manufacture |
| *mare* ⎫ | sea | marine, marina, mariner, submarine |
| *marinus* ⎭ | related to the sea | |
| *medius* | middle | median, mediate, medium |
| *migrare, migratus* | move from one place to another | migrant, emigrate, immigrate, migratory |
| *mille* | thousand | millimeter, millennium, millionaire |
| *mittere, missus* | send, throw | missionary, emit, missile, mission |
| *minor* | smaller, inferior | diminish, minimize, minimum, minority |
| *monere, monitus* | warn | premonition, admonish, monitor |
| *mors, mortis* | death | immortal, mortality, mortuary, postmortem |
| *mur* | wall | immure, mural, intra-mural |
| *mutare, mutatus* | change | immutable, mutation, commute |
| *nascor, natus* | bear, be born | renaissance, native, innate, cognate |
| *nocere* | harm | innocent, innocuous |
| *nomen, nominis* | name | nominee, nominal, misnomer, nomenclature |
| *nox, noctis* | night | nocturnal, equinox, nocturne |
| *ordo* | rank, order | ordinary, subordinate, coordinate |

(Cont.)

| Root | Meaning | English Derivatives |
|------|---------|---------------------|
| *pater* | father | patrimony, patricide, patriotic |
| pax, *pacis* | peace | pacific, pacify, pacifist |
| *pellere, pulsus* | drive | repulsive, compulsion, impel |
| *pendere, pensus* | hang, weigh | appendage, impending, ponderous, pensive |
| pes, *pedis* | foot | quadruped, pedestrian, centipede, pedagogue |
| *petere, petitus* | strive for, seek, ask, attack | petulant, impetus, perpetual, petition |
| *placere* | please | placate, complacent, complaisant, implacable |
| *planus* | flat, level | plane, explanation, plain |
| *plenus* | full | plenteous, replenish, plenipotentiary, plenitude |
| *plicare* | fold | duplicate, explicate, complicated |
| *ponere, positus* | place, put | postpone, dispose, component, position |
| *populus* | people | populous, population, popular |
| *portare* | carry | portable, import, deportment, porter |
| *potens* | powerful | potent, potential, potentate, omnipotent |
| *primus* | first | prime, primeval, primary, primitive |
| *proprius* | one's own | property, appropriate, proper, expropriate |
| *proximus* | nearest | proximity, approximate |
| *regere, rectus* ⎱  *rectus* ⎰ | rule, direct, manage / right | incorrigible, regulate, rectify, rectitude |
| rex, *regis* ⎱  *regula* ⎰ | king / rule | regal, regent, regime, regulate |
| *rumpere, ruptus* | break | rupture, disrupt, interruption, erupt |
| *sagax, sagacis* | wise | sage, sagacious, sagacity |
| *sanctus* | holy | sanctum, sanctimonious, sanctuary, sanctify |
| **scendere** (*scend-*) | climb | ascend, descendant, scan |
| *sciens* | knowing | science, scientist, omniscient |
| *scribere, scriptus* | write | prescribe, proscribe, script, inscription |
| *sedere, sessus* | sit, sink down | sedentary, session, sediment, recession |
| *sentire, sensus* | feel | sentiment, sensation, resent, sensitive |
| *sequi, secutus* | follow | sequence, subsequent, sequel, consecutive |
| *similis* | like | similar, assimilate, simile, similitude |
| *solus* | alone | solo, solitary, desolate, soliloquy |
| *solvere, solutus* | loosen, free | solvent, dissolve, solution, resolve |
| *specere, spectus* | look | spectator, circumspect, spectacular, perspective |
| *spirare* | breathe | respiration, inspirational, expiration, aspire |
| *stringere, strictus* | draw tight | astringent, stringent, strict, stricture |
| *tangere, tactus* | touch | tactile, intact, tangent, tangible |
| *tenere, tensus* | stretch | tension, intention, retension, tensile |
| *tempor-, tempus* | time | temporary, contemporary, extemporaneous, tempo |
| *torquere, tortus* | twist | torque, distort, contort, extortion |
| **trahere, *tractus*** | pull, draw | traction, distract, retract, intractable |

(Cont.)

| Root | Meaning | English Derivatives |
|------|---------|---------------------|
| *vacuus* | empty | vacuum, evacuate, vacuous |
| *valere, valutus* | be strong, have worth | valiant, validate, evaluate, valuable |
| *venire, ventus* | come | convene, souvenir, contravene, circumvent |
| *vertere, versus* | turn | versatile, extravert, diverse, adversity |
| *verus* | true | verify, veracity, veritable |
| *videre, visus* | see | visible, evident, television, audio-visual |
| *vincere, victus* | conquer | victorious, invincible, convict, vanquish |
| *vivere* | live | vivid, vivacious, revive, survive |
| *vocare, vocatus* | call | irrevocable, vociferous, invocation, evocation |
| *volens* | willing, wishing | benevolent, volition, malevolent |
| *volvere, volutus* | turn, roll | revolve, convolution, involved |
| *vorare* | devour | carnivorous, voracious, herbivorous |

# Index